Our American Awakening

Restoring the Republic

Chris Hambleton

Congratulations on winning the Goodreads giveaway! I hope you enjoy the book!

Best Regards,

Connect with Me Online:
Website: http://www.cwhambleton.com
Facebook: http://facebook.com/cwhambleton
Twitter: http://twitter.com/chris_hambleton
Blog: http://fictionsoftware.wordpress.com

Discover Other Titles by the Author

Speculative Fiction Titles

"The Seed of Haman" (2013)
"The Exchange" (2012)
"The Castors of Giza" (2012)
"The Cell" (2010)
"Endeavor in Time" (2008)

The Time of Jacob's Trouble Trilogy (2011)
"The Last Aliyah" (Book 1)
"The Son of Shinar" (Book 2)
"The Siege of Zion" (Book 3)

The Days of Noah Series (2013)
"Rise of the Anshar" (Book 1)

Non-Fiction Titles

"Our American Awakening" (2013)
"The American Tyrant" (2012)
"Ezekiel Watch" (2012)
"On the Precipice" (2011)

To learn more about Chris Hambleton and his other books, please visit his author website at http://www.cwhambleton.com.

To my children and the next generation. May the difficult lessons we are learning today not be wasted, and may you make America a better nation than the one you inherited. May the America that you help build finally become that "shining city on the hill" that she has always yearned to be.

Table of Contents

"Nil desperandum – Never Despair. That should be a motto for you, me, and all liberty-loving people! All are not dead, and where there is a spark of patriotic fire, we will rekindle it."
— Samuel Adams

Foreword

Wednesday, November 7th, 2012

Last night, I went to bed with the news that we have re-elected Barack Obama as President in these United States of America, and I can't help but grieve for my country. Last night, America declared that it had turned from a center-right nation to a center-left nation.

Yesterday, we came to the proverbial fork in the road of American history and veered sharply left. While Mitt Romney may not have been the best alternative to Barack Obama, he did present a distinct contrast and emphasized a return to traditional American values and governance. And last night, a majority of Americans rejected him and those values he represented. Romney is a good man with solid values and has a great history of bringing bankrupt, dying companies and organizations back to life. Now we'll never know if he could have done the same for our declining nation.

As a conservative American, the last four years have been filled with regret, frustration, and too often anxiety. There have been many times in which I could only hang my head in sorrow and ponder what has become of this great nation which was once based upon liberty and limited government. As a result of this election, I fear there will only be more of the same. This great country which was founded and guided by liberty-minded men and women knowingly voted in a radical who had promised to "fundamentally transform" her – and has been succeeding in that transformation these last four years. And despite knowing all this, a majority of Americans still re-elected him.

Over the last four years, many Americans admitted
regretting their first vote for Obama because what he
campaigned on and how he governed were completely different.
However, after yesterday's elections, that excuse can no longer
be made. Fool me once, shame on you; fool me twice, shame on
me – and after yesterday, shame on us. Regardless of the
effectiveness of the opposition (or lack thereof), America failed
to recognize who Obama is, what he believes, and what he
ultimately wants to accomplish: tearing down America's values,
denigrating our rich heritage of faith and liberty, and changing
the United States into just another failing Western socialist
democracy.

Yesterday, the American voters consciously made several
critical decisions that will impact this nation for generations to
come:

We chose to pursue collective equality instead of
individual liberty.

We chose Socialism and Progressivism instead of
Americanism.

We chose to support gay-marriage instead of traditional
marriage.

We chose to support state-funded contraception and
abortion instead of protecting life.

We chose to support more dangerous federal borrowing
and reckless, wasteful spending instead of responsible fiscal
policies.

We chose to support the expanding welfare state at the
expense of the shrinking working state.

We chose to allow the government to make our healthcare
decisions instead of ourselves.

We chose to continue the policies of irresponsible waste
and mismanagement of our resources.

We chose to abandon Israel and support pro-Islamic, anti-
American policies and sentiments.

Over the last four years, we have watched as Barack Obama apologized to lesser, barbarian nations on behalf of America, allowed our embassies to be overrun by terrorists, one of our ambassadors to be slain, strangled our abundant energy supplies, seized control of numerous private industries, businesses, and even our entire healthcare system. But yesterday, the American majority forgot that any of those incidents happened and rewarded him with another term in office.

In only four short years, Obama and the obstructionist Senate – and enabled by the House of Representatives – has added more to the national debt than the first two hundred and fifteen years of our history, more than the first forty-two presidents combined. Under his administration, the Financial Crisis of 2008 turned into the Great Recession which has lasted for more than four years, with the unemployment rates double or even triple what they have been in a generation. The small businesses that haven't closed their doors are barely surviving because of high energy prices, rising taxes, and crushing regulation – with only more of the same on the horizon.

Today, I feel a tremendous sense of trepidation for the future of this country. With no concerns about another re-election, what accountability will Obama really have? By their votes, the American people overwhelming want the federal government to continue the self-destructive policies of the last four years. After just one term of Obama's socialist policies and overreaches of power, the United States has all but become a republic in name only – the Great Banana Republic of the United States of America. From now on, perhaps we should all face the Capitol and bow when we recite the Pledge of Allegiance.

While America has been on the dangerous road of Progressivism and even socialism for much of the last century, Barack Obama greatly sped up the transformative process. Obama's re-election guarantees that he and the Congress will only continue the self-destructive policies of the last decade – at the expense of the rest of our country. We Americans can no longer allow a handful of people in a distant capital far removed from real accountability (and often even reality) to intrude upon our daily lives as it has for far too long.

The United States of America is – and always has been – a free nation with tens of millions of well-armed and highly individualistic citizens. The only entity in America which We the People really need to fear is our government, regardless of who's in charge of it. Democrat and Republican politicians alike have trampled our God-given rights for their own ends and benefits. And over the past two decades, dangerous amounts of power have been accumulated by our federal government to the point that the States have become almost meaningless.

Many of us are exhausted from the past four years and want to return to our normal lives of not having to deal with politics, debating, and haggling all the time. But the honest assessment is that our work of restoring the American Republic will not revolve around elections, but around our everyday-lives. We must create the nation we desire from the grassroots up, full of liberty and justice for all, and no longer just hope for the best and entrust that vision to others, especially those we elect. If we are to truly restore this nation to her former greatness, we must accept much of the same responsibility that the Founding Fathers did. That generation laid the foundation for the Republic, but after a century of failed Progressivism, it falls upon our generation to restore it.

John Adams once said, "I must study politics and war that my sons may have liberty to study mathematics and philosophy. My sons ought to study mathematics and philosophy, geography, natural history and naval architecture, navigation, commerce and agriculture, in order to give their children a right to study painting, poetry, music, architecture, statuary, tapestry, and porcelain." However, that's only half the cycle of democracy – eventually, another generation must study politics and war again because tyranny always rises when the people become apathetic and negligent. That is where we are today: we must study politics and war so that our children have the liberty to study what they desire.

Are we prepared to accept those same responsibilities that our Founders did? They chose the path of liberty and sacrifice which was often fraught with terrible struggles and suffering. They could've just as easily shrugged their shoulders and bowed their knees to the king and submitted to his tyrannical rule. But they didn't – they chose liberty. The motto of "Liberty or Death!" wasn't just a clever rallying cry; they really meant it, and thousands willingly gave their lives for the Cause.

Today in the early Twenty-First Century, we Americans are once again faced with the same basic choice: liberty or tyranny, freedom or servitude. However, the attitude of far too many Americans towards our problems is one of both ignorance and apathy: "I don't know and I don't care."

Today in this great republic that our Founding Fathers created, what would they say if they saw their creation in its present circumstances? How would they react to the millions of pages of laws and regulations that govern us? Would they be ashamed that their posterity has betrayed everything they fought and bled and died for in the name of mere creature-comforts and convenience? What would they write to the people of this nation that they loved so much and sacrificed everything for? What would they do to restore justice and sensible governance in this land that they and their own forefathers settled and tamed with little more than their bare hands and stubborn will?

The terrible truth about our modern federal government is that it has turned into the very sort that our Founders rebelled against two centuries ago. But it did not happen all at once – we (through our elected officials) did it gradually, vote after vote, election after election, Congress after Congress, and President after President. Mark Levin contends that America has already become "a post-constitutional country" – the Constitution we continue to live under has not been repealed or replaced, as much as it has been rendered largely irrelevant by our own government and courts. By us through our negligence.

Were our Founders all that different than us? Yes and no. Yes, in the fact that they did not remain apathetic, silent, and submit to the tyranny that was being imposed upon them. No, in that they were ordinary men and women like you and me. The difference is that when their natural rights were repeatedly violated, they did not sit idly by and take it – they stood up and defended what was theirs, that which has been given to all mankind by our Creator, that which no king, legislature, or government has the right to take from anyone.

After four years of unrestrained borrowing, spending, and multitudes of new regulations from the federal government, millions of people were looking forward to the 2012 elections and the prospect of placing a new president in the White House. But while changing presidents may slow our current rate of decline, many long-term measures must be immediately taken in order to ensure that such encroachments from our federal government never occur again. And those drastic measures begin with us – in our homes, in our families, and in our private lives.

Early in our history, Alexis de Tocqueville wrote, "America is great because Americans are good." But skim any newspaper in the country or visit any news-website. Is that still true? Are Americans still good by any standard of morality? Could it be that our nation's greatness is waning because our "goodness" has faltered? Are we prepared to ask those difficult questions and honestly examine what has happened – and what is happening – to our country from the highest offices of the land down to the average citizen?

Much of this book was initially written as part of "The American Tyrant" which was specific to the background, philosophy, and political history of Barack Obama. However, due to time constraints (namely, the 2012 elections), the book was split into two: one concerning American tyranny and the other concerning American restoration. As a result of that division, some of the content in the early chapters may sound familiar if you've read "The American Tyrant."

13

The primary goals of this book are to accurately assess the current state of America, as well as rekindle a deep appreciation and love for our country, our shared heritage and history, our national ideals and character, and our unique American identity. Americans tend to have short memories, and after the last four years, far too many Americans have forgotten what it really means to be an American, and exactly why the United States of America is a very special nation. The United States of America is an exceptional country because of her people, not because of our government – and we are a much better people than what we have become.

As you read this book, please understand that I am not a lawyer, nor a scholar, nor am I very eloquent at times, but I deeply love my country, her history, and her people, and I grieve for her in her current state of decline. If these clumsy words can help awaken the love of America in just one person, the effort will have been worth it. Our Declaration of Independence and Constitution were not written just for lawyers, judges, academics, or scholars, but for everyday people like you and me. That is one of the many things that makes our founding – and our Founding Fathers – extraordinarily special and breathtaking to contemplate.

Lastly, I feel compelled to offer a brief word of caution: this book is not for the faint of heart. It is certain to offend some of the sensibilities of most readers. But that's okay – we all need to be shaken up from time to time. And regardless of how dark the days ahead may become, America will always be a country worth fighting for – not because of her resources, land, or her wealth, but because of her ideals and heritage.

"The time is now near at hand which must probably determine whether Americans are to be freemen or slaves; whether they are to have any property they can call their own;

whether their houses and farms are to be pillaged and destroyed, and themselves consigned to a state of wretchedness from which no human efforts will deliver them. The fate of unborn millions will now depend, under God, on the courage and conduct of this army. Our cruel and unrelenting enemy leaves us only the choice of brave resistance, or the most abject submission. We have, therefore, to resolve to conquer or die." – George Washington

Chapter 1 - Our Current Crisis

"THESE are the times that try men's souls. The summer soldier and the sunshine patriot will, in this crisis, shrink from the service of their country; but he that stands it now, deserves the love and thanks of man and woman. Tyranny, like hell, is not easily conquered; yet we have this consolation with us, that the harder the conflict, the more glorious the triumph. What we obtain too cheap, we esteem too lightly: it is dearness only that gives every thing its value. Heaven knows how to put a proper price upon its goods; and it would be strange indeed if so celestial an article as freedom should not be highly rated." – Thomas Paine, "The American Crisis"

In the closing days of 1776, five months after America had declared its independence from Great Britain, it appeared that the American Revolution had failed. What had begun with a resounding cry for liberty seemed to be ending with a whimper. The Continental Army was more of a stumbling, bungling, ragtag group of vagabonds than an army – by anyone's measure. Enlistments, gunpowder, supplies, and fortitude were rapidly running out; Congress had little power to finance the war and soldier after soldier slunk away from the war-effort or simply didn't reenlist. General George Washington was battling his detractors in the Congress nearly as hard as the British. By all accounts, the noble quest for American independence seemed to be falling apart before it had even found it's stride.

In those fading days of 1776, the Signers of the Declaration of Independence must have wondered where they had gone wrong. Where were the brave patriots who had sworn to give all to the glorious Cause? In those dark days, it seemed as though the only thing they could do was pray – yet not even God was answering their pleas for help. But then one week before

Christmas, Thomas Paine published the first of his "The American Crisis" pamphlets, which was read aloud to the Continental Army mere hours before the Battle of Trenton in the desperate hopes of bolstering morale among the wavering soldiers. And bolster them it did; after retreating from the British time after time in 1776, Washington and his army launched a surprise attack on the Hessians the day after Christmas – and to everyone's surprise, won the battle and likely saved the revolution.

According to numerous first-hand accounts from the Revolutionary War, God frequently moved in the hearts and minds of both the Americans and their enemies, and sometimes even in the very winds, waves, and weather itself. Bizarre winds and storms that would suddenly arise, as well as unusual occurrences of thick fog to confound the British and aid the Americans gave credence to the belief that God wanted America to be independent – though they still had to fight for their freedom. The long, trying years of the Revolution forged a new nation out of thirteen very different Colonies, and thus America was born. George Washington would credit the moving of this Invisible Hand in America for the remainder of his life.

Throughout most of the Revolutionary War, America faced a threefold crisis: lack of soldiers, lack of supplies/money, and lack of allies. But one by one, God provided for those needs – first in Valley Forge and the months that followed, then with our newfound allies from France and Prussia. Would Americans have won their freedom had those allies never joined us? I contend that we would have, though it would've probably taken longer due to the limited numbers of soldiers and a negligible navy. Once the fires of independence were set ablaze in the peoples' hearts, it is nearly impossible to extinguish.

Today in America, we too face a threefold crisis, but one which has been slowly constructed by the hands of our own public trustees – and our own negligence – over the last century: exploding public debt (and soon, inflation), vast

17

government regulations/bureaucracy, and the trampling of the Rule of Law by our officials in the highest offices of the land. And while those challenges are daunting, there is really no reason why they cannot be overcome. America has faced and defeated similar challenges before – she only needs the will and the vision.

The last two presidents, George W. Bush and Barack Obama, have tripled the national debt in less than fifteen years. When President Bush took office, the national debt stood at under $6 trillion; when he left office eight years later, the national debt had nearly doubled to almost $11 trillion. President Obama has outspent his predecessor but in half that time. At the end of Obama's first term in office, the national debt will be well over $16 trillion. The government has been running annual deficits of over $1.3 trillion since 2009. To put this in perspective, Obama has borrowed and spent more in one term in office than all the previous presidents before him combined (excluding Bush 43) – four years versus two hundred and fifteen.

The president is not only the highest elected official in our land, but the foremost representative of our people. When foreigners think of America, the current president typically comes to their mind. Presidents set the standard whether they like it or not, and not only for their administrations, but for the rest of the country as well. What becomes permissible for a president to do while in office, the same often becomes permissible in our society. When a president lies under oath and says that oral sex with an intern in the Oval Office wasn't really sex or even wrong, promiscuity and immorality spread throughout the culture; after all, if such acts are excusable for the Commander-in-Chief, then they are excusable for average citizens. When a conservative president appears to not be concerned with running government efficiently and fails to keep expenditures and debt to a minimum, government waste, fraud, and bureaucracy quickly expand throughout not only the federal government, but throughout the corporate world as well. When a president ignores the Constitution, the Separation of Powers, and the Rule of Law in the name of "getting things done," corruption and lawlessness explode like wildfire and can engulf the entire nation.

While every president has had their faults, Barack Obama is an entirely different sort of president than we've had before. In late 2008, Obama was elected under the banner of reuniting the country, restoring fiscal sanity and efficiency, somehow ending institutionalized racism, and even reversing global warming (which has turned out to be a twenty-year fraud). However, he has not only failed in those grand promises, he has exacerbated the problems by repeatedly violating the Constitution, ignoring the role of Congress and the Courts, and mocking the very notion of the Rule of Law. The mainstream media has been entirely complicit in both the election of and the tyranny of Barack Obama because of their intentional protection and shielding of him from any real accountability. When the average American knows more about the forty-year-old Watergate Scandal of Richard Nixon but not Obama's scandals of "Fast and Furious" and the "Benghazi Attack," it's a clear indication of the media being little more than puppets or even mouthpieces of the Obama administration.

By abandoning most of the constitutional restraints on the Executive Branch and ruling by Executive Orders and his unelected, unconfirmed, unaccountable advisors (known as "czars"), Obama has repeatedly trampled the Constitution and all but negated the need for the Legislative Branch or the Judicial Branch. Increasingly, he has begun ruling simply by fiat, creating new laws, regulations, agencies, and even treaties out of thin air, despite the fact that he has absolutely no power to do so under the Constitution. Past presidents from time to time have differed with Congress and the Courts and have even tried to skirt the Rule of Law, but never as blatantly and willfully as this president.

Needless to say, because of such flagrant, public violations of the Constitution and the Rule of Law, millions of Americans are getting informed and involved in the political process. Many of these violations – especially healthcare reform – will affect our personal lives in very dramatic ways. Never before has so much of our individual sovereignty been threatened and violated by our own government, and now many people are genuinely frightened about what is happening to the country they have known and loved their entire lives. Most Americans don't want throw away everything that we and our ancestors have fought and bled and died for over the last three centuries, but far too many continue to ignore the threat of our current circumstances. However, the good news is that after decades of apathy and abstaining from politics, American citizens are waking up to the awful consequences of our elected officials' decisions and who we put in the White House.

America After Obama

After more than four years of Obama's presidency and the culmination of a century of Progressive policies, America has been experiencing unbelievable economic damage. There is no end in sight to the Great Recession that began in 2007-2008, though the Obama administration claims it ended in 2010. Today, the financial crisis that exploded in the fall of 2008 is no longer confined to Wall Street, the banks, and the mortgage industry, but has spread throughout the economy. Bankruptcy, bailouts, insolvency, and sky-rocketing public debt now stalk the land and continue to strangle the U.S. economy.

Consider just a few of the current economic highlights after Obama's first term in office:

- Unemployment has been over 8% for 44 straight months – since the very beginning of Obama's first term. But more importantly, the true unemployment rate (which includes the under-employed and those who have given up looking for work) is in the range of 15% to 20%. That mirrors the range of the worst years of the Great

Depression in the 1930s. The numbers decreased slightly just before the election, but remain close to the 8% level.

- The Labor Force Participation Rate among men is the lowest since 1948.
- The U.S. manufacturing activity has plummeted to the lowest level in three years.
- The housing collapse that began in 2008 is now deeper than at the peak of the Great Depression.
- There are 46 million Americans now on food-stamps, and record others are on welfare.
- There are nearly 11 million Americans now on disability, more than the entire population of New York City.
- Over 100 million Americans now get some form of entitlement checks like Social Security or Medicare (almost 1 out of every 3 Americans).
- The net worth for American families is down 40% from 2008.
- New business startups are at the lowest level in 30 years.
- The U.S. credit rating has been downgraded for first time in history – twice.
- More than $6 trillion has been added to the national debt in four years – a 50% increase in the entire national debt.
- More than 1.4 million businesses filed for bankruptcy in the last year alone (2011). Not since the staggering 330,000 businesses that filed for bankruptcy during Jimmy Carter's final year in office have so many businesses closed down.
- Last but certainly not least, with the upholding of ObamaCare in the Supreme Court, a recent survey shows that more than 80% of all doctors are considering leaving their practices or simply retiring early. This comes at the same time that the Baby Boomers have begun retiring, when over 30 million new patients are being added to the Medicare rolls. Between ObamaCare

and our rapidly-aging population, we should expect much poorer quality of care, poorer service, European-style waits in diagnosis and treatment, and looming bankruptcy in our healthcare system.

Because of the utterly reckless spending that began under George W. Bush and then exploded under Barack Obama, the national debt has nearly tripled in less than fifteen years, with Obama spending more in one term in office than Bush did in his two terms. Though tax revenues dropped in 2009, rather than cut government spending to reduce our liabilities, Obama put federal spending into overdrive, resulting in deficits over $1.3 trillion per year. With massive deficits, no sensible budget, complete gridlock in Congress, and the skyrocketing public debt, the United States government is now borrowing – or rather printing via the Federal Reserve – 46 cents for every dollar spent. Imagine borrowing almost the same amount of money you made every paycheck with no end in sight and then saddling your children and grandchildren with that outrageous debt (along with the interest). That is the fiscal policy of the federal government of the United States of America today.

A Nation Divided

One of the reasons why so many people voted for Barack Obama in 2008 is that they were sick and tired of the bitter partisanship that has divided the country since the 1990s, though it dramatically increased after the contentious 2000 election of George W. Bush. While the raw partisanship was bad, the constant agitation by the mainstream media only exacerbated the national divide, especially after the invasion of Iraq in 2003. Americans in both parties wanted the nation to be healed, and Obama was promising to do just that.

Not only was Obama promising national unification and healing, he was also holding out the promise of racial and cultural healing to a nation plagued by racial strife since the days of the Founders. Slavery has been called America's "original sin," and our bitter, bloody Civil War was fought over the issue; but even after slavery had been vanquished, the suppression of liberty, racial tensions, and class warfare continued. The Civil Rights Movement of the 1960s tore down most of the Jim Crow laws and regional/ racial barriers, but still the feeling remained that America had not been completely absolved of her terrible sin of slavery.

When Obama burst onto the national political scene at the Democratic National Convention in 2004, many saw that perhaps he was the one to finally fix the racial problems in America. After all, he appeared to be the ultimate African-American, being the son of a black man from Kenya and a white woman from America. And by his campaign, Obama was only too happy to absorb the hopes and dreams of so many Americans in finally bringing racial harmony to the United States. But has he? Not by any measurable means. If anything, racial tensions have only worsened because of his repeated use of class warfare tactics between the rich and the poor and between the minorities and the whites for purely political purposes. When politicians can't (or won't) unite their constituents, they divide and conquer – which is what Obama has been doing for most of his public life. What's truly tragic about Barack Obama is that he has enormous potential to heal many of this country's wounds, but he has squandered that potential for cheap political gains.

Today in early 2013, America has not been this politically (or culturally) divided since the days of the Revolutionary War and the Civil War. Yet we're not divided between various regions or States in our time, but citizen against citizen, neighbor against neighbor, and brother against brother. For the past century, too many of our politicians have divided us in order that they might be elected into office and acquire power – to conquer us without firing a shot, to subject us to servitude without cracking a whip. Rather than seeing ourselves as Americans with our common bonds of morality, culture, traditions, language, and history, and heritage, too many of us see ourselves as Democrats and Republicans. By their policies and actions, our politicians have successfully divided Americans into warring political parties, classes, and subcultures. But not only have we been divided politically, but we are now deeply divided culturally between traditional America and pop-culture America – and as evidenced in the last election, pop-culture America appears to be winning the battle for the heart of the nation.

Throughout our history, America has been roughly a nation of thirds – one-third has a particular opinion, another third has the opposite opinion, and the last third is undecided. In the Revolution, a third of the people supported the independence effort, a third wanted to remain loyal to Britain, and the other third was on the fence. The divisions during the Civil War were similar, and in both cases, the leanings of the undecided third helped determine the outcome of the war. The undecided third is usually drawn to one side by the successful efforts of one or the other.

The same remains true in our politics today, with many of the politicians spending the vast majority of their time, money, and efforts trying to win the support of the moderate/undecided third. Yet both the Founding generation and even the Civil War generation had numerous advantages that we in modern America are sorely lacking today: a strong identity as Americans, strong homes and communities, large families, and most importantly, a common set of values and moral standards. Though the Continental Army was forced to retreat from the British time and time again and was severely outgunned and outmanned, they continued fighting the war. And of course, there was no guarantee of the outcome – Americans were fighting the strongest army and navy in the world. But they continued to fight for what they held dear, for what they believed in. There was no alternative – and the same later held true for the Civil War. But today, far too many Americans seem to just shrug their shoulders at our problems and go back to

24

watching TV or surfing the Internet, as if our problems are so great and deep that they either can't be fixed or that they must be left to others, to the experts or the politicians.

We not only have a crisis in our government and public institutions, but we also have a threefold crisis throughout our society: exploding depravity, lawlessness, and violence, millions of broken homes, and an absence of basic moral standards and even the values which produce them. The basis for every society, culture, and nation is the family, and the foundation of every family is the marriage. The United States of America today has the highest divorce rate in the world (4.95 divorces per 1000, half of all marriages end in divorce) – is it any wonder our nation is in a shambles? If our homes are breaking apart and crumbling, then so follows our civilization. When our homes are divided, our nation becomes divided.

Another reason America is faltering is because the country is dramatically changing due to the long march of Progressivism and Leftism through our public institutions. Our American civilization is based upon the concepts of limited government as defined in the Constitution which emphasizes individual liberty, individual responsibility, and individual, localized self-government; meanwhile, the American culture and public institutions are increasingly centralized, bureaucratic, and collectivist/socialist. The federal government itself teaches and reinforces collectivism in our education system, mass-media, and pop-culture which has resulted in growing numbers of people who want socialism instead of republicanism, while the rest of us want to remain governed by the concepts of limited government set forth by our Founders in the Constitution.

William Penn once said, "If we will not be governed by God, then we will be ruled by tyrants." In America today, we have refused to submit to the light governance of God and His eternal standards for just, orderly societies, and now we are being ruled by the heavy hand of tyrants in the White House, the Congress, the Courts, and countless other agencies of our governments, the greatest being the federal government today.

25

The State of the Union

Even before the Financial Crisis of 2008, America's financial system had been on shaky grounds by our loose monetary policy after 2001 and the record-low interest rates. If America was not in economic decline before Barack Obama took office in 2009, it certainly is after four years of his radical Progressive social and economic policies.

The following are the fifty economic numbers from 2011 that should shock every American (via The Economic Collapse):

1. A staggering 48% of all Americans are either considered to be "low income" or are living in poverty.

2. Approximately 57% of all children in the United States are living in homes that are either considered to be "low income" or impoverished.

3. If the number of Americans that "wanted jobs" was the same today as it was back in 2007, the "official" unemployment rate put out by the U.S. government would be up to 11%.

4. The average amount of time that a worker stays unemployed in the United States is now over 40 weeks.

5. One recent survey found that 77% of all U.S. small businesses do not plan to hire any more workers.

6. There are fewer payroll jobs in the United States today than there were back in 2000 even though we have added 30 million extra people to the population since then.

7. Since December 2007, median household income in the United States has declined by a total of 6.8% once inflation is accounted for.

8. According to the Bureau of Labor Statistics, 16.6 million Americans were self-employed back in December 2006. Today, that number has shrunk to 14.5 million.

9. A Gallup poll from earlier this year (2011) found that approximately one out of every five Americans that do have a job consider themselves to be underemployed.

10. According to author Paul Osterman, about 20% of all U.S. adults are currently working jobs that pay poverty-level wages.

11. Back in 1980, less than 30% of all jobs in the United States were low income jobs. Today, more than 40% of all jobs in the United States are low income jobs.

12. Back in 1969, 95% of all men between the ages of 25 and 54 had a job. In July, only 81.2% of men in that age group had a job.

13. One recent survey found that one out of every three Americans would not be able to make a mortgage or rent payment next month if they suddenly lost their current job.

14. The Federal Reserve recently announced that the total net worth of U.S. households declined by 4.1% in the 3rd quarter of 2011 alone.

15. According to a recent study conducted by the Black Rock Investment Institute, the ratio of household debt to personal income in the United States is now 154%.

16. As the economy has slowed down, so has the number of marriages. According to a Pew Research Center analysis, only 51% of all Americans that are at least 18 years old are currently married. Back in 1960, 72% of all U.S. adults were married.

17. The U.S. Postal Service has lost more than $5 billion over the past year.

18. In Stockton, California home prices have declined 64% from where they were at when the housing market peaked.

19. Nevada has had the highest foreclosure rate in the nation for 59 months in a row.

20. Once the third largest city in America, the median price of a home in Detroit is now less than $6000.

21. According to the U.S. Census Bureau, 18% of all homes in the state of Florida are sitting vacant. That figure is 63% larger than it was just ten years ago.

22. New home construction in the United States is on pace to set a brand new all-time record low in 2011.

23. Currently, 19% of all American men between the ages of 25 and 34 are now living with their parents.

24. Electricity bills in the United States have risen faster than the overall rate of inflation for five years in a row.

25. According to the Bureau of Economic Analysis, healthcare costs accounted for just 9.5% of all personal consumption back in 1980. Today they account for approximately 16.3% (and with the passage of Obamacare, those costs will only continue to increase).

26. One study found that approximately 41% of all working age Americans either have medical bill problems or are currently paying off medical debt.

27. One out of every seven Americans has at least 10 credit cards.

28. The United States spends about $4 on goods and services from China for every $1 that China spends on goods and services from the United States.

29. It is being projected that the U.S. trade deficit for 2011 will be $558.2 billion.

30. The retirement crisis in the United States continues to worsen. According to the Employee Benefit Research Institute, 46% of all American workers have less than $10,000 saved for retirement, and 29% of all American workers have less than $1,000 saved for retirement. ($1,000 is about one month's worth of minimum wages)

31. Today, one out of every six elderly Americans lives below the federal poverty line.

32. According to a study that was just released, CEO pay at America's biggest companies rose by 36.5% in just one recent twelve-month period.

33. Today, the "too big to fail" banks are larger than ever. The total assets of the six largest U.S. banks increased by 39% between September 30, 2006 and September 30, 2011.

34. The six heirs of Wal-Mart founder Sam Walton have a net worth that is roughly equal to the bottom 30% of all Americans combined.

35. According to an analysis of Census Bureau data done by the Pew Research Center, the median net worth for households led by someone 65 years of age or older is 47 times greater than the median net worth for households led by someone under the age of 35.

36. Today, 37% of all U.S. households that are led by someone under the age of 35 have a net worth of $0 or even less than $0.

37. A higher percentage of Americans is living in extreme poverty (6.7%) than has ever been measured before.

38. Child homelessness in the United States is now 33% higher than it was back in 2007.

39. Since 2007, the number of children living in poverty in the State of California alone has increased by 30%.

40. Tragically, child poverty is exploding all over America. According to the National Center for Children in Poverty, 36.4% of all children that live in Philadelphia are living in poverty, 40.1% of all children that live in Atlanta are living in poverty, 52.6% of all children that live in Cleveland are living in poverty and 53.6% of all children that live in Detroit are living in poverty.

41. One out of every seven Americans is on food stamps and one out of every four American children is on food stamps.

42. In 1980, government transfer payments accounted for just 11.7% of all income. Today, government transfer payments account for more than 18% of all income.

43. A staggering 48.5% of all Americans live in a household that receives some form of government benefits. Back in 1983, that number was below 30%.

44. Right now, spending by the federal government accounts for about 24% of GDP. Back in 2001, it accounted for just 18%.

45. For fiscal year 2011, the U.S. federal government had a budget deficit of nearly $1.3 trillion. That was the third year in a row that our budget deficit has topped $1 trillion.

46. If Bill Gates gave every single penny of his fortune to the U.S. government, it would only cover the U.S. budget deficit for about 15 days.

47. Amazingly, the U.S. government has now accumulated a total debt of $16 trillion (2013). When Barack Obama first took office the national debt was just $10.6 trillion.

48. If the federal government began right at this moment to repay the U.S. national debt at a rate of one dollar per second, it would take over 440,000 years to pay off the national debt.

49. The U.S. national debt has been increasing by an average of more than $4 billion per day since the beginning of the Obama administration.

50. During the Obama administration, the U.S. government has accumulated more debt than it did from the time that George Washington took office (1789) to the time that Bill Clinton took office (1993).

Of course, after going through all these numbers, the obvious question is: "How has it come to this?" The simple answer is that the United States government has been spending (and promising to spend) trillions of dollars it does not have, and is enabled to do so by the nation's central bank: the Federal Reserve.

At the core of our economic problems is the Federal Reserve, which encourages a debt-based economy rather than an asset-based economy, along with irresponsible government borrowing and spending. Like most central banks, the Federal Reserve is a perpetual debt machine, and will continue creating debt until it's either severely regulated or put out of existence. The Federal Reserve not only enables, but encourages our government to be wasteful and spend vast amounts of money it does not have.

The Federal Reserve creates money out of nothing and floods our banks and economy with their banknotes, which has almost completely destroyed the value of the U.S. dollar. The real value of the dollar has dropped more than 95% since the Fed was created in 1913. The Federal Reserve has a nightmarish track record of incompetence and is largely responsible for causing both the Great Depression and the recent Great Recession by its monetary policies. If the Federal Reserve System had never been created, the U.S. economy would be in far better shape and far more stable.

But our flailing economy is only the surface indicator of the decline of our great nation – the much more tragic decline of America can be seen in our cities, communities, schools, churches, families, homes, marriages, and our children. From "America: To Pray or Not to Pray" by David Barton of WallBuilders:

- For 15 years before 1963, pregnancies in girls ages 15 through 19 years had been no more than 15 per thousand. After 1963, pregnancies increased 187% in the next 15 years.
- For younger girls, ages 10 to 14 years, pregnancies since 1963 are up 553%.
- Before 1963, sexually transmitted diseases among students were 400 per 100,000. Since 1963, they were up 226% in the next 12 years.
- Before 1963, divorce rates had been declining for 15 years. After 1963, divorces increased 300% each year for the next 15 years.
- Since 1963, unmarried people living together is up 353%
- Since 1963, single-parent families are up 140%.
- Since 1963, single-parent families with children are up 160%.
- The educational standard of measure has been the SAT scores. SAT scores had been steady for many years

31

before 1963. From 1963 they rapidly declined for 18 consecutive years, even though the same test has been used since 1941.

- In 1974-75 the rate of decline of the SAT scores decreased, even though they continued to decline. That was when there was an explosion of private religious schools. There were only 1000 Christian schools in 1965. Between 1974 to 1984 they increased to 32,000. The SAT scores for private schools were nearly 100 points higher than public schools.
- Of the nation's top academic scholars, three times as many come from private religious schools, which operate on one-third the funds as do the public schools.
- Since 1963, violent crime has increased 544%.
- Illegal drugs have become an enormous and uncontrollable problem.
- The nation has been deprived of an estimated 55 million citizens through legal abortions just since 1973.

On the Road to Tyranny

High budget deficits and skyrocketing public debt are not only recipes for a national financial disaster, but our gigantic federal debt has put America on the road to tyranny. When a government can't pay its bills and manage its debts, it has two choices: collect more taxes or default on the debt – and defaulting on the debt is never really an option because it destroys the nation's credit. In order to collect more taxes, the government can encourage economic growth (and therefore increase tax revenues) by relaxing regulation and actually lowering the tax rates as was done in the 1980s under Ronald Reagan. By lowering the marginal tax rates and streamlining the tax code and other regulations, economic growth exploded and the revenue to the Treasury nearly doubled in only eight years.

However, encouraging economic growth to raise more tax revenue is not the instinctive response of most governments – raising taxes on the populace is. Under this policy, tax revenues will initially increase, but then steadily decrease because taxes are always a drag on the economy. And depending on the tax burdens placed on the citizens – especially the wealthier citizens who invest their money in businesses and investments that spur economic growth – the financial consequences can quickly turn catastrophic.

The former policy is the route that Ronald Reagan and George W. Bush took in the tax reforms early in their administrations and both led to steady, solid economic growth. However, Jimmy Carter, Barack Obama, and other liberal presidents have taken the latter route, which produces economic stagnation – if not worse. The high tax rates that the "Bush Tax Cuts" slashed were introduced in the latter years of Bill Clinton's term in office, which initially produced increased revenue to the Treasury, but by 2000 had led to a recession. The only positives that came out of the recent Fiscal Cliff negotiations were that most of the reduced rates were made permanent and the AMT (Alternative Minimum Tax) was finally indexed to inflation.

By nationalizing the healthcare system, strangling economic growth through massive federal regulations, and maintaining deficits well over one-trillion dollars each year, Barack Obama has created the conditions for a future economic disaster that will make the 2008 mortgage meltdown look like a walk in the park. As the government grows increasingly desperate to balance the budget (or at least bring more revenue into the Treasury), their instinctive response is to dramatically raise taxes. But that response will only exacerbate America's economic problems because people will further hunker down and try to protect their financial assets rather than risk them through making investments and building small businesses that promote economic growth. And as the desperation grows, so will tyranny from the government.

Those familiar with early American history know that it was Britain's doubling of their national debt in the Seven Years War (the French and Indian War in America) that led to the tough new taxes and onerous regulations imposed on the American Colonies. The British government became increasingly aggressive in raising revenue and dug in their heels to enforce the new taxes, and the king and the Parliament became tyrannical towards the Colonies. When the Americans finally had enough, they rebelled against the British tyranny and claimed their independence – and the rest is history.

Today, our own federal government is leading America down the same path that our Founding Fathers first rebelled against: tyranny from high taxes and infuriating regulations that resulted from vast, wasteful government overspending. But even those challenges could be overcome if our communities and families were as stable and strong as they once were. Marriages and families are the foundation of every society, and when they are strong, the society is strong – but when they are weak, the society crumbles and declines. Nations are only as strong and stable as their families, and America is no different.

If America is to really recover and be restored, we not only need to get our fiscal house in order, but our homes and families in order as well. But first, we need to know where we came from and how we got to where we are today.

Chapter 2 - Where Did We Come From?

*"Last and not least, they cherished a great hope and inward
zeal of laying good foundations, or at least making some ways
toward it, for the propagation and advance of the gospel of the
kingdom of Christ in the remote parts of the world, even though
they should be but stepping stones to others in the performance
of so great a work."* – William Bradford

Since the early 1960s, something has dramatically changed
in the deepest levels of American society. After the brief period
of Pax Americana in the 1950s, it seemed as if some invisible
switch was flipped in the heart of the United States and the very
fabric of the nation began quickly unraveling. Almost overnight
we went from light to darkness, from optimism to pessimism,
and from America the Great to America the Guilty.

Some cite the shocking assassination of John F. Kennedy as
the trigger which threw the nation into a cultural upheaval,
while others cite the urban race-riots, civil rights and anti-war
protests, and the unpopular Vietnam War. Others say that
American finally woke up from the idealistic Fifties to the
"realism" of the Sixties. However, those suggestions are only
the surface indicators of a much deeper, more fundamental
change within the heart and soul of our nation.

On June 17, 1963, America's highest court in the nation –
the Supreme Court of the United States – declared that America
was now independent of God. In the case of "Abington School
District v. Schempp" the use of Bibles in public school was
ruled unconstitutional by the Court appointed by FDR, the
Hugo Black Court. As Chief Justice, Hugo Black popularized
the notion of the "Separation of Church and State" used so often
today in ruling against any (and all) religious influence in the
country. This phrase has been quoted and cited so often that

35

many Americans believe that it's part of the Bill of Rights, namely the First Amendment.

Surprisingly, the term "Separation of Church and State" is nowhere in the Constitution, but originated from a letter that Thomas Jefferson wrote to the Danbury Baptists, who were concerned about the free exercise of their beliefs. There were rumors circulating that the State of Connecticut was going to make one denomination the official state denomination, and the Baptists wanted to have the President give them his written guarantee of their freedom to worship as they saw fit. Jefferson wrote that the First Amendment in essence created a wall of separation of Church and State. It wasn't that the Baptists were pressuring the State, it was that the State (of Connecticut) was pressuring the Church.

The First Amendment clearly states that "Congress shall make no law respecting an establishment of religion, or prohibiting the free exercise thereof..." Contrary to modern revisionism, the Founders weren't attempting to extinguish religion, as much as prevent a state-preferred religion from dominating the nation, as was commonplace in England and throughout much of Europe. The Founders were protecting the freedom to worship as everyone saw fit, not destroy religion or even isolate it from the public square. In fact, religion plays a critical role in every government and society, as it's the primary means of establishing and communicating the moral values/code of a society.

There are five pillars in every society that are responsible for preserving and passing along its history and values: the families, the religious institutions, the media (in various forms), the educational system, and the government. Some societies blend one or more of these pillars together while others separate and isolate them. In the ancient world, the government, educational system, and religious institutions were often combined into some form of state-religion structure. Modern societies typically separate these pillars so they function independently, though over the last century, many societies

36

have been steadily returning to the state-religion model under the banner of secular humanism.

The teaching of history plays a vital role in communicating, validating, and reinforcing a society's values. If a nation's values are directly attacked, the societal pillars and values themselves are often sufficient to repel the frontal assault and the foreign ideas are rejected. However, if the history of a society is gradually corrupted in a continuous series of small, indirect revisions, people begin to question where they came from, and soon they will start questioning and even rebelling against the society's long-held values and eventually accept the foreign values. For much of the last century, but in particular the last fifty years, the history and faith of America's Founding Fathers have been under constant attack from secular revisionists, who are committed to replacing our traditional Judeo-Christian values of America with the values that more closely match their own: secular humanism.

When a nation forgets – or is purposefully made to forget – their own history and heritage, they will soon forget their traditions and values. Eventually, the nation becomes unglued and unanchored and can be twisted and turned by whatever cultural or political winds are blowing. One of the first targets of the American secularists was the "Father of our Country," George Washington, who came under assault by the revisionists in the early 1930s. A picture of George Washington (and Abraham Lincoln) used to be proudly displayed in every schoolroom in the country – but today they have been either thrown out or replaced by the portrait of the current president. Why? Could it be that the secular educrats want whoever our current president is to be our standard rather than the Father of our Country? Could it be so our children are not prompted to ask about who our most prominent Founding Father was? Could it be so they are not prompted to ask where we came from?

In American society, the educational system (especially the public schools), the media, our churches, and our families are responsible for teaching America's history, about our Founders, and their rich heritage of faith and character that guided them. But sometime in the last century, the ties that bound those societal pillars together came undone, and suddenly they went their separate ways. The families stopped teaching their children and left that up to the schools, they stopped passing on their faith and values and left that up to the churches, and then soon the children began hearing contradictory messages between their families, the schools, the churches, and the media.

Today, the five pillars that were once bound together so tightly to keep America strong and united have completely broken down. Good families are few and far between, the churches are confused, weak, and behave more like social clubs than religious institutions. The educational system and media not only refuse to accurately teach about our history and our Forefathers, they often teach the exact opposite, painting Washington, Jefferson, and Madison as wealthy, white (and therefore racist), slave-owning hypocrites.

If America's values are to be restored, then her history and her heroes must be restored. Most people need heroes – living or dead – that they can draw upon for encouragement and examples to follow during their own daily struggles. Who could not be encouraged by the stories of how George Washington refused to give up and surrender after suffering terrible defeats and retreating from the British time and time again? And what about Lincoln's firing of general after general until he found the one to defeat the Confederate Army?

But now that such real American heroes have been denigrated and removed from our history books, what heroes do our children look up to? They look up to the ones they see on television and in magazines, most of whom aren't real heroes at all, but merely the most popular pop-culture icons of the week. Traditional American heroes like Washington and Lincoln were ordinary people with extraordinary character, who made impossibly difficult choices and then stood by those decisions. Most modern American heroes merely scored more points than the other players in a game or had more #1 songs on the music-charts. Modern liberals like to call everyone "heroes" and proclaim that everyone is special; and as others have observed: "When everyone is special, no one is."

So who are America's real heroes? What is America's history? Where did we come from? What circumstances and past leaders made us into the nation that we are today, or at least the nation that we once were? What made America, "America?" Before the 1960s, the very word "America" evoked smiles and eye-twinkles, and looks of beaming pride and boundless optimism. But since then, that same word provokes scorn, frowns, and often derision. Even our current president – Barack Hussein Obama – frequently apologizes for our country's past sins while abroad and declares that America is not special or exceptional any more than France, Spain, or Japan are special in their own right. While it's sad enough to hear a fellow American voice such feelings, it's even more maddening when our own sitting president and representatives announce them publicly for all the world to hear, mock, and amplify. And yet to our shame, that same president was re-elected and most of those same representatives and Senators hold office year after year.

Could it be that we have forgotten what makes America unique and exceptional among all the other nations of the world? Why did people even come to this new land? What were they seeking? Were they merely chasing after gold, silver, and precious stones like the other Europeans did to our south? Or did those early Americans sacrifice for something much more important – something much greater?

Settlers of Faith

After the discovery of the Americas by Christopher Columbus in 1492, the first attempts to colonize North America came mostly from England, which had sought to rival Spain's successes in the southern hemisphere of the New World. Sir Walter Raleigh sent an expedition that landed in Roanoke (Virginia) in July of 1584, but the colony vanished within several years. In 1607, the Virginia Company settled Jamestown, but it was met with disaster after disaster such as pestilence, starvation, and Indian attacks. It wasn't until 1624 when the King of England took over the colony that it finally stabilized and began to grow on its own.

The Pilgrims of Plymouth were the first to successfully establish a self-sufficient colony in America in 1620, though they lost nearly half their number within the first few years. Under the leadership of William Bradford, the colony survived, established itself, and slowly grew. The Pilgrims (formerly known as the Separatists) came to America seeking religious freedom from the terrible persecution under the Church of England. The Pilgrims had originally signed a charter with the Virginia Company, but when they landed north in Cape Cod, they forged a new charter amongst themselves called the Mayflower Compact, the first form of civil government created in North America.

> *In the name of God, Amen. We, whose names are underwritten, the loyal subjects of our dread Sovereign Lord King James, by the Grace of God, of Great Britain, France, and Ireland, King, defender of the Faith, etc.*
>
> *Having undertaken, for the Glory of God, and advancements of the Christian faith and honor of our King and Country, a voyage to plant the first colony in the Northern parts of Virginia, do by these presents, solemnly and mutually, in the presence of God, and one another, covenant and combine ourselves together into a civil body politic; for our better ordering, and preservation and furtherance of the ends aforesaid; and by virtue hereof to enact, constitute, and frame, such just and equal laws, ordinances, acts, constitutions, and offices, from time to time, as shall be thought most meet and convenient for the general good of the colony; unto which we promise all due submission and obedience.*

*In witness whereof we have hereunto subscribed our
names at Cape Cod the 11th of November, in the year of the
reign of our Sovereign Lord King James, of England,
France, and Ireland, the eighteenth, and of Scotland the
fifty-fourth, 1620.*

In 1628, a much larger group of persecuted Christians left
England for the New World and settled near the Pilgrims on the
Northeastern coast. Though they held similar religious views as
the Pilgrims, they were Puritans but not Separatists. From 1630
to 1640, over 20,000 Puritans settled the Massachusetts Bay
Colony and built numerous farms, villages, and towns, notably
Salem and Boston. In the following decades, tens of thousands
more colonists came to New England and established the
colonies which would later become the States of Pennsylvania,
New York, Rhode Island, Connecticut, Delaware, and
Maryland.

With the establishment of the much larger Massachusetts
Bay Colony, soon the original settlers of Plymouth were
absorbed and simply became part of New England. With their
high ideals of education, religion, and hard-work, the Puritans
established many of the early laws, doctrines, and civil
institutions in New England. However, due to their strict
religious practices and intolerance for other faiths, other more
tolerant colonies and villages were soon established nearby,
notably the Anglicans, Quakers, and Baptists.

While the Pilgrims were few and had sought peace with the
surrounding Indian tribes, the much greater numbers and
settlements of the Puritans (as well as the nearby growing Dutch
colonies) exacerbated relations and soon wars broke out
between the colonists and the natives, as in the Pequot War and
King Philip's War. By the late Seventeenth Century, most of the
natives had been either pacified, killed from war, integrated into
the Colonies, succumbed to foreign diseases, or had been driven
away. The mistreatment of the Indians was one of the first

declarations of "white man's guilt" by the Progressives – and rightly so in some cases.

Over the course of the last century – particularly the last fifty years when American history began being rewritten by the secularists – the Puritans have been portrayed as religious extremists on the order of the Taliban, as if most of the Puritans constantly ran around with torches hunting down witches and anyone else who broke their religious code. The Puritans did have very strict standards with regards to education, society, and their strong work-ethic, which later became extremely legalistic and caused many to depart from their congregations. As a result, the Puritan churches mostly either softened or died out within the Seventeenth Century, though many of their standards for the society remained. If there is one group to be credited with laying the foundations of the American civil society, justice system, reverence for education, and work-ethic, it's the Puritans. And while the Puritans may have been wrong or extreme in their later religious practices, they were certainly right in most of the civil institutions they founded and the legacy they left behind.

One question seldom asked today is why the Pilgrims and the Puritans succeeded in their northern colonies while the southern colonies all but failed. In fact, it was only by their continual re-supplements that the southern colonies survived as long as they did. The settlers of Jamestown and Roanoke were better prepared and supplied than the Pilgrims, yet their mortality rates were nearly 90% as opposed to the 50% of the Pilgrims. Not only that, but the Pilgrims and Puritans became self-sufficient within a matter of years while the settlers at Jamestown took decades.

The answer lies in their purposes and intentions for coming to the New World. The settlers of Jamestown were mostly men intent on finding the fabled riches and gold of America like the Spanish had discovered to the south, and many presumed to return to England with their newfound fame and fortune. But the Pilgrims and Puritans had no such delusions – or intentions.

They came to settle a new land and create a nation of faith. The Pilgrims saw themselves as literal stepping-stones for their children, grandchildren, and the generations to follow, but not for wealth, but liberty and religious freedom. They gladly sacrificed everything so their posterity could live in a free land and live according to their dictates rather than under the tyranny of the king and the state-church.

The Great Awakening

As time went on and the Colonies were established and rapidly spread, the fervor and the first ideals of the Puritans began to wane, and the spirit of the faith and unity which motivated the early settlers was replaced by a growing apathy. Familiarity breeds lethargy, apathy, and later even contempt and disdain, and the Colonists were no different. And while their religion had not changed much, by the early Eighteenth Century, the people were still going through the motions of the religion, but its spirit was fading. New England was gradually becoming more and more like Old England.

In the late 1730s, a handful of preachers began traveling up and down the coast, preaching the Gospel to the Colonists. Men such as George Whitfield and Jonathan Edwards re-ignited the flames of faith which had once burned so brightly in the New World, but had steadily dimmed over the decades. This grassroots revival later became known as the "Great Awakening" which lasted nearly thirty years, and roughly ended with the passing of George Whitfield.

During the Great Awakening, the Gospel and the teachings of the Bible rang throughout the Colonies once again. People in the tens of thousands heard the Good News, repented, and were spiritually reborn. But the transformation wasn't just in the churches, but throughout their society. Homes were renewed, parents were changed, families were improved, and children were raised with the wisdom of the knowledge of the Bible and what was expected of a decent, orderly society and a people who wished to live free and remain free. The principles and truths which had first established the Colonies in the New World were rediscovered and began to spread anew.

Another effect of the Great Awakening was that the cold traditionalism was countered with individual religious experience, which undercut the authority and power in the larger denominations, some of which tended to be more loyal to the king of England. The fiery messages of individual salvation and societal revival preached up and down the coasts also unified the spirit of the Colonies, further dismantling the differences between not only denominations, but entire regions and colonies. The Great Awakening also produced a fresh crop of pastors who spread out and planted churches, as well as produced new orators who would later speak out against the growing tyranny of the king in the years ahead.

Late in the Great Awakening, a series of conflicts between the English, the French, the Colonists, and the Indians broke out in the New World: the French and Indian War. It was in these conflicts that the future American military leaders and the first soldiers of the ragtag colonial army began to emerge, namely George Washington, Ethan Allen, Horatio Gates, and Charles Lee. While the Colonies had raised militias before, the side-by-side fighting next to the British exposed the inexperienced Colonists to their military strategy and the modern practices of warfare at that time.

Many of the Founding Fathers were young men and children during the Great Awakening, such as the Lees of Virginia, Patrick Henry, Samuel Adams, and his younger cousin John Adams. Benjamin Franklin printed several of Whitfield's sermons which also spread the Gospel message throughout the Colonies. But it wasn't the generation of the Great Awakening that was awakened to the idea of independence from Great Britain – that happened years later in the generation of their children. The generation of the Great Awakening laid the spiritual foundations and further developed the principles of faith, liberty, and self-government which would later culminate in the rally for independence.

The Cry for Independence

On the heels of the Great Awakening came the French and Indian War, which laid the groundwork for eventual American independence. In Europe, Britain and France were fighting the Seven Years' War (1756-1763) which spilled over into their colonies in North America. As a consequence of the long, expensive war that spanned the Atlantic, the British had doubled their national debt. In order to pay those debts, the new King George III and the Parliament imposed new taxes on the Colonies, which the Americans immediately protested. For the next decade, the Americans and the British Crown sparred over taxes and regulations, until matters finally came to a head in New England with the Boston Massacre, the Boston Tea Party, and the Intolerable Acts.

When the British first began passing the various tax-acts, there were no real cries for independence as much as demands for proportional representation in Parliament. In fact, most Colonists couldn't imagine being independent from Great Britain; after all, they were still British citizens and under the authority of the Crown. It took several years for men like James Otis, Samuel Adams, John Adams, Patrick Henry, the Lees of Virginia, and the writings of Thomas Paine to finally convince a plurality of the Colonists that independence from Great Britain was the only answer to subjugation.

One of the most widely debated matters during this time (especially in the churches), was whether the Colonists should remain loyal to the Crown and continue to submit to the king's rule as the Scriptures decreed, or if they should rebel and become a new nation. The early Pilgrims and Puritans testified in their writings and journals that they had been called out of their native lands to forge a new nation: a nation of laws rather than men, and a nation of people that would be self-governed by the Ten Commandments and the Golden Rule. The Great Awakening served to re-ignite that Puritan vision and inspired the Colonies to separate themselves from the Old World once and for all.

Another change that led up to the Revolutionary War was the attitudes and the hardening-of-hearts of the British themselves. Soon after the French and Indian War, King George, Parliament, and the British people began to consider the Colonists to be their subjects rather than their fellow citizens. Meanwhile, the Colonists had been re-awakened to the knowledge that all men were equal under God – including the king and Parliament – and that they had the right to determine their own form of government. What once had been unthinkable mere years earlier became the only option for the Thirteen Colonies as they banded together and produced one of the greatest documents in the history of the world: the Declaration of Independence.

Genuine faith always bears fruit, though sometimes it may not be seen until years afterwards, and often the other fruits of revival may be entirely unexpected. In the case of the Great Awakening, the spiritual revolution eventually led to the cry for independence from an ever-encroaching British king and Parliament which had grown indifferent to the Colonies. And when this spiritual heritage had matured, it led to the Revolutionary War and then later gave birth to the Constitution, which this country has maintained ever since. Today, the United States maintains the oldest working constitution in the world.

The French and Indian War that ended a decade before the rumblings for independence began not only exposed the Colonists to the art of war, but also provided dozens of forts that they didn't have to build themselves – the British and French had done that for them. Later, many of those forts would be used to secure the frontier against the Indian tribes as Americans expanded westward. The war also weakened several of the stronger Indian tribes which further aided westward expansion during the early years of the American republic. But more than anything, the French and Indian War – coupled with their faith and sense of a righteous cause – gave the Colonists the courage to rebel against the foremost military power on the earth.

The innate desire for independence and freedom is one of the deepest ambitions of the human spirit, especially after enduring a "long train of abuses." An independence movement typically starts very slowly, like a tiny though relentless trickle. Then it picks up speed, depth, power, and eventually becomes a mighty, unstoppable river. Such was the case with the American Revolution: a mere handful of men like Samuel Adams, John Adams, and Patrick Henry kept pounding away from the pulpits and meeting-halls until the people agreed that independence was the answer.

The issuance of the Declaration of Independence was not a united declaration of war against Great Britain as much as a declaration that Americans were seizing their natural, God-given rights that the king had been taking from them through laws and taxation. And once they had agreed on independence and reasserted their rights, the Colonists had to defend those rights against a power that had become tyrannical.

The Revolutionary War

The Revolutionary War began over a year before the signing of the Declaration of Independence when the British soldiers marched to Lexington and Concord. The purpose had been twofold: to confiscate the gunpowder and munitions that the Colonists had stashed there and also arrest Samuel Adams and John Hancock, Boston's leaders of the patriots. After Paul Revere's famous night-ride to rouse the countryside, the Minutemen repelled the British troops who retreated to Boston. A few months later in mid-June, the Battle of Bunker Hill marked the first major battle of the Revolutionary War, after which George Washington was appointed to be the Commander-in-Chief of the American forces.

Not only did Washington have to organize an army with very little funding (since the Continental Congress had no power to tax), he had to do so while fighting the greatest military force of that time: the British Army. The British used their superior navy to quickly transport soldiers and supplies throughout the Colonies, whereas the Americans had no navy except for a handful of private merchant-ships. The farmers, merchants, and shopkeepers of America pitted themselves against the professional, highly-disciplined British regulars. The very notion that the American "rustics" could even take up arms against Her Majesty's Army was laughable – but they did.

By all accounts, Great Britain should have crushed the American resistance within the first few months, before the First Continental Congress even had a chance to draft the Declaration of Independence. While the Americans rallied at first, a series of defeats and lack of powder, supplies, food, and even enlistments discouraged them. But Washington and the ragtag colonial army kept fighting, or rather, kept attempting to slow down the British invasion and then retreating to fight another day. For the first year of the war, defeat stalked the Colonial Army at every turn. But Washington's surprise attack on the Hessians the day after Christmas showed that he and the American army were capable of besting the British.

The following year (1777) gave Washington another major victory, one which turned the tide of the Revolutionary War: the Battle of Saratoga. Not only did Saratoga bolster much-needed confidence and enlistments in the American war effort, the victory convinced France to finally agree to an open alliance with the Americans against the British Empire. In the late fall, it appeared that the Americans were finally on their way to winning their independence – and then came the long, terrible winter at Valley Forge. Over the winter of 1777, one-fifth of the Continental Army was lost to exposure, disease and starvation – roughly 2,500 of the 12,000 soldiers quartered at Valley Forge.

Time and time again during the early days of the Revolutionary War, it was clear that Providence was with

Washington and the Americans. There are numerous accounts of strange yet providential weather such as fog, wind, rain, and even storms at sea that clearly aided the Americans and hampered the British. Many felt that God was with them, and they relied on their belief that the war they were fighting was just – especially after the victory at Saratoga. But the long winter in Valley Forge shook their confidence; men ate literally anything they could find to alleviate their suffering, from the tattered rags they could spare to leather, paper, and tree-bark. Many were dressed in little more than rags and some were even naked during the dead of winter. Amputations were frequent because of exposure, gangrene, and frostbite, especially since they were drilled relentlessly by their new drillmaster Baron Von Steuben. Whereas Providence had once been aiding them, now it seemed as if He was crushing them. But when the long winter was finally over, the Continental Army was entirely different – the crucible of Valley Forge had not been used to punish them, but refine and mold them into a disciplined, committed army. Out of the fires of Valley Forge, the new American Army had arisen.

What had happened during that winter of hell at Valley Forge? From the Book of Romans, we know that "tribulation produces perseverance; and perseverance, character; and character, hope." When the winter had ended, the Continental Army marched out of Valley Forge with a confidence and character that could not have been formed by any other way than suffering and perseverance. Whereas desertions, quarrels, and differences had been many and frequent before the winter of 1777, such were greatly reduced afterwards. The tribulations of Valley Forge had indeed produced perseverance, and then character, followed by hope. Even secular historians cite Valley Forge as the primary event the forged the Continental Army into a unified body – into the American Army. Though the war did not end until several years later at Yorktown in 1781, the tide of the war had actually turned in late 1777.

The modern anti-war cry, "War is not the answer!" is not only simplistic, but overlooks the good that can come from war, such as the judgment of wickedness and evil, freeing those who are enslaved, tearing down entrenched differences and traditions, forcing people to choose sides and defend their beliefs, molding character, exposing and removing corruption, producing leaders, and removing the opportunists. The six long years of the Revolutionary War transformed thirteen separate colonies into the American nation, and the soldiers who endured the terrible war were trained for future national defense.

The Revolutionary War forged a new nation from many different peoples – e pluribus unum – and created a new country based on common creeds rather than by tribe, race, class, or ancestry. However, there were still many differences and divisions between the new States which had to be overcome.

The Early Republic

Before the Treaty of Paris was signed by Great Britain and the Thirteen States in 1783, the infant nation of America was already fracturing. States were quarreling and threatening one another, people were suffering the after-effects of the war with staggering inflation and debt, soldiers who had been promised pay and land were demanding to be paid, and others were rioting and stalking the countryside. In less than five years after finally winning their freedom, America seemed to be on the verge of self-destruction.

In the spring of 1787, several members of the Continental Congress concluded that the Articles of Confederation that the States had previous agreed to were too weak and needed to be reformed. Another convention was called to meet that summer at Independence Hall at Philadelphia, with George Washington presiding. Soon after concluding that the Articles were un-reformable, the delegates fell to squabbling and division, until Benjamin Franklin beseeched them to begin each session with prayer and look regularly to history, the Scriptures, and to Providence to help them resolve their differences.

Slowly but steadily, the Constitution took shape, and through a series of compromises and agreements, most of the delegates' demands were satisfied. By mid-September of 1787, the new Constitution was signed and finally revealed to the public. The convention had produced a model for limited federal government: a constitutional republic which left most of the power of the nation in the hands of the States and the people. Wisdom, patience, civility, and compromise after compromise had created the Constitution, but the States and the people still needed to ratify it.

Following the Constitutional Convention, several delegates proceeded to write a series of articles in the newspapers which explained and argued for ratification of the new Constitution. These articles became known as the "Federalist Papers," which were written by Alexander Hamilton, James Madison (the primary author of the Constitution), and John Jay. The Constitution and these articles were widely distributed and discussed throughout the country. Several of the Framers were surprised to hear them being frequently debated by common laborers at the taverns, in the shipyards, and throughout the land. Though there were a number of Founders who opposed the new Constitution (the Anti-Federalists), the Constitution was ratified and went into effect in early 1789.

The first president of the newly created United States of America was George Washington, who many already referred to as the "Father of our Country." Since Washington D.C. had not been built nor even planned yet, the President and Congress resided in New York City. Interestingly enough, Washington was first inaugurated at Federal Hall near St. Paul's Church which faced a large open field owned by the church. When the inauguration concluded, Washington and the rest of Congress went into St. Paul's to worship. Nearly two hundred years later, part of this field became the site of the World Trade Center. St. Paul's Church still stands (though it faces away from the site) and was saved from destruction on September 11th, 2001 due to a large sycamore tree which blocked the flying debris from the church.

During the first years of the new nation, the basic departments of the government were created, such as the Treasury Department, the State Department, the War Department, and the Attorney General. The New York Stock Exchange was also created in those early years, which later formed the backbone of the financial institutions we have today. But the new administration was not without its problems – Washington's Cabinet was fraught with strife between Alexander Hamilton and Thomas Jefferson, who always seemed to be in opposition to one another, especially with regards to the new French Revolution and the First Bank of the United States, the nation's first central bank. Jefferson wanted to aid the French and was opposed to a central bank, while Hamilton was the opposite. Washington's position was especially difficult because all the institutions were new and untested, and there were few he could look to for advice (like former presidents and former Cabinet members).

George Washington ran unopposed for a second term but decided not to seek a third term, a tradition which was upheld by all future presidents until Ulysses Grant nearly a century later, who failed to win the GOP nomination. Teddy Roosevelt also ran for a third term but lost to Woodrow Wilson in 1912. It wasn't until FDR that a president ran for and was successfully re-elected to a third (and fourth) term in office. However, only five years after FDR's death, the Twenty-Second Amendment was passed and ratified, which permanently limited the occupation of the presidency by one individual to only two terms.

John Adams (Washington's Vice President for both terms) was the second president of the United States and his political opponent, Thomas Jefferson, was his vice president. The quarrels that plagued Washington's Cabinet only worsened in the Adams administration, and the two men who had once been steadfast friends became bitter enemies. Adams successfully kept America out of the French Revolution and signed the Alien and Sedition Acts, which gave the government sweeping powers over the press, naturalization, and non-naturalized residents. The Acts expired just before Adams left office, except for the law that authorized the president to deport resident aliens if their country of origin was at war with the United States.

Thomas Jefferson succeeded Adams as president in 1801 and served two terms. He is best known as the author of the Declaration of Independence, the first Secretary of State, and the sponsor of the Expedition of Lewis and Clark. During his presidency, Jefferson also oversaw the Louisiana Purchase from France which doubled the size of the United States at that time, which makes up nearly a third of the continental states today. Adams and Jefferson reconciled in later years, and both died on July 4th, 1826 within hours of one another, exactly fifty years after the signing of the Declaration of Independence. The last words of John Adams were, "Thomas Jefferson still survives," though unknown to him, Jefferson had died five hours earlier on that same day at Monticello.

After Jefferson left office in 1809, James Madison, the primary author of the Constitution and the Bill of Rights, became president and guided the country through the War of 1812. Napoleon Bonaparte, who had risen to power late in the French Revolution, was rapidly sweeping through Europe, with Great Britain as his main opposition. The British began seizing American ships trading with France and were pressing captured American sailors into their Navy, and soon war was declared upon the British and their territories in Canada. During the War of 1812, the new capital of Washington D.C. was raided by the British and the new White House was burned, along with the Capitol Building and other public buildings.

James Madison was the last of the Founding Fathers to hold high office, though John Adams' son, John Quincy Adams, was president for one term in 1825 and served in Congress until his death in early 1848. Once the Founders passed away and especially after the invention of the cotton-gin, the nation began dividing deeply along regional lines, particularly between the North and the South.

Another spiritual revolution known as the Second Great Awakening began in the late Eighteenth Century soon after the new American Republic had been founded. War debt, regional divisions, political squabbling, as well as rampant inflation and alcoholism plagued the young country. What began as a handful of preachers praying for spiritual revival soon spread through their churches, then their communities, and then across the countryside. By the 1820s, church-growth throughout the nation was exploding, particularly in the Methodist and Baptist denominations. Of the two great spiritual revivals in America, the Second Great Awakening has had the longer lasting impact.

While the First Great Awakening had been mostly one of revitalizing existing churches and causing people to return to their churches, the Second Great Awakening was one of exponential church growth, with millions of the "unchurched" becoming active Christians, especially on the frontiers and more rural areas. And like the First Great Awakening that stirred Americans' hearts towards independence, the Second Great Awakening stirred them towards another revolution in society: the abolishment of slavery.

One curious effect of the race to add slave-states and free-states to the Union in the first half of the Nineteenth Century was that the Midwest and part of the West were quickly settled...and "Christianized." New England in particular set out multitudes of missionaries – sometimes even entire churches – to settle the Midwest and propagate the Gospel as the new foundation of the land.

The Civil War

The tensions that led up to the Civil War were long in coming. Even at the drafting of the Declaration of

Independence, the stormclouds over slavery were present and growing ominous. The fractures which would later split the nation between North and South had always existed in the young nation, but had been previously contained by commonalities such as language and culture, external threats and wars, and also mutual dependence. For the first fifty years of the nation's history, the Union between the North and the South was steady, though the divisions between the two had already begun to grow and deepen.

In the early Nineteenth Century after the War of 1812, both regions boomed, expanded, and prospered, but their economies went in opposite directions. The North embraced industrialism and built many factories, and was soon rapidly expanding due to immigration from Europe. The South continued to base their economy on agriculture (and slave-labor), and with the invention of the cotton gin, they shifted their crops over to a larger percentage of cotton, which was in ever-increasing demand by the industrial textile-mills of Great Britain. These textile-mills in Great Britain paid more for the cotton than those in the North, which led to cheaper foreign goods that also competed with those made in the North. Soon federal tariffs were slapped on the goods which helped the factories of the North, but hurt the consumers and businesses in the South. As both regions developed and expanded, the North and South began to compete with one another rather than compromise and resolve their differences.

Before the Tariff of 1828, the questions of nullification and even secession had been bandied about but never on a widespread, regional basis. The tariffs helped the Northern factories but hurt the South, which prompted Senator John Calhoun of South Carolina to introduce a bill which would allow states to nullify federal laws that hurt their state/constituents, and South Carolina promptly passed the bill into law. President Andrew Jackson immediately disputed the notion of nullification and announced that the Constitution had not created a Union of States but a single nation, in which federal laws had to be obeyed by all the States – without exception. The situation grew so heated that Jackson threatened the use of federal force and even martial law if South Carolina refused to collect the taxes defined in the Tariff of 1828. Several months later, South Carolina backed down and withdrew the ordinance, but the rift between the North and the South had greatly increased.

The political pressures inside the nation continued to build during 1830s and 1840s, boiled throughout the 1850s, and then finally exploded in 1860 after the election of Abraham Lincoln. Compromise after compromise had been tried for years, and still tensions had continued to rise. Often a new compromise or agreement would cool the tensions for a while, only to have them resume a short time later. When the Democrat Party split and Lincoln was overwhelming elected by the Northern and West Coast states (the "free" states), South Carolina and the rest of the South saw that it was pointless to remain in the Union because they would always lose future elections. Lincoln won 180 electoral votes to Breckenridge's 72 (the Democrat/Southern candidate), and 51 electoral votes were won by other candidates in the border states between the North and the South. The South realized that even if those border states voted with them (in defense of slavery), they would still forever lose elections to the Northern anti-slavery states. In particular, the three Northern States of New York, Ohio, and Pennsylvania held nearly as many electoral votes (85) as the entire South combined (87), excluding the border states of Kentucky, Missouri, and Tennessee.

Even today, many debate whether the South seceded over the issue of States' rights or in order to protect the institution of slavery (upon which their economy was largely based). The answer is both: the South seceded from the Union in order to protect their States' rights to own slaves. One of the South's primary accusations against the Northern States was their flagrant violation of Article IV of the Constitution, which stipulated that runaway slaves from one state could not be freed by another, and that they had to be returned to their state of origin.

With the election of an anti-slavery president, the South felt helpless to stem the abolitionist tide and decided to leave the Union while they could. One of their other sticking points was that Lincoln himself had said, "Government cannot endure permanently half slave, half free." The South interpreted that to mean that Lincoln intended to end slavery by any means possible in order to protect the federal government. Was South Carolina rash in their decision to leave the Union? Probably, but many around the country were acting out of years of anger and pent-up frustration at the time – on both sides of the Mason-Dixon Line.

The Civil War began four months after South Carolina seceded when the South began taking over existing federal buildings and forts. After all, since they were no longer in the Union, they couldn't have foreign offices throughout their new nation – especially the forts and garrisons. South Carolina demanded that the federal garrison at Fort Sumter surrender (which could easily fire upon the city), but they refused and South Carolina began bombarding them. After several weeks, the commander of the fort surrendered and the federal soldiers were sent home to the North.

In late July of 1861, the federal army of the North attacked Confederate troops stationed in Virginia – the First Battle of Bull Run. The North thought they would easily win the first battle, which would quickly put down the rebellion/insurrection of the South and compel them back into the Union. Congressmen and their families held picnics in the hills above the battlefield, only to flee in terror when the South forced the North to hastily retreat and clogged the roads with the wounded and dying. With that battle, the terrible four-year Civil War began, which would take the lives of between 620,000 to 750,000 American soldiers and tens of thousands of other lives.

Both the North and South had advantages and disadvantages in the Civil War, though the North had all the necessary ingredients to win a long war. The North was far more populated than the South (22 million versus 9 million), was much more industrial, had better infrastructure, had faster/greater transportation (railroads), and also had many more miles of telegraph lines. The North also had much stronger financial institutions, an established government, a strong army and navy, and the rest of their national infrastructure. However, the North was fighting a primarily offensive war in the unfamiliar territory of the South, which required more men. Many of the more experienced military leaders and soldiers sided with their home-states in the South, and since most of the federal revenues were funded by Southern tariffs (an astounding 87% before 1860), those sources of revenue dried up when the Southern States seceded.

For the South, their advantages in the Civil War were that they were initially better funded, they were fighting a defensive war over a larger, more primitive area, as well as fighting on their home turf. Also, the South had more experienced military leaders and soldiers than the North, they were fighting to preserve their homes, nation, and culture, and they felt justified in both seceding from the Union and fighting the war. For the South, they wanted to be free just like their forefathers had against Great Britain, and they drew courage from the examples of the Founders and the Revolutionary War. Tragically, the primary institution the South was fighting to protect was slavery, which was diametrically opposed to the founding ideal of America that "all men are created equal."

The weaknesses of the South were deeper and more difficult to remedy than those in the North. The South was extremely reliant upon imports and foreigners for support, as well as supplies, arms, and equipment which never really emerged. The South also terribly lacked the modern forms of communication and transportation that were prevalent in the North, as well as having government and military institutions which were new and not well-established. In the end, the South suffered from having far fewer men, little to no industrial strength, too much dependency on imports for their necessities and agricultural exports for their revenue.

In the Civil War, the South won battle after battle against the North, and the war didn't turn against them until Robert Lee changed the Confederate strategy and invaded Pennsylvania in 1863. The idea had been to wear down the North until they gave up and went home, but the South was wearing out faster due to lack of money, infrastructure, and manpower. Lee decided that invading the North was the only way to get the North to back down quickly, but their superior numbers and infrastructure prevailed. After Gettysburg, the tide of the Civil War turned and the South never recovered.

An infamous observation about history is that "the victors write the history books," and the Civil War is no exception to that rule. Many of the actions taken by President Lincoln in the North during the Civil War were unconstitutional, but temporarily excused due to the war. By Executive Order, he suspended the writ of habeas corpus and trial-by-jury. Lincoln also used the war to weaken and pressure his political enemies, since they could easily be painted as American traitors, or at least Southern sympathizers.

Most modern history books claim that the Civil War was all about slavery, but that is only half-true. While the protection and abolition of slavery did play a big role in inflaming both sides of the conflict, the primary reason the South seceded was because they felt increasingly helpless against the majorities of the larger states in the North. By 1860, the balance of power had shifted so dramatically that the South felt they had little to no say in selecting presidents (and therefore the Courts) because their electoral votes no longer mattered, as well as crafting and passing legislation because they had fewer representatives in Congress.

For the North, the Civil War wasn't really about slavery until after Gettysburg and Lincoln's Emancipation Proclamation. For the first three years of the war, Lincoln and other Northerners refused to let the South leave the Union, even though many in the North didn't want the slaves freed because cheap labor would take away their jobs and businesses. Pride, hard-hearts, and the inability to negotiate and compromise any longer – on both sides of the conflict – led to the devastating Civil War. Tragically, we see many of those same feelings, divisions, and conflicts throughout America today, but between the political right and the political left rather than between the secessionists and the abolitionists.

The four-year Civil War literally ripped the nation apart and set state against state, neighbor against neighbor; and brother against brother. While the War hurt the North, it ended up all but destroying the South – economically, culturally, and spiritually. Lincoln may have preserved the Union, but he destroyed half the country in the process. If not for slavery, did the Civil War really need to be fought? Why couldn't Lincoln have just let the South go? At the time, many Northerners also favored secession of the South because it would finally put an end to the bitter political divisions and never-ending quarrels.

Like the Revolutionary War, the Civil War didn't need to be fought – Lincoln and the Congress could have simply released the Southern States from the Union and let the institution of slavery collapse on its own, or let the South decide to get rid of slavery themselves. The South could have used their vast wealth to free the slaves on their own and preserve their States. Would Lincoln have had the support for the Civil War if anyone had known the consequences of utter devastation, loss of rights, and the blood of over 650,000 American soldiers? Consider how much history, culture, knowledge, and lives were lost in the Civil War – one wonders what America would look like today had it never been fought. Two hundred years of development in the South was destroyed in a matter of months, especially under Sherman's horrific marches that ripped the South apart. Pride and stubborn, hard hearts on both sides almost destroyed the nation.

Even after the war was over and the slaves had been freed, most former slaves continued to live in squalor, with a significant percentage of them becoming share-croppers for the same masters, another form of economic slavery. They were free, but their conditions were not much better, especially since many in the South wanted to continue to oppress them. And were the former slaves welcome in the North? Not so much, because the lower paid workers and immigrants didn't want to compete with the former slaves for jobs.

During and after the Civil War, Northerners frequently referred to the Southerners as "traitors" and "rebels." But in a voluntary union under the Constitution that the States had been free to join – no one had conquered them and forced them to ratify the Constitution – they couldn't be considered traitors nor rebels any more than a spouse can be considered that if they want out of their marriage union. If any group could rightly be considered to be called rebels, it was the Colonists who rebelled against Britain, because they were indeed under the authority of the British Crown.

But the South was under no one's authority except their own as sovereign States; they voluntary joined the Union by ratifying the Constitution, and they felt they could voluntarily leave it. After all, they too cited the words of the Declaration of Independence in their enumerated reasons for secession:

> *"That to secure these rights, Governments are instituted among Men, deriving their just powers from the consent of the governed. That whenever any Form of Government becomes destructive of these ends, it is the Right of the People to alter or to abolish it, and to institute new Government, laying its foundation on such principles and organizing its powers in such form, as to them shall seem most likely to effect their Safety and Happiness."*

If the Civil War had not forced the South back into the Union, it's very likely that slavery would have died off within the next several decades anyway. Would the South have dug in their heels so much to protect an institution they knew was cruel and inhumane, if not for the constant quarrels and demands from the North? Slavery was already ending in much of South and Central America, and was dying as an institution, especially when compared to the laborers of the North. Men work harder to earn their own wages voluntarily than with a whip on their backs. With the invention of machines and steam engines that were already expanding the industrial might in the North, it would've likely been only a matter of time before the South would've freed their slaves in exchange for machines and automation. But greed, expediency, impatience, and pride took them to war instead.

After the Civil War, Lincoln and Johnson had wanted to be merciful to the South in restoring them to the Union, but many in Washington did not – especially after a Southerner had assassinated the sitting president after the war had ended. Once the Confederacy had finally surrendered, the Radical Republicans in Congress punished the South and encouraged carpetbaggers to take advantage of their defeated neighbors and brothers. Should we wonder why Southerners were bitter for so many years afterwards? What kind of Union destroys half the country and then in the name of Reconstruction, keeps them in deplorable conditions? It took decades for the South to rebuild and return to their former economic levels.

Once the dust settled and Americans began to rebuild their lives, many took advantage of the Homestead Act and moved West, which now held more promise than the South. It's often easier to build anew rather than rebuild that which has been destroyed, especially with all the racial tensions that remained and the bad memories of what had once been, but was now forever lost because of the war.

Soon after the Reconstruction had formally ended, the nation experienced a long boom and a flurry of inventions such as the telephone, the incandescent light-bulb and electricity, and later, the automobile and then the airplane. Again, it's highly likely that these inventions and the spread of the Industrial Age would have naturally ended slavery without the loss of over 650,000 men and the accumulated wealth of two centuries of development in the South.

One of the consequences of the Civil War was the destruction of federalism as it had been originally implemented in the American Republic. Before the Civil War, America was referred to as "*these* United States," denoting a union of sovereign States confederated under a strictly federal system of government. But after the Civil War, the reference was changed to "*the* United States," which describes a national government rather than a federal government. States were no longer sovereign entities granting a portion of their sovereignty to the federal power, but had rather become regional entities within America with their own governments which were subject to the national government. Today if a State really considers themselves to be sovereign, they only need to reject federal decrees and see what happens.

As a result of the forced Reconstruction and the loss of state-sovereignty, the ill-feelings left from the Civil War continued and soon domestic terrorist groups arose like the Klu Klux Klan. The feelings of racism between the whites and the blacks deepened in the South and then later emerged in the Jim Crow laws that sought to disenfranchise the blacks in any way they could. To be fair, racism also plagued the North but was usually not codified as in the South.

In the end, all Americans have paid dearly for the sin of slavery, which brutally enslaved millions of people while living in the freest nation on earth. The North, but especially the South, paid more than enough for the sin of slavery in their slain fathers, brothers, and sons in the Civil War. And while the North first fought mostly to keep the Union together, one cannot help but observe that despite their numerous advantages, the North stumbled from battle to battle until Lincoln issued the Emancipation Proclamation and the purpose of the war changed from restoring the Union to finally ending slavery.

The Great Melting Pot

From the very beginning of the United States in 1776, "*e pluribus unum*" – "out of many, one" – has been our national motto. That Latin motto has been printed on our coins and currency since soon after the Constitution was ratified, much longer than "In God We Trust." For many years, America was known as the "Great Melting Pot" where immigrants came from all over the world to settle here and become Americans, merging their distinct cultural flavors and traditions with our own. This practice of many people melting into one country largely held until the multiculturalism of the 1970s, when immigrants were encouraged to retain their own nationality though living in America.

Aside from the native Americans (who themselves immigrated to America thousands of years ago), all Americans today are a mixture of English, Scotch, Irish, French, Dutch, Germans, Swedes, Mexicans, and a slurry of other nationalities. Much of the East Coast of America was settled during colonial times by the English and other Europeans, and by the beginning of the Eighteenth Century over 250,000 people lived in the American colonies. By the beginning of the American Revolution less than a century later, the number had climbed to about 2,500,000. Due to the French Revolution and the initial building of the country, immigration slowed until the early Nineteenth Century.

After the War of 1812 until Reconstruction following the Civil War, nearly 7.5 million immigrants came to the United States. A significant portion of the newcomers were Irish who were fleeing the Great Famine, and most settled in the larger cities along the East Coast. Another significant portion of the immigrants during that period were Germans who settled the nation's interior and began farming, especially in portions of the Midwest such as Ohio, Indiana, Illinois, and Michigan.

Following an economic depression in the 1870s, immigration boomed again until 1920, which brought more than 23 million immigrants to America. This third wave of immigrants was mostly from Eastern and Southern European nations such as Denmark, Norway, Sweden, Switzerland, the Netherlands, Italy, Russia, Poland, and Austria/Hungary, as well as those from Asia which settled in the West Coast.

After 1920 due to WWI, the Great Depression, WWII, and then the vast worldwide rebuilding after WWII, immigration slowed until the mid-1970s. America is currently in a fourth wave of immigration, with nearly 10% of all American residents being foreign-born today. Immigrants from Latin America now account for about half of all new arrivals, another quarter are from Asia, and the rest are either from Europe, Africa, or other nations.

The steady influx of immigrants is the lifeblood of a nation, which often brings fresh perspectives, gratitude, and new life into the country. However, when such an influx is not managed properly and becomes a deluge, the nation can be quickly overwhelmed financially, culturally, and politically by the mass immigration. Such was the case in the ancient Roman Empire, and such is the case in America today. Because of federal negligence coupled with petty political wrangling, another 11-12 million "undocumented residents" (illegal immigrants) are dwelling inside the United States with both political parties trying to out-maneuver one another to capture the new voting bloc.

When immigrants are blended into a modern nation, they help revitalize it and give those around them a new appreciation for their country and a renewed patriotism. America's long history of immigration has caused the United States to be much more tolerant of those from different cultures, races, and backgrounds than most other nations. Immigrants have made America great – when they were stirred into the Great Melting Pot and left their previous national identity and allegiances behind – when they became full-fledged Americans. But due to illegal immigration, multiculturalism, and political correctness, our immigration policies (or lack thereof) are dividing and crippling the nation instead of revitalizing it.

Without a steady stream of fresh immigrants, nations tend to turn inward and become very self-centered, with little regards to helping spread freedom and democracy to other nations.

Chapter 3 - How Did We Get Here?

"I believe there are more instances of the abridgement of the freedom of the people by the gradual and silent encroachment of those in power, than by violent and sudden usurpation." –
James Madison

After the Civil War and the Reconstruction had ended in the 1870s, America stabilized and embarked on a fifty-year entrepreneurial, industrial, and economic boom. The incredible innovations in transportation, communications, automation, and industrialization swept over America at the time when "laissez faire" policies (low taxes, low regulation) were widespread throughout the local, state, and federal governments. The discovery of oil and its refinement into petroleum drove industrial expansion at the same time that multitudes of life-changing inventions and innovations were blossoming. As America's industrial strength grew, instability in Europe and Asia were increasing and the promise of a better life in the New World caused immigration to the United States to boom.

In that fifty year period, more than 23 million immigrants flocked to America, first to the coasts and the metropolitan areas, and then millions resettled throughout the country. Those from Europe mostly settled on the East Coast and east of the Mississippi River, while the immigrants from Asia settled along the West Coast. As the immigrants settled in the East, others from the East and the Midwest pushed westward across the continent. Not only did the immigrants bring their rich, diverse cultures, traditions, and work-ethics, they also brought some of their political philosophies, namely the new Progressive philosophies which were sweeping through Europe.

The industrial boom, laissez faire mentality, and nearly endless supply of fresh, cheap labor created vast amounts of wealth which rapidly accumulated in the hands of the infamous bankers and industrialists of the period such as J.P. Morgan, John D. Rockefeller, Henry Ford, and Andrew Carnegie, as well as the various railroad tycoons. However, while incredible amounts of new money were being created, a huge underclass of poor laborers was also being created – which did not go unnoticed by opportunists hungry for new power and wealth of their own: political power. The millions of poor, largely-uneducated immigrants created a huge new class of "easy votes" – as well as deep, widespread feelings of envy and resentment against the wealthy. The shrewd politicians realized they just had to say the right words and the poor masses would place them in office and help them stay there in perpetuity.

From the widening wealth-disparity between the rich and the poor and the opportunists all too happy to prey upon the masses, the principles of collectivism emerged in America and took shape. Socialism, Statism, and Communism have existed in one form or another since the days of the city-states in the ancient world but had declined after the Fall of the Roman Empire. In the Middle Ages, feudalism and the monarchies of Europe had all but contained those forces and philosophies until the days of the French Revolution in the late Eighteenth Century when the notion of "equality" in society arose, which promised hope to the multitudes of poor, starving masses. A few decades later, this philosophy of a new, centrally-managed, entirely-equal political state was further refined and codified by Karl Marx in his book, "Das Kapital."

The Marxist creed, "From each according to his means, to each according to his needs," was incredibly appealing to the huge, poor underclass who constantly saw the vast excesses of the rich, the royalty, and the aristocracy.

Equality Versus Liberty

The political philosophies of equality and wealth-redistribution did not really take root in America until the industrial boom and vast amounts of wealth began being created. With little aristocracy and a loosely-defined class structure – as well as cheap land and boundless opportunities – such philosophies couldn't take hold as quickly in America as they had in Europe. However, the rapid accumulation of incredible wealth amidst the terrible working conditions of the poor opened the doors for the organizing of worker's unions in order to improve pay, hours, and working conditions. As the unions spread and grew in power, they became a growing political force which embraced the principles of equality and the various political philosophies that promised to implement it: communism, socialism, and collectivism. In America, these philosophies and their implementation in the American republic became known as "Progressivism."

Progressivism is the Western political philosophy which seeks to institute social, political, or economic reforms on the basis of equality rather than liberty. It was largely natural that the Progressive Era arose after the Industrial Age had matured as a response to the incredible inequalities in wealth between the industrialists and the workers. The first labor unions mostly sought to improve working conditions in the factories, mines, and mills, and soon moved towards fewer working hours and better wages. However, like most movements for reform, they didn't remain confined to solving the specific problems for which they had been created, but soon morphed into a full-blown political philosophy that became a powerful force in Western industrialized nations. As in the French Revolution, the idea of collective equality in American society began to take precedence over individual liberty.

In order for collective equality to prevail in a society, the power of government must necessarily be used to coerce the wealthy to give a significant portion of their wealth to the poor or the lower classes. Collective equality – and the redistribution of wealth which attempts to create it – is a direct violation of individual liberty, though it's often felt to be justified because of the vast disparities between the rich minority and the poor majority. Under such equality, "Give me liberty or give me death!" becomes "From each according to his means, to each according to his needs." However, in order for the government to remain strong enough to redistribute the wealth (especially during economic downturns), the government needs a predictable, stable, and ever-growing source of revenue: the income tax. Not only that, but by implementing the "progressive" income tax (under which the wealthy pay a much higher percentage of taxes than the poor), the two primary requirements of wealth-redistribution are met: the wealthy are punished according to their riches and the poor are given that which they did not earn. The various forms of Marxism depend upon their primary enemy to survive: capitalism. The foundation of Marxism is built upon the very economic principles it despises.

Though Progressivism may have the best of intentions, the last century has proven time and time again that it doesn't work because it only tries to solve the surface problems of inequality and poverty, and must do so by violating individual liberty and human behavior. If wealth-redistribution works, then why are the rich richer and the poor poorer than ever before? The socialists would argue that it's because there's not enough redistribution – but it wasn't even enough in the former Soviet Union! If the Progressives really wanted to help the poor, they would teach them how to become self-sufficient and how to accumulate individual wealth, rather than become dependent upon welfare and wealth-redistribution from the government. In the end, only the size and scope of the government has grown under wealth-redistribution and the progressive income tax – at the terrible expense of individual liberty and self-sufficiency.

Because of the greed and the lack of charity on the part of some of the industrialists – as well as the greed and jealousy of the poor – the ideas of Communism, Socialism, Fascism, and Progressivism became more popular and Progressive tyrants arose. Since the early Twentieth Century when Progressivism took hold in America, one class of citizens has been pitted

70

against another in the name of equality and fairness: the rich versus the poor, the men versus the women, the old versus the young, the blacks versus the whites, and so on. One of the first actions of the Progressives was to add the progressive income tax to the Constitution to permanently change the federal tax structure, and thereby create the means by which to fund the Progressive State. As long as the federal progressive income tax is cemented in place in the United States, liberty will always take a backseat to equality.

Compared to other Western nations, America has been slower to adopt Progressivism and socialism, although many of the same reforms have been made, especially with the recent nationalization of the healthcare system. The generation at the turn of the Twentieth Century experimented with Progressivism, the WWII generation reluctantly embraced Progressivism and accepted it with the New Deal in the Great Depression, and then the majority of the Baby Boomer generation demanded Progressivism mixed with Constitutionalism. Lastly, by electing Barack Obama, the Millennial generation openly supported the fundamental transformation of America's constitutional republic into a Western socialist democracy. Since the popularization of Progressivism at the turn of the last century, each generation in American has grown increasingly comfortable with soft tyranny and wealth-redistribution in the name of equality and fairness. Where liberty and independence once ruled, egalitarianism and equality now reign supreme.

The Natural Rights of Man

In contrast to collectivism and other forms of economic and social equality is individual liberty, which is perhaps the foremost principle that founded America. Religious freedom, economic freedom, and self-governance are all based upon individual liberty and the concepts of mankind's "natural rights" (or "inalienable rights"). Where there was equality in

America, it was under the Rule of Law in which the law is blind and everyone is to be given equal justice. But that in itself is another natural right.

John Adams rightly defined the American notion of equality when he said, "All are subject by nature to equal laws of morality, and in society have a right to equal laws for their government, yet no two men are perfectly equal in person, property, understanding, activity, and virtue, or ever can be made so by any power less than that which created them ... all are subject by nature to equal laws of morality, and in society have a right to equal laws for their government."

The philosophy of natural rights declares that every human being is endowed with a particular amount of sovereignty and individual power by our Creator. Every person is equally free, and if not for other men and their institutions, every person could do as they pleased. But because men are not angels but rather fallen creatures, by our individual consent we give up a portion of our individual sovereignty to submit to laws and other social contracts for the benefit, peace, and prosperity of the societies in which we live.

When a person first settles a land, they have complete sovereignty over that area. However, when another settles nearby, soon basic laws and rules must be established so one doesn't violate the other's property and natural rights. Consequently, each must voluntarily give up a small portion of their rights so they can live in peace and without fear from the misdeeds of others: "that to secure those [natural] rights, governments are instituted among men." As a population expands in a given area, more laws and more complex social contracts are needed to keep order and protect the natural rights which have not been voluntarily surrendered by the people.

Though these concepts and rights may not have been clearly defined when America began being settled by the Puritans and other Europeans, they were nonetheless known and actively being practiced. When the movement for independence and self-government arose during the 1770s, the American

Colonists drew upon the writings of John Locke and Edmund Burke to explain, refine, and validate the principles of natural rights that they already knew and held dear. However, like most people in free countries, the Colonists often took their natural rights for granted – until those rights began being violated by the British king across the sea.

While taxation under British rule had been nearly non-existent before King George III, after his coronation and the French and Indian War, Britain thought it was only proper that the American Colonies pay some of the expenses for their defense and the wars/uprisings fought in the New World. However, the British refused to allow the Americans to have any representation in Parliament, and the Americans and their supporters strongly protested. By the end of the decade, the mood towards the Colonies had soured in Britain and they began seeing the Colonists as their subjects rather than as their fellow citizens.

Since all taxation is the coerced surrender of one's property, the dispute over taxation without representation was essentially an argument over natural rights and God-given sovereignty. The "natural rights of men" writings and speeches of Edmund Burke and John Locke, two famous philosophers of the period, inspired the American Colonists in their quest for independence and provided the foundations for many of their arguments. Thomas Paine rose to prominence with his own writings on individual sovereignty and natural rights, and his pamphlet "Common Sense" finally convinced the American public that they needed to fight for their independence if they were to secure their God-given freedoms from the king of Britain.

When King George III and Parliament began passing taxation laws without the consent or representation of the Colonies, their natural rights were violated, which became the primary reason for our Declaration of Independence. However, the Signers of the Declaration did not declare war on Great Britain in order to be free – war with the British Empire had already been fostered upon them at Lexington and Concord, and then in various cities, towns, and ports throughout America. The Declaration of Independence was America's response to the British Empire's repeated violations of their natural rights and their sovereignty.

After the Revolutionary War was fought and won, the Treaty of Paris was signed by the Thirteen Colonies – thirteen small, sovereign nations which then became the States. Four years later after the Articles of Confederation proved to be a failed compact/confederated form of government, the Constitution of the United States of America was drawn up in the summer of 1787, published in September, and then ratified by the States on June 21, 1788. Rhode Island was the last state to sign the Constitution in May of 1790, and the Bill of Rights (the first ten amendments) was ratified in 1791.

The guiding principles common to both the failed Articles of Confederation and the Constitution were the primary reasons why the Colonies had issued the Declaration of Independence in the first place: to prevent tyranny and the loss of individual, natural rights. Barack Obama and other anti-Constitutional scholars have called the Constitution a compact of "negative liberties," i.e. what the government cannot do TO you, rather than "positive liberties": what the government can do FOR you. But that was no oversight on the part of the Framers – that's precisely the point of the Constitution: to protect our natural rights from our government, which we have regardless of what political party or form of government is currently in power. Government cannot give one group of people anything it doesn't first seize from another.

The primary confusion and debate about natural rights, liberty, and government today is: "Where do our rights come from: the Creator or the State?" This is one of the many reasons why the Creation-Evolution debate and religious teachings are so important. If we believe in a Supreme God and Creator who created us in His Image, then our rights as men and women inherently come from Him and therefore cannot be taken away from us – regardless of what laws are in effect. For example, no

74

government has the authority to restrict what we say, though there may be consequences to our use (and abuse) of that freedom. Conversely, if one believes that there is no Creator (as in Evolution, Marxism, Atheism, Communism, Socialism, and Fascism), then the State is the Highest Authority over mankind and is the entity which bestows rights upon men. Under that philosophy, our individual rights come from the government and therefore can be given or taken away at any time by other men via the legal system.

At the heart of individual rights and philosophies lies an over-arching religious debate: "Do we derive our liberty from God or from men, from the Rule of Law in which all men are created equal, or from the Rule of Tyrants in which some men are 'more equal' than the rest?"

The Revolutionary War was fought to free Americans from the Rule of Man (King George III) and restore the Rule of Law, which they had been living under since they had settled in the New World. With the hard-fought struggle to secure their natural rights still fresh in their minds, the last thing the Framers of the Constitution wanted to do was construct a form of government that would quickly lead to tyranny. In fact, the very foundation and structure of the Constitution – the Separation of Powers and the system of Checks and Balances between Three Branches of government – were designed solely to minimize and distribute power throughout the government in order to prevent tyranny from ever taking hold in America again. The Framers knew that all men – even the best of men – are prone to tyranny and therefore sought to prevent it.

Under the Constitution, tyranny from one branch of the government is very difficult to achieve if the other branches are functioning properly. The Framers rightly understood that power always corrupts, so they fashioned the Constitution in such a way that the three branches would challenge, compete, and contend against one another. The Constitution was not written to make government powerful and efficient, but quite the opposite – the Founders wanted America to have the minimum amount of government necessary in order to protect their rights. The notion that "The government which governs least, governs best," was prevalent in the minds of the Framers and most Americans in that era and embodied in the very structure of the Constitution. All three branches were to be equal in power and be able to prevent one branch from becoming tyrannical and thereby threatening the natural rights of the American citizens. And for most of the last two centuries, the Constitution has protected Americans' individual rights far better than any other form of government in history.

But over the last century as more and more Americans embraced collective equality in contrast to individual liberty, self-governance began to erode and has been increasingly replaced with state-governance. As the State grows, the Citizen becomes smaller, weaker, less-important, and more dependent on the State to care for him and administer his rights, rather than him taking care of himself. As more and more people rely on the State, the Rule of Man grows at the expense of the Rule of Law, and individual liberty shrinks while State-power balloons. Naturally, the State quickly becomes antagonistic to individual liberty and often implements policies which promote immorality, crime, and instability, which only feed State growth and the accumulation of power.

Corruption of the Constitution

A society based upon the Rule of Law and self-governance can only function properly when individual morality and virtue are upheld by all, or at least a solid majority. Correspondingly, when personal virtues and moral standards crumble, so does the Rule of Law. The Progressive State only tolerates individual liberty among the citizenry as long as it doesn't interfere with the State's power. Drawing upon their study of history and personal experiences with Great Britain, the Framers of the Constitution feared the accumulation of power by the State (the new federal government) and sought to keep it as weak as possible, while still being able to preserve the Republic and the citizenry's natural rights. In order to disburse and restrict the power of the new government, the Framers devised a system of Checks and Balances and Separation of Powers to keep the new government from growing too powerful too quickly.

Unfortunately, because of the degradation and laxity of our personal values and standards of morality over the years – as well as our increasing demands for equality rather than liberty – the carefully-designed system of Checks and Balances in the Constitution has been subverted by at least two amendments: the Direct Election of Senators (the Seventeenth Amendment) and the federal Income Tax (the Sixteenth Amendment). Next to those two amendments, the establishment of the central bank (the Federal Reserve) removed the power to print/coin money from the Congress and gave it to a group of unnamed, unaccountable private banks, thus removing and obscuring any accountability and oversight for managing the nation's money supply. Not only that, but the monumental "Marbury v. Madison" ruling in 1803 established the Supreme Court as the ultimate authority over both the Executive Branch and the Legislative Branch – and thus, the seeds of judicial activism (or "legislation from the bench") were sowed.

Not only does power tend to corrupt those in elected office, but power always tends to accumulate into the hands of corrupt people. As the population grows, more power is available for abuse/accumulation, whether it be through labor, property, money, or authority, though such power is typically collected in the form of money through taxes or tariffs. But despite the careful Separation of Powers and the system of Checks and Balances, ultimately the people should still retain their power – especially where the Judicial Branch is concerned, which is not elected by the People.

After Marbury v. Madison in 1803, James Madison, the primary author of the Constitution, regretted that another Check was not included to diffuse the Court's power. The very idea that a handful of unelected, unaccountable men having the sole

77

authority over the interpretation of the Constitution, the law, and the other two branches of government was anathema to the Framers. Madison even suggested that such an amendment be added to the Constitution to restore the ultimate arbitration of the law to the People via a solid majority vote in Congress, not the Court.

The battle in the federal court system during the last several years has been over Obama's national healthcare law, which the Supreme Court recently ruled as constitutional. However, under the Constitution, that decision was not theirs to make, nor even in the Congress's authority to seize those natural rights of life, liberty, and property from the American people. The Tenth Amendment clearly states that "The powers not delegated to the United States by the Constitution, nor prohibited by it to the States, are reserved to the States respectively, or to the people." Of all the Amendments, the Tenth Amendment is the one that Congress, the president, and the rest of the federal government trample the most.

Healthcare legislation, as well as any legislation regulating the environment, energy, resources, and welfare are the responsibilities of the States, not the federal government. The Tenth Amendment is just as important as all the others (if not more-so); Thomas Jefferson even declared that "The Tenth Amendment is the foundation of the Constitution." If the government sees fit to repeatedly ignore the Tenth Amendment, then why can they not just as easily ignore the Fourth, Second, and even the First Amendments?

Presidents Who Redefined the Republic

As the Constitution was being drafted (as well as afterwards), the branch of government the Framers feared the most was Congress, the Legislative Branch. If America was to be based upon the Rule of Law, then the laws and those who created them had to be watched very carefully and constantly held accountable. If a president or Justice ignores laws or rules by fiat rather than the Rule of Law, corrective action must be taken to restore order under the Constitution and the Rule of Law. However, if the laws themselves are tyrannical and unjust, then people stop following the Rule of Law and tyrants arise (the Rule of Man).

By and large, America has had an extremely stable federal government over the past two centuries, especially when compared to most other countries in the world. The three branches of federal power were designed to contend with one another (the Checks and Balances) under the assumption that elected officials would not typically surrender their power to others in another branch of government. The Framers figured that when (not if) unforeseen events arose and two or more branches of the government agreed with one another on new legislation, then those laws should be upheld. However, it's highly unlikely that they would agree with unconstitutional laws being passed and signed – even if it was by the constitutional process. Usually the Congress and the President are at odds with one another (by design), and typically keep one another in check. When there have been significant changes or alterations to the American Republic, it's been at the hand of a strong president and either a weak or culpable Congress, and often during a time or war or economic upheaval – when the People are more willing to trade a portion of their liberty for temporary security (economic or political).

The following analysis of the American presidents – as well as the Congresses and Courts that enabled them – and descriptions of their alterations of the American Republic are intended primarily to compare and contrast their words and actions with regards to the Constitution, rather than insult or denigrate those individual leaders who many of us hold dear. Most American presidents have been very honorable men who deeply loved their country and presumably had the best intentions for the American people in mind – and for that we should be eternally grateful. However, that cannot and should not excuse these presidents' breaking of faith with the

Constitution they swore to defend and uphold – and the American people.

Andrew Jackson (1829 - 1837)

Andrew Jackson was the first president who really departed from the Constitution in several significant ways, primarily in that he pushed for the abolition of the Electoral College and supported the direct election of presidents, especially after winning the popular vote in 1824 but losing the Electoral College vote. Jackson also strongly supported a more democratic form of government rather than the democratic republic that the Founders had created. One of his main accomplishments as president was that he put the national central bank (the Second Bank of the United States) out of business and subsequently paid off the entire national debt. Unfortunately, those actions led to the Panic of 1837 and doomed the presidency of his successor, Martin van Buren.

While in office, Jackson greatly expanded the Spoils system in Washington D.C. ("to the victor go the spoils") and corruption immediately followed. Jackson also laid the unconstitutional groundwork for the Civil War by his response to the Nullification Crisis with South Carolina. Due to the high tariff prices on European goods, South Carolina wanted to nullify the Tariff of 1828, citing that the nullification of unjust federal laws was within a State's sovereign rights. From their writings, both Jefferson and Madison supported South Carolina's arguments for nullification. Jackson strongly disagreed and threatened to send federal troops to South Carolina to enforce the law if the state legislature nullified it. South Carolina begrudgingly backed down, but the precedent for the trampling of States' rights by the federal government had been set. Because of this showdown, it should be no surprise that South Carolina was the first State to secede from the Union in 1860.

Lastly, Andrew Jackson is credited with forming the modern Democrat Party out of the former Democratic-Republican Party of Madison and Jefferson. And since his opponents frequently referred to him as a "jackass," he gleefully adopted that as the symbol for the new party – which is still in use today.

Abraham Lincoln (1861 - 1865)

As time goes on, the story and intentions of Abraham Lincoln become more complex and interesting, to say the least. In our public schools and history books, Lincoln is portrayed as one of the greatest American presidents; after all, he saved the Union, freed the slaves, and initiated the settlement of the West through the Homestead Act. However, since the victors write the history books, are those portrayals we take for granted really accurate? It's no accident that the Civil War is known as the "War Between the States" in the South, while known as the "Civil War" in the rest of the nation.

Abraham Lincoln was personally against slavery, but he showed no intentions of abolishing it, at least until he unilaterally issued the Emancipation Proclamation. However, the slaves were not legally freed until the ratification of the Thirteenth Amendment after Lincoln's death. The Emancipation Proclamation was an Executive Order issued by Lincoln that only applied to the slaves in the Confederate States, not the Union States nor the Border States. And since the Confederate States had left the Union three years earlier, they of course refused to recognize the proclamation by a "foreign" leader. The slaves were not physically nor legally freed until after the Civil War had ended and the Thirteenth Amendment had been ratified. The Emancipation Proclamation appears to be more of a political or even military maneuver than one of conscience, morality, or liberty.

The Homestead Act in one form or another had been introduced since the 1840s in an attempt to quickly bring more free/non-slave States into the Union, and therefore shifting the balance of power away from the slave-States of the South. The Southern States defeated the Homestead/Free Soil bills several times, and the Homestead Act wasn't passed in Congress until they seceded from the Union. However, the law excluded "anyone who had taken up arms against the United States" and thus excluded the Confederate citizens. After the Civil War ended, the Confederates were pardoned and that portion of the law doesn't appear to have been enforced.

Slavery and its evils often cloud the causes, intentions, and circumstances surrounding the Civil War. Given the complexity of the events, emotions, and politics that led up to the Civil War, the one certainty that can be concluded about Lincoln was that his primary motivation was to keep the Union together. He was determined to bring the Confederate States back into the Union by any means necessary and regardless of the cost to the country. By the end of the Civil War, over 620,000 American soldiers had been killed, though the actual number may be closer to 700,000. And those figures don't take into account the thousands of noncombatants who died from disease, starvation, and other effects of the war.

Lincoln and the Congress that enabled him is responsible for turning "these" United States of America into "the" United States of America – from a confederated republic of states into a nation with a strong central government. Until the Civil War, America consisted of a federal union of several independent, sovereign States; after the war, America was a nation consisting of a national government that really governed one large nation-state. By waging the Civil War against the South, Lincoln destroyed States' rights and effectively nullified the Ninth and Tenth Amendments which guaranteed the States' rights. The relationship between the federal government and the States has never been the same; since the Civil War, the States are independent and sovereign in name only.

Sovereignty in any union, whether it be a marital union or federal union, is meaningless if one or both entities cannot voluntarily leave the union and are forced to remain in the union against their will. But that's not a union – that's a prison, which is the primary reason the Southern States gave for declaring their independence and seceding from the Union.

The Southern States looked to the Declaration of Independence when asserting their right to secede, specifically its introduction: *"When in the Course of human events it becomes necessary for one people to dissolve the political bands which have connected them with another and to assume among the powers of the earth..."* The South's argument for leaving the Union was the same the Signers cited for dissolving the relationship between the Colonies and Great Britain. Yet Lincoln and his supporters frequently referred to the Confederates as "rebels" in the same manner as King George and the British soldiers did with the Colonists. When half the country dissolves the union/agreement, it's called "independence" or "secession," not "rebellion." Rebellions and insurrections involve tiny factions and groups of people, not entire sovereign states.

In the Constitution, secession was not explicitly forbidden, nor was it even mentioned. From the ratification of the Constitution until the time of the Civil War, it was widely taken for granted that a State had the inherent right to peaceably secede from the Union. Before ratifying the Constitution, New York, Virginia, and Rhode Island even wrote into their own state constitutions that they had secession rights and thus they were conditionally joining the Union. Also, under the Ninth and Tenth Amendments, the States had the inherent power to secede. Thomas Jefferson and James Madison both assumed that States – as sovereign entities who had voluntarily entered the Union – had the right to secede, along with the right to nullify federal laws that violated their sovereignty.

When the Southern States finally seceded in 1860-1861, many Northern newspapers were in favor of simply letting them go, but Lincoln would have none of it. After the politics had become so bitter and so divided for decades, many felt that the long political battles had finally ended. And while Lincoln did not expressly declare war on the South when they seceded, he helped trigger it by refusing to remove the Union soldiers from Fort Sumter.

The fundamental principles of the American Experiment are self-government and self-determination, as declared in the Declaration of Independence. However, could these principles really be espoused by the Union during the Civil War if millions of people and entire States were not allowed to determine their own government for themselves? Certainly not! Another supporting argument for the secession of the Southern States was that they were the original signers of the Treaty of Paris that freed them from Great Britain – at which time they were sovereign nation-states. If they voluntarily joined the federal union in order to become part of the "United States," then they could voluntarily leave it as well. It's likely that the Constitution would have never been ratified had the States known the agreement was permanent – and unbreakable.

Abraham Lincoln – and the Congress that authorized the war – could have simply just let the South go rather than expend hundreds of thousands of lives and destroy half the country. Consider how many homes, families, wealth, and history was obliterated in the Civil War. Consider the vast bloodshed, pain, and suffering that the war cost. Having a divided America would not mean perpetual war between the North and South; after all, the American Loyalists fled to Canada after the Revolutionary War and the last conflict we've had with Canada was in 1812 when the British tried to retake America. Regardless, the Civil War likely was a Divine judgment upon America for the horrible evils of entrenched slavery. There didn't have to be a Civil War if the hotheads in both the North and South would've humbled themselves, repented, and voluntarily ended slavery – while they could. The dirty little secret is that racism was just as pervasive in the North as it was in the South, and that the North was somewhat hypocritical in that while they thought the slaves should be free, they didn't think that the blacks should be first-class citizens like the whites. Even after the war had ended, racism was just as entrenched in the North as it was in the South.

More than sixty years passed between the Twelfth Amendment (Choosing the President and Vice President) and the next three amendments which were ratified following the Civil War in order to abolish slavery, grant the former-slaves citizenship and natural-born rights, and ensure the right to vote among citizens.

Theodore Roosevelt (1901 - 1909)

Teddy Roosevelt kicked off the Progressive Era in America with a bang and was one of the few widely popular Progressive presidents. He began his political career in the liberal wing of the Republican Party and continued moving left before finally leaving and forming the Progressive Party. After serving two consecutive terms as president, he ran for a third term under his new party, which later became known as the Bull Moose Party.

As New York governor and later as president, Roosevelt became the country's foremost "trust-buster," warring against the "robber-barons," railroads, trusts, and other corporations/wealthy individuals he didn't like. He greatly expanded federal regulations and effectively ended the laissez faire period in America. He pressed for more democracy and the direct election of Senators over the Constitutional republic, created the Square Deal (the forerunner of FDR's New Deal), and greatly expanded national parks which locked land away from future private use. His blatant, unconstitutional actions effectively split the Republican Party between the Progressives and the conservatives.

After Roosevelt's second term, the GOP was deeply divided but was growing more conservative, exemplified in that they elected William Taft as president after Roosevelt declined to run in 1908. In order to split the GOP vote and propel Woodrow Wilson into office, a number of prominent Wall Street backers convinced Roosevelt to run for president as a third-party candidate in 1912. Though Wilson and Roosevelt were nearly identical on most Progressive issues, Wall Street preferred to have Wilson in the White House. And by splitting the GOP vote with the semi-popular third-party, the Progressives and Wall Street bankers succeeded.

His Progressive Party laid the planks of socialism which would soon be rolled into the Democratic Party under Woodrow Wilson: a national healthcare system/insurance, social insurance/security, limited court-power over strikes, minimum-wage and an eight-hour workday, the federal securities commission, farm relief/subsidies, inheritance taxes, the federal (progressive) income tax, direct election of senators, women's suffrage, and judicial recall. By playing favorites and wielding unconstitutional federal power through taxes and regulation, free-market capitalism and competition were damaged and the modern era of "big business" was born under Roosevelt.

As president, Roosevelt re-interpreted the Constitution to mean that the president could exercise any powers not explicitly forbidden to him, blatantly violating the Tenth Amendment and Article II of the Constitution. The Square Deal exemplifies his vast expansion of executive powers, and he set the example for future Progressive presidents to follow, namely the rigid conservation of natural resources, control of corporations, and consumer protection. Until Roosevelt, those responsibilities had been handled by the States – and rightly so.

Woodrow Wilson (1913 - 1921)

Woodrow Wilson was the first intellectual elected as president, previously holding the office of President of Princeton University before serving one term as governor of New Jersey. As president, he filled his administration and Cabinet with like-minded Progressive academics and created a slew of new federal agencies and departments such as the Federal Reserve Board, the Federal Trade Commission, the Food and Drug Administration, the Federal Fuel Administration, and numerous others. Nearly everything that Teddy Roosevelt wanted to accomplish in office, Wilson actually implemented. Just because an agency is prefaced with the word "federal" does not mean it's constitutional, but the public will get the impression that it is.

Like Roosevelt before him, Wilson ran for a third term by deadlocking the Democratic Convention in 1920, though he was unsuccessful. In 1919, he suffered a debilitating stroke which he, his wife, and his chief of staff concealed from the public (and the Congress), isolating him from the Cabinet and even the Vice President for the remainder of his term. His wife Edith would sometimes even guide the pen for him while he was signing major pieces of legislation so they would still be technically signed "by his hand." Wilson also issued his "Fourteen Points" after the Great War (WWI) and helped create the League of Nations, which was replaced by the United Nations in 1946.

During Wilson's tenure in office, four Progressive Constitutional Amendments were ratified: the Sixteenth (the federal Income Tax), the Seventeenth (Direct Election of Senators), the Eighteenth (Prohibition), and the Nineteenth (Women's Suffrage). The Sixteenth Amendment gave us the income tax system we have today, which permanently altered the system of taxation in America, causing the size and scope of the federal government to greatly expand. The Seventeenth Amendment, while at first-glance appearing relatively innocuous, profoundly altered the relationship between the States and the federal government, effectively rendering the Ninth and Tenth Amendments powerless – and almost meaningless. The Eighteenth (Prohibition) had nothing to do with government and was repealed by the Twenty-First Amendment thirteen years later in 1933.

Last but certainly not least, Wilson pressed for the Federal Reserve Act, which was passed during his first year in office. This act transferred control of the United States' money supply from Congress (Article I, Section 8) over to the Federal Reserve Board, which is a group of unelected, unaccountable, private bankers. The truth about the Federal Reserve is that there's nothing "federal" nor "reserve" about the Federal Reserve – it's simply a huge central bank but much larger and vastly more powerful than the previous central banks, the last of which President Andrew Jackson defeated in the 1830s. A Progressive state needs complete control of the money supply to succeed, and the Federal Reserve Act did just that. By providing a nearly endless supply of "instant money" to the federal government, the Federal Reserve enabled Wilson to institute the draft and push America into the Great War (WWI) even though he had explicitly campaigned as the candidate "who had kept us out of the War."

Today, the Federal Reserve is the most powerful entity in the nation and is the largest creditor to the United States Treasury (not China nor Japan). The Federal Reserve creates money out of thin air (they don't even have to print it) and then loans it to the Treasury – with interest, though most of the interest is paid back to the Treasury. Central banks always cause the national debt to explode, which is why Jackson was able to pay off the national debt after eliminating the central bank. By mismanaging the nation's money supply, the Federal Reserve is directly responsible for some of America's biggest booms and busts, such as the Financial Crisis of 2008 and even the Great Depression. Ben Bernanke, the current Fed Chairman admitted as such in 2008 when he publicly apologized for it: "Regarding the Great Depression. You're right, we did it. We're very sorry. But thanks to you, we won't do it again." The Great Depression was partially caused by deflation (the collapse of prices/costs), and the Fed's drastic tightening of the money supply when they should have loosened it. The Fed's only weapon against deflation is inflation, which is what they're employing today by creating trillions of dollars in a desperate effort to restart (and now sustain) our economy.

Whoever controls the money supply of a nation effectively controls the entire economy AND the government of the country. As Mayer Amschel Rothschild (the founder of the Rothschild banking dynasty) once declared, "Let me issue and control a nation's money and I care not who makes its laws."

The Founders perfectly understood this principle and how money really worked (especially paper money), which is specifically why they placed that responsibility under the peoples' control via the Congress. Those who control our money should be directly accountable to the people, which is much too important to be left up to unknown, unaccountable corporations or individuals.

Franklin D. Roosevelt (1933 - 1945)

When the Crash of 1929 hit Wall Street and the Great Depression began, the Progressive Republican Herbert Hoover proved to be powerless in addressing the economic crisis. The governor of New York, Franklin D. Roosevelt, ran against him and made grand promises to restart the economy – namely, the New Deal.

After easily winning the 1932 elections, FDR continued in Woodrow Wilson's and his cousin Teddy's footsteps by greatly expanding the federal government, creating dozens of new federal agencies and departments which now regulate nearly every facet of American life. Through his enactment of widespread public works and welfare programs during the Great Depression and later WWII, FDR won an astounding four consecutive terms in office before dying from a cerebral hemorrhage in 1945. After his death, the Twenty-Second Amendment was ratified which limited presidential service to two terms.

Roosevelt's signature legislation was the New Deal, fashioned after the Square Deal but greatly expanded in size and scope. The New Deal created the vast union/city political machines which are still in place today – and which have also led to their dismal crime, poverty, and corruption. Throughout the Great Depression, FDR blamed bankers, investors, our financial system, and even capitalism to further his Progressive agenda. However, by the end of his first term, the Depression had not lifted and the economy crashed again in 1937 because of his New Deal policies which had failed to restart the American economy.

Over the last decade, a number of historians and economists have revisited the New Deal and examined FDR's big-government policies, and have concluded that they prolonged the Great Depression by at least seven years. FDR, not being one to let a good crisis go to waste, saw the Depression as an opportunity to quickly enact as much of the Progressive platform as possible, such as excessive federal taxes on income, onerous regulations on businesses, collective bargaining and unionization, crony capitalism between businesses, banks, and government, the federal minimum-wage, price-controls, wage-controls, and massive taxation on the wealthy (who created the jobs to pay for his outrageous spending in the first place). Does this sound eerily familiar? It should – Barack Obama has been pushing for many of the programs and reforms of the New Deal but under different terms/names.

When FDR's opponents finally woke up and realized what he was doing, much of his New Deal legislation was struck down in the courts as unconstitutional and an overreach of the Executive Branch. FDR responded by packing the Supreme Court with Progressives and appointed eight of the nine justices by 1941, along with reshaping much of the federal appellate system. FDR also appointed Hugo Black as the Chief Justice, who coined the phrase "Separation of Church and State" and ruled that pornography was protected under the First Amendment. Hugo Black also wrote the majority opinion for the ruling that declared prayer in public schools was unconstitutional in 1962.

Despite the facts, FDR remains one of America's more beloved presidents for leading the country through the Great Depression and WWII. He was confident and optimistic and helped Americans gather their bearings during the dark days of the Depression, even though his policies were in fact worsening and prolonging their suffering.

FDR's lasting legacy (aside from dramatically liberalizing the Supreme Court) includes the creation of the Federal National Mortgage Association (Fannie Mae), the FDIC, Social Security, Selective Service, and the WPA, as well as numerous other agencies and departments. He also wanted to nationalize healthcare but felt it was an overreach, which was surprising restraint for a Progressive. Of special note, FDR also helped Joseph Kennedy (the patriarch of the Kennedy political dynasty) enter American politics, who was a bootlegger during Prohibition and who later served as one of FDR's ambassadors.

FDR also seized all non-jewelry, non-collectible gold and made its ownership illegal, and even arbitrarily set the price by his own authority. After the attack on Pearl Harbor, FDR unilaterally interned over 120,000 Japanese-American citizens without cause from 1942-1945, as well as drafting over 10 million men for service in WWII. Under FDR's authority, at least one boatload of Jewish refugees from Europe were turned away from the United States and sent back to the gas chambers and death-camps of the Nazi's.

Lyndon B. Johnson (1963 - 1969)

Lyndon Johnson was first elected to Congress during the waning days of the New Deal and often seemed to see himself as the next FDR. After becoming president following John F. Kennedy's shocking assassination, he quickly continued implementing the planks of the Progressive platform where FDR had left off. During his term in office, the Medicare/Medicaid programs were created, as well as his "Great Society" legislation and the "War on Poverty" welfare programs. Prior to Barack Obama, modern Progressivism peaked under LBJ, who was renowned for his heavy-handed control of the Senate and for exerting massive political pressure on both his allies and his enemies.

Though LBJ signed the Civil Rights Act of 1964 and created the Great Society, ostensibly to lift the poor out of their poverty, he did more-so for political reasons rather than out of

91

compassion and personal convictions. One of LBJ's seldom-publicized quotes from that time was: "I'll have those n*ggers voting Democratic for the next 200 years." And tragically, he has – today, black Americans vote Democrat about 90% of the time, even though Democrat policies have consistently harmed their families and communities since LBJ's Great Society legislation became law.

From the days of Lincoln to the Great Society of LBJ, most black Americans (especially in the South) voted Republican because Lincoln was credited with freeing the slaves. But with the advent of the Civil Rights Movement and the Great Society, Martin Luther King, Jr. changed his party affiliation from Republican to Democrat, and many blacks followed his lead. The new welfare policies of LBJ and the Democrat Party not only cemented the newly-acquired black vote, but politically, socially, and economically re-enslaved blacks and destroyed millions of black families.

Along with the vast expansion of the federal welfare state, LBJ's time in office was one of anger, riots, and cultural upheavals. While JFK favored leaving Vietnam, LBJ greatly expanded the war-effort and instituted the draft which sent over 550,000 troops overseas. His policies created the anti-war movement that spawned the radicals and the countercultural movements that are plaguing America even today through the likes of Saul Alinsky, Hillary Clinton, Bill Ayers, and of course, Barack Obama.

Barack Obama (2009 - ??)

Barack Obama is by far the most divisive, most radical individual to preside over America as President and Commander-in-Chief. With the recent passage of the Progressives' century-long dream of nationalized healthcare, Obama has effectively completed the primary goals of the Progressive Party and also the Communist Party of the 1950s.

By playing to Americans' desire to end the foreign wars and campaigning on a vague message of "Hope and Change,"

92

Obama successfully won the presidency despite very little being known about him. Since even before his nomination in 2008, he has been extremely deceptive about his radical background and roots. While running for office, he portrayed himself as a social moderate and fiscally responsible liberal, but refused to provide even basic documents such as school/college transcripts and even his own birth-certificate. Even before running for office, he sealed nearly all of his family and personal history, but the media was so enamored with a "clean, articulate, black man" (in the words of his Vice President Joe Biden), that they didn't care. When he later became President, he sealed the rest of his personal records by Executive Order 13489, one of his very first acts of office.

Before running for public office in Illinois, Obama had worked as a "community organizer" and was an ardent disciple of Saul Alinsky. He was extremely unqualified for the presidency, holding no executive or leadership roles other than the editor of the Harvard Law Review. When he was a State Senator and a U.S. Senator, he had legislative experience but no executive experience. As for his vetting, Obama wrote two memoirs which have been found to contain numerous factual errors, along with some personal friends in his books that he's admitted to making up out of "composites."

Upon taking office, Obama immediately pushed through a $787 billion stimulus package that did very little to restart the economy. Once the package was passed, he quickly moved onto pressing for national healthcare reform, though no one could really agree on what those reforms should actually entail. Later in 2009, through repeated backroom deals and blatant acts of corruption and manipulation, the Democrat-controlled Congress passed the "Affordable Care Act" on Christmas Eve and he promptly signed it, effectively nationalizing one-sixth of the entire American economy and placing it under executive control via the Department of Health and Human Services. Most of the Congressmen didn't even read the 2400-page bill, with House Speaker Nancy Pelosi brazenly declaring, "We have to pass the bill in order to find out what's in it." To say that the ACA was an unconstitutional act would be an understatement, but on June 28, 2012, the Supreme Court upheld the law in a 5-4 split decision, with Chief Justice John Roberts (a Bush appointee) casting the deciding vote.

Next to FDR, Woodrow Wilson, and Teddy Roosevelt, Obama has been the most anti-Constitutional president in the nation's history, frequently acting far outside the bounds of the Constitution and the President's specific, enumerated powers. In the name of expediency ("getting things done"), he has taken to bypassing Congress altogether and simply issues edicts, policies, and decrees in order to accomplish his will. There are even rumblings of his support for a Constitutional amendment to abolish the Twenty-Second Amendment which would allow him to stay in office for more than two terms.

Apart from issuing over one hundred far-reaching Executive Orders, Obama has surrounded himself with more than forty unelected, unappointed advisors referred to as "czars," many of which hold to the same radical, ultra-Progressive (if not anti-American) views as he does. Van Jones, Obama's "green jobs czar" was dismissed from office because he was an avowed, unrepentant communist who thought the Islamic terror attacks of September 11th were a conspiracy created by the government under the previous Bush administration.

The Obama administration's constitutional violations go on and on, from its blatant disregard for the Rule of Law, to its refusal to enforce the borders/immigration laws, suing numerous states for a variety of reasons, widespread corruption in the Department of Justice, crony capitalism with green-energy companies, cap-and-trade regulations, illegal EPA/interior mandates and regulations, ignoring of federal court rulings, and numerous other scandals and illegal activities.

Just before the last election, the American consulate in Benghazi, Libya came under a coordinated terrorist attack on September 11th, 2012. But instead of even offering a basic response, the Obama administration ordered those defending the compound to "stand down," as well as refusing to send reinforcements to assist them. In the end, our ambassador was sodomized, tortured, and dragged through the streets after succumbing to his injuries. The ambassador's assistant, along with the two Navy Seals who disobeyed orders and defended the compound, were also killed in the attack. The Obama administration has been attempting to stonewall the Benghazi investigations since October, 2012.

Dishonorable Mentions

Both Richard M. Nixon (1969 - 1974) and William J. Clinton (1993 - 2000) both overreached in their presidencies, but their scandalous actions were primarily abuse of power violations rather than blatant acts against the Constitution. Nixon took the United States off the Gold Standard which gave the Federal Reserve even more power to create money than it already had. The Watergate Break-in and the subsequent cover-ups/scandals were quite isolated and did not affect the American system of government (at least not directly). The same held true with Clinton's numerous scandals, cover-ups, and even the perjury/impeachment proceedings.

Several acts of Clinton's time in office which could be construed as tyrannical was the siege against the Branch Davidians at Waco, Texas, as well as the firing of all ninety-three U.S. attorneys soon after taking office. Clinton also signed Executive Order 13083 which nullified the Tenth Amendment and gave the President (himself) broad new executive powers over most of the federal government, though the Congress and States pressured him to suspend it. Clinton's administration played an instrumental role in crafting the national healthcare legislation, though the bill was promptly defeated in 1994, causing the Democrats to lose control of the House of Representatives for the first time in over fifty years.

All debt eventually enslaves, and that holds true for the national debt as well as personal debt. The borrower is always a slave to the lender, and under George W. Bush, the national

debt increased from $5.7 trillion when he took office to over
$10.6 trillion when he left. In a mere eight years, Bush added
nearly $5 trillion, which almost doubled the national debt. After
holding both the Executive Branch and the Legislative Branch
for six years, as well as overseeing a good economy, the
Republicans should have been paying down the national debt as
quickly as possible instead of doubling it.

Tragically, Bush's massive deficit-spending set the
precedent for Barack Obama, who has managed to add more
than that amount but in only half the time (four years). Not only
did Bush dramatically increase spending, he also filled his
administration with czars. At one point, he had thirty-three
czars (in contrast to Clinton's eight, Reagan's one, and Bush
Sr.'s two), but they didn't attract much attention until Obama
expanded the number after taking office to more than forty
czars. Whereas the Founders typically disbursed federal power,
Bush consolidated it and gave us the DHS, ICE and TSA. In
many cases, Bush set the precedent for what was acceptable for
the president to do, and Obama expanded it and then radicalized
it.

To Bush's credit, he did provide the strength, resolve, and
reassurance that was desperately needed in the wake of
September 11th. However, aside from the lack of fiscal
discipline, his biggest shortfall was his lack of ability to
communicate. After eight years of Bill Clinton's shenanigans,
scandals, and juvenile behavior in the White House, America
could have greatly benefited from a president who could
communicate American values. Good leaders live out their
personal convictions and conduct themselves with integrity;
great leaders not only live their values, but communicate their
values to those they lead and serve.

Presidents must be able to effectively communicate, which is
one of the reasons why Obama is so revered by his constituents
but Bush was not – despite their actual records on leadership,
economics, and integrity. By his failure to communicate, Bush

allowed the media and his opponents to define him, while Obama constantly defines (and redefines) himself.

Progressive Presidents and the Republic

Notice that most of the presidents on the list lean heavily towards Progressivism, which is simply another name for modern Liberalism, Statism, Socialism, and Marxism. Progressivism is diametrically opposed to the Constitution and the Republic it created because Progressives exalt equality and State power rather than individual liberty. Francis Fox Piven – a radical Marxist professor at Columbia University – declared in 2012 that Democrats equal Progressives, Socialists, Communists, Marxists; they are all one and the same now, and that they must all work together to transform America and the world. And though they may prefer different labels, names, and titles, politically and morally, they are the same.

Following the revolutionary counter-culture and anti-war movements of the 1960s, the New Progressives and their allies sought to permanently change the political structure of the United States. But the Communist Party and Progressive Party were simply too unpopular and too heavily monitored by the federal government to be viable candidates for their support. That left only the Republican Party (which was unthinkable to the Progressives) and the Democrat Party, which they decided was more aligned with their values, goals, and politics. Following their success of demonizing the traditional Democrat leadership under Lyndon Johnson because of the Vietnam War, the New Progressives began infiltrating the Democrat Party in droves, though cleverly masking their revolutionary ideas and motives in traditional liberalism and even patriotism.

Soon the Communist Party in America was no longer of any concern, especially after the fall of the Soviet Union. But where did all the American communists go? Surely the vast majority of those radicals didn't see the error in their ways and become capitalists, yet communism appeared to simply vanish into thin air. Or did it only seem like that because the radicals and

97

communists had so thoroughly and completely infiltrated the Democrat Party that it had become the Democrat Party "in name only" (the DINOs).

Watch and listen to some of the famous Democrat speeches before 1970 – they sound like Republicans by today's standards, but they were Democrats. They dearly loved their country and usually wanted what was best for America, even if their ideas didn't always make sense or add up on paper. Consider how little Marxism and communism were in the speeches of FDR, Truman, Kennedy, and even LBJ, and then compare those speeches by those of today's leading Democrats, particularly Nancy Pelosi, Harry Reid, and Barack Obama – they are like night and day.

Today's Democrat Party leaders – though certainly not most Democrat voters – are ideologically the Party of Marx, Lenin, and Stalin, not the Party of Jefferson, Jackson, and Kennedy.

Chapter 4 - The Progressive Transformation

"You Americans are so gullible. No, you won't accept communism outright. But we'll keep feeding you small doses of socialism until you finally wake up and find you already have communism. We won't have to fight you; we'll so weaken your economy until you fall like overripe fruit into our hands." – Soviet leader Nikita Khrushchev

One of the great curiosities of history is the propensity for history to repeat itself, despite our best efforts not to repeat the same mistakes. Such an axiom has been proven so often throughout history that it led Georg Wilhelm Friedrich Hegel to declare, "The only thing man learns from history is that man learns nothing from history."

During the 2000 presidential campaign, one of Al Gore's talking points was about the wealth-disparity gap between the rich and the poor, particularly demagoguing the Top 1%, the Top 2%, and the Top 5%. I remember being surprised at first, because didn't most Americans aspire to achieve those levels of wealth? In fact, didn't many in our political class often seek audiences and photo-opportunities with those Top 1-5%? And yet here he was trying to stir up jealousy and envy between the average voters and the "privileged few," though they were the very people that Clinton, Gore, and other politicians frequently rubbed elbows with – their biggest supporters. More surprising was that those people with the enormous wealth continued supporting the Progressive politicians even after months of criticism and insults! But it wasn't until Barack Obama was elected by a wide majority – and re-elected – did I realize that history was repeating itself in the early Twenty-First Century eerily similar to what had occurred in the early Twentieth Century.

Our American Awakening

In the late Nineteenth Century after the Industrial Age had matured and incredible amounts of wealth had been created, the Progressive Era arose as a response to those enormous wealth-inequalities. In the late Twentieth Century after Progressivism had waned for years, it then was reignited by those same tensions, though due to the Information Age and the advent of personal computers and the Internet. History was (and is) repeating itself with respect to the laissez faire policies in the technology sectors over the past thirty years which created several hundred billionaires and at least five million millionaires, followed by a rise in Progressivism as a response to that inequality. Just as the Progressives Teddy Roosevelt and Woodrow Wilson fostered class envy between the rich and the poor to sweep themselves into power, so have Barack Obama and the Progressive Democrats of today.

History is repeating itself – and we are demonstrating once again that mankind learns nothing from history. And just as the rise of Progressivism in the Twentieth Century led to the rise of horrible tyrants who slaughtered tens of millions of their own people and two world wars, one can only wonder what horrors the new rise of Progressivism will usher in.

One of the more comical (and rather hypocritical) reports from the Occupy Wall Street protests were all the luxury electronics that the downtrodden, unemployed activists had at their disposal, such as the newer laptops, tablets, and smart-phones, particularly the new iPads and iPhones. The OWS activists were protesting the vast wealth-gap between what they called the Top 1% and the 99%, even though many in the Top 1% earned their wealth by creating and selling the very products those activists were using at their protests! If the Progressives and the OWS protesters really want to make American capitalism more equal and fair, then they should demand that we go back to the 1970s, shut down all the cellular-networks, dismantle the Internet, and outlaw personal computers, laptops, tablets, MP3-players, eReaders, and all the other luxury items they enjoy. While they're at it, they might as well get rid of

100

automobiles, electricity, factories, tractors, and anything else that has dramatically improved the quality of life for the past two centuries. Who enabled most of the Top 1% to get to where they are today? We did, because we bought their products and services.

Since the early Twentieth Century when Progressivism took hold in America, one class of citizens has been pitted against another in the name of inequality: the rich versus the poor, the men versus the women, the old versus the young, the blacks versus the whites, and so on. The feelings aroused by such class warfare prevents any significant reforms of our tax system, which is favored by the majority to punish the rich, even though the wealthy help create most of the jobs. As long as the federal progressive income tax is cemented in place in the United States, liberty will always take a backseat to equality. Not only that, but Progressivism never stands still – it steadily marches ever leftward towards Communism and other forms of Marxism, though Progressives are careful to avoid such terms and definitions.

As mentioned in the last chapter, America has been slower to adopt full-blown socialism compared to other nations in the West, although many of the same Progressive reforms have been made, especially with the recent nationalization of the healthcare system. The generation at the turn of the Twentieth Century experimented with Progressivism, the WWII generation hesitantly embraced Progressivism and accepted it with the New Deal in the Great Depression, and then the majority of the Baby Boomer generation preferred Progressivism instead of Constitutionalism. Lastly, by electing Barack Obama, the Millennial generation (and most of Obama's supporters) openly supported the fundamental transformation of our constitutional republic into a Western socialist democracy.

How did Progressivism rise to power so quickly and completely in America and turn our nation inside out? By the negligence and apathy of the Judeo-Christian majority. In a democracy, the majority always rules and holds the influence of the minority in check – unless they stop acting like the majority. When the majority is weakened or becomes demoralized, the vocal minority rises up and purports to be the majority, even though their actual numbers and power may be quite small. Though America has been a center-right country for decades, it is now governed by a radical Progressive, Leftist administration. Though Woodrow Wilson was one of the major Progressives who pushed America towards socialism, he accurately diagnosed what was happening with the radical elements at that time: *"A little group of willful men, representing no opinion but their own, have rendered the great government of the United States helpless and contemptible."*

With the popularization of Progressivism at the turn of the last century, each generation in American has grown increasingly comfortable with soft tyranny and wealth-redistribution in the name of equality and fairness. The last several political campaigns by the Democrat Party have openly pushed for vast wealth-redistribution and other Marxist policies – and they are winning. Now that Progressivism has been rejuvenated in America, it's become the majority political view of voting Americans.

But what really is Progressivism? Where did it originate, and more importantly: where is it taking us?

The Foundation of Progressivism: Communism

In 1848, Karl Marx wrote "The Communist Manifesto" and outlined the Ten Planks of Communism, a set of guidelines to change a nation/economy from capitalism to Communism. Socialism, Progressivism, communism, and modern liberalism are all forms of Statism in which the State is ultimately in control of the people, rather than the people being in control of the State. And since these political philosophies are all based upon some form of Marxism, they eventually end in communism or totalitarianism. But neither socialism nor communism "sold" very well in America as they had in Europe, so the early liberals and "statists" in the late Nineteenth Century rebranded their version of democratic socialism to be called "Progressivism," and therefore made it more palpable to the American public. However, Progressivism is still socialism and communism, though in a milder form – at first.

The Ten Planks of Communism (and also Progressivism) are:

1. Abolition of private property and the application of all rent to public purpose.
2. A heavy progressive or graduated income tax.
3. Abolition of all rights of inheritance.
4. Confiscation of the property of all emigrants and rebels.
5. Centralization of credit in the hands of the State, by means of a national bank with state capital and an exclusive monopoly.
6. Centralization of the means of communication and transportation in the hands of the State.
7. Extension of factories and instruments of production owned by the State, the bringing into cultivation of waste lands, and the improvement of the soil generally in accordance with a common plan.
8. Equal liability of all to labor. Establishment of industrial armies, especially for agriculture.
9. Combination of agriculture with manufacturing industries; gradual abolition of the distinction between town and country by a more equable distribution of the population over the country.
10. Free education for all children in government schools. Abolition of children's factory labor in its present form. Combination of education with industrial production.

While several of the Ten Planks of Communism were enacted during the Progressive Era from Teddy Roosevelt through FDR, their influence was not really felt until much later because most of these laws were at the federal level and did not immediately filter down to the state and local levels. Also, the Ten Planks of Communism were very broad and tended to be harder to enact. But during the late 1950s, the Communist Party in America came up with a specific set of goals to transform not only the American government, but permanently alter American society. These grassroots-level goals were publicized in a book called "The Naked Communist" by Cleon Skousen in 1958 and then read into the Congressional Record by U.S. Congressman Albert S. Herlong, Jr. on January 10, 1963.

The Naked Communist

The following is the list of specific Communist Party goals outlined in "The Naked Communist." These proved to be far more effective than the Ten Planks of Communism because they were very specific and spanned so much of American society rather than only at the top/federal level. The *italicized items* are those which have been successfully implemented in American society to one degree or another:

1. *U.S. acceptance of coexistence as the only alternative to atomic war.*
2. U.S. willingness to capitulate in preference to engaging in atomic war.
3. *Develop the illusion that total disarmament by the United States would be a demonstration of moral strength.*
4. *Permit free trade between all nations regardless of Communist affiliation and regardless of whether or not items could be used for war.*
5. *Extension of long-term loans to Russia and Soviet satellites.*
6. *Provide American aid to all nations regardless of Communist domination.*

104

7. *Grant recognition of Red China. Admission of Red China to the U.N.*

8. *Set up East and West Germany as separate states in spite of Khrushchev's promise in 1955 to settle the German question by free elections under supervision of the U.N.*

9. Prolong the conferences to ban atomic tests because the United States has agreed to suspend tests as long as negotiations are in progress.

10. Allow all Soviet satellites individual representation in the U.N.

11. *Promote the U.N. as the only hope for mankind. If its charter is rewritten, demand that it be set up as a one-world government with its own independent armed forces.*

12. *Resist any attempt to outlaw the Communist Party.*

13. Do away with all loyalty oaths.

14. Continue giving Russia access to the U.S. Patent Office.

15. *Capture one or both of the political parties in the United States.*

16. *Use technical decisions of the courts to weaken basic American institutions by claiming their activities violate civil rights.*

17. *Get control of the schools. Use them as transmission belts for socialism and current Communist propaganda. Soften the curriculum. Get control of teachers' associations. Put the party line in textbooks.*

18. *Gain control of all student newspapers.*

19. *Use student riots to foment public protests against programs or organizations which are under Communist attack.*

20. *Infiltrate the press. Get control of book-review assignments, editorial writing, policymaking positions.*

21. *Gain control of key positions in radio, TV, and motion pictures.*
22. *Continue discrediting American culture by degrading all forms of artistic expression. An American Communist cell was told to "eliminate all good sculpture from parks and buildings, substitute shapeless, awkward and meaningless forms."*
23. *Control art critics and directors of art museums; promote ugliness, repulsive, meaningless art.*
24. *Eliminate all laws governing obscenity by calling them "censorship" and a violation of free speech and free press.*
25. *Break down cultural standards of morality by promoting pornography and obscenity in books, magazines, motion pictures, radio, and TV.*
26. *Present homosexuality, degeneracy and promiscuity as "normal, natural, healthy."*
27. *Infiltrate the churches and replace revealed religion with "social" religion. Discredit the Bible and emphasize the need for intellectual maturity which does not need a "religious crutch."*
28. *Eliminate prayer or any phase of religious expression in the schools on the ground that it violates the principle of "separation of church and state."*
29. *Discredit the American Constitution by calling it inadequate, old-fashioned, out of step with modern needs, a hindrance to cooperation between nations on a worldwide basis.*
30. *Discredit the American Founding Fathers. Present them as selfish aristocrats who had no concern for the "common man."*
31. *Belittle all forms of American culture and discourage the teaching of American history on the ground that it was only a minor part of the "big*

picture." Give more emphasis to Russian history since the Communists took over.

32. *Support any socialist movement to give centralized control over any part of the culture–education, social agencies, welfare programs, mental health clinics, etc.*

33. Eliminate all laws or procedures which interfere with the operation of the Communist apparatus.

34. *Eliminate the House Committee on Un-American Activities.*

35. *Discredit and eventually dismantle the FBI.*

36. *Infiltrate and gain control of more unions.*

37. *Infiltrate and gain control of big business.*

38. *Transfer some of the powers of arrest from the police to social agencies. Treat all behavioral problems as psychiatric disorders which no one but psychiatrists can understand or treat.*

39. Dominate the psychiatric profession and use mental health laws as a means of gaining coercive control over those who oppose Communist goals.

40. *Discredit the family as an institution. Encourage promiscuity, masturbation and easy divorce.*

41. *Emphasize the need to raise children away from the negative influence of parents. Attribute prejudices, mental blocks and retarding of children to suppressive influence of parents.*

42. *Create the impression that violence and insurrection are legitimate aspects of the American tradition; that students and special-interest groups should rise up and use "united force" to solve economic, political or social problems.*

43. Overthrow all colonial governments before native populations are ready for self-government.

44. *Internationalize the Panama Canal.*

45. Repeal the Connally reservation so the United States cannot prevent the World Court from seizing

jurisdiction over domestic problems. Give the World
Court jurisdiction over nations and individuals alike.

As of 2012, 37 of the 45 goals specified in "The Naked
Communist" have been achieved, with most of the unmet goals
relating specifically to the old Soviet Union and the Cold War.
Before the Soviet Union collapsed in 1991, the Communist
Party in the United States was operating as just another political
party. However, after the collapse of the USSR, the Communist
Party all but disbanded and disbursed; communism had been
defeated without a shot being fired. Or had it? Rather than
continue under the Communist Party banner (which had been
rendered irrelevant), the American communists simply changed
hats and political party affiliations. Most simply became further
entrenched and involved in the Democrat Party (the quickest
avenue for their success), the universities and education system,
the regulatory agencies of the federal government, and the
mainstream media. But the communist migration had begun
years earlier in the 1960s, when the Progressive wing of the
Democrat Party moved from any notion of protecting individual
liberty to desiring equality above all – with the exception of sex,
non-moral religions, drug-use, and morality.

Robert Bork's "Slouching Towards Gomorrah" explains in
depth what happened during the transformative years of the
1960s: the pounding waves of radical individualism and radical
egalitarianism finally burst through the dams of moral and
cultural restraint and overwhelmed the American universities.
Yet the foundations for the rebellion of the 1960s were laid
much earlier in the century, though they were largely held in
check by WWI, the Great Depression, and then WWII. The
prosperity and comforts (and therefore cultural laxity) of the
1950s were immediately followed by the cultural upheavals of
the 1960s. Suddenly, the radical political philosophies that were
once mocked and ignored became embraced by the rising
counter-culture of the anti-war youth movements.

What happens when a generation of people who had little but was required to give much (the WWII generation) is immediately followed by a generation that had been given much yet had very little required of them? The generation that was given much tends to take that hard-won prosperity for granted and becomes extremely self-centered, and then licentiousness (known in religious circles as 'sin') becomes widespread. And as sin is ignored and spreads, its terrible effects and consequences deepen.

At the root of all our nation's problems (and all the other nations, in fact) is the sin and immorality of us – her individual people. For example, when men abandon their families or a couple has a child out of wedlock, the government is often looked to in order to provide assistance for the mother and child. Government takes on the role of the 'father' or 'provider' rather than the negligent man and therefore must grow larger to assume its new responsibilities and expenses. Soon others realize these "benefits" and "entitlements" and the welfare-state explodes. Prior to secularism and the welfare-state (which go hand-in-hand), various religious, family, and cultural pressures were put on negligent fathers (and irresponsible mothers) to take responsibility for themselves. And when that wasn't possible, the families, churches, and communities stepped in to help – not the government. The government's primary responsibility is to govern, not to be our parents.

The welfare policies of the federal and state governments since the time of the Great Society of LBJ have all but destroyed poorer minority families, especially those living in the inner-cities. If the government offers to pay unmarried women more money a month than her boyfriend makes, then why would it make any sense for her to marry him? And when more money is offered for each out-of-wedlock child, then isn't that simply encouraging her to have more children and never marry? As the children grow and mature in that environment, how can they realistically break the cycle of poverty and dependency when that's all they've ever known? If the money is good, why would they ever want to? Rather than encouraging immorality and irresponsible behavior through its policies, the federal government should be discouraging it or not even get involved at all and leave welfare up to the States and the local governments.

When individuals refuse to self-govern themselves, they essentially cede their God-given rights of self-governance to the State, such as when they break the law. And this is what has been happening at every level of Western society – person by person, family by family, city by city, state by state, and in country after country since the cultural revolution of the Sixties. And what a cultural revolution it has been – it's all but destroyed the distinctly American culture that took centuries to build.

Progressivism Leads to Communism

Even if Barack Obama had not been elected President and another milder, more typical liberal or Progressive was in his place, the results would still eventually end up the same. Under Progressivism, the State always becomes nearly all-powerful and the citizens merely exist to further the State (and at the behest of the State); therefore, the State's power becomes almost unlimited while the people's rights are severely restricted. Under the Constitution and the American model of limited government, the exact opposite occurs: the State exists solely to protect the people and their natural rights, and therefore its powers are clearly defined and limited, so as to not infringe upon the peoples' inherent rights and freedoms.

While Progressivism at first seems innocent enough, in the end it always evolves (or devolves) into other forms of Marxism, depending on the society or culture. Nazi Germany espoused socialism while hating the communism of the Soviets, even though both were quite similar in that they elevated the State far above the Individual. All forms of Marxism are in direct opposition to the constitutional republic erected by the

Founding Fathers; the embracing of Progressivism has created such deep divisions and fissures within the country that now many Americans are being pitted against one another through numerous "divide and conquer" schemes and class warfare from the highest offices in the land.

Progressivism is always much easier to implement in a democracy rather than a constitutional republic. This is where the Seventeenth Amendment fits into the Progressive plan which was pushed for by Teddy Roosevelt and enacted by Woodrow Wilson. According to Article I, Section 3 of the Constitution, Senators were to be chosen by the legislatures of the States or appointed by the governors (such as during a recess). The Senators were intended to directly represent the States and the States' interests before the federal government, and not the people thereof directly. Not only that, but Senators were supposed to be considered "super legislators" for their State and foster competition from their respective State legislatures, with State politics and their governor keeping them in-check. Many of the Founders feared direct-democracy because they knew how quickly and thoroughly large groups of people could be manipulated. The purpose of the Senate was to slow down the legislative process and carefully consider the needs and desires of the States, while the House was to enact the desires of the People. The Senate was to be the guardian of the constitutional republic and protector of State sovereignty.

Most Americans have been mistaught that the United States is a democracy – it is not, nor was it ever intended to be a democracy. The United States is a constitutional republic with democratic institutions. The Founders feared democracy and rightly so, because democracies have a terrible history of trampling minority rights in favor of the majority. In a democracy, the majority can pass whatever laws they want, even if those laws violate others' rights. Benjamin Franklin quipped that "Democracy is two wolves and a lamb voting on what to have for lunch. Liberty is a well-armed lamb contesting the vote!" While the saying is memorable enough, there's a great deal of truth behind it, as well as being quite revealing about how the Founders felt about democracy and what they desired for America.

First and foremost, the Founders wanted America to remain a land of liberty. They were quite familiar with other forms of government – especially democracy – and its shortcomings and dangers were very well-known. In order to protect their liberty, they devised a constitutional republic which used democracy in a limited fashion to represent the people but also to prevent the government from becoming too powerful. In a democracy, people often vote away their own political power, freedom, and sovereignty for short-term benefits, especially during turbulent times like war, economic downturns, etc. However, in a constitutional republic, political power remains mostly with the people, because it's more difficult for them to vote away their own sovereignty. Constitutional republics are based upon the Rule of Law which often isn't easily or arbitrarily changed and is therefore usually quite stable. Democracies are based upon the turbulent Rule of Man and are usually dependent upon the whims and emotions of the people, and therefore often quite unstable.

With the ratification of the Seventeenth Amendment, the fundamental structure of the Legislative Branch (if not the foundation of the Constitution) was changed which transformed the United States from a republic into a democracy. With that seemingly minor change, the State legislatures no longer have a direct voice in the federal government, which has all but obliterated the concept of States' rights and State sovereignty. Because of the Seventeenth Amendment, Senators now behave more like exalted representatives than the representatives of their States, and they have also become more focused on national issues rather than state issues. If the Seventeenth Amendment had been in place when the Constitution was drafted, it probably wouldn't have been ratified because the States were sovereign entities at that time and highly protective of their rights. In fact, the entire purpose of the Constitution was to confederate the States into a peaceful union under a federal government, not obliterate them as under a national government.

Through Progressivism, the American republic is being forced into the mold of a socialist democracy, which is diametrically opposed to everything she's stood for since her founding, with the recent healthcare law being the best example. Though the nationalized healthcare law has been found to be constitutional by the opinion of five Supreme Court justices, over the long haul it will either be repealed, defunded and picked apart, or will simply become meaningless because it goes against all the characteristic natures of Americans to choose their own treatments, select their own doctors, and be treated in their own timeframes – especially when Americans are used to being treated right away for most medical procedures. Taking a pain-pill or being put on a twenty-four month waiting list simply won't be tolerated in America – at least not at first. Sooner or later, Progressivism fails and the people turn against it.

Progressives will argue that nationalizing the healthcare system is in the country's best interests to make it more efficient and fairer to those who can't afford good coverage. However, that argument assumes that the issue is about providing quality healthcare and that the federal government is only trying to look out for the well-being of the citizenry – which is where they would be mistaken. If the federal government really wanted to provide affordable, quality healthcare to as many citizens as possible (including the poor), they would be deregulating the healthcare industry, introducing competition, and encouraging private investment – the exact opposite of what the Affordable Care Act has done. Widespread competition and sensible regulation makes any product or service more affordable and of better quality, not another bloated, bureaucratic monopoly that resides in Washington D.C.

In the end, the issue with the healthcare system is primarily about money and control, and about the federal government trying to patch and plug failing systems created by Progressive legislation generations ago. Like every other creature, self-preservation is what's ultimately behind all the power-grabs by the federal government – and that means cutting costs and becoming financially solvent without losing political power. Consider the following scenario with regards to Social Security and our healthcare system:

1. A person retires at age 65.
2. He/She receives an average of $1,500 per month in Social Security and Medicare benefits
3. He/She lives to age 85; resulting in $360,000 in benefits ($1,500 x 12 months x 20 years)
4. For every 3 retirees, it costs the government $1,080,000 over the next 20 years
5. There are approximately 72,000,000 retirees in 2012
6. $360,000 x 72,000,000 = $25.92 trillion over the next 20 years
7. There are only 109,000,000 workers in 2012
8. Since 70% of the money borrowed has been from Social Security, 100% of the money to be paid to Social Security must come from current workers
9. $25.92 trillion / 109,000,000 is $238,000 per worker or nearly $12,000 per year per worker or $1,000 per month per working citizen
10. For every 3 citizens the government refuses to treat (and dies), it will save $1,080,000 that it was obligated to pay over that 20-year period

With that scenario in mind, understand that in twenty years (by 2033), the national debt will be over $43 trillion because of Social Security and Medicare obligations alone (assuming we haven't paid down any part of the current national debt)! Is it starting to make sense now why the government has a vested interest in completely controlling the healthcare system and have a handful of unelected, unaccountable bureaucrats deciding who gets what medical treatments? As fiscal pressures inside the federal government continue to grow, the people who will suffer the most will be the poor, the elderly, and the sick.

Though they may have the best of intentions, Progressives ultimately seek to impose equality (specifically, equal outcomes), but can only do so by seizing and accumulating power, wealth, or property from the people and then redistributing it – in theory, equally (with the distributors and elites in charge, of course). However, Bill Clinton and most of the Twentieth Century liberals were traditional Progressives as opposed to the radicals and revolutionaries who now hold office, such as Eric Holder, Nancy Pelosi, and Hillary Clinton, who wrote her college thesis on the Marxist community organizer Saul Alinsky. Barack Obama would later become an ardent disciple of Alinsky and even teach his thuggish "community organizing" tactics in Chicago before running for public office.

The difference between traditional Progressives and radical Progressives is that traditional Progressives typically respect the traditional institutions but seek to heavily reform or remake them and continue to operate within most Constitutional boundaries. Radical Progressives are driven revolutionaries who refuse to govern according to the Constitution if it interferes with their goals. When Teddy Roosevelt, Woodrow Wilson, FDR, and LBJ introduced their Progressive changes and legislation, they usually operated within the system of Separation of Powers and pushed their legislation through Congress, even if their bills were unconstitutional. Sometimes their bills passed, other times they failed, but they still operated within the basic framework of the Constitution.

However, Barack Obama and the new Democrats are not traditional Progressives, but radical Progressives, indicative of their disregard for the Constitution and the Separation of Powers. In truly radical fashion, Obama sees no need to operate within those restrictive boundaries of the Constitution – he just enacts and enforces (or refuses to enforce) the policies and laws he chooses. Though what he is doing may sound just and fair (at least to one group of citizens), it's tyrannical to others because it violates their equal protection under the law and their constitutional rights. Tyranny is still tyranny, regardless of what it's called and how it's dressed up.

Presidents prior to Obama had their moments of tyranny, but with him, tyranny has become commonplace and his standard operating-procedure – and it will only grow worse since his re-election. Consequently, our republic which is based upon the Rule of Law is being turned into one of lawlessness, corruption, and crony capitalism. Democracies – especially republics – must require strict adherence to the Rule of Law or they will collapse/degenerate into chaos or dictatorships. Once our elected officials stop adhering to the Constitution and behave like thugs, there is little that can be done to stop their abuse of power – as we have recently seen. History is replete with examples of how republics are corrupted from within and then turn into dictatorships, monarchies, or empires when a strong leader comes to power under the banner of saving the country. When that occurs, the Rule of Law is cast aside and the Rule of Man – tyranny – commences.

Before Barack Obama, the United States was steadily rolling towards Communism due to the welfare laws, Progressive programs like Social Security and Medicare/Medicaid, and the ever-expanding size and scope of the federal government. But once in office, Obama vastly sped up the process and has implemented deeper, more sweeping policies of Statism and Communism more than any other president since FDR.

Communism: American Style

After the Soviet Union collapsed in 1991 and the Iron Curtain fell, most Americans thought that communism had been finally defeated. However, only "organized communism" had been defeated; the communists in America and throughout Europe, Russia, and the rest of the world simply changed hats and went underground. Today, America is infected with "disorganized communism" which is proving to be much more parasitic and dangerous – before, we could at least identify the radicals and their organizations. Now they operate under a variety of titles, names, and patriotic-sounding organizations throughout our media, universities, schools, unions, and governments. But their statist ideologies have not changed – just their nametags and affiliations. And many of them operate in the same circles that Barack Obama and others running our government today emerged from.

In his "Communist Manifesto," Karl Marx describes the Ten Planks (steps) which are necessary to destroy a free-enterprise system and replace it with a system of statism or totalitarianism, which will eventually produce a communist/socialist state. Not only are these planks a guide for transforming a nation, they can also be used as a test to determine precisely how communist a society has become. Understand that even if communism is wrapped in the Stars and Stripes and called by a different name, it's still communism. With that in mind, how does America measure up? How communistic and socialist – or Progressive – have we become?

The following is the original Ten Planks of the Communist Manifesto with their American counterparts for each plank (LibertyZone: http://www.libertyzone.com/Communist-Manifesto-Planks.html)

1. *Abolition of private property and the application of all rent to public purpose.*
   The government implements this critical plank with actions such as the misuse of the Fourteenth Amendment of the U.S. Constitution (1868) and various zoning laws, school and property taxes, and also the Bureau of Land Management. Zoning laws are the first step to government property ownership – government regulation usually leads to government control as the government expands.

2. *A heavy progressive or graduated income tax.*
   Americans know this as the misapplication of the
Sixteenth Amendment of the U.S. Constitution, the Social
Security Act of 1936, Joint House Resolution 192 of 1933,
and various State income taxes. Progressives call it "paying
your fair share." This is also what Barack Obama and
modern Progressives refer to as "social justice."

3. *Abolition of all rights of inheritance.*
   Congress has enacted this plank as the Federal & State
Estate Tax (1916), reformed Probate Laws, and limited
inheritance via arbitrary inheritance tax statutes. Though
portions of the estate tax laws were suspended several years
ago, under the Obama administration they are back in full-
force.

4. *Confiscation of the property of all emigrants and rebels.*
   These are better known as government seizures, tax liens,
Public Law 99-570 (1986); Executive Order 11490, sections
1205, 2002 which gives private land to the Department of
Urban Development; the imprisonment of "terrorists" and
those who speak out or write against the government (1997
Crime/Terrorist Bill); or the IRS confiscation of property
without due process. Asset forfeiture laws are used by DEA,
IRS, ATF, DHS, ICE, and other agencies to seize private
property.

5. *Centralization of credit in the hands of the State, by means
   of a national bank with state capital and an exclusive
   monopoly.*
   This is the Federal Reserve System, which is a privately-
owned credit/debt system created by the Federal Reserve Act
of 1913 (originally several banks on Wall Street). All local
banks are members of the Federal Reserve System and are
regulated by the Federal Deposit Insurance Corporation
(FDIC), another privately-owned corporation. The Federal

Reserve Banks issue fiat paper money and practice economically destructive fractional reserve banking, in which 10% or less is held by the bank as reserves and the other 90% is used to finance new loans. The Federal Reserve literally creates money out of nothing and loans that money out to other banks, businesses, people, and even other governments.

6. *Centralization of the means of communication and transportation in the hands of the State.*
   This is the Federal Communications Commission (FCC) and the Department of Transportation (DOT), mandated through the ICC Act of 1887, the Commissions Act of 1934, the Interstate Commerce Commission established in 1938, the Federal Aviation Administration, and Executive Orders 11490 and 10999, as well as State-mandated driver's licenses and various DOT and DHS regulations.

7. *Extension of factories and instruments of production owned by the State, the bringing into cultivation of waste lands, and the improvement of the soil generally in accordance with a common plan.*
   This is administered by the Desert Entry Act and the Department of Agriculture. Again, "controlled or subsidized" is essentially the same as being "owned," but without possessing the title-deed. Land and industrial control also fall under the Department of Commerce and Labor, Department of Interior, Environmental Protection Agency, Bureau of Land Management, Bureau of Reclamation, Bureau of Mines, National Park Service, and the IRS-control of business through corporate regulations and punitive taxes (income, payroll, etc.) and non-compliance/violation fines.

8. *Equal liability of all to labor. Establishment of industrial armies, especially for agriculture.*

This is essentially the Minimum Wage Act, which equalizes/mandates the minimum wage for all "legal" workers. This is also administered via the Social Security Administration and the Department of Labor. Equality is also enforced/enacted by the Nineteenth Amendment of the U.S. Constitution, the Civil Rights Act of 1964, assorted public/corporate unions, affirmative action, the Federal Public Works Program and Executive Order 11000.

9. *Combination of agriculture with manufacturing industries; gradual abolition of the distinction between town and country by a more equable distribution of the population over the country.*

This is the Planning Reorganization Act of 1949, zoning laws (Title 17 1910-1990) and Super Corporate Farms, as well as Executive Orders 11647, 11731 (ten regions) and Public Law 89-136.

10. *Free education for all children in government schools. Abolition of children's factory labor in its present form. Combination of education with industrial production.*

Americans are being taxed to support public schools/universities, but these have actually become "government schools." Even private schools are now government-regulated. Before the Progressive Era, most children were educated by cooperatives and religious schools in their communities. The purpose of our public school system used to be to educate the children, but today is used to train them to fit into the government/corporate system. This is administered by the Department of Education and pushed by the NEA and Outcome Based Education. Terms like "social justice," "majority rules," and "paying your fair share" are all Marxist ideologies taught to American children in the public school system every day for the thirteen most formative years of their lives. If one wants to capture the next generation, all they have to do is write (or choose) the public-school curriculum and the text-books.

In America today, the Marxist Creed, "From each according to their ability, to each according to their need" is not only alive and well (and enforced), but sounds like a good idea to most Americans, especially after being educated by our public schools over the last forty years. Some have been so mis-educated and propagandized that they think it came from the Bible! As Norman Thomas, the Socialist Party presidential candidate of the 1940s once said:

> *"The American people will never knowingly adopt socialism. But under the name of Liberalism, they will adopt every fragment of the socialist program until one day America will be a socialist nation without knowing how it happened."*

With the election – and re-election – of Barack Obama, that day has come to America.

Communism Always Ends in Misery

At first glance, communism may sound like a reasonable theory for fostering equality and governing society, but it always ends in misery for every nation that attempts to implement it. The reason for its consistent history of failure (and incredible suffering) is because communism is diametrically opposed to human nature – namely, our deep-rooted sense of property-rights and possessions. Whether you take something from a two-month-old, a two-year-old, a twenty-year-old, or an eighty-year-old, the reaction is always the same: a deep, profound sense of injustice coupled with anger and resentment. It's in our very nature to desire property and possessions, and people will always grow to hate whatever or whoever takes their property away from them. Even most

121

animals have those inherent instincts, yet communism foolishly tries to dispel them!

Since people tend to rebel against communism, the societies based on it always have to enforce it – usually by massive suffering, state-sanctioned mass-murder, and brutal authoritarian control. The only people who really like communism are those who are administering it – those who are in control and in power – those who possess what others cannot. Because communism is highly collective and redistributive, people have little incentive to work hard to grow crops, become educated, build businesses, etc., and therefore must be threatened or even compelled to labor for the State. But the lack of incentives and authoritarian government control always lead to terrible shortages in food, energy, water, and other critical resources, which only causes the central authority to increase their pressure on the people in a vicious, never-ending cycle of tyranny and suffering. Eventually, all communist governments collapse, are abandoned for a less-authoritarian model, or the people rebel in a bloody coup or civil war.

The only nation in which communism appears to be "working" is in Communist China, which has implemented a capitalist form of communism, by which the government allows the corporations to do what they want, as long as the communists remain in control. However, China would resemble North Korea if not for the trillions of dollars of goods imported annually by the United States. China also uses their mastery for duplication and reverse-engineering to steal many products and designs from other nations, as well as employs millions of workers who work under horrible slave-labor conditions. How can any other industrialized country compete in manufacturing when their competition uses slave-labor and they do not?

In America before Barack Obama, we had an abstracted form of redistribution of wealth through the Social Security and Medicare programs (as well as other forms of welfare), but we never had a president who openly pushed for wealth-redistribution as being truly wonderful for American society.

It's one thing to laud the benefits of various entitlement programs, but quite another to purposefully grow the welfare state at the expense of the country's producers. Obama and his various advisors consistently reject sound social and economic policies in order to further their transformative agenda – like most other authoritarian regimes.

Such revolutionaries are infinitely more dangerous than liberals and even traditional Progressives, particularly when they're in power – especially when they sit in the highest offices in the most powerful country in the world.

The Rise of the Radicals

There are two ways to overthrow a society or a government: from the outside by sheer force or from the inside by treason and diabolical subversion.

In the very beginning of the Progressive Era, the Progressives may have started out with the best of intentions, but they were seriously misguided as to their understanding of human nature and the fallen state of man. Our Founders viewed mankind as sinful and prone to corruption and therefore in need of checks and balances, with the understanding that "If all men were angels, no government would be necessary"; in essence, government is a necessary evil to restrain more undesired evil. The Progressives viewed mankind as mostly good, with flawed elements that could be expunged with enough education, psychology, and reason. After all, mankind was evolving, wasn't he? However, history has proven time and time again that some of the worst tyrants have been the best educated and the most "sound of mind." The horrors of WWI and WWII, the Nazi death-camps, gas-chambers, and Soviet gulags demonstrated the utter fallacy of Progressive evolutionary philosophy.

Teddy Roosevelt was one of America's most beloved presidents, but acted far outside the constitutional bounds for the office of the President. In fact, he personally re-interpreted

Article II of the Constitution to mean that the president could exercise any powers not explicitly forbidden to him, rather than the opposite as the Ninth and Tenth Amendments specified. The powers of the federal government are expressly limited to those specifically enumerated in the Constitution, and of the three branches of the federal government, the Executive Branch is the one specifically limited to executing the laws of the Constitution and the government.

After Teddy Roosevelt, the first real Progressive in American politics proved to be so successful, other Progressives followed on the trail he had blazed. First came Woodrow Wilson who saw the Constitution as an antiquated, outdated document that was full of "negative liberties"; it specified only what the government could NOT do to the people, rather than what the government could do FOR them. He viewed the Founders as being simplistic and paranoid about the evils of government and rather extreme about liberty. Following in Wilson's footsteps came FDR who implemented the next phase of Progressive reforms during the Great Depression (Social Security, vast expansions of federal power, and numerous public works projects). Then LBJ took over where FDR had left off by implementing the Great Society and creating Medicare and Medicaid. But their greatest Progressive goal remained unmet – nationalized healthcare – until Barack Obama came to power in 2008 and signed it into law in 2010 through a series of backroom deals and promises that were soon broken.

Why has nationalized healthcare been the dream and goal of the Progressive movement since Teddy Roosevelt? Because by controlling the healthcare system, the government has complete power and authority over every aspect of peoples' lives – what they eat and purchase, what medical treatments they can receive, and whether they are even "worth" treating. By controlling the healthcare system, they can dictate what consumers can buy, what producers can grow, create, and sell, and even who gets what type of care. Nationalized healthcare is about having unlimited power and control over the people – not healthcare or medicine. Not only that, but the party or politicians who deliver the most benefits (or just the most promises) will stay in office/power in perpetuity.

When the Progressive reforms didn't occur fast enough or go far enough (or were simply rejected by the people), the communists soon infiltrated and took over the Progressive movement or the Progressives simply realized the logical conclusion of their goals: communism. Whether intentional or not, the Progressives aligned themselves with the communists and simply continued to implement their Progressive/socialist agenda in the universities, the schools, the churches, the media, and the government. And though they were known by different names, they were all Statists at heart and in action. In their worldview, it is the State which is all-important, not the Individual, and the Individual exists solely to benefit the State, rather than the State existing to protect and benefit the Individuals that comprise the State. But at the heart of the Individual vs. State argument is a more fundamental debate: Man vs. God or Evolution vs. Creationism.

In the late Nineteenth Century, once the teachings of the Theory of Evolution had matured and sufficiently spread to the universities and schools, it began producing fruit, namely secular humanism, atheism, communism, Nazism, fascism, abortion, and environmentalism, just to list a few. The Theory of Evolution would be relatively harmless if it were just confined to the realm of science-books and the study of origins, but soon after it was popularized, it became an all-encompassing philosophy for economics, law, psychology, sociology, and politics. One of the first practical actions of Progressives, socialists, and communists when taking over a country is to permeate Evolutionary teaching throughout all the primary and secondary schools. And why shouldn't they? If the children grow up believing that the Highest Authority is not God or the Creator, then the Highest Authority must be the State – and therefore must be obeyed. If man is an evolving or progressing creature that can "evolve," then they can be manipulated and "guided" along in their evolution. When Hitler was slaughtering millions of innocent people, he genuinely thought he was helping the human race – and Evolution – by ridding Europe of her "undesirables," which wasn't just confined to the Jews, but the Gypsies, blacks, Slavs, communists, Poles, homosexuals, the handicapped, and many others.

The Marxist Antonio Grasci postulated that the West could only be secularized (de-Christianized) by what he termed "a long march through the institutions": the cinemas, theaters, schools, universities, seminaries, and the news agencies (along with television and radio). In order for the goals of secularism to be made permanent, every institution that made the Western culture what it was would have to be changed from the bottom up, rather than just at the government level downward – and that meant starting with the philosophy of man's origins: by a Creator. By replacing the Creator with the teaching of the Theory of Evolution, the secularists were able to justify their authority over natural rights.

Following in Grasci's footsteps, Adolph Hitler declared, *"Let me control the textbooks and I will control the state."* The Humanists, Progressives, and Leftists of the Twentieth Century understood that as well, and have almost accomplished just that. In less than twenty years after the 1960s, America turned from nominal Christianity to fully embrace secular humanism: the worship of man. From the beginning, some of the Statists knew they could never radically change America from the outside – it would have to be done from inside the very institutions they despised. They have been very patient in their "long march through the institutions."

Over the last hundred years, but especially since the 1960s, secular humanism has pushed Christianity out of the public square and relegated it to a minority of churches. Just before the turn of the Twentieth Century, the Supreme Court emphatically declared that the United States of America was an unabashedly Christian nation, though not due to its churches as much as by the vast majority of individual beliefs, values, and behaviors. Less than eighty years later, that same judicial body declared that secular humanism was now the national religion of the country. America became a different nation from the inside-out in less than two generations.

Abraham Lincoln once said, "The philosophy of the classroom today will be the philosophy of government tomorrow," and the more centralized a nation's education system is, the faster the implementation of those philosophies occurs. During the 1960s after the public education system began being centralized to counter the Soviets in the Cold War, the political Left (the Progressives) essentially took over the nation's education system at the university level. Their philosophy was that the State, not the individual people who comprise the State, is of the utmost importance – the individuals only exist for the benefit of the 'collective'. Their doctrines then permeated through the rest of the education system from primary school upwards, and now saturate nearly all facets of American society. Television, newspapers, and much of the mass media further propagate and reinforce the humanist principles espoused in the universities, which today resemble little more than sacred temples of secular humanism.

Some memorable quotes from the founders of communism and humanism demonstrate that a centralized education system plays directly into the hands of those who yearn to mold and shape the next generation into adopting their own tyrannical philosophies:

"Education is a weapon, whose effect depends on who holds it in his hands and at whom it is aimed." – Josef Stalin

"The education of all children, from the moment that they can get along without a mother's care, shall be in state institutions at state expense...My object in life is to dethrone God and destroy capitalism." – Karl Marx

127

Our American Awakening

"If our generation happens to be too weak to establish Socialism over the earth, we will hand the spotless banner down to our children." – Leon Trotsky

"Destroy the family, you destroy the country...Give me four years to teach the children and the seed I have sown will never be uprooted." – Vladimir Lenin

Over the years, the American Progressives were seldom able to be completely honest about what their intentions were and where they wanted to take the country. Whenever their true aims for America were discovered, they would change their labels, organizations, or affiliations. Since the 1960s, they've seen fit to even twist or pervert the meaning of popular, well-known words to fit their own ideology (like 'liberty,' 'tyranny,' 'progress,' 'equality,' etc.). This allowed them to sound like traditional Americans with traditional values but espouse completely different ideas, especially to young, impressionable minds in their classrooms, marches, protests, and literature.

In the counter-culture that arose in the 1960s, the predominant political philosophy was one of revolution rather than reform. One of the side-effects of the Great Depression and the Progressive Era was that communism and socialism attracted more people and steadily grew. But the Progressives and the communists had been working hard for sixty years and America still had not been turned into a socialist utopia like those of Europe. The fundamental transformation of America was simply taking too long, and the youth movement was too impatient to wait for it any longer. The counter-culture of the generation that had been given so much after WWII wanted to overthrow all that their parents and grandparents had built and fought and died for.

With their overwhelming numbers and vast amounts of youthful energy with no viable outlets, the young Progressives in the SDS (Students for a Democratic Society) and other groups were radicalized and became advocates of revolution

128

rather than reform. Within the new political movement, there were two divergent philosophies about exactly how to conduct their revolution: by violent means of anarchy and overthrowing the institutions from the outside, or by stealthily infiltrating the institutions and quietly conducting the revolution from the inside. Of the two groups, the latter has proven to be far more effective, because that which cannot be seen on the inside is much harder to defend against than outside, tangible threats. If accused, those operating from the inside would either scream "McCarthyism!" or state that they just have a different point of view and are expressing their opinion – and exercising their First Amendment rights.

The Sixties revolutionaries like Bill Ayers, Jerry Rubin, Bernadine Dohrn, Abbie Hoffman, and Tom Hayden operated against the system from the outside and were often subsequently identified and arrested for domestic terrorism and other crimes. But what about the other camp of revolutionaries, the ones who decided to operate within the system and subvert it from within? Many of these revolutionaries now hold powerful, influential positions within our media, universities, and government institutions.

The New Progressives: Clean-cut Radicals

Along with the subversive revolutionaries, there arose a segment of the radicals who had no end-goal in mind. This breed of radical doesn't tear down something so they can then rebuild it according to their own ideas – these radicals only exist to destroy. These radicals live and breathe revolution and derive their very purpose in life by tearing societies and institutions down. Regardless of what the institution is – even if it agrees with their philosophies – they are only there to distort and destroy. Their struggle and justification for their actions is against the "Haves" on behalf of the "Have-nots"; the radicals exist to take power, money, property, or influence away from the Haves and redistribute it to the Have-nots, while accumulating a portion of whatever they're taking for themselves – like typical socialists and communists.

The foremost of these new revolutionaries was a community organizer from Chicago named Saul Alinsky, one of the few intellectual radicals who codified his anarchist/revolutionary philosophy so that others would carry on his life's work. Alinsky was trained in a wide variety of shakedown techniques and mafia-style thuggery by Frank Nitti, Al Capone's "enforcer." Though not directly affiliated with the mafia-machine, Alinsky learned their ruthless, unorthodox methods and then applied them to his new movement of community organizing, such as provoking his opposition to overreacting and then publicly discrediting them, if not just humiliating them for the sheer joy of it.

Alinsky wrote "Reveille for Radicals" in 1946 and then "Rules for Radicals" in 1971, which is a comical misnomer (the only real rules for radicals is that there are no rules). Today, "Rules for Radicals" is the community organizers', anarchists', and radicals' manual of standard operating procedures. Since the early 1970s, "Rules for Radicals" tactics have been used to extort money from numerous banks, corporations, and of course, various state and local governments – and even the federal government. When they're not extorting money from their enemies, Alinskyite radicals are busy infiltrating our government institutions in order to change our laws in the name of social justice and redistribute our wealth to their causes – taking from the Haves and giving it to the Have-nots.

Outside the radical Progressive movement, Saul Alinsky and his writings didn't receive widespread attention until one of his early admirers became the First Lady: Hillary Clinton, who was Barack Obama's first Secretary of State. Clinton was so enamored by Alinsky's teachings that she wrote her thesis on him and his legacy. However, Alinsky's most famous, most powerful disciple is not Hillary Clinton, but Barack Obama, our sitting President. The rebel has now become the ruler, and has brought with him his revolutionary bedfellows and Marxist comrades. Ironically, the Sixties radicals now find themselves in control of the very agencies and departments they had once sworn to tear apart. Given that radicals and community organizers are now running much of the federal government, it should be no wonder that America is in a shambles.

It's unknown exactly when Obama was exposed to Alinsky's writings, but considering who his mother and grandparents were (committed communists) and who he surrounded himself with in college, grad-school, and law-school, it's likely that he was exposed to Alinsky at a very young age. Alinsky's teachings had such an influence on Obama that upon graduating from college, he became an Alinskyite community organizer and taught others to use the pressure tactics espoused in "Rules for Radicals" to help fellow organizers succeed in their shakedown efforts. And make no mistake – they did succeed.

Other radicals are merely "useful idiots" (so aptly named by Vladimir Lenin) and are used as the ground-forces, infantry, and shock-troopers by the radical leaders. The 2011-2012 Occupy Wall Street protesters were primarily composed of these individuals, who were simply used by the movement's organizers for their own political purposes, namely Van Jones – Obama's former "green jobs czar" who also happens to be a radical communist community organizer.

Several ways to distinguish between traditional liberals (and Progressives) and their radical counterparts is to evaluate their ideology and identify their end-goals. Liberals tend to be more specific with their reforms, whereas radicals will give fewer specifics and offer no real substantive plans. Liberals are often more honest and civil, whereas radicals will use any means necessary to achieve their goals because the ends are all that really matters. Liberals will debate and attempt to draw others to their side; radicals vilify and use character-assassination techniques (like depicting their opponents as being racists or Nazi's) not to win the argument, but in order to destroy their opposition. Radicals usually cannot win when playing by the rules, so they must destroy – which comes naturally to them because their underlying philosophy is anarchy and revolution. Revolutionaries do not build because it's not in their nature, they can only destroy. Most people love to build or at least reform, reinvent, or recreate in order to feel as though they've achieved something worthwhile. However, there is a tiny minority (revolutionaries and anarchists) who view destruction and chaos as their "creations," tearing down the old so that others who come after them may build anew. Alinsky himself said that before any change can occur, the current order must become disordered and the current organization must become disorganized. The Revolutionists in early American history were the exception rather than the rule, in that they sought to create a freer, more prosperous society rather than simply tearing down the old one. The French Revolutionists who came only a decade later were much different and slaughtered tens of thousands of their own people and turned Paris into a bloodbath.

The new revolutionaries – the radicals like Alinsky – are only there to destroy, regardless of what the institution is. Even if America fully implemented communism and created the utopian Worker's Paradise of the Soviet Union, they would still be driven to tear it apart for their simple love of revolution and anarchy. These radicals are societal parasites, feeding off institutions, nations, and societies like termites. The most shocking aspect of such radicals is that they're not tearing down in order to build anything – they just like tearing down. They are driven by the bloodlust of revolution and the raw pursuit of power. They're not being radicals – they ARE radicals. That's who they ARE. Once they reach the pinnacle of their power and their goals have been attained, they don't know what to do except accumulate more and more power – the pursuit never ends. These radicals make great revolutionaries but terrible leaders, often because they don't know what to really do with power once they attain it. This is one of the reasons why Obama was such a superb campaigner but a failed president – he is incapable of organizing for leading, only organizing for revolution and taking power. They know how to accumulate power, but not how to utilize it effectively.

In the minds of radicals and other extreme Progressives, the "ends" is all that matters; the "means" is of no concern because it might interfere with achieving their "ends." To such radicals, the "ends" doesn't even have to justify the means, because no justification or rules matter. The radicals and revolutionaries in our modern era revolt and rebel for the simple sake of rebelling, no matter how good the system is or even if it agrees with 99% of their ideologies. They feel compelled to hone in on that 1% that irks them and will do literally anything and everything possible to "fix" that 1%, even if it means destroying the other 99% in the process. Radicals are tyrants at heart and will do whatever it takes to achieve and hold onto power.

Preceding the recent clamor for gun-control legislation after the horrible massacre at the Sandy Hook Elementary School, Barack Obama signed twenty-four Executive Orders regulating and restricting firearms and ammunition, mostly directed to the various regulatory agencies under his control. Since he took office in 2009, gun ownership has nearly doubled, along with the number of firearms sold also doubling. Ammunition sales have also been incredible, with most stores having difficulty remaining stocked. Many people even believe that Obama might attempt to launch a national gun confiscation program, but that's unlikely because it goes against his Alinskyite training. One of Alinsky's rules was that "The action is in the reaction," which means that instead of planning a strategy around what action will work best against your adversary, the trick is to decide how you want your adversary to react and then plan a strategy that will provoke that reaction. With that in mind, Obama may be making various moves to provoke a mass-revolt, which he can then act against with public support. This is another stark difference between typical Progressives and radical Progressives – the former seeks actions, while the latter seeks reactions.

Consider the stark differences between Bill Clinton (a typical Progressive) and Barack Obama (a radical Progressive). Though he and his party lost control of the Congress in 1995, Bill Clinton drew others to his party and built it, even amidst embarrassing scandal after scandal. He compromised and learned to work with a Congress that opposed him – even one that impeached and humiliated him. However, Obama is destroying his party rather than building it, alienating people rather than drawing them in, and hurting the country rather than helping it. Many who voted for Obama on the platitudes of "Hope and Change" have seen him only make things worse and recently voted against him – or didn't bother to vote at all.

To get an idea of what motivates Saul Alinsky and his fellow radicals is best described as a sheer lust for power. One day while he was training a new batch of starry-eyed radicals, they were arguing about what they were really trying to achieve: money, fame, reform, etc. He jumped up and screamed at them, "It's about power, you idiots! It's all about the power!" The same holds true with Obama and other radical Progressives – they're not interested in fame, money, reforms, or politics – they're only concerned with gathering and holding power! And what better place to do that than in the regulatory offices and elected positions of the federal government – or even as the President of the United States of America?

Without power, radicals are an annoyance and a plague upon society, creating discontent, waging class warfare, and generally making a nuisance of themselves. In order to obtain power, radicals are not merely content to defeat their opponents, but must destroy them through manufactured scandals, lies, and character assassination. This is largely how Obama rose to power so quickly in Illinois: he destroyed his opposition by character assassination, the legal system, and various scandals that caused them to withdraw from the race, leaving him to be the only viable candidate.

Though the presidency of Barack Obama has been an unprecedented disaster for America economically, morally, and

134

internationally, he has merely caused the long Progressive transformation that America has been on to speed up. Whereas the United States was thirty to fifty years away from the financial "point of no return," the policies of Obama and the 111th Congress have cut that time in half.

Chapter 5 - Our New Slavemasters

"There are two ways to enslave a nation. One is by the sword. The other is by debt." – John Adams

The United States of America has stood strong for more than two centuries. We have lasted through one revolution, one foreign invasion, one civil war, two world wars, and a host of other foreign wars both near our shores and on the other side of the world. We have gone through cycles of booms and busts, prosperous times and years of recessions, depressions, and bank-panics. But the crisis looming before us is one that has the greatest potential to crush America and destroy everything we have grown accustomed to: the exploding national debt.

The Exploding National Debt

Over two hundred years ago, John Adams observed, "There are two ways to enslave a nation. One is by the sword. The other is by debt." At this point in our history, it appears that we are about to be enslaved by the latter. Our last two presidents – in a mere twelve years – have nearly tripled the national debt from $6 trillion to over $16 trillion. At the rate the federal government is spending money they don't have, the national debt will cross the $18 trillion mark by 2015. However, our true national debt (which includes unfunded liabilities) is an astounding $200 trillion – and that's the conservative figure! Because of our unfathomable accumulation of public debt, a complete economic collapse is more likely – and if that's the case, then how do we prepare for it, if not try to lessen the blow?

One of the foremost principles of debt comes from Proverbs 22:7: *"The borrower is the slave of the lender."* When you borrow money, you voluntarily indenture – or enslave – yourself to the one who extends credit to you for the privilege of using their money. The principles of public versus private credit and borrowing are no different – if you borrow money, sooner or later you will have to repay it. With private or personal debt, you can borrow without payment for only so long before you ruin your credit and are then unable to borrow more. And if you die before repaying your debts, your creditors have first claim upon your assets and your estate, not your family and other heirs.

Public debt is more onerous because one group of people can borrow the money today for their own use, but not necessarily pay it back within their time; they can leave that for another generation to pay back. In America, we have been borrowing without repaying for decades, but the national debt didn't begin skyrocketing until the early 1980s and especially after 2000. And while George W. Bush's spending was terrible, it has been incomparable to Barack Obama's, who has borrowed the same amount of money – more than $5 trillion – but in half the time! The Founders understood the intrinsic link between debt and tyranny; if a nation wants to remain free, it must have a free-market, robust economy and low government debt:

> *"The principle of spending money to be paid by future generations, under the name of funding, is but swindling futurity on a large scale...I place economy among the first and most important virtues, and public debt as the greatest of dangers. To preserve our independence, we must not let our rulers load us with perpetual debt."* – Thomas Jefferson

Given the bad economy and the exorbitant, reckless spending, a number of people have come to believe that the flagrant mismanagement and huge, rapid accumulation of debt has another purpose: to increase and cement our poor economic conditions in place for generations, so America never again recovers and can wield such enormous influence over the world.

Not only is this administration failing to turn the American ship away from the rocks, they're making the ship go full-speed ahead so the inevitable collapse will be larger and more painful. Granted, that is quite an accusation to make, which even borders on conspiracy. But can there be any other reasonable explanation for what this administration is doing?

In 1966, two radical sociology professors at Columbia University named Richard Cloward and Frances-Fox Piven formulated the "Cloward-Piven Strategy," a political strategy that sought to overload the welfare system in order to replace it with a national system of guaranteed annual income. Their theory was that if the poor had a guaranteed income, they wouldn't be poor any longer. However, what they were really advocating was vast wealth-redistribution from those who worked and produced to those who did not. After all, if your annual income is guaranteed by the federal government regardless of whether you work or not, what incentive do you have to find and retain any form of employment, much less grow your skills in order to grow your income?

Though the Cloward-Piven Strategy did lead to a dramatic increase in the welfare rolls during the late-1960s and early 1970s, it never fully succeeded, which would have transformed the American economy from capitalism to socialism. But the strategy did lay the groundwork for what appears to be in use by the Obama Administration and the more radical members of the Democrat Party today: overload the system until it collapses, demagogue the greed and unfairness of the former failed system, and then use the crisis to replace free-market capitalism with socialism. It's the only plausible explanation for why Obama is exploding the national debt and increasing dependency on welfare programs, while keeping his boot on the necks of small businesses and energy producers – the institutions that help America function. The end-goal of the American socialists has always been to fully implement socialism in the United States, but first the existing system of capitalism and free-markets must be discredited and abandoned,

138

if not destroyed. And from the last few years, it appears that they are succeeding.

Free-market economies like America's function best when taxes are low and regulation is kept to sensible levels. By dramatically inflating our deficits and the national debt, the politicians then demand that taxes (especially on the wealthy and the corporations) need to be increased to pay for their reckless borrowing and spending. But do these politicians – often the same ones who borrowed and then wasted the money in the first place – have any intention of using those higher tax revenues to pay down the debt they created? Of course not – they will simply continue mismanaging the public funds and wasting our tax-dollars.

Not only do we have the national debt dragging down the economy and our incentive, but the steadily rising interest and servicing of the national debt will also consume more and more of the federal budget. Currently, the Federal Reserve is keeping interest rates artificially low, but what happens if – and when – they return to normal? The CBO estimates that by 2020 (on a projected national debt of $23 trillion), that half of all income tax revenues will go to paying just the interest alone on the national debt. Who wins in the end? The banks, countries, and others who are financing the federal government's massive debts. The question that no one in office wants to consider today is: "What happens when America's creditors demand to be repaid?" The other question yet to be asked is: "What happens when America cannot even afford to pay the interest on the national debt?"

Is there a purpose behind Obama's (and Congress's) outrageous spending? And if so, then what is it? Since our politicians are seldom forthright with us, we only have to look at the effects of their policies: the permanent reduction of America's influence around the world and the transition from a constitutional republic into another failing Western socialist democracy. Obama and his supporters may dispute that statement, but his actions speak far louder than his teleprompted words. Even one of the books the president was caught reading was "The Post-American World" by Fareed Zakaria, which describes the steps that America should take in gracefully stepping down from being a super-power. In fact, soon after he took office in 2009, someone asked one of his advisors what their administration's purpose/vision in office was, and they essentially said, "Our purpose is to manage America's decline."

Imagine any other official in that position saying those treasonous words! What kind of captain purposefully beaches their ship instead of turning it around while they can? Instead of setting out to solve our problems and fix the economy, this administration has determined to let our problems slowly but steadily crush us and turn the United States into just another nation that stumbles along the inevitable path towards collapse.

Inflation: The Silent Thief

As frightening as the national debt is, the massive deficit-spending, borrowing, and interest-servicing is only one side of the "enslavement coin" – the other is devalued currency and inflation due to creating vast amounts of money that cannot be adequately absorbed by the economy. What is inflation? It's not simply a rise in prices, but the decrease in value (or purchasing power) of our currency. Inflation is the purposeful manipulation of our currency by our government via our central bank, the Federal Reserve. Inflation managed by the Federal Reserve effectively allows Congress to borrow money in perpetuity – and with little accountability. After all, by 2015 the national debt will have tripled in less than fifteen years, and more than 11% of that is owned by the Federal Reserve – and growing!

As Ayn Rand has observed, "Inflation is not caused by the actions of private citizens, but by the government: by an artificial expansion of the money supply required to support deficit spending. No private embezzlers or bank robbers in history have ever plundered people's savings on a scale comparable to the plunder perpetrated by the fiscal policies of statist governments."

But what really is inflation and why is it theft? Walter Williams explains inflation and its causes/effects as follows:

"Pretend several of us gather to play a standard Monopoly game that contains $15,140 worth of money. The player who owns Boardwalk or any other property is free to sell it for any price he wishes. Given the money supply in the game, a general price level will emerge for all trades. If some property prices rise, others will fall, thereby maintaining that level.

Suppose unbeknownst to other players, I counterfeit $5,000 and introduce it into the game. Initially, that gives me tremendous purchasing power, whereby I can bid up property prices. After my $5,000 has circulated through the game, there will be a general rise in the prices – something that would have been impossible before I slipped money into the game. My example is a highly simplistic example of a real economy, but it permits us to make some basic assessments of inflation.

First, let's not let politicians deceive us, and escape culpability, by defining inflation as rising prices, which would allow them to make the pretense that inflation is caused by greedy businessmen, rapacious unions or Arab sheiks. Increases in money supply are what constitute inflation, and the general rise in the price level is the result. Who's in charge of the money supply? It's the government operating through the Federal Reserve.

There's another inflation result that bears acknowledgment. Printing new money to introduce into the game makes me a thief. I've obtained objects of value for nothing in return. My actions also lower the purchasing power of every dollar in the game. I've often suggested that if a person is ever charged with counterfeiting, he should tell the judge he was engaging in monetary policy.

141

When inflation is unanticipated, as it so often is, there's a redistribution of wealth from creditors to debtors. If you lend me $100, and over the term of the loan the Federal Reserve increases the money supply in a way that causes inflation, I pay you back with dollars with reduced purchasing power. Since inflation redistributes (steals) wealth from creditors to debtors, it helps us identify inflation's primary beneficiary. That identification is easy if you ask: Who is the nation's largest debtor? If you said, 'It is the U.S. government,' go to the head of the class."

Since QE1 in 2009 ($1.5 trillion), QE2 ($2 trillion) in 2010, and now QE3 ($85 billion per month) the Federal Reserve has been creating money out of thin air in order to buy massive amounts of assets, treasuries, and even stock, which artificially inflate the economy – and keep it inflated. However, just as the artificially-low interest rates and over-leveraging in the years leading up to the sub-prime mortgage meltdown of 2007-2008 created the housing market bubble and then the bust, these "quantitative easing" policies (currency injections) only delay the inevitable day-of-reckoning caused by poor monetary policy, and have also made it much worse than if the free-market was allowed to balance itself. Bubbles and busts are a part of every capitalist-based economy, but those created by currency injections, inflation, and artificial economic stimuli only make the bubbles bigger and the busts longer and more catastrophic.

When governments borrow more money than is absolutely necessary and they begin to collapse under the weight of their own financial obligations, what they do is inflate (or devalue) the currency. Rome did it, Germany did it, and now the United States is doing it. Rapid inflation causes a loss of confidence in a currency and can easily and quickly spiral out of control. The reason why paper-money can function in society is largely because people place their confidence in it and agree that a particular banknote has some intrinsic value, such as $1 for a loaf of bread. But what happens when that confidence erodes or is shaken by poor monetary policy and bad economic forecasts? As instability rises, so do prices.

Massive currency injections coupled with increasing instability is only a recipe for an economic disaster. Suddenly, that $1 loaf of bread next week can cost $2, then $5, then $10 – or higher. When the forces of inflation are no longer able to be contained, panic ensues and hyperinflation kicks into high gear – and overnight, that $1 loaf of bread can cost $100, $500, $1000, or even much more. At that point, people are carting loads of worthless paper-notes to buy bread and basic staples. Think it can't happen in modern-day America? It occurred only a few decades ago in Argentina, Russia, and Mexico. One of the most famous examples of hyperinflation was in Germany during the days of the Weimar Republic after WWI. After the Great War had ended in 1919, the German mark had exchanged at 12:1 marks/dollar. When hyperinflation ravaged the country only a few years later, workers were often paid daily with bags full of cash and their wives would run to the shops to buy whatever goods they could – while the goods were still there. At the peak of hyperinflation in the Weimar Republic in November 1923, a loaf of bread cost 200,000,000,000 marks. Hyperinflation continued in the Weimar Republic until sound monetary policies were enacted and confidence was restored. Inflation became the great equalizer, because everyone's wealth was wiped out in only a matter of months.

If the huge national debt and taxes won't get us, then inflation and America's ruined credit will. All the socialists have to do to ensure America's decline (if not collapse) is to explode the spending in the name of fixing the bad economy and then let the economic forces they have unleashed run their course. When the government attempts to pay down its massive debts through currency inflation, confidence collapses and the wealth of the nation is wiped out. Financial laws and the consequences of our reckless spending can sometimes be delayed for years, but they cannot be avoided forever. Sooner or later, debts must be repaid – one way or another. Whenever a nation breaks or twists those laws, calamity eventually ensues; in the case of massive borrowing and spending, the longer the consequences are delayed, the worse and more painful they will become.

Though the Federal Reserve has recently created and invested trillions of dollars in order to prop up American and European banks and economies, we have yet to feel the real effects of inflation, though prices have increased on many commodities over the last few years. Why? Mostly because the American dollar is the world's reserve currency. When the value of the dollar decreases because inflation is increasing, Americans feel a small pinch in their pocketbooks, but foreigners feel it much more because their currency doesn't inflate at the same rates as the dollar. This leads to large jumps in the prices for food and other commodities they depend on, and leads to shortages, then instability, and then even uprisings and political revolutions.

Inflation in America dramatically rose soon after Richard Nixon took the dollar off the Gold Standard in 1971, enabling it to "float" the value of the dollar relative to other currencies. This allowed the Federal Reserve to create as much money as they desired, but the value of the dollar dropped from 900 mg of gold in 1969 to under 100 mg in a mere ten years. The real purchasing power of the American dollar collapsed in only one decade; people today marvel when their grandparents used to buy a gallon of gasoline or a loaf of bread for a quarter, but today those same commodities cost at least ten times that amount. What happened? The removal of the Gold Standard and the inflationary policies of the Federal Reserve, as well as massive government borrowing and spending. And though on the surface it appears that prices are rising, they are not – there is no shortage of bread, milk, energy, or other commodities; the sole reason why prices are higher is because our currency is worth much, much less.

When Jimmy Carter was president in the late 1970s, inflation was raging at 13% (it's usually at 2-3%) and the prime interest rate was at a whopping 21.5%. With rising taxes, high inflation, and astronomical interest rates, much of America had lost confidence in the economy and in Washington D.C. People stopped buying houses, cars, and investing in general (other than in basic savings accounts and bonds) because they simply couldn't afford to make big-ticket purchases with those interest rates and that inflation. A general feeling of pessimism and malaise set in, and when people looked to their leaders to fix the economy, they were answered with shrugged shoulders, somber speeches, and a bungling president who appeared to have no clue what he was doing – because he didn't. Today, we have a similar situation and a similar president, except that this one perpetually lies through his teeth instead of just bungling his way through office.

Inflation is partly driven by monetary policy but also by public optimism and confidence in the economic outlook, such as whether tax-rates are rising or falling. A typical scenario that can trigger inflation is when Congress passes a large tax increase or commodity prices (like oil) skyrocket. Knowing that their expenses will increase, businesses then raise their prices to offset the increase in taxes or the cost of doing business, and the increases then ripple through the economy from there. Inflation is typically inversely proportional to national confidence – when confidence falters, inflation rises and people restrict their spending; when confidence is restored and people spend and invest, inflation falls.

When Ronald Reagan took office in 1981, he immediately pushed for across-the-board cuts in the marginal tax-rates and simplification of the tax-code, as well as reducing regulation and federal administrative expenses. He also pushed for the reduction of the prime interest rate and other key rate reductions from the Fed to get the economy running again. And though there was a tough recession in 1982 that rivaled the one in 2008, by 1983 the recession had ended and both inflation and the prime interest rate had been cut in half. Why? Because through his policies and character, Reagan restored confidence in the American economy, which encouraged businesses to expand and hire new employees, investors to invest in businesses, and people to spend their money on houses, cars, and investing instead of sitting on their money in fear of inflation and taxes.

But today, thirty years after the Reagan Revolution, inflation is back and is growing (as of 2011); recently it's dipped as a result of the economy gradually improving. Unemployment remains around 8% (though the true number is at least 11%) and America is experiencing the longest recession since the Great Depression. Though the stock market is now at all-time highs, unemployment is still very high and average Americans are still experiencing tremendous amounts of uncertainty – what the Obama administration calls a "jobless recovery." What happened to trigger such a dramatic decline in employment and small businesses? The lack of confidence and anti-business policies (high taxes, high energy costs, and crippling regulations) and socialist rhetoric coming from the White House. The passage of the healthcare reform law and huge increases in the deficits ensure that huge tax increases are coming to us very soon, and both people and businesses are afraid to spend their money and make long-term investments. Through his policies and speeches, Obama has single-handedly strangled consumer confidence, investing, and American optimism across the board.

If American confidence – as well as the economy – is to be restored (or even just turned around), then Barack Obama's Progressive policies must be stopped and countered with sound economic policies and reduced regulations.

The Federal Reserve

No discussion on the national debt or inflation in the United States would be complete without taking a close look at the Federal Reserve, because the central bank is where all the

146

money originates from. In Walter William's Monopoly game explanation of inflation, who's the culprit regularly (and sometimes willy-nilly) introducing new money into the economy? The Federal Reserve. Also referred to as "the Fed," the Federal Reserve creates new money primarily in two ways: direct money creation which is loaned to the government and other banks, and also fractional-reserve banking, which magically turns every $1 into $10.

In the mind of most Americans, the Federal Reserve is the federal agency which oversees the interest rates and the nation's money supply. However, the Federal Reserve is not federal, and it's certainly not a reserve. The Federal Reserve was purposely named to obscure its true identity: the central bank of the United States. In its organization and complexity, the Fed looks, acts, and feels "federal" and official, but is not – the Federal Reserve is simply another central-banking system like the First and Second Banks of the United States, but organized in such a way as to not seem like a bank. Americans traditionally have been extremely distrustful of banks (especially central banks), and the very structure, name, and daily-operations of the Federal Reserve are designed to avert that distrust – and avoid the blame when their policies wreak havoc on the economy.

The main responsibility of the Federal Reserve is to contain inflation (and deflation) and provide a stable supply and flow of money in the United States economy. In order to perform those responsibilities, the Fed has two primary weapons at its disposal: it can tighten or loosen the money supply throughout the nation's banking system, and also raise or lower key interest rates which affect deposits and loans. When interest rates rise, borrowing decreases but saving increases. When interest rates are lowered, borrowing increases but saving decreases. However, since inflation is mostly caused by more money circulating in the economy than it can absorb, that's like putting the fox in charge of the hen-house. Since 1913 when it was created, the Federal Reserve and its policies are primarily responsible for creating inflation in the first place.

147

The primary way the Fed controls the money supply is through the buying and selling of government bonds. When the Fed buys government bonds through the private banking system, the private bank takes the money, adds the cash to its reserves, and begins loaning out the new money at a 10:1 rate to other businesses, banks, and individuals – quickly expanding the money supply tenfold (and more as the process is repeated). When the Fed sells some of its government bonds, the money supply contracts in a similar fashion, but in reverse.

So what really is the Federal Reserve? The Federal Reserve is a private banking corporation which Congress has granted the sole authority to manage the country's money supply. In essence, the Federal Reserve is a huge banking cartel, which means they are in complete control of not only the money supply, but the entire banking system. The Federal Reserve Act of 1913 made all other forms of currency in the United States illegal except for Federal Reserve Notes, the very goal that the Wall Street banks had been trying to accomplish for years. This monopoly destroyed the competition between the Wall Street banks and the West Coast banks, which were rapidly growing and threatening their market at the time. When the Federal Reserve Act was enacted, the West Coast banks lost and decided to cooperate in order to stay in business.

Mayer Amschel Rothschild who essentially created the central banking systems in use today, is infamously quoted as saying, "Let me issue and control a nation's money and I care not who makes its laws." The Rothschild banking cartel occupied most of the banking houses in Europe during the Nineteenth Century and still has an untold amount of holdings, with estimates ranging anywhere from $10 billion to over $1 trillion.

How did the Federal Reserve come about? Before the Federal Reserve, a variety of currencies were used in the United States and the country went through banking "panics" every few decades when people would lose confidence in the economy and pull all their money out of the bank. The two banking powerhouses on Wall Street, the Rockefellers and the Morgans, were often at war with one another, vying for financial supremacy. For decades, the larger banks of Wall Street had wanted to create a new central bank, but were unable to due to the smaller banks and the current national-bank system.

But at the turn of the last century, Wall Street began losing to the banks on the West Coast and the Rockefellers and the Morgans decided to form an alliance to completely reform the nation's banking system – with their banks being forever protected from bankruptcy and panics. Also, they wanted to devise a way to wipe out most of their competition – the growing West Coast banks and the thousands of smaller banks along with their banknotes. To avoid damaging their own reputation and the possibility of having their own banking charters revoked (as well as avoid Teddy Roosevelt's trust-busting), they decided to have the federal government implement their vision for them. During the Progressive Era, large businesses and banks learned an important lesson: if you can't eliminate your competition through your own products, services, and practices, you can just as effectively manipulate public opinion, influence politicians, and lobby for regulations in the name of the "public good" to eliminate your competition for you. Many of the big businesses that exist today are a result of the regulations, lobbying, and elimination of competition rather than natural growth from producing better products and services.

On November 22, 1910, Senator Nelson W. Aldrich, with a handful of companions, took a private railroad car from Hoboken, New Jersey to the coast of Georgia, allegedly on a duck-hunting expedition. The tiny group of powerful Wall Street bankers, the Assistant Secretary to the U.S. Treasury, and Senator Aldrich met at J. P. Morgan's plush retreat at the Jekyll Island Club on Jekyll Island, Georgia to hammer out the new banking reforms. After a week of intense work, the group produced the Aldrich Plan, which was later modified and

149

renamed as the Federal Reserve Act. On December 22, 1913, the Federal Reserve Act was passed, signed by Woodrow Wilson, and went into effect the following year. These same banks had encouraged Teddy Roosevelt to run as a third-party candidate in 1912 to ensure that the conservative Republican President William Taft was defeated, who would've never signed their bill.

Within a few short years, the passage of the Federal Reserve Act changed America from an asset-based economy to a debt-based economy. The Wall Street banks were able to eliminate all forms of competing banknotes and much of their competition – and later caused gold and silver to be removed from circulation – in favor of their Federal Reserve Notes. America's new banking cartel, the Federal Reserve, was now in control of all the other banks in the United States.

And while the creation of the Fed didn't create the explosive national debt we have today, the Fed gave Congress the mechanism to borrow and spend tremendous amounts of money, often during recessions, wars, and other crises (real or manufactured). Before the Federal Reserve was created, the Treasury had to borrow money by issuing bonds and then convincing banks, corporations, or individuals to buy them. With the creation of the Federal Reserve, the Treasury simply makes a phone call and requests the money it wants, which the Fed creates literally out of nothing. And while the Federal Reserve has no cash, they have a huge blank checkbook with an infinite amount of zeros.

The Fed's constant meddling in the American economy helped create the sub-prime mortgage meltdown of 2008, the high-inflation, high-interest rates, and the economic misery of the 1970s, as well as extending and deepening the Great Depression by making the wrong adjustments to the money supply too quickly or too broadly. In November, 2002 at a conference to honor the late Milton Freeman, Ben Bernanke (the current Chairman of the Federal Reserve) stated, "I would like to say to Milton and Anna: Regarding the Great

Depression. You're right, we did it. We're very sorry. But thanks to you, we won't do it again." Would there have even been a Great Depression if not for the Federal Reserve's destructive actions of the 1920s through the 1930s? There may have been a sharp downturn in 1929, but the lasting economic effects were directly caused by the Federal Reserve and the Progressive policies of FDR.

Another contributing factor to the growing national debt and ever-increasing power of the Federal Reserve is the removal of the Gold Standard in 1971. Under the Federal Reserve Act, all gold in the Treasury and the banks was placed into the vaults of the Federal Reserve, since the Federal Reserve Notes were backed and partially-redeemable by gold. The Fed took control of the rest of the gold in America after 1933 when FDR made owning gold illegal, except for jewelry and collectible bullion. With the entire nation's gold supply in their vaults and monopolization of the nation's money supply, the banking cartel was complete. When Nixon finally removed the United States from the Gold Standard completely, the last economic restraints of the Federal Reserve's power and accountability were removed.

The Gold Standard prevents central banks – or any other banks – from inflating the currency as high as they want because it's real and limited in quantity. Also, that prevents governments from borrowing as much as they want because the currency has to be backed by real gold (which they usually don't have). With the Federal Reserve System in place, it was only a matter of time before the Gold Standard was eliminated because it interfered with their monopoly over the currency. The creators of the Federal Reserve System had two desires in mind when conceiving the central bank: to be able to inflate the currency during recessions and depressions and to have their own private banks bailed out whenever they busted. We have repeatedly seen both actions firsthand since 2007, when the Federal Reserve and the Treasury have spent trillions of dollars bailing out busted domestic banks and even foreign banks.

151

Many accuse the Federal Reserve and the Wall Street banks of being driven completely by greed and focused completely on getting rich, but that's not the case. After all, they're already infinitely rich because they control the money supply and can create as much of it as they want. As Saul Alinsky once screamed at his disciples, "It's all about power!" If you have money but no power, you really have very little because that money can be easily lost or taken away – but if you have enough power, you can create all the money you desire and never worry about losing it. For those who desire power above all else, it doesn't really matter what they have power over, as long as they have power.

Given the vast power, wealth, and unaccountability of the Federal Reserve, it's subject to all sorts of speculation, from being the driving force behind the New World Order to the Kennedy assassination. In 1989, Jim Marrs published a book called, "Crossfire: The Plot that Killed Kennedy," which accused the Federal Reserve of assassinating JFK because he had ordered the Treasury to begin issuing and circulating silver certificates which looked exactly like Federal Reserve Notes. The conspiracy is that he was trying to abolish the Federal Reserve, which would be possible once enough of the new silver certificates were in circulation. Less than a year after issuing the executive order, Kennedy was assassinated.

President Kennedy may have had the right idea of how to restrain the Federal Reserve, but the entirely wrong reasons for issuing the silver certificates. If anything, his Executive Order 11110 increased the power of the Federal Reserve rather than decrease it, because by issuing silver certificates (most of which would never be redeemed), he ceased the direct sale of silver from the Treasury which was competing with the Federal Reserve. The Federal Reserve Notes were never at risk at all; the silver certificates were designed to look like Federal Reserve Notes to get people to accept the Federal Reserve Notes in place of their silver, rather than the other way around.

If we want to reduce the debt, we must severely restrict the government's ability to borrow money – which begins with constraining the Federal Reserve. Half the purpose of the Fed is to provide Congress with an endless supply of money that it can create from nothing. The other purpose of the Fed is to keep their banks solvent forever – often with bailouts from the federal government as seen in 2008-2009. Also, the Fed helps keep inflation rates high – which helps the government reduce the true value of its debt by devaluing the currency. Inflation always benefits the borrower, because loans are not indexed to inflation; as inflation rises, more money is available to service the debt. Any nation with a central bank typically has a large national debt – the two go hand-in-hand because one enables and drives the other.

"Banking was conceived in iniquity and was born in sin. The bankers own the earth. Take it away from them, but leave them the power to create money, and with the flick of the pen they will create enough deposits to buy it back again. However, take it away from them, and all the great fortunes like mine will disappear and they ought to disappear, for this would be a happier and better world to live in. But, if you wish to remain the slaves of bankers and pay the cost of your own slavery, let them continue to create money." – Sir Josiah Stamp, Director of the Bank of England (appointed 1928).

The first step in returning the federal government to fiscal sanity is to stop borrowing money – especially from the Federal Reserve. The next step is to put America back on the Gold Standard and return us to a stable form of currency, one that cannot be easily inflated or created out of nothing. Once the currency has stabilized and the federal government has overcome its addiction to the easy money from the Federal Reserve, they need to dismantle it and return the power of money creation back to the Congress and the States, and decentralize the monetary system away from Washington D.C.

and Wall Street. In order to make the transition easier, the Treasury should re-issue U.S. Treasury Notes backed by gold and silver as were issued before the Federal Reserve, and then fractional-reserve banking needs to be reduced to a 5:1 rate or lower. The last step will then be to actually start paying down the national debt.

Until the Progressive Era and its push to centralize everything, people were typically very wary about getting into any sort of debt and were outraged when the government spent more than it took in. Before the Sixteenth Amendment was ratified and the federal income tax took effect, the size and scope of the federal government was very limited because it was primarily funded by consumption-based taxes such as tariffs. When the economy did well, imports increased and the government revenues increased. When the economy contracted, so would government revenues, and they were forced to spend less because revenue was limited and the people and banks were less likely to buy government debt during a bad economy.

But with the passage of the Federal Reserve Act and the Sixteenth Amendment, the spending and borrowing constraints on the federal government were greatly reduced, and now the Congress can spend any amount of money it wants to on whatever it wants, from buying votes, creating stimulus packages, and bailing out banks and corporations for billions of dollars. But without the Federal Reserve, such irresponsible actions would be very difficult, if not impossible. Of course, countries can accumulate large national debts without a central bank, but it's much more difficult – especially if your currency is not the world's reserve currency like the American dollar. Recently, there's been more and more talk outside the U.S. of getting rid of the reserve currency, which would doom the U.S. to the same inflation problems that the Fed creates in the rest of the world.

The Founders hated public debt because they understood that it would enslave them just like a tyrannical king. They also hated paper money and banknotes, of which they'd had a belly-

154

full from the days of the Revolution when Congress was issuing tons of worthless Continentals. Their hatred of paper money caused them to specify that in the Constitution, Congress alone has the power and responsibility of coining money – not an unaccountable central bank – so ultimately the people could retain control of the money supply and directly hold their leaders accountable for their monetary policies every two, four, and six years.

As the first Secretary of the Treasury, Alexander Hamilton pushed for central bank, but they had charters and expired after twenty years. The Federal Reserve has no explicit expiration date in its charter, but it can be dissolved at any time by Congress. One of the few good things that Andrew Jackson did during his presidency in the 1830s was that he refused to renew the charter for the Second Bank of the United States and let it die, and then he immediately paid off the national debt of $58 million ($1.4 billion in 2010 dollars). The national debt had been about $80 million ($1.8 billion adjusted) in 1793, mostly due to the Revolutionary War debts, and the federal government soon began paying it down; by 1812, it stood at $45 million ($741 million adjusted). By the middle of his second term in office, Jackson had completely paid off the national debt, but unfortunately, he put many of his cronies in charge of the newly-acquired federal surplus and soon the country was back in debt.

In mid-2012, Ron Paul introduced a bill that would require the Federal Reserve to be audited, so they could presumably be held accountable for their management of the American currency. Unfortunately, the measure overwhelmingly passed in the House but died in the Senate under the leadership of Harry Reid. Even if the measure would've passed the Senate, it would've never been signed by Obama, because the Federal Reserve issues the money for the Progressives' spending. The Fed is regularly audited, but usually by its own people, its banks, and others that can hardly be considered "independent." A limited audit of the Fed a few years ago discovered that between 2007 and 2010, the Federal Reserve loaned out more than $16 trillion dollars to the "too big to fail" banks and other banking institutions. It's no wonder that the Fed doesn't want to be audited – because then they could be held accountable for their monetary misdeeds.

Would the Congress ever dissolve the Federal Reserve? We can only hope, but it's not likely because the Federal Reserve enables the federal government to freely borrow and spend money they don't have. Socialism, wealth-redistribution, and government expansions all feed at the trough of the Federal Reserve and would soon starve if the central bank was ever dismantled. That's why Congress, the President, and the rest of the federal government need to return to fiscal sanity first. However, if there is a huge economic collapse or hyperinflation sets in, people may just stop using the worthless Federal Reserve Notes and use forms of real currency again like silver, gold, and copper.

In closing, carefully consider the words of Thomas Jefferson, who understood banking systems all too well:

"And I believe that banking institutions are more dangerous to our liberties than standing armies. If the American people ever allow private banks to control the issue of their currency, first by inflation, then by deflation, the banks and corporations that will grow up around the banks will deprive the people of all property – until their children wake-up homeless on the continent their fathers conquered... The democracy will cease to exist when you take away from those who are willing to work and give to those who would not." – Thomas Jefferson

Chapter 6 - The Death of Morality

"We have no government armed with power capable of contending with human passions unbridled by morality and religion. Avarice, ambition, revenge, or gallantry, would break the strongest cords of our Constitution as a whale goes through a net. Our Constitution was made only for a moral and religious people. It is wholly inadequate to the government of any other." – John Adams

While rising inflation, the exploding national debt, and the monetary policies of the Federal Reserve are extremely dangerous to America, those threats are more "external" to our civilization rather than "internal." When the United States encounters another economic crisis, the nation will suffer, but she won't be mortally wounded. The mismanagement of her resources affects the nation's body, but not her soul – not her national spirit and character. The nation's character is being terribly wounded from within by moral confusion, widespread immorality, abandonment of commitments, and negligence of our families, homes, churches, and schools. America is not only being torn apart by her own leaders, but by her own people: us. As Proverbs 14:34 declares, "Righteousness exalts a nation, but sin is a reproach to any people." Moral character begins with individual virtue, which builds nations, but individual immorality tears them down.

America's moral character is but a shadow of what it once was. Until roughly fifty years ago, Americans' sense of what was right and what was wrong was quite clear and consistent. There were such things as moral absolutes, and most Americans agreed on what those moral standards were. Much of America's moral standards were based upon the Bible, but now those standards can't even be read, spoken, or heard in our public

157

squares and schools. In the past, the majority in the society set the moral standards, but now the minority prevents any such standards from taking hold, especially through the tyranny of political correctness. Throughout America today, moral absolutes have been replaced by moral relativism: "What's right or wrong for you isn't right or wrong for me."

The decline in moral standards and rise in moral relativism has not occurred suddenly, which would've likely been recognized and subsequently defeated. America's moral decline is like that of a frog in a pot of water which is slowly being boiled. It's only by looking back to where we came from can we see how far we've declined. As the standards in our society have crumbled, immorality has increased to the point that we can barely even recognize immorality for what it is. Now the caldron is boiling and we seemed trapped by our own inability to identify what's right and what's wrong. And even when we can identify it, too many of us are too afraid of political correctness or "offending someone" to speak out.

As immorality increases, so does the size and scope of government that is needed to contain such evil and countermand the effects of immorality. As Americans have traded their individual religion for the secular state, they're starting to realize what previous generations intrinsically understood: with sin comes tyranny. However, even with that realization, few Americans know how to escape the caldron that is boiling us alive. Like the Roman Empire and other infamous civilizations that fell, the American Republic will collapse under the weight of her own immorality – unless we dramatically change course.

When did America lose her morals and how can they be regained? The following are the major events of how and when America turned from her Judeo-Christian moorings and towards secular humanism:

1859 – The Origin of Species (Theory of Evolution)

During the first half of the Eighteenth Century, the winds of revolution were howling throughout Europe and the lower classes were rising up against the monarchies, oligarchies, and aristocracies. The first principles of Socialism had been introduced and were spreading rapidly, along with the new philosophies of secularism and humanism which were aspiring to dethrone Christianity and the Church. However, the new philosophies had a fundamental flaw: they couldn't answer the question of origins – where did mankind (and the rest of the universe) come from? If that question couldn't be reasonably answered apart from supernatural Creation, their new philosophies would have no basis for authority.

This philosophical problem began being solved by reinterpreting the Creation account of Genesis, first by proposing that the literal six-days of Creation could also mean "ages," and then the notion that the Creation occurred over a period of thousands of years. Coupled with the day-age theory was the reinterpretation of the Flood of Noah, which was postulated as being a regional or even a local Flood rather than a global deluge. Once such liberal reinterpretations were increasingly accepted, the rest of the Bible could be similarly reinterpreted. With their principles of textual criticism in hand, the skeptics arose and called in to question everything in the Bible, and even questioned established history.

In 1831, Charles Lyell, the founder of modern geology and the often-cited Geologic Column, popularized the new Uniformitarian theory in his book, "Principles of Geology." This theory proposed that the earth was very old and that the same geologic processes existing today have existed for all history. Rather than the various geologic features being formed suddenly by a catastrophic global Flood, Lyell speculated that those features were formed slowly over very long periods of time. But even with the Uniformitarian theories, the secularists still couldn't quite formulate a materialistic or Uniformitarian version of origins that would be acceptable to the general populace – until Charles Darwin's infamous book was published: "The Origin of Species."

Darwin's new Theory of Evolution followed many of the principles of Uniformitarianism but was applied to biology rather than geology. The theory speculated that over long periods of time, species would mutate, change, and adapt to their environment and entirely new species would arise. While it's observed that many small changes and adaptations frequently occur within kinds and species (micro-evolution), changes that transform one species into another (macro-evolution) have never been observed. Unfortunately, the evolutionary processes occurred so slowly that they could not be readily observed, which is why Darwin's theory required the Geologic Column. Darwin postulated that if Evolution were true, it should be recorded in the fossils found in the various geological layers.

Ironically, in geology the Geologic Column dates the rock layers according to the index fossils found within them, while in Evolution the fossils are dated by the rock layer they are found in – which is circular reasoning. When one is used to date the other and vice-versa, any age can be assigned to the rocks and the fossils from thousands to millions to billions of years, which is precisely what the evolutionists have done.

When first published in 1859 (at the personal urging of Charles Lyell), the full title of Darwin's book was "On the Origin of Species by Means of Natural Selection, or the Preservation of Favoured Races in the Struggle for Life." However, the title was soon shortened because some people were uncomfortable with the blatant racism embodied in the phase "Preservation of Favoured Races" in their new favorite science book. However, the book only reinforced the existing racist ideas of the time that black people and others from less-developed regions of the world were primitives or even subhuman species. This also provided another justification for slavery, because the slave-owners frequently argued that their slaves were incapable of living side-by-side with more advanced peoples, and therefore, they were helping society by keeping them in chains.

Though "The Origin of Species" was published as a scientific book, Darwin actually had very little scientific training, as with most of the early evolutionists. In fact, only one founding evolutionist, Jean Lamarck, was an educated, trained scientist. Charles Darwin was an apostate Divinity student while Charles Lyell was a lawyer who utterly despised the Bible and Christianity. Darwin was heavily influenced by the writings of Lyell, who repeatedly encouraged Darwin to publish "The Origin of Species" and therefore support his theoretical Geologic Column and refinements of Uniformitarianism. The two theories – Uniformitarianism and Evolution – must go hand-in-hand; neither theory can survive without the other.

The Theory of Evolution was crafted (whether intentionally by its founders or not) with one underlying purpose: to supplant the Bible and the Creator from Western society, and thereby free the populace from the moral constraints of religion at large. The new secular philosophies required a theory of origins, and the theories of Darwin and Lyell emerged at just the right time to meet that need. The teaching of the Theory of Evolution single-handedly dethroned Christianity in a matter of years, first in Europe and then later in America. Once a nation or people have turned away from their Creator, they are then inherently freed from any self-imposed moral boundaries or guidelines that once governed their personal behavior. And not only are individuals then freed to engage in any activity they see fit, so is the State.

Various flavors of the Evolution theory had existed prior to Darwin, with some of the origin debates going all the way back to the Greek Stoics and Skeptics. But the reason why the modern Evolution theory has had such a huge impact on Western society and thought is because it left the realm of origins and was applied to many of the other secular institutions and philosophies which were being developed at that time.

Evolution theory would've been mostly harmless if it were just confined to the realm of science-books and the study of origins, but it became an all-encompassing philosophy for economics, law, psychology, sociology, and politics.

In the worldview of Progressivism, Secularism, Socialism, and Communism, Evolution is their foundation of origins, redistribution and equality are their creeds, secular professors are their priests, universities are their temples, and abortion and euthanasia are their sacraments.

1890s – Psychoanalysis

As a result of the Age of Reason and the rise of secular humanism, doctors and scientists began applying the Scientific Method and other principles to human behavior, mental illness, and sociology. However, they approached their fields of study with an increasingly humanistic and evolutionary reproach; soon crime, evil, and other anti-social behaviors were reclassified from being spiritual in nature to being a disease to be treated and possibly cured.

Rather than emanating from man's sinful nature, crimes were now the result of socio-economic circumstances such as a poor family upbringing, poverty, and lack of education. Instead of individual repentance as with most religions, now only rehabilitation was necessary. The spiritual nature of man was tossed aside and man became little more than an advanced animal in the eyes of modern psychology. If man is an evolved, sophisticated beast, then reason holds that with enough therapy and rehabilitation, man can be repaired. The psychology book soon replaced the Bible and other religious writings to cure peoples' mental and spiritual ills, much to the delight of the secularists and Progressives.

Psychoanalysis often shifts the responsibility for misbehaviors from the individual who committed the crime elsewhere (typically to their parents, childhood, or environment). Even society is blamed for the individual misdeeds of the criminal, and eventually the criminal becomes viewed as the victim even in the most heinous of crimes. After all, who would demand that someone be put to death for their crimes if they are merely sick rather than evil? In reclassifying evil as mental-illness, psychoanalysis has greatly contributed to the denigration of the death-penalty and has encouraged the early-release of murderers, rapists, child-molesters, and other criminals back into society, where they often continue their crimes.

While the principles of psychoanalysis and various therapies have helped doctors better understand the human mind and have in fact helped many people, the denial of the spiritual, eternal element of man has terribly hurt both our society and multitudes of people over the last century. Using psychoanalysis alone to treat all forms of behavioral problems is as counterproductive as using the Bible for Alzheimer's or dementia. Crimes of the heart (or spirit) need "spiritual" remedies, not physical remedies.

1920 – The American Civil Liberties Union (ACLU)

The American Civil Liberties Union was formed in 1920 under the banner of protecting civil liberties and civil rights of various minority groups. The roots of the ACLU go back to 1915 (during the Woodrow Wilson administration) as an anti-war group called the American Union Against Militarism, a movement composed mostly of Marxists, anarchists, and radical immigrants. Soon it broadened its mission and identity and became the National Civil Liberties Bureau (NCLB), which maintained very close ties to the Communist Party USA.

As a result of the rise of Progressivism and then Communism in the 1920s and 1930s, the ACLU soon became a thoroughly anti-Judeo-Christian organization which uses the legal system to subvert the Constitution and various moral laws at every level of society. The Constitution assumed a religious and moral citizenry, and many of our laws were written not to force new standards of morality, but to simply codify what behaviors the citizens had already decided were not acceptable, beneficial, or tolerable to their society.

By misusing the Equal Protection Clause of the Fourteenth Amendment (which was originally intended to only be applied to racial matters), the ACLU has forced a secular moral code upon the United States and all but purged America of its Judeo-Christian heritage. The ACLU is not concerned with whether or not moral laws are beneficial to society or not – they simply cannot tolerate religious-based laws that attempt to govern individual behavior. Even the Progressive Teddy Roosevelt referred to the ACLU as the "enemies within." The ACLU is one of the greatest threats to the United States because it distorts and uses our own laws and Bill of Rights against America in order to purge its Judeo-Christian heritage from within.

The following are highlights from the stated goals of the ACLU's published "Policy Issues" which undermine morality in America:

- The legalization of prostitution (Policy 211)
- The defense of all pornography (including child pornography), as "free speech" (Policy 4)
- The decriminalization and legalization of all drugs (Policy 210)
- The promotion of homosexuality (Policy 264)
- The opposition of rating of music and movies (Policy 18)
- Opposition against parental consent of minors seeking abortion (Policy 262)
- Opposition of informed consent preceding abortion procedures (Policy 263)
- Opposition of spousal consent preceding abortion (Policy 262)
- Opposition of parental choice in children's education (Policy 80)

- The defense and promotion of euthanasia, polygamy, government control of church institutions, gun control, taxpayer-funded abortion, birth limitation. (Policies 263, 133, 402, 47, 261, 323, 271, 91, 85)

To make matters worse, over the last several decades the ACLU and other activist lawyers have discovered that they can often achieve the same results by merely threatening a lawsuit, without ever having to go to court and sometimes without ever settling. This has proven to be far more effective in removing statutes, plaques, and memorials from schools and public property – as well as intimidating fellow citizens – than filing expensive lawsuits and having to go to trial.

Ironically, the ACLU is strongly against all forms of capital punishment, even though they support abortion (partial-birth and taxpayer-funded), euthanasia, and birth-control with equal ferocity. In summary, the ACLU supports preventing or extinguishing most forms of life except that of criminals. They are able to rationalize such double-standards because of their greatly distorted values concerning life (especially innocent life), justice, and victims. On capital punishment, the ACLU sees the murderer on death-row as the victim instead of the people they killed, while for abortion, the ACLU sees the victim as the woman who terminates her fetus instead of the innocent, unborn child. In both cases, the ACLU shows little regard for justice or the sanctity of life, particularly with their stand against the death-penalty in which the murderer gets to live while their victim does not.

The ACLU has done a small measure of "good" at times, but their organization has severed the intrinsic link between religious-based morality and our constitutional, limited government. Both go hand-in-hand and one cannot exist without the other. The ACLU may try to keep the letter of the law and the Constitution, but they definitely do not encourage the spirit of the law from which it came.

165

1925 – The Scopes' "Monkey Trial"

While the Theory of Evolution had existed since 1859, it had been making only gradual inroads into the American textbooks. The Theory of Evolution and its pseudo-Biblical counterpart, Theistic Evolution, was progressing in the universities, seminaries, and also in the more liberal churches and denominations. Most public schools at the time steered clear of the rising Creation-Evolution debate and taught little of either one. Because liberalism was sweeping through so many churches, a reactionary Christian Fundamentalist movement arose, and some of these fundamentalists introduced legislation (such as the Butler Law) to ban the teaching of the Theory of Evolution in public schools.

Tennessee was one of the States in the "Bible Belt" which banned the teaching of Evolution in public schools, which worried the ACLU and the secular humanists. But it wasn't the exclusive teaching of Creationism that concerned them, as much as the absence of Evolutionary teaching which underpins secular humanism. In early 1925, the ACLU decided to challenge the statute and found a teacher willing to break the new Butler Law, John Scopes, and guaranteed to cover his legal fees and provide financial assistance if he taught Evolution in the classroom.

The infamous Scopes' "Monkey Trial" (as it became known) soon turned into a media circus and a larger debate ensued: the debate between science and religion and what place religion should hold in public schools. At that time, most public schools were secular in nature but posted the Ten Commandments and often said a short daily prayer along with the Pledge of Allegiance. Much of the country was drawn into the debate which continued to grow even beyond the science vs. religion argument towards one of values: the rural fundamentalist values versus those of the more secular city dwellers.

Though John Scopes and the ACLU lost the trial, the underlying purposes of the debate were met: the derision, isolation, and removal of fundamentalism from public discourse and later, the public square. The Scopes Trial changed how religion affected schools and made Americans rethink what was being taught in the schools and how it influenced students. In 1955, the movie "Inherit the Wind" was produced which was based upon the Scopes Trial, but portrayed the fundamentalists as illogical, vengeful extremists, while depicting the evolutionists as rational, logical, and noble. Evidently the real Scopes Trial didn't portray Christians the way Hollywood saw them or wanted them to be portrayed. Meanwhile, most public schools have shown "Inherit the Wind" to generations of American students, undercutting religion and pushing them towards secularism. If we are to maintain a strict wall of Separation of Church and State, then why is that piece of secular propaganda shown in our schools every year? Shouldn't we at least be consistent?

In the end, the Butler Law backfired and caused Evolutionary teaching to explode throughout America, though the amount of Evolution and origins in the public school science curriculum remained miniscule until 1959. Another significant impact of the Scopes Trial and the "Inherit the Wind" movie was that a new generation of Americans arose which was much more willing to question authority of any sort, whether it was the religious, civil, or parental.

1933 – The Humanist Manifesto

The Humanist Manifesto was a document that codified the new religion of Secular Humanism, a product of the Humanist movement and the rise of secularism throughout the West. The Humanist Manifesto formally rejected all religious beliefs and teachings, as well as denied the presence and power of God or any other supernatural being. Many of thirty-four signers were university professors, Unitarian ministers, editors, and other humanists.

Forty years later in 1973, the Humanist Manifesto was appended and then superseded by the Humanist Manifesto II, which supported the new human "rights" of no-fault divorce, birth-control, and abortion on demand. Two infamous lines in the revised Humanist Manifesto are, "No deity will save us; we must save ourselves," and "We are responsible for what we are and for what we will be." In 2003, the Humanist Manifesto III was signed, which refines and builds upon the previous versions.

The Humanist Manifestos all deny the Creation and the existence of a supernatural Creator. Human rights are therefore granted by other humans or their institutions rather than a Creator, and therefore our destiny as a race is completely up to us. As an anti-religious belief system, the humanists have only two real ways of propagating their secular religion to the general population: through the press and through the public education system. However, early on they realized that the public school system was the key to transforming the religious-based society into one based upon secular humanism. One of the signers of the Humanist Manifesto, John Dewey, built upon Horace Mann's public education system which was modeled after the secular institutions in Prussia and successfully transformed America's public education system into one based completely on secularism.

Both Mann and Dewey sought to permanently end education by Christians and Jews, and their success is evident in almost every school – public and private – in America.

1940 – Planned Parenthood

Planned Parenthood was formed by Margaret Sanger, a committed eugenist, anarchist, racist, and evolutionist. Among Sanger's first publications was her monthly newsletter, "The Woman Rebel" whose slogan was, "No Gods, No Masters." Her stated goals were to limit the number of "racially-inferior" children born into poverty in order to create a "pure race" – and in her eyes, those of "black" and "yellow" skin were primary candidates for birth-control, sterilization, and also abortion.

By its own actions and its published agenda, Planned Parenthood is one of the most vile, murderous organizations in America. Planned Parenthood promotes dangerous sexual activities among teenagers and even actively aids child-molesters by deliberately concealing their crimes and identities. From 1973 when abortion was legalized to 2012, there have been approximately 55 million abortions, with Planned Parenthood being the largest abortion provider in the United States.

Planned Parenthood is partially funded by the federal government, along with various state governments and other contributions, along with private revenue. While it also provides birth-control, adoption services, STD-testing, and other women's health services, the bulk of its funding comes from providing abortions, which comprise over 95% of its income.

1946 – Permissive Parenting

In 1946, Dr. Benjamin Spock published his book, "The Common Sense Book of Baby and Child Care," which became an instant bestseller as the post-WWII baby-boom erupted. Spock was referred to as the "father of permissiveness" by Vice President Spiro Agnew because Spock recommended acquiescing to the demands of infants and children rather than ignoring or punishing their tantrums. His new book and liberal parenting advice ushered in the era of permissive parenting which promoted instant gratification during children's formative years with very little discipline (if any). Eleven years after the first edition had been released, Spock released a second edition which tried to correct some of the errors of the first edition, but by then the damage had already been done.

Some of Dr. Spock's reasons for originally writing the book were to correct some of the problems he had noticed with child-rearing at the time, such as cold/aloof parenting and the overuse of spanking and other forms of corporal punishment (some of which were abusive). However, rather than administer corporal punishment in the proper way or reserve it for the worst of offenses, many parents took Dr. Spock's advice to the extreme and never administered it. Soon spanking was considered to be child abuse and the parents who spanked their children were seen as bullies who resorted to using violence to control their children.

Since its publication, Dr. Spock's book on parenting has been the second-best-selling book in the country (the Bible is the first). Dr. Spock was among the first pediatricians to study psychoanalysis in order to understand children's needs and family dynamics, and therefore applied a humanistic standard to child-rearing rather than the Bible or other religious books and traditional parenting. His ideas about childcare influenced succeeding generations of parents to treat their young children as individuals, which led to the parenting relationship being altered into one based upon equality and friendship rather than parental authority, training, and guidance.

When the generation raised with Dr. Spock's parenting methods matured, the negative results of his advice began to be seen. The Baby Boomer generation which had been given so much had been fed a steady diet of instant gratification and had a sense of entitlement, and then rebelled against society upon attending the universities. During the violent Vietnam anti-war protests of the 1960s, Dr. Norman Vincent Peale declared that society was now paying the price of following Dr. Spock's parental advice of instant gratification. The rebellious youth were often even referred to as the "Spock Generation," since the magnitude of the anti-war protests and youth rebellions were unlike any America had ever seen before.

In addition to his writing and pediatric work, Dr. Spock was also a committed left-wing activist and was deeply involved in the Vietnam War protest movements during the 1960s and early 1970s. During his latter years, he advocated a vegan/vegetarian diet for children, which proved to be quite unpopular.

1947 – Separation of Church and State

Before the case of Everson v. Board of Education was decided by the Supreme Court in 1947, few Americans had ever heard the phrase "Separation of Church and State." However, over the course of the last sixty years, that phrase has become part of our national psyche, with many Americans even assuming that the phrase is part of the Bill of Rights or the Constitution. Since 1947, the phrase has been cited in hundreds of court-cases, though it is nowhere to be found in the Declaration of Independence, the Constitution, the Bill of Rights, or even the Federalist Papers.

Though the concept of "Separation of Church and State" was certainly embraced by many of the Founding Fathers, it was more of a one-way street – that the State cannot be intertwined with the Church such that a national religion is established by the State – instead of the forbidding of all religious influence in government and public institutions as it's used today. The First Amendment stipulates that "Congress shall make no law respecting an establishment of religion, or prohibiting the free exercise thereof" and Article VI specifies that "no religious Test shall ever be required as a Qualification to any Office or public Trust under the United States." The First Amendment keeps the State out of the Church while Article VI is intended to prevent a State religion from ever taking root in the government.

The phrase "Separation of Church and State" is traced back to a January 1, 1802 letter by Thomas Jefferson to the Danbury Baptist Association in Connecticut, which was later published in a Massachusetts newspaper. Jefferson wrote, "I contemplate with sovereign reverence that act of the whole American people which declared that their legislature should 'make no law respecting an establishment of religion, or prohibiting the free exercise thereof,' thus building a wall of separation between Church & State."

Among Alexis de Tocqueville's numerous observations of America in the 1830s was how intimately intertwined our ideas of liberty and practice of Judeo-Christian principles were. Both

171

pillars supported one another and made America into the great bastion of freedom, liberty, and justice for all that she has been renowned for. As one of America's corner-stones, this "Separation of Church and State" kept the State completely out of personal and even community religious affairs – not the reversed situation we have today in that the Church is kept out of most public affairs.

And so it was throughout most of our history until the Supreme Court of Progressive Hugo Black, who essentially redefined what the "Separation of Church and State" meant. Before the Supreme Court rulings, the Church and the State were on nearly equal footing and neither could hold sway over the other – if a community wanted to put a Nativity scene on public property, they were more than welcome to do it. But after the rulings, the State became superior to the Church and began dictating its actions on public property, regardless of what the majority of the people in that community wanted. Today, all it takes for a religious display on public property to be banned is one voice of dissent, even if tens of thousands of residents support it. That is tyranny by the minority.

Before the English philosopher John Locke wrote of the secular government, the State and the Church were often two sides of the same coin – which frequently led to persecution (by the State) for those who did not agree with the Church. It was this sort of state-sanctioned, state-enforced religion that the Founders feared, not the people freely exercising their religion while in office or on public property. There was also the concern of States' rights, since many of the States had different denominations and they were concerned that the federal government could establish a national religion (or national denomination) over time if not specifically restricted from doing so. The Bill of Rights was intended to limit the scope of the federal government, not the State governments. The First Amendment declares that "*Congress* (i.e. the federal legislature) shall make no law respecting an establishment of religion," – if the States wanted to establish a state-religion or state-denomination (which several had at the time), they were free to do so under the First, Ninth, and Tenth Amendments. Tragically, in our hyper-sensitized culture (and due to the actions of activist lawyers, judges, and the ACLU), any mention of God, the Bible, or any sort of religious code or standard in the public square is seen as the "establishment of a state-religion," even though it's nothing of the sort. The concept of the "Separation of Church and State" was intended to keep the government out of the churches, though not necessarily God or personal convictions and personal religion out of the government – especially the state and local governments. Many of the Founding Fathers repeatedly even declared that without the widespread practicing of religion that encouraged individual morality – particularly the Judeo-Christian religion – that the American Experiment in self-governance would undoubtedly fail. In fact, the Continental Congress approved a resolution to import or print 20,000 Bibles on September 11th, 1777 (however, it's unknown how much of that request was fulfilled). Limited government and self-government begin with the citizenry's governing of their individual selves – which is best accomplished with an active, personal practicing of religion.

The reason why the Everson v. Board of Education ruling changed the concept of the "Separation of Church and State" in the United States was because the Supreme Court led by FDR-appointed Hugo Black misapplied the Due Process Clause of the Fourteenth Amendment (which was primarily concerned with voting rights) with the First Amendment. After that ruling, the religious rights of the States and local governments began being stripped away because now the First Amendment applied not only to the federal government, but to ALL the governments in the United States of America. Until that ruling, it was relatively common for States and local municipalities to grant religious denominations legislative or effective privileges – which were completely within their rights under the American model of federalism embodied in the Constitution.

With regards to the re-interpretation of the First Amendment, Hugo Black's language was sweeping:

"The 'establishment of religion' clause of the First Amendment means at least this: Neither a state nor the Federal Government can set up a church. Neither can pass laws which aid one religion, aid all religions or prefer one religion over another. Neither can force nor influence a person to go to or to remain away from church against his will or force him to profess a belief or disbelief in any religion. No person can be punished for entertaining or professing religious beliefs or disbeliefs, for church attendance or non-attendance. No tax in any amount, large or small, can be levied to support any religious activities or institutions, whatever they may be called, or whatever form they may adopt to teach or practice religion. Neither a state nor the Federal Government can, openly or secretly, participate in the affairs of any religious organizations or groups and vice versa. In the words of Jefferson, the clause against establishment of religion by law was intended to erect 'a wall of separation between Church and State.'" *330 U.S. 1, 15-16.*

The Due Process Clause of the Fourteenth Amendment prohibits state and local governments from depriving people of life, liberty, or property without certain steps being taken to ensure fairness and justice. This clause has been used to make most of the Bill of Rights applicable to the States, as well as to recognize substantive and procedural rights. However, the Bill of Rights does NOT apply to state and local governments – only to the federal government, because the scope of the Bill of Rights is the federal Constitution.

After this landmark case, the Fourteenth Amendment – particularly the Equal Protection Clause – was reinterpreted by the courts to require each State to provide equal protection under the law to all people within its jurisdiction. This clause was the basis for Brown v. Board of Education (1954), the Supreme Court decision which precipitated the dismantling of racial segregation in the United States education system. However, under the Tenth Amendment, the federal government has no jurisdiction over any education system – that is a responsibility left up to the States, or the People.

1948 – The Kinsey Reports

In 1948, Alfred Kinsey published his widely acclaimed report, "Sexual Behavior in the Human Male"; this was later followed in 1953 with the companion book, "Sexual Behavior in the Human Female." Although it was later revealed that much of his research for the "male" book was conducted on sexual predators in prisons, the Kinsey Report was (and still is) considered to be the standard study of human sexuality in America. The effects of these books were that the vile perversions of these convicted sexual predators and child molesters became the supposed "normal" standard of human sexuality and therefore the perversions were normalized.

The impact that the Kinsey Reports had on the American public are nearly impossible to measure. Before the Kinsey Reports, Americans assumed that most people conformed to what was considered traditional sexual morals and that those who didn't (the deviants and perverts) were a very tiny minority. Prior to 1948, most discussions of sexuality were limited to moralists and ethicists who based their work on assumptions and impressions of what they thought transpired behind closed doors. Suddenly, all forms of sexual-behavior – including the degrading, abhorrent forms – were open for discussion, examination, and even observation (under the banner of "science," of course).

In the name of research, Kinsey threw off all morality and standards, such that he not only theorized about sexuality and interviewed numerous subjects, but actively observed and even participated in the sexual activity of his subjects, sometimes

175

even with his own co-workers. He justified his behavior as being necessary to gain the confidence of his research subjects and to further understand their feelings and responses. Kinsey also encouraged his staff to follow his methods and engaged in a wide range of deviant sexual activity in order to help the interviewers understand the participants' responses.

Literally no deviant sexual behavior was "taboo" to Kinsey during his research, including pedophilia, homosexuality, pre-marital sex, extra-marital sex, and group sex. Much of Kinsey's data-samples were skewed to the deviant side of the spectrum because he used prisoners and co-workers in his samples; when the data was re-examined and resampled twenty years later, the deviant effects of the reports had already dramatically altered society and few differences were found.

Before Kinsey's reports, the majority of sexual activity in America was traditional and confined mostly to marriage; when sex outside marriage did occur, it was frowned upon by society and usually kept quiet. But after his reports were made public, the sexual constraints were thrown off and deviant sexual behavior became widely accepted. After all, if "everyone was doing it," then certainly such infidelities and behavior was excusable, right? Since the Kinsey Reports and the loosening of sexual restraints, America has literally become sex-crazed.

Sex in society can be likened to a powerful river – when its energy and power are properly harnessed, the society greatly benefits and thrives. However, if left unrestrained, that incredible energy can completely flood and destroy that same society. When sex is constrained to marriage, families are built, children are more likely to be raised in more-secure, loving, two-parent homes, and the overall society is stable and thrives. However, when sex is unrestrained, it soon becomes worshipped and essentially becomes the idol/god of that society. As a society becomes flooded with sex, it soon becomes an all-consuming, self-destructive force; sex becomes all everyone thinks about. Also, unrestrained sex usually becomes highly addictive and progressive in society, requiring more and more variety and deviancy in order for the participants to feel the same excitement as in previous encounters, just like many other forms of entertainments, pleasures, and substance-type addictions.

1953 – Popularization of Pornography

In 1953, Hugh Hefner launched the "Playboy" magazine, which first featured Marilyn Monroe and became an overnight sensation. Considering the effects that the Kinsey Reports had on American curiosity towards sex, the consumption of other pornographic material became more widespread, though still not widely acceptable. However, Playboy helped change that with the inclusion of exclusive interviews on a variety of subjects, and also their portrayals of the models as "the girl next door." Playboy changed America's attitudes toward pornography and made it more acceptable instead of simply being "dirty magazines."

As with other forms of illicit sexual content, pornography preys upon the consumer's thought-life and attitudes towards women. As pornography became more popular in America, women were no longer viewed as sweethearts, wives, mothers, sisters, and daughters to be protected and cherished, but were demoted to sex-objects to lusted after. When women become fantasy sex-objects in the eyes of men, they stop being real people with thoughts, feelings, needs, and dreams of their own. Pornography feeds men's lusts, which then contributes to pre-marital sex, extra-marital affairs, and other illicit relationships. The more that lust is fed – especially in men – the greater it grows.

Not only were men's attitudes towards women terribly damaged with the popularization of Playboy, but women's attitudes towards men were damaged as well. After pornography became widely available, no longer could women be as trusting towards men as they once were, because they were no longer certain whether men were really being genuine towards them or not. Now there was an unsaid "expectation" on the part of women after a date, which the men usually paid for. Also, the airbrushed pictures in the pornography magazines set unrealistic and unattainable standards of feminine beauty and sexuality that women then had to compete with. Now in order to be thought of as beautiful, women felt they had to measure up to the fake images and sexually aggressive behaviors portrayed in those magazines.

When men consume pornography, not only are tremendous feelings of betrayal, anger, and hopelessness generated in women, it also opens them up to rebellion against the societal norms of marriage and family. After all, why should the women work hard in the home raising the kids if her husband is constantly lusting after fantasy women or even having affairs outside the home? Affairs don't begin with the simple act of physical betrayal; they start with lust and covetousness in the mind and heart. Is it any wonder that the feminist movement soon became radicalized and gender confusion set in after pornography became widespread? For the women who couldn't possibly measure up to the impossible standards set by pornography and other magazines, many simply gave up and sought to be equal with men in society in every way possible.

Pornography may not have been solely responsible for America's sexual debasement, but it certainly contributed to the problem (along with many other societal ills). How can a society properly function when so many of the males are consumed with lust for every other woman that they encounter? The human male thinks about sex enough as it is without being continually fed illicit, degrading, unrealistic images of women and sexual situations. People often wonder when exactly chivalry died and often blame feminism – but it wasn't feminism that was ultimately responsible for the death of chivalry and the noble treatment of women, but the widespread consumption of pornography by the men and boys.

1959 – Evolution in Public Schools

In October 1957, the Soviet Union surprised the world by announcing they had placed Sputnik, the first unmanned space satellite, into orbit. The United States was shocked – how had the Communists beaten them into space? How had the American scientific community failed, and how had their intelligence networks not known about such a monumental undertaking by their Cold War enemy? In response to the very real threat of the Soviets, the United States drew the completely wrong conclusions when they examined the public school curriculum: the science textbooks had very little Evolution content (or Creationist content either).

Though the American attitude towards space exploration had been one of leisure, the sudden realization that they had both lost the "high ground" and that the Soviets had accomplished a technological feat that the Americans had not nearly created a national emergency. And even though the nation's education system had been continually improving, President Eisenhower called for an immediate overhaul to the nation's education system, with a renewed emphasis on science, math, and foreign languages. Reforms were to be made at every level of the education system, particularly in primary schools and high schools. In 1958, the National Defense Education Act was passed and with it, the National Science Foundation started the Biological Sciences Curriculum Study, which emphasized the teaching of Evolution in high school biology textbooks.

Because of the Scopes Trial and the controversy created by the Creation/Evolution debate, most high school biology and life-science textbooks contained little mention of the various origins theories – a precautionary approach taken by publishers avoid raising the controversial topic. Eisenhower and Congress somehow determined that the lack of "proper scientific education" (i.e., lack of Evolution in textbooks) in schools was the primary reason why America was falling behind Russia in terms of science, math, and technology. They reasoned that the Creationism taught to children created an inherent inability to

179

comprehend hard sciences, which was needed to win the Cold War. However, the math and science scores didn't support those conclusions. If the students were falling behind in the math and hard-sciences needed in the Cold War, then why would adding more information on Evolution – an unobservable, untestable theory of origins – or even biology help America regain the technological advantage?

Not only did the over-reaction to Sputnik dramatically increase the amount of Evolutionary content (along with expelling Creationism) in the public school textbooks, it also effectively nationalized the education system. Before Sputnik, local communities and the States had been able to exert nearly complete control over their own schools. By exerting local control over the textbooks being used to teach their children, the people had been able to keep Evolution out, if that was what they wanted. But after Sputnik, the federal government poured millions of dollars into new textbooks that made Evolution one of its foundational themes. The new Biological Sciences Curriculum Study made Evolution one of the guiding principles of science, as most mainstream scientists since the Scopes Trial had insisted. With the federal government now determining what textbooks would be used, the publishers became more immune to pressure from the market (the States and local districts). After 1960, if communities objected to the inclusion of Evolution in the textbooks, they were essentially ignored because the federal government now set the standards.

It cannot be emphasized too strongly about the negative effects that the reaction to the Sputnik incident had in the public schools, particularly with the destruction of one of the primary Judeo-Christian pillars in America. In the 1930s, Adolph Hitler declared, "Let me control the textbooks and I will control the state" – after Sputnik, the secular humanists seized the opportunity to control the textbooks of the entire nation from the federal level. In less than twenty years, America turned from nominal Christianity to fully embrace secular humanism: the worship of man. Since the increase in Evolutionary content in schools and rejection of religion (along with other factors), moral values in America have dramatically declined. After all, if students from their earliest years through college are taught they are the product of pond-scum and the offspring of monkeys, apes, and toads, then that's how they will act. And according to Evolution, secular humanism, and moral relativity, they are entirely within their rights to act like animals.

Proverbs 23:7 declares that, "For as a man thinks in his heart, so is he." It matters where people think they came from and what their place and purpose in the universe is. People think of themselves differently – and will therefore behave differently – if they believe they are a cosmic mistake or the progeny of earthworms and monkeys instead of a unique, special creation of God. Instilling the notion that individuals are essentially meaningless and purposeless is as foolish and self-destructive as a society that uses tax revenue from crime and anti-social behavior (drug-abuse, gambling, and prostitution) to fund their education, incarceration, and rehabilitation systems. Societies are built by the character of their people and families and then reinforced by their institutions – how can immorality possibly build a better society? It can't! And how can teaching that humans came from cosmic burps and rocks possibly elevate mankind and cause us to even want to improve our character and destiny?

Despite the decades of Evolutionary teaching in the public schools, the Creation/Evolution debate continues to rage. In fact, the longer that Evolution has been taught, the more often it's been questioned and carefully investigated. Today, the Theory of Evolution is a theory in crisis because of the tremendous advances that have been made in molecular biology, biochemistry, and genetics since the Sputnik crisis. What were once viewed as basic forms of life and simple-cells are now known to be comprised of thousands of irreducibly complex systems at the smallest levels. Carefully designed, irreducible complexity pervades the microscopic biological world.

Also, much of the supposed evidence for the transitory forms from primates to humans in Evolution has been shown to not only be false, but purposely fraudulent in order for the perpetrators to receive fame, money, or simply to keep the theory alive. The Theory of Evolution would've been abandoned years ago if there were a better alternative to supernatural Creation, but there isn't. So the secular scientists (and school systems) must continue teaching a theory that many of them know is patently impossible (or simply false), but teaching the alternative is unthinkable. In math terms, what would the answer to 2 + 2 be if the correct answer (4) was simply not allowed? The given answer – whatever the teachers determine it should be (other than 4) – could be anything.

1960 – The Birth-Control Pill

In 1960, the birth-control pill was introduced which made contraception convenient and affordable. Women no longer had to worry about inadvertently becoming pregnant, especially outside of marriage. As far as the liberal feminist movement was concerned, women were now freed from the shackles of sexual consequences. One of Margaret Sanger's primary purposes of Planned Parenthood was to encourage widespread contraception – especially among what she saw as the "inferior" races (Africans and Orientals). Planned Parenthood was instrumental in obtaining the initial funding for the research and development of the birth-control pill in the 1950s.

Initially, the birth-control pill only inhibited fertility, but later another component was added to the pill to prevent implantation of the fertilized egg. In 2006, emergency contraceptives (the "morning-after" pill) were approved by the FDA and made available over-the-counter, which cause even the implanted embryo to be aborted. Since the introduction of "the pill," life has been terribly cheapened and children have come to be viewed as burdens rather than blessings. Marriage has also been cheapened because the pill allowed couples to live together and "play house" without the normal consequences of marriage (i.e., children) and the legal ramifications of being married.

With the invention of the birth-control pill, feminist groups immediately claimed that women's reproductive rights were their own business and groups such as Planned Parenthood began dispensing birth-control pills free of charge to women and even underage girls without spousal (or parental) knowledge or consent. Since reproductive rights were now solely determined by the women rather than the couple, the stage was set for the next form of birth-control: abortion. Now that women had the "right to choose" if and when to conceive, it was only a small step to then decide to end an unwanted pregnancy by abortion. In the modern feminist movement, pregnancy, babies, and children have come to be viewed as their enemies (along with men) because they interfere with their freedom.

Feminists argue that the birth-control pill was the key player in forming women's modern economic role because it prolonged the age at which women first married, thereby allowing them to invest in their education and become more career-oriented. Soon after the birth-control pill was legalized, there was a sharp increase in college attendance and graduation rates for women as the pill was effective, cheap, and widely-available. The ability to control fertility without the concern of having children indeed allowed women to make long-term educational and career plans.

Coupled with the spreading of male lust through pornography, the pill also changed America's views on the moral consequences of pre-marital sex and promiscuity. The pill effectively divorced sexual activity from reproduction, the natural consequences of sexual activity. But not only did the pill divorce sex from reproduction, but it also divorced sex from morality. With the use of the pill, women could now be as promiscuous as men without worrying about inadvertently becoming pregnant, and could therefore have as many different partners as they chose. Rather than remaining exclusive and special for married couples, sex became just another recreational activity that could be freely enjoyed by any couple, regardless of how fleeting or superficial that relationship was.

1962 – Public School Prayer Outlawed

After the secularization of the public schools and the federalization of the school curriculum, it was only a matter of time before lawsuits against daily prayer and Bible-reading in public schools were instigated. With the activist, liberal majority on the Supreme Court and throughout much of the appellate system, the anti-religious groups saw their window of opportunity to permanently sever America's religious moorings and "set her free."

In 1962, several families of public school students in New Hyde Park, New York complained that the voluntary prayer to "Almighty God" contradicted their religious beliefs (secular humanism and atheism). The prayer in question was non-denominational and read:

> *"Almighty God, we acknowledge our dependence upon Thee, and we beg Thy blessings upon us, our parents, our teachers and our country. Amen."*

The case, Engel v. Vitale, that was brought about by the parents soon reached the Supreme Court, which was the very intention of the lawsuit. Following their earlier ruling in 1947 that popularized the phrase "Separation of Church and State," the Supreme Court (still chaired by Hugo Black and other Progressive FDR appointees) ruled that the daily prayer violated the Establishment Clause of the First Amendment. Despite the fact that the prayer was entirely voluntary, the Court held the opinion that the mere promotion of a religion is sufficient to establish a violation of the Separation of Church and State.

Beginning in the late 1940s, Hugo Black wrote many decisions relating to the Establishment Clause, in which he consistently insisted on the strict Separation of Church and State. Under Chief Justice Hugo Black, both prayer and Bible-reading were outlawed in the United States public school system.

1963 – Public School Bible-reading Outlawed

Following on the heels of the ruling against public school prayer, required Bible-reading in public schools was banned by the Supreme Court. On June 17, 1963, the Supreme Court ruled against the school district in Abington School District v. Schempp – and American schools have been declining ever since, and along with them, American society. Test scores and numerous other measurements of society had been gradually improving until this fateful decision – then the indicators exploded off the charts in the opposite direction. Rapes, murders, divorces, substance-abuse, unwanted pregnancies and other indicators began skyrocketing within months of this Supreme Court decision.

The Abington case began when Edward Schempp, a Unitarian Universalist in Abington Township, Pennsylvania, filed suit against the Abington School District in the United States District Court to prohibit the enforcement of a Pennsylvania state law that required his children to hear and sometimes read portions of the Bible as part of their public school education. The Bible formed much of the basis of Western civilization and government, philosophy, and history, and it was often read in that context in the schools, rather than in a religious context. Soon the case advanced to the Supreme Court, which ruled that prayer or the reading of Scripture in public schools was unconstitutional. The case received even more attention after it was combined with Murray v. Curlett which was initiated by the American Atheist founder, Madalyn Murray O'Hair.

185

Like a handful of other states, Pennsylvania law contained a statute that compelled school districts to perform brief Bible-readings in the morning before class. Twenty-five other states had laws allowing for "optional" Bible-readings, while the other states had no laws supporting or banning Bible-reading. At the time, several State courts had already ruled Bible-readings in public schools unconstitutional as the result of the Supreme Court's earlier rulings on school prayer and the Separation of Church and State.

While the Supreme Court (again led by Hugo Black) ruled that the compulsory Bible-reading was unconstitutional because it violated the Establishment Clause, it did so primarily because the state law was compulsory. The Bible was not banned from public school, but students could not be compelled to read it; they could still read it voluntarily, of course, as any other piece of historical or religious literature. However, the ACLU again intentionally misconstrued the ruling and has now effectively banned all Bible-reading in public schools through intimidation and the threat of expensive lawsuits and negative publicity. To the secular humanists' delight, the nation which was founded on the idea of "freedom of religion" has become the nation "free of religion." But has the removal of the Bible, the moral foundation of America, been good for the country? Certainly not! Just pick up the newspaper or turn on the news!

Before the Bible was expelled from public schools, the main behavioral problems were gum-chewing, horse-play, and sometimes (though rarely) smoking. Today, the main behavioral problems in schools are drugs, alcohol, assaults, mass school-shootings, and even gang-rapes. When God was expelled from America's schools, He was all but expelled from the rest of society as well. When God is removed from a segment of society, a spiritual vacuum is created which is immediately filled by whatever the society worships besides God: money, power, fame, lust, etc.

How do most un-churched children receive moral values if the primary source of moral values is removed? They now

186

receive them mostly from television, their peers, and to a minor extent, their parents. Is it any wonder that America has lost her character and spiritual moorings since that fateful decision? After that decision, America experienced one of the worst periods in her history which included the assassination of her beloved president, JFK, other political assassinations, race-riots, revolutionary groups, and the creation of radical philosophies that we are still struggling with today.

When America – as represented by the Supreme Court – asked God to leave the public schools, He politely obliged and took with Him the protections and blessings He had bestowed upon America for most of its history. America sowed the wind, but has been reaping the whirlwind ever since.

1964 – Sex Education in Public Schools

With the invention of the birth-control pill, the Kinsey Reports, the increasing availability of pornography, and no more moral responsibilities imposed on the schools by the Bible, it was only natural that sex education began being taught in the public schools.

In 1964, SIECUS (Sexuality Information and Education Council of the United States) was founded by Dr. Mary Calderone, the medical director of Planned Parenthood. As the educational arm of Planned Parenthood, the stated purpose of SIECUS was to promote sex education in all public schools and educate students in order to allow them to freely explore their own sexuality in any manner they may choose.

Before SIECUS, sex education was the sole responsibility of parents, and abstinence before marriage was usually taught. Not only that, but discussions about sex were usually reserved for older teens, not for children. But this conflicted with Planned Parenthood's interests – in terms of money, Planned Parenthood and other groups saw teenagers and even children as a huge untapped market, and they realized that if they could educate

187

the children about sex rather than the parents, their business would boom. And it did.

In 1977, Mary Calderone stated that a child has a fundamental right "to know about sexuality and to be sexual." In fact, encouraging the sexuality of children was a primary goal to Calderone, since she believed that children are sexual from birth and saw no reason to restrict the sexual behaviors in children. If sex education is taught for one or two months for several years with little or no moral structure, how can parents or churches possibly compete for the children's value system? Which is precisely the point – in terms of education, parents and churches cannot compete with the public schools; there simply aren't enough hours in the day.

SIECUS still exists today and has the goals of actively opposing programs that try to teach abstinence, encouraging childhood sexuality, and forcing widespread acceptance of the homosexual agenda. The public schools are SIECUS's main classrooms and they tirelessly promote their immoral agenda at the expense of the parents and other taxpayers.

1969 – The Gay Rights Movement

The "Gay Rights Movement" (or Gay Liberation Movement) began with the Stonewall Riots in New York City. For most of America's history, sodomy and other homosexual activities were illegal – and seldom practiced (or at least done so in secret). However, with the fraudulent statistics cited in the Kinsey Report and the explosion of the Sexual Revolution, homosexual activity increased also. The Stonewall Inn was a homosexual bar owned by the Mafia that violently resisted the frequent police-raids against gay-bars and gay-hotels. The riots in Greenwich Village lasted several days before the situation was diffused. A year later, the first Gay Pride marches occurred in Chicago, Los Angeles, New York, and San Francisco which commemorated the anniversary of the riots.

Our American Awakening

Today, Gay Pride events are held annually throughout the world toward the end of June to mark the Stonewall Riots. Since that time, the Gay Rights Movement has become yet another Civil Rights Movement that seeks to press its own set of values upon America through the media, the education system, the arts, and other avenues of society. Over the last two decades, the legalization of gay-marriage has become the foremost civil rights issue of our era, with a majority of our youth strongly favoring gay-marriage in the name of equality and fairness.

1970 – "No-fault" Divorce

In 1970, "no-fault" divorce became a reality in the United States. Previously in order to obtain a divorce, evidence of abuse, adultery, abandonment, felony, or other grounds for divorce had to be given before a divorce could be granted. However, people began manufacturing evidence and testimonies to obtain a divorce, and various lawyers and judges objected to the legal requirements for divorce. In essence, people had to prove "breach of contract" in order to leave the marriage, since marriage is essentially a social and financial contract between a man and a woman. Just like business contracts cannot be easily broken or disregarded on a whim, neither could marriage contracts.

Once "no-fault" divorce became legalized, the institution of marriage in America became even more devalued than it already was after the Sexual Revolution of the Sixties. People began divorcing because they were no longer in love, because their feelings had changed, or simply because of "irreconcilable differences." Carrie Lukas of the Independent Women's Forum, has stated that "no fault divorce makes the marriage contract effectively no contract at all." She has also stated, "People wonder why marriage as an institution is in trouble. One reason could be that the legal system has devalued the marriage contract and made marriage a less attractive institution."

189

The ease of divorce also helped trigger the rise of live-in relationships, in which a couple simply lives together with no legal requirements or responsibilities – or protections. Marriage is the most basic, fundamental contract of society and in the West, it usually protects women and provides security and helps prevent poverty, and especially financial security in the event of divorce.

Many people today question why marriages must be granted by the State when it has no business in that civil institution. However, it became involved to protect those harmed by divorce or abandonment – usually the women and children – who had no recourse when their husbands and fathers left them with no means to provide for themselves. Again, the State became involved when people abandoned or violated their commitments.

After the advent of "no-fault" divorce, the divorce rates declined, but mainly because fewer people were getting married.

1972 – Hardcore Pornography Goes Mainstream

As the pornography industry matured and grew, the progressive, addictive nature of pornography worsened. In 1972, the movie "Deep Throat" was produced by members of the Colombo Mafia family, which only fed more perverted fantasies and mainstreamed oral sex. After the movie became popular, women were increasingly pressured by boyfriends and husbands to perform similar degrading acts on demand.

Because of the movie's popularity and the widely publicized extra-marital affairs of former President Bill Clinton in the Oval Office, America's younger generations don't even consider these degrading acts as sex. Planned Parenthood and other groups encourage the practice of oral sex – especially among teens – as a safe alternative to sexual intercourse. With groups like Planned Parenthood advertising directly to teens and writing the sex education curriculum in our public schools, is it any wonder why America has lost all moral common-sense and self-restraint?

Along with the mainstreaming of hardcore pornography, adult bookstores, massage parlors, strip clubs, and gay bathhouses began to proliferate across the United States. Since unconstrained sex is addictive and progressive, more illicit sexual experiences are required for the participants to get the same "high" as before. Soon wild, unrestrained sexual perversions with multiple partners, homosexual and bisexual behaviors, orgies, and other depraved forms of sexual activities became more and more commonplace – especially with the new videotape technology introduced in the early 1980s.

Because videocassette players were cheap, portable, and easy to use, pornographers immediately began producing and distributing thousands of pornographic videos. More than any other technology, videotapes caused the pornographic industry to boom; by 1998 there were more pornography outlets in the United States than McDonald's restaurants. In modern pornography, literally no form of sexual behavior is too illicit for sale.

1972 – Adult-Child Sex Relations

After the Gay Rights Movement had become more tolerated and accepted in the American culture, the National Coalition of Gay Organizations adopted a platform that included this demand: "Repeal of all laws governing the age of sexual consent."

Emerging from the Gay Rights Movement, the North American Man-Boy Love Association (NAMbLA) was born, though most homosexual groups deny any link between the two. NAMbLA, the primary group for man-boy relations has one stated goal: to remove any and all restrictions against adult/child sex. David Thorstad (one of their spokesmen) states that their ultimate objective is the "freedom of sexual expression for young people and children," a goal unchanged

191

since the founding of their wicked, perverted organization. Former ACLU attorney Ruth Bader Ginsberg (one of our sitting Supreme Court justices) co-authored a report recommending that the age of consent for sexual acts be lowered to 12 years of age. It should be noted that Planned Parenthood and SIECUS have pushed for lowering the age of consent throughout their history as well.

1973 – Abortion is Legalized

On January 22, 1973, the Supreme Court ruled on two highly controversial decisions in the same day that made abortion legal in the United States: Roe v. Wade and Doe v. Bolton. Both cases were later proven to be all but manufactured in order to create a court-case that could be appealed to the Supreme Court. Both were based on lies and false testimonies which were later recanted; the plaintiff Norma McCorvey (known in the trial as "Jane Roe") returned to obscurity after the case was decided. In 1994, McCorvey converted to Christianity and expressed deep remorse for her part in the Supreme Court decision. Since her conversion, McCorvey has worked in the pro-life movement.

Though the Supreme Court ruled that women had the "right" to terminate a pregnancy at any stage of development up to the point at which the unborn child could survive outside the womb (even with medical assistance), abortionists can still legally abort infants up to the moment before actual live birth. Since this ruling, abortion has been protected under the Privacy Clause of the Fourth Amendment and the Equal Protection Clause of the Fourteenth Amendment of the Constitution. In the forty years of legalized abortion, over 55 million infants have been aborted – at least two generations of Americans. In 2011, it was revealed that in New York City alone, 41% of all pregnancies end in abortion. Approximately 90% of all abortions occur during the first trimester, before the 13th week of gestation.

As if a typical abortion wasn't grotesque enough, in 1992, William Mudd Martin Haskell invented the Intact Dilation and Extraction (IDX) abortion procedure, better known as partial-birth abortion. In this horrible, tortuous procedure, the baby is manipulated to be delivered feet-first ("breach") and then the entire body of the baby is delivered – except for the head. The abortionist then jabs a pair of scissors into the base of the baby's skull and severs the brainstem, and then proceeds to suck out the brains with a high-suction vacuum, causing the baby's head to collapse before finishing the "delivery." Partial-birth abortion was banned in the United States in 2003, though other methods of late-term abortions have been invented.

It should be noted that Barack Obama has skirted the issue of the ban on partial-birth abortions by voting "present" whenever the legislation has been put before him (as per Planned Parenthood's advice), though he voted several times against the "born alive" bill in Illinois. He has also voiced personal concerns whether the partial-birth abortion ban is unconstitutional, though he didn't explicitly declare his support for or against the ban. However, his wife Michelle has strongly voiced her opinion that partial-birth abortions are a "legitimate medical procedure" in a 2004 fundraising letter.

1980 – Ten Commandments Outlawed

In 1980, as the battle over the Separation of Church and State continued, the Supreme Court struck down a state law that required a copy of the Ten Commandments to be posted on the wall of each public school classroom in Kentucky. As in previous cases, the Establishment Clause of the First Amendment (coupled with the Fourteenth Amendment) was cited. Because the Ten Commandments display in the classrooms lacked a secular legislative purpose, they were deemed to be violating the First Amendment.

The latest battle over the Ten Commandments occurred in the courtroom itself, in which several Kentucky courthouses prominently displayed the Ten Commandments, which of course the ACLU objected to. The ACLU sued and the case went to the Supreme Court in McCreary v. ACLU of Kentucky. In 2005, the Supreme Court again ruled that the display was unconstitutional and ordered that the Ten Commandments be removed. Meanwhile, those same Ten Commandments remain prominently displayed on the wall behind the justices on the Supreme Court, as they have been for the last two centuries.

1994 – Free, Instant Pornography

In the mid-1990s, the Internet was launched and quickly became the latest and greatest form of information medium. As with videotapes, pornographers immediately established a foothold on the new medium, claiming that their "speech" (displaying and offering pornographic material on the Internet) is protected by the First Amendment. With the advent of the Internet, the most vile, depraved expressions of human perversion are only a click away and instantly available to everyone. In 2012, polls show that over 50% of the pastors in the United States regularly view pornography on the Internet. Another Christian survey reveals that approximately 70% of men and 20% of women polled are addicted to pornography. Pornography sites encompass 12% of all the sites on the entire Internet, and searches for pornography constitute more than 25% of all search-engine requests.

2003 – State Sodomy Laws Overturned

Though most states had already abolished or repealed their sodomy laws since the 1960s, the Supreme Court in a 6-3 decision (Lawrence v. Texas) overturned the remaining sodomy laws in fourteen Southern and Western States. Justice William Kennedy (who wrote the majority opinion) declared that no state has the right to interfere with the private sexual activities of homosexuals. However, seventeen years before the 2003 decision, the Supreme Court had ruled in Bowers v. Hardwick that states do indeed have the right to restrict certain kinds of sexual conduct. The Tenth Amendment also clearly leaves these decisions to the States – or the people.

In his dissent against the majority opinion, Justice Antonin Scalia declared: *"State laws against bigamy, same-sex marriage, adult incest, prostitution, masturbation, adultery, fornication, bestiality, and obscenity are sustainable only in light of Bowers' validation of laws based upon moral choices. Every single one of these laws is called into question by today's decision."*

Indeed – by ruling against the States' sovereignty in governing one form of sexual behavior, the States no longer have any basis for prohibiting any other form of sexual behavior, including polygamy, bestiality, and pedophilia. The rulings of the Supreme Court since the Progressive Era have turned the United States of America from a nation based upon liberty and individual morality into one based upon licentiousness and depravity.

2004 – Same Sex Marriage

Since the normalization of homosexuality, advocates of civil unions and same-sex marriage have been pressing for equal rights for gays and lesbians to marry. In order to protect traditional marriage, the Defense of Marriage Act (DOMA) was enacted in 1996, which prevents the federal government from recognizing same-sex marriages and allows each State to not recognize same-sex marriages performed in other States. Since same-sex marriage is debated just as much as abortion, leaving the matter up to the States is far less contentious than the Supreme Court ruling one way or the other (as they did with many other hot-button social issues). However, though DOMA is still on the books and supposed to be enforced as the law of the land, Barack Obama and his Justice Department has refused to defend the law in court.

Since 2004, Connecticut, Iowa, Massachusetts, New Hampshire, New York, Vermont, and the District of Columbia have legalized same-sex marriage. Several other states have ballot initiatives to legalize same-sex marriage, while many other states have amended their constitutions to ban same-sex marriage. Given the consistent overreaching of the Supreme Court, it's likely only a matter of time before same-sex marriage is legalized – and constitutionally protected – in the United States of America.

2010 – Affordable Care Act

In 2010, the Affordable Care Act was signed into law and later upheld by the Supreme Court in 2012, effectively nationalizing the healthcare system in the United States. Not only will the federal government have complete control over the healthcare of individuals, the ACA constitutes the largest expansion in both contraceptives and abortion in history. From LifeNews.com:

Firstly, the Act will permit health insurance plans that provide abortion coverage to participate in the state Exchanges. This means that health insurance plans that provide coverage for abortion services will be federally subsidized with your tax dollars.

Secondly, in order to give the perception that the federal government is not paying for the abortions, the Act requires that EVERY enrollee in plans that cover abortion— regardless of his or her sincerely held religious or moral convictions—must pay a separate insurance premium that will be pooled and used to pay for abortion services for other enrollees. The "abortion premium mandate" and the federal subsidization of health insurance plans that cover abortion expand the government's involvement in abortion coverage beyond anything that we have seen before.

The "preventive care" mandate in the ACA is also a great expansion of abortion because it is being used to require nearly every health insurance plan to pay for coverage for all FDA approved "contraceptives" without co-pay. This includes drugs with known life-ending mechanisms of action—including the abortion inducing drug "ella."

Further, the ACA does not comprehensively prohibit the funding of abortion with the federal tax dollars that are authorized by and appropriated through the Act. This is a loop-hole that several states tried to exploit when they sought funding for abortion by including it in their "high-risk" insurance pool proposals. Once these attempts were exposed by pro-life groups, the Department of Health and Human Services issued regulations to prohibit abortion coverage through the pools. However, the White House was clear that these restrictions did not set a precedent for restrictions on abortion for other ACA programs. And, since there is no express prohibition on funding of abortion in the Act, there is nothing to stop states, pro-abortion groups, or the Obama Administration from trying to exploit other loop-holes.

Because of the outrage over the unpopular healthcare law and the recent upheavals in American politics, several Republicans (and even some Democrats) have vowed to repeal and replace the healthcare law in order to put individuals – rather than bureaucrats in the federal government – back in control of their healthcare.

For the past century, America's broken moral compass and rising tide of immorality has been responsible for creating most of the cultural and national problems that are now overwhelming us. Our declining national character and our collapsing civil institutions are intrinsically joined – as one decreases and declines, so does the other. And as our problems increase and our civil institutions collapse, more Progressive, authoritarian government institutions are needed to combat our lack of self-governance and rising dependence. For the last century, too many Americans have come to believe that more money, more government, and more education will solve our problems, but they've only continued to make them worse. Whenever there's a problem in education, defense, or energy, the immediate answer from Washington is to haphazardly throw billions of dollars at it and hope it goes away before the next election cycle begins.

In our desperate search for answers, we have become more and more debased and foolish, while the solution – national repentance and a revival of our Judeo-Christian character – is now nearly unthinkable. G.K. Chesterton summed up America's moral decline when he said, *"When people stop believing in God, they don't believe in nothing – they believe in anything."*

When a civilization collapses, it usually doesn't happen all at once, but is merely the grand finale after a long period of decline, of rampant immorality, loss of national identity, and lack of purpose. If America is to endure, we must rediscover who we are as Americans and what makes America a truly extraordinary country.

Chapter 7 - Who Are Americans?

"America is great because she is good. If America ceases to be good, America will cease to be great." – Alexis de Tocqueville

During his high-flying presidential campaign of 2008, Barack Obama declared that he was going to "fundamentally transform America." As typical at the time, the crowds cheered wildly and some even fainted at his carefully-chosen words and manufactured charisma. However, what did he really mean by that statement? Isn't America her citizens – We the People – us and our fellow Americans? Would his supporters have cheered (and fainted) as they did if he would've promised to "fundamentally transform Americans" – the people rather than the abstract nation? And after more than four years of his presidency, has he succeeded in his goals?

In the traditional measure of presidential success, Obama has been an utter failure. But he never said he wanted to become the best president – he said he wanted to transform the nation. With that standard in mind, he has been an incredible success. He has kept very few of his campaign promises, often methodically, deliberately going against his own speeches, promises, and platform. Rather than have one of the most transparent presidencies, his has been rife with misdirection, corruption, and crony capitalism. That's another sign of a declining republic: the election (and re-election) of willful, lesser men and women to high office who keep few of their promises and fill the government with corruption.

But throughout his presidency, Obama has been consistent in that one, broad, over-arching goal: to fundamentally transform America – and fundamentally transform Americans. And he has been doing just that.

Today in America, poverty has increased over 15% since Obama took office, the national-debt for the entire nation's history has risen an astounding 50% in four years, college tuition and health insurance costs have risen 25%, gas prices have doubled (though they are slowly decreasing), America's credit-rating has slipped from AAA to AA, the average family's net-worth has dropped 39%, and the number of long-term unemployed has doubled to over 5.4 million people. The Misery Index has increased by 65% and the number of food-stamp recipients has risen nearly 50%. Like it or not, this is now Obama's America.

After four long years, Americans are growing accustomed to being miserable, paying high prices for gas, food, and energy, taking government subsidies/welfare benefits without a second thought, and not working or being productive. Indeed, Obama IS fundamentally transforming America – by fundamentally transforming Americans. And while he may still blame his predecessor George W. Bush for the dire economic problems, his own policies have greatly exacerbated and prolonged them – just like FDR's policies during the Great Depression. Obama is changing Americans into the very people he and his wife regularly insult and denigrate: fat, lazy, over-indulgent consumers. But shallow, unaware, dependent voters are what he wants more of because they always vote for his party and other Progressives.

After 20+ years of multiculturalism run amuck, people have either forgotten – or are forgetting – what it means to be an American. Our pathetic public education system, politically correct media, nanny-state governments, and twisted/perverted Hollywood entertainment industry have tragically altered Americans' self-image. We are becoming the very caricatures the mainstream media portrays us to be.

Appallingly, Barack Obama – as the President of the United States of America – has frequently echoed those same remarks, saying that America is just as special as every other nation is, meaning that American exceptionalism is all in our heads. And

200

of course, when everyone is special, no one is. Not only that, Obama has remarked several times that America is not an exceptional nation. If he thinks that, then why did he even bother running for the Senate or the Presidency? Who wants to help run a country they don't love with every fiber of their being? Unless they mean to harm or "fundamentally transform" that nation by holding a powerful leadership position. Most Progressives may say they love America, but their reasons behind that affection are different than most traditional Americans. Progressives love America for her radical individualism and what they think it could be (another utopia) instead of what it is and its heritage.

In 1831, a young Frenchman named Alexis de Tocqueville toured America and sought after the source of her greatness. After all, France and America had been allies during the American Revolution, and France had soon followed in her footsteps with a revolution of her own. However, the two upheavals could not have been more different. The French Revolution was lawless, tyrannical, and extremely bloody, whereas America's was relatively confined to the battlefields. When the fighting was over and the Constitution was ratified, Americans settled down and quickly rebuilt their nation. Meanwhile, France continued to experience political upheavals that eventually culminated in a dictatorship under Napoleon.

Though the original source of this quote from Alexis de Tocqueville has been recently called into question, it still bears a great amount of truth in rediscovering who we are as Americans – and what makes America special among all the other countries in the world:

"I sought for the greatness and genius of America in her commodious harbors and her ample rivers, and it was not there. I sought for the greatness and genius of America in her fertile fields and boundless forest, and it was not there. I sought for the greatness and genius of America in her rich mines and her vast world commerce, and it was not there. I

*sought for the greatness and genius of America in her public
school system and her institutions of learning, and it was not
there. I sought for the greatness and genius of America in
her democratic congress and her matchless constitution, and
it was not there. Not until I went into the churches of
America and heard her pulpits flame with righteousness did
I understand the secret of her genius and power. America is
great because America is good, and if America ever ceases
to be good, America will cease to be great."*

If we are to heal our nation and restore America's national
soul, we must first rediscover who we are as Americans.
Because of a century of Progressive revisionism, we cannot rely
upon the media or our schools to accurately tell us, which
means we need to relearn our history and our traits for
ourselves. At the heart of relearning what it means to be an
American is understanding the concepts of "Americanism."

Americanism can be summed up by what Dennis Prager
refers to as the "American Trinity": individual liberty, belief in
God, and "e pluribus unum" ("out of many, one"). These three
fundamental concepts define both the nation and the idea of
America and undergird her very foundations and institutions. If
any of those three American fundamentals fall, the other two
are greatly weakened and Americanism falters. The three
fundamentals check and balance one another, yet also support
one another. But at the center of the American Trinity is the
belief in God, by which the other two cannot exist – the very
"leg" that the Progressives and the secularists have been
attacking for the last century.

In conjunction with Americanism, what defines us as
Americans? Deep down in our hearts and souls, what makes
Americans different from other peoples of the earth? What are
our traditional character traits from our earliest days through
most of our history? When illegal aliens sneak across the
borders into the United States, does that instantly make them

Americans? No, it does not – no more than you stepping into a garage makes you a car.

So what makes Americans "American"? The traits/characteristics which follow are not implied to mean that ONLY Americans have these traits, but that more often than not, we exhibit these traits more than other peoples. Also, these are meant to be broad and general observations, and by no means all Americans throughout all our history have exhibited these traits.

It must also be noted that each one of these American character traits are under assault by the federal government, the politically-correct media, and much of our education system.

We are Independent

The foremost defining American character trait is independence, stemming from long before the days of the Revolutionary War. We don't like being told what to do, and we tend not to take orders very well. We bristle when ordered around, even though we will still often obey those orders. We don't like being "put in a box" and ruled by distant, elitist central-planners and inherently distrust "kings" and those who imagine themselves to be such.

The primary means by which our American spirit of independence is under attack is our recent acceptance of and growing reliance on government subsidies, welfare, and entitlements. All these "benefits" make us dependent on someone else (usually the central-planners in Washington D.C.) and steadily crush our spirit of independence and self-reliance. And the central-planners inherently know that; it's hard to enact meaningful reforms, much less conduct revolutions, if most of the populace is cashing government checks every month.

Since the advent of the Progressive Era, we have been slowly but steadily forging our own chains of slavery and dependence by the Progressive candidates we put into office and by embracing their programs and policies.

We are Creative/Inventive

Americans are – and always has been – one of the most entrepreneurial peoples in the world. In many parts of the country, "Yankee ingenuity" is still alive and well even far outside New England where it originated. From simple modifications in our tools (like the Yankee screwdriver) to the numerous inventions over the past three hundred years, America has been an astoundingly inventive nation. Hundreds of thousands of inventions (at least) which have improved life all over the world have been invented in America, such as the cotton gin, the Franklin stove, the steamboat, air-conditioning, the telephone, the telegraph, the light-bulb, the assembly line, the airplane, nuclear energy, the space shuttle, the personal computer, the Internet, and countless others. And then there are the vast amounts of art, paintings, buildings, sculptures, and millions of books that have come from America.

Why have so many of these inventions occurred in America? Most occurred here because of our system of limited government, individual desire to learn and improve ourselves, the widespread availability of books and education resources, equal protection under the law, the free-market (capitalism), the protection of private property, and our traditional Judeo-Christian work-ethic of "If you don't work, you don't eat."

We are Entrepreneurial

From her earliest days, a significant portion of Americans were entrepreneurs, primarily out of necessity. When the first settlers came to America from across the sea, they encountered new lands with new creatures, fertile soils, unique foliage, and climates that were different than those they were used to. And given the vast distance between the New World and their home countries, they had no other choice than to experiment, discover, and refine what crops grew in which climates and soils, which domesticated animals thrived in each climate, and how to survive in the unique new land they found themselves in. If they couldn't quickly adapt to their surroundings, they would starve or die, as happened in several of the early colonies.

Not only did the farmers have to adapt their skills to function in the New World, but so did the other settlers, creating shops and businesses to enable people to buy and sell their products and services. At first, many supported the agricultural industry, but soon created other industries used to build villages, towns, and then cities. The settlers took their knowledge and skills from the Old World and adapted them to the New World, creating new products, methods of production, and industries to help them survive and later thrive. Along the way, they discovered more efficient ways of creating their products, and new inventions and production methods only deepened America's entrepreneurial spirit.

Since Americans tend to be independent-thinkers and creative/inventive, it's only natural that they would also apply their skills and knowledge to starting businesses of their own or finding a way to sell their inventions rather than rely on others for their employment/survival.

We are Individualistic

Individualism is a close brother to independence and in America, the spirit of individualism runs very deep. Our Declaration of Independence reinforces this character trait in decreeing that all men are created equal, meaning that we all have inalienable rights as humans created in God's image. Individualism is rooted in individual freedom, which bristles at the notion that people can be lumped into categories and groups and therefore considered to have the same feelings, hopes, and desires as everyone in that class. Individualism asserts that everyone is unique and free to express their ideas and pursue their own path in life. Traditionally in America, people are free to embark on their individual pursuits up to the point where they interfere with other people's pursuits, which are then resolved through the law and the courts.

The greatest enemy of individualism is egalitarianism (complete equality throughout society) and Marxism in any form, especially socialism and communism. Marxism spurns the very idea of individualism, desiring to treat all people the same so they may have equal outcomes: the same amount of education, consume the same amount of food, fuel, and other resources, and have the same standard of living. While Marxism attempts to resolve societal inequalities and provide "social justice," it always fails because it acts contrary to human nature, namely individuality. We as people are NOT all the same, regardless of whether there are two of us or two billion.

Individualism functions best under the Rule of Law and under a simple set of broad yet well-known moral common laws, such as: don't steal, don't murder, etc. Radical individualism occurs when individualism is exalted above the needs/well-being of the society, which often leads to selfishness and ingratitude, as people tend to only think of themselves and their own needs/wants instead of the others around them. Individualism can often be a double-edged sword, especially when economic and social disparities become increasingly pronounced, such as the wealth-gap and the "evil rich" that the Progressives continually vilify (though most Progressive leaders happen to be quite wealthy).

We are Adaptable

Along with being inventive and entrepreneurial, Americans tend to be highly adaptable to whatever situation they find themselves in. Rather than sit around and wait for someone else to come along and take care of a problem, Americans will often find a way to get it done themselves – and often cheaper, faster, and better. Again, this characteristic is deeply entrenched in the American psyche. When our ancestors were settling the New

World, they had no alternative but to figure out how to solve most problems on their own – their very survival depended on it.

In later times because of costs, shortages, and limited time/money, Americans had to adapt the resources and parts they had in order to solve their problems. Often, new inventions, processes, or even industries were created by this compulsion to adapt. This characteristic of Americans seems to hold true whether they find themselves on the frontier, on the farm, at the office, or on the battlefield.

Americans tend to enjoy learning (though not necessarily in the classroom) and typically had a solid foundation in the "3R's": reading, writing, and arithmetic, as well as the physical sciences. Having broad, practical, applied knowledge is critical in being able to adapt to new, unpredictable situations/problems. One of the reasons why Americans have been becoming less adaptive, creative, and entrepreneurial is likely due to the 18+ years we're spending in the classrooms (13 years in public school, ~5 in college) learning theories instead of applying our knowledge in the "real world."

We are Practical

Traditionally, Americans have tended to be practical and prudent with their money, time, and resources. This was another byproduct of living in the New World and then later on the frontier with very limited supplies, money, man-power, and time. The practical nature of Americans is revitalized during economic downturns, which forces them to make do with what they have for as long as possible. Especially on farms and rural areas, Americans will find ways to fix broken equipment themselves, or rig up some means to get the job done rather than sit around and do nothing about it.

Since the Baby Boomer generation of the 1960s onward, the practicalness of Americans has steadily waned, with millions of families taking on vast amounts of personal debt. Consequently,

207

our government has followed suit and has tripled the national debt in less than fifteen years. However, due to the extended years of the Great Recession with high gas prices and high unemployment, it appears that America's practical side is starting to show again.

We are Informal

Americans from most eras have tended to be informal, both in dress and mannerisms. Such informality is sometimes construed by others as being backwards, rustic, rude, uncaring, or improper, but those are typically not intentional. Americans reserve their formality for special occasions, holidays, and religious observances, but like to relax and be informal most other times, choosing comfort and practicality over formality at work and in public.

We also tend to be rather informal in our speech and our writing, preferring to quickly communicate our ideas without regard to their "properness." This has led to a wider acceptance of American English as opposed to British English, though the English language as a whole is still rather cumbersome and convoluted.

We are Stubborn

Stubbornness, which could also be construed as "being committed" is another deep-seated American trait. Being stubborn was needed to settle the New World in which few conveniences existed, and later in settling the frontier, fighting the French, the Indians, the Spanish, the British, and later, ourselves in the bloody Civil War. Time and time again when facing incredible odds, Americans stuck with it and pressed forward, refusing to give up and turn back. Americans hate surrendering, losing, and giving up, even if it's when the conflict ended in a stalemate or truce. This is one reason the Korean War and the Vietnam War left such a bad taste in our mouths: we were committed but not allowed to fully win those wars.

The Revolutionary War in particular required an incredible commitment, as Washington and his ragtag army continued to fight though they lacked supplies, training, and even much hope at times. But through their commitment to freedom and their refusal to surrender, as well as a healthy measure of Divine providence, they won their independence from the Old World – and ours. The same would hold true in the Civil War, the Great War, and in WWII.

This American characteristic would also prove critical to our inventors, businessmen, entrepreneurs, and other laborers, from the invention of the electric light-bulb in which thousands of combinations were tried without success, to the building of the transcontinental railroad, the Golden Gate Bridge, the Brooklyn Bridge, the Empire State Building, the Hoover Dam, inventing the airplane, the automobile, the personal computer, and the endless list of other inventions and efforts that required sheer determination and stubbornness to succeed.

We are Religious

In their book "The Light and the Glory," Peter Marshall and David Manuel make the case that America was intended to be settled by religious people. Expedition after expedition tried to settle North America without success – like Jamestown, Roanoke, and others – but it wasn't until devout Christian people fleeing persecution and seeking to shine the light of the Gospel in the New World that the settlements succeeded and became permanent. Early America was predominantly settled by men and women who came seeking God rather than gold, as was the case in South America. Compare the history of the two hemispheres of the New World – they are like night and day, with Central and South America being plagued with invasion after invasion, revolution after revolution, and much of which remains in terrible poverty despite their vast wealth of gold and other natural resources.

It was in America that the Judeo-Christian variation of Christianity took root, flourished and grew, and soon spread over the continent. Rather than being plagued with endless religious wars as Old Europe, Americans learned to be tolerant of other beliefs and live in peace and prosperity with those who held vastly different beliefs than they did. The practical application of Judeo-Christian principles in everyday life blessed America and enabled it to become a great nation despite its many challenges.

Tragically, the religious character of America has been waning over the last century with the state-enforced teaching of secularism and Evolution. But despite the culture, media, and education being quite anti-religious, roughly 60% of Americans still pray every day, and less than 50% believe in Evolution. A high proportion of Americans still regularly contribute to religious organizations and charities, though the Obama administration is trying to discourage this by attempting to limit or remove the tax deductions for such giving. Since the Progressive Era, the steady creep of socialism in the United States has also caused our religious character to decline, at least until recently; the aggressive policies of the Obama administration have driven many Americans back to their roots of religion, independence, and limited government.

For the last century, America has been the predominant missionary nation to the rest of the world. Even today, America sends out more Christian missionaries and financial aid to poverty-stricken nations than any other country around the globe.

We are Risk-takers

From the first pilgrims who decided to leave everything they knew to come to the strange, unknown New World, Americans have been risk-takers. Time and time again, Americans have been known to literally "put everything on the line" for what they believed in, whether it's settling the frontiers, investing in their own inventions or businesses, or fighting wars where they were severely outmanned and outgunned.

Our "put it all on the line" mentality is what has helped lead to our incredible inventions and developments throughout our short history, as investors are willing to risk their capital on new ideas, inventions, and businesses. Great risks often promise great rewards, and those possibilities still drive multitudes of Americans today.

American risk-taking frequently leads to economic booms, but also to economic busts, such as recessions or even depressions. That is the nature of risk-taking – sometimes we win and sometimes we lose. But at least we try over and over, rather than lie down and let someone else take care of us. Most Americans would still rather gamble their futures in order to pursue their dreams and aspirations than live a comfortable, secure, shackled existence under an all-knowing, all-providing, all-powerful State.

We are Dreamers

Like every generation of Americans, we are still a nation of dreamers – through good times and bad. We still hope for a better future for both ourselves and the generations to come. The American Dream to many is home-ownership, but that is far too narrow. The American Dream is a set of broad ideals that at their core revolve around liberty and self-determination – and with those freedoms, we are able to work hard and be upwardly mobile in our society. The American Dream means that if you apply yourself, you can become anyone you want to be – you are not confined to one particular class or sector of society. Some of our most successful people came out of severe poverty and overcame incredible odds. But because we are a free country governed by the Rule of Law and the principle that all men are created equal, Americans have the opportunities that most of the rest of the world does not.

Sadly, there is a significant portion of America which is losing the American Dream and is even becoming disenchanted with it. Why? Primarily because of government interference and exploding personal and national debt. When people no longer have the freedom to administer their own property the way that they see fit or have to comply with endless regulations and costs, they begin to see their situation as hopeless. Now they must not only overcome the typical odds of risk-taking, but they must also overcome government policies and structures that are working against them. The other source of disenchantment is due to the recent trivializing of the American Dream, which renders it in only materialistic terms, such as buying a new home or a new car. Those are by-products of the American Dream, not the dream itself.

As the federal government expands its scope of power and influence, jobs and investment opportunities are drying up because the people who have money are trying to protect their wealth from onerous taxes and unfair bailouts rather than invest/risk their savings. Why invest your hard-earned money if it's going to be confiscated from high capital-gains taxes, even though that money has already been taxed? Why invest in a car company if the company goes bankrupt and the government then bails them out, while throwing away the corporate bonds? Why sell your house in order to buy a better one if you have to pay rising federal sales taxes on it? Capitalism and wealth-creation only thrive under the consistent, even-handed Rule of Law, equal protection, limited government, and limited taxation.

And that doesn't even begin to take into account the crushing problems that inflation and an exploding national debt are creating. Why should young people save for retirement if their savings are going to be inflated away before they even reach middle age? Why should students go to college if their education costs a fortune but there are limited opportunities for employment when they graduate? Why go to work if you can make more in food-stamps and disability/unemployment benefits than you could at a job? Why should people think about tomorrow when the economic conditions demand that they only think about today?

If the American Dream is to be revived, then both the people and their governments need to behave responsibly and live within their means. Rather than take out enormous debt to go to a university you can't afford, find the best job you can and work your way through school – even if it takes longer. Rather than buying a big new house you can't afford, buy a smaller fixer-upper, improve it and raise its value yourself. As far as the government is concerned, the economic obstacles that continue to be thrown up in our path need to be reduced if not eliminated, and both spending and regulations need to be restored to much lower, common-sense levels. The government can only work against its people for so long before some form of a political revolution – violent or non-violent – occurs.

We are Diverse

Given the sheer variety of the people and the cultures from which they came, Americans have always been very diverse. Even in the colonial days, there were a significant number of blacks who were full citizens under the law (at least in the Northern states). Later, waves of English, Irish, Germans, Italians, Poles, Jews, Chinese, Mexicans, and others from all over the world came to America to forge new lives and seek out new opportunities for themselves and their families.

The sheer diversity of our citizens has helped America become a more tolerant nation, and has helped many different people from all over the world build better lives for themselves and create futures and dreams that would've never been possible. America was once referred to as "the Great Melting Pot" because people who immigrated here adopted American customs and merged them in with their own; the Polish would

213

become just as American as the Irish, the Africans, and the Asians.

However, over the last several decades, multiculturalism has taken root and has rapidly spread, which disparages the notion of the Melting Pot as being racist or intolerant. But the Melting Pot cannot be racist because Americans are not a race – we're a nation of many races. Now immigrants are encouraged to retain their cultures, traditions, and even their native language, while the established Americans are supposed to change to adapt to them, rather than vice-versa.

We are Tolerant

Since the colonial days, as a people Americans have been quite tolerant of those who are different from themselves, despite the decades of slavery and the post-Civil War era. And while there were indeed periods of racial and religious intolerance throughout our history, we have always managed to move past those periods and have learned to tolerate others different from ourselves. Compared to most other nations, America is still one of the most tolerate nations on earth.

The reason for our tolerance goes back to our Judeo-Christian foundations and even to the principles set forth in the Declaration of Independence, namely that "all men are created equal." Over the years, this has led to women's suffrage and equality in society, as well as tearing down the racial barriers that existed even before the Civil War. Rather than blindly persecute others who are different than us, we recognize that they are different and are entitled to their opinions, views, and beliefs.

Throughout our history, we have been encouraged to judge others by their character, their morals, and their ideas rather than on the basis of their religion, their race, their gender, their family/culture, or their background. This stands in stark contrast to most of the world throughout history, even today.

We are Impatient

Americans are impatient – probably more-so today than in other generations. We are naturally restless anyway and hate to wait for much of anything. We tend to want to live life to the fullest, which means often filling our lives with more activities and commitments than we have time for. We always seem to be "on the go" and get very impatient when our time is wasted in traffic, at the DMV, or waiting senselessly in long lines (unless it's for a concert or other entertainment event).

A stereotype of Americans is that we get many of our meals at fast-food places and drive-thrus, and get upset if we have to wait more than sixty seconds for our food, even though it's better than what most of the rest of the world could even imagine. It's often hard for us to slow down and savor the little things in life, like quiet moments and everyday times with our families and loved ones.

Impatience is also characteristic of how we fight our wars, or at least how we expect our wars to be fought. American soldiers like to move fast, strike hard, and then go home. Standing guard during long, drawn-out wars and being on the defensive rather than the offensive is not a characteristic of many American soldiers. Our tolerance for wars is typically five years or less, and we expect to have won the conflict in half that time.

Endless wars or "police actions" with no clear victory in sight discourage not only American soldiers, but their families, friends, and the general population. If we're not in a war to win it, then we shouldn't be committing the lives of our young men and women to it in the first place. Otherwise, people will stop sacrificing their lives for their country if it's obvious that their sacrifice isn't appreciated or is going to be wasted.

We are Patriotic

Along with independence, patriotism is at the core of the vast majority of Americans, or at least it was until the Vietnam War. From the earliest days of the Colonies, Americans have fought to protect their families, their property, and their freedoms from any threat. We deeply love our country and our independence, and most of us are willing to sacrifice our lives to protect our land, our freedom, our property, our families, and our way of life.

Since WWII and the advent of the Cold War, patriotism in America has been faltering. The Vietnam War, the Korean War, even the recent wars in Iraq and Afghanistan run counter to America's character, which is why they become increasing unpopular the longer they continue. Americans are more than willing to go to war after we've been attacked or when our way of life has been threatened, but we are very wary and suspicious of leaders and military actions which push us into unnecessary wars and long, senseless conflicts.

The unpopularity of the Iraq War resulted in a Democrat-controlled Congress with an extreme Progressive Speaker of the House, along with another Progressive controlling the Senate. Then in 2008 as the war continued, Barack Obama ran on an anti-war "Hope and Change" message and was swept into the White House. When the electorate is highly charged due to a divisive war or bad economic conditions, we tend to vote with our emotions rather than our heads – simply because we want "change."

Were American freedoms really threatened during the Korean War, the Vietnam War, and the Iraq War? Not directly, which is the main reason that many view those wars as unnecessary. Each time we fight an unpopular foreign war, the country's radical elements are emboldened and increase their power and standing in our society. Would the Democrat Party have taken such as hard-left turn in the 1960s and 1970s if it wasn't for the Vietnam War and the subsequent anti-war protests and riots?

The rise of the current crop of Progressives, radicals, and revolutionaries are the direct result of the bitter and widespread Vietnam anti-war protests. Progressivism was steadily dying in America until the 1960s and the counter-culture movements.

Would the SDS and Saul Alinsky have been so highly-revered and influential if the Vietnam War had ended earlier or had never been fought? Not likely. Would Barack Obama have been elected president if the Iraq War had never occurred or at least had been better explained? Probably not.

Our Founders were very wary of getting involved in foreign wars and entangling alliances and repeatedly warned us against getting involved in other nations' conflicts. Early in the American republic, George Washington and John Adams struggled to keep America out of the French Revolution even though they were our ally and many Americans wanted to help them. If our homeland has not been attacked or invaded, then what exactly are our soldiers fighting for? Freedom, they say, but freedom exactly for whom? Do the Afghans or Iraqis want freedom? If so, then why aren't they more supportive of our actions?

Not only are foreign wars detrimental to our national morale and values, but they can also be a tyrant's way of eliminating the patriots and those who are willing to sacrifice everything for their country. How many of our young men and women have sacrificed their lives in foreign wars that were not fought with victory in mind? That's something to think about as our soldiers are deployed all over the world with few clear objectives and little direction of victory.

We are Open-minded

Along with being tolerant, Americans often tend to be open-minded in accepting new ideas and new ways of doing things. Of course, this varies from person to person, but as America has become more diverse, we've become more open-minded. Unfortunately, sometimes Americans can be so open-minded that their brains are at risk of falling out (especially with regards to religion and politics)!

Americans are typically quick to embrace new ideas and better ways of doing things, as long as they make sense, are practical, and not overly-expensive. We aren't locked into the notion of "this is the way it's always been done, so this is the way we're always going to do it" mentality, at least in recent generations. As more conveniences and inventions have improved our lives, Americans have become more adaptable and open to new ideas.

We are Charitable

Though our religious makeup has been changing over the last several decades, Americans remain very charitable. As of 2012, the United States is the most charitable nation in the world – and that's after four long years in the Great Recession. During times of hardship, Americans surprisingly tend to give more than during times of prosperity; more churches were planted during those difficult years of the Great Depression than during the Roaring 1920s, even though grander and more extravagant churches were constructed.

Charity and liberty walk hand-in-hand, and having healthy free-markets cause both to increase. The biggest enemies of charitable giving are high taxation and socialism, which rob people of their income and property which they would normally give to help others. Also, as socialism in a society grows, people feel less and less obligated to help their fellow citizens because "someone else" – the government – will take care of them.

One of the widely-popular tax deductions that Barack Obama and other Progressives have pressed for eliminating are the deductions to charity. While some people may give at the end of the year in order to reduce their tax burden, millions more give out of habit and their conscience, with little thought to giving simply to save money on their taxes. After all, if one is greedy or stingy, does it really make sense to give $10,000 away just to save $1,000 in taxes?

Regardless of the reasons why people give to charity, the important thing is that they are giving, and any policy that

218

hampers charitable giving should be prevented or at least discouraged. Encouraging individual people to give makes better and more compassionate societies because giving makes better people.

We are Honest

For most of American history, honesty was just as sacred as property and liberty. Until the last generation or two, shaking hands or giving your word in order to make a commitment was almost as reliable as a signed contract. Our leaders and presidents were famous for their honesty, and telling the truth was not only encouraged, but expected. In the past, companies and banks made multi-million dollar deals with one another simply on a handshake and the understanding that "My word is my bond." It's much faster, easier, and cheaper to make those types of business agreements than it is to bring in high-paid lawyers and draw up long, complicated contracts.

Since the 1980s onward, honesty has given way to legality; "My word is my bond" has been replaced with "So sue me!" Today, contracts and lawsuits clog the legal system and pervert the Rule of Law, as well as encourage the mentality that easy money can be obtained by simply suing someone or a corporation. In the end, the lack of honesty and integrity in our society enriches primarily the lawyers and a tiny group of people willing to exploit the justice system.

Honesty goes hand-in-hand with Judeo-Christian ethics, and as that belief system declines, so does honesty. That's not to say that most other religions do not value honesty, but few are as clear and concise as the commandments of "Thou shalt not steal" and "Thou shalt not bear false witness."

As other moral traits, our honesty has been declining as Progressivism has been increasing in the country. One of the tenants of Progressivism is the redistribution of wealth, by which the government takes from the rich via taxation and then redistributes to the poor via welfare. As wealth-redistribution becomes more entrenched in a society, a sense of "entitlement" settles in, until the poorer people feel they are entitled to the public benefits that are seized from their fellow citizens. Honesty and integrity soon depart, as the wealthier people attempt to retain more of their money while the poor demand more benefits.

Redistribution of wealth – even when done with the best of intentions – always corrupts a society from within because it's essentially stealing (legalized theft) regardless of what sophisticated title it's given or how it's framed. And when the State isn't honest, then that only encourages the people to become dishonest.

We are Skeptical

Americans traditionally tend to be skeptical of "new-fangled" ideas or products, wanting to see things for themselves before supporting them. "Trust but verify" is one of our creeds, and such skepticism has prevented many bad ideas from ever seeing the light of day.

The bulwarks of healthy skepticism are rationalism, common-sense, practicality, and a fair understanding of human nature. Especially in a free-market economy, people have learned to be careful with their time, money, resources, and labor. Skepticism often quickly separates the good ideas and products from the bad, as well as the serious entrepreneurs from those who are out just to make a quick profit. Such skepticism is also used to refine promising ideas into viable products, services, and processes.

We are Compassionate

Even during tough times, Americans are typically compassionate people. The Golden Rule of "treating others the way you wish to be treated" is still widely known and more or less followed in our nation, despite several generations of secular education. However, like charity and patriotism, compassion is slowly but steadily waning as the American society cools towards Christianity, Judaism, and religion in general. When love grows cold in a nation, compassion, manners, and empathy are among the first victims.

As previously mentioned, Americans are usually still the first ones on the scene to rescue, provide emergency supplies, and help rebuild whenever and wherever disaster strikes. When earthquakes or tsunamis occur, people immediately ask "Where are the Americans?" above any other nation or relief group, including the United Nations. Yet when disaster strikes the United States, few countries send us aid – nor do we expect them to.

American compassion doesn't just extend to others during tragedies and calamities, but also during wars. Our soldiers frequently pass out their own water and food to those who have none, as well as candy and treats to children who have never had such luxuries before. How many other foreign soldiers have done that in history – did the Romans? What about the British, the Germans, the Russians, the French, the Japanese, or the Chinese? There are very few that have been known do that, and frequently they have done quite the opposite. And aside from a handful of widely-publicized, disgusting incidents in foreign prisons, Americans treat their prisoners and enemies far better and with much more compassion than other armies – past or present.

We are Hard-working

Americans typically aren't satisfied unless they're steadily, gainfully employed. Most of us find great satisfaction in our employment, as well as wanting to take personal pride in our work. America was built from an untamed land full of potential to be the most advanced nation on the face of the earth. How? With countless years of hard work: clearing the land, preparing the soil, planting and harvesting the crops, and then building villages, towns, cities, and the endless miles of roads that connect them.

From our earliest days, the Judeo-Christian principle that "If a man does not work, he shall not eat" has been firmly entrenched in our society. Even today in our advanced society, people work just as hard and as long today as when our ancestors were clearing the land, though the effort and type of work has changed. And though during the Great Recession, where good jobs are often difficult to come by, most people still want to work and earn a decent living rather than live off the welfare system.

Today, our American work-ethic is under assault from three enemies: labor unions and the sense of entitlement, lax parenting, and growing government welfare programs. Those three enemies discourage hard work at both the expense of the individual and at the expense of the society. America was built upon faith, determination, sweat, toil, honesty, and hard work – and by those characteristics, she will continue to prosper.

We are Restless

Along with hard work, Americans are traditionally restless, with some having an insatiable wander-lust, to others who are serial entrepreneurs, to others who devote their time and energy to their career or hobbies. An old American trait was that they would start building the next house before the roof of the previous one was even finished.

It was this restlessness that quickly settled the frontiers, with Americans taming and civilizing an entire continent in less than a century (not counting the original Thirteen Colonies). This restlessness continues to be a driving characteristic in many Americans today, motivating them to take up new hobbies, see more of the world, or change jobs or even careers when it may not make the most sense.

Americans have a hard time sitting still, at least while they're still fairly mobile and typically need to be doing something, though we do spend far too much time in front of our computers and televisions. Time is precious, and we have a sense that we need to fill it up and keep busy – almost to a fault.

We are Courageous

Like the other character traits that helped us explore the New World and then settle the vast, wild frontiers, Americans are courageous. During the colonial days, we were courageous in our demands for liberty and independence, and then we fought for our beliefs, property, and our way of life – and won that freedom in the face of incredible odds.

Courage is signing a document addressed to your former king that declares your nation to be now free – and knowing that you've essentially signed your own death warrant.

Courage is storming the beaches of Normandy and Omaha Beach, despite knowing that you may not live to see the next sunrise.

Courage is facing your greatest fears and yet remaining in the ranks, even though you want to run for your very life.

Courage is facing down other world leaders, though a devastating nuclear war may be triggered as a result of your actions.

Courage is refusing to take your "designated place" in the back of the bus and surrendering your seat to someone else.

Courage is raising Old Glory on an unprotected hill under heavy artillery fire, knowing that at any moment you could die for your country.

Courage is marching down the street in the face of fire-hoses, police dogs, and the National Guard.

Courage is fighting to the last man and never, ever surrendering.

These are the kinds of courage that American after American has shown during times of war and terrible battles both at home and far away in strange, foreign lands.

Today, our soldiers continue to carry America's heritage of courage and refuse to buckle under tremendous pressure, even when the pressure comes from those in their own government – the very ones they've sworn to protect.

It is these traits and characteristic which have made Americans an exceptional people and the United States of America an exceptional nation:

We are Independent.
We are Creative and Inventive.
We are Entrepreneurial.
We are Individualistic.
We are Adaptable.
We are Practical.
We are Informal.
We are Stubborn.
We are Religious.
We are Risk-takers.
We are Dreamers.
We are Diverse.
We are Tolerant.
We are Impatient.
We are Patriotic.
We are Open-minded.
We are Charitable.
We are Honest.
We are Skeptical.
We are Compassionate.
We are Hard-working.
We are Restless.
We are Courageous.

Many of these traits were ingrained in Americans even before the United States of America came into existence. At that time, however similar we were, America was still a disunited, disparate group of Thirteen British Colonies – until the Declaration of Independence transformed us into a new country.

Chapter 8 - The Appeal and Declaration

"The highest glory of the American Revolution was this; it connected in one indissoluble bond the principles of civil government with the principles of Christianity. From the day of the Declaration...they (the American people) were bound by the laws of God, which they all, and by the laws of The Gospel, which they nearly all, acknowledge as the rules of their conduct." – John Quincy Adams

The document that first bound the Thirteen Colonies together into one new body – one new country – is the Declaration of Independence. In the preface to the Declaration, it doesn't read, "The Thirteen Colonies," but "The Thirteen United States of America," with each State essentially being its own sovereign entity. On July 4th, 1776, thirteen new nation-states proclaimed together in unison that they were declaring their independence from Great Britain. On that day, a new country was born: the United States of America.

Not only did the Declaration of Independence bind Americans together as one country and permanently sever our ties to Great Britain, it defined who we are as a people and our highest ideals, namely our reliance upon God as our Creator and our Provider, our inherent right to self-government, and our belief that all men are created equal – and therefore are all equal in the eyes of God and are to be treated equally under the law. And when our natural rights as a people are grievously and repeatedly violated by our existing government, we have the right to cast off that government and devise another that is better suited to protecting our rights.

Why did our Founders appeal to the Creator in their cry for independence? Because the Creator is the Highest Authority over both Man and his governments. When someone cannot petition their government for a redress of grievances, they must then petition their Creator. The Continental Congress had sent letters and delegations, held peaceful protests, and had attempted every way possible to petition King George and the Parliament to reconsider their arguments, but they had been rebuffed time and time again. The British left the Colonists no alternative other than rebel.

The Founders also frequently referred to God as their "Providence" or their "Provider." But for many in the secular West today, the term "Providence" is the State, not God our Creator. Under Progressivism and Statism, there is no room for God or for "Providence," because that's solely the role of the State. Do we really want our neighbors or some group of distant, largely unaccountable politicians to be our Provider, or do we want God to be our Provider? That is the question that divides the West in the Twenty-First Century, and especially America today.

The worst kind of slavery is that in which one cannot even see or acknowledge that they are essentially serfs or slaves, all the while thinking that they're free. Though we have lost unfathomable freedoms over the last century under Progressivism and the idea of "moving forward," we Americans are still relatively free in comparison to most other Statist-type totalitarian governments. However, our freedoms steadily seep away every time we demand that our government take care of us or give us another benefit. The primary lesson that Americans need to re-learn is that we cannot be free from government intrusion and yet beg that same government to take care of us. If we are to remain a free society, we must also be personally responsible and provide for ourselves and those in need around us.

When we pay taxes, we voluntarily surrender part of our personal property for the government to keep order and justice, uphold the laws, and protect our nation. But when the government grows far beyond its limits and demands that we surrender more and more of the income that we have earned by

227

our own labors and then uses that money to fund institutions we find abhorrent and immoral, our natural rights are not only being violated, but trampled. And with the passage and implementation of the healthcare law, our natural rights are being violated even more than when we were ruled by an arrogant, pompous king three thousand miles away.

The Seeds of the Declaration

When King George III took the throne, the British Empire was deeply in debt from the Seven Years War (the French and Indian War). In order to raise revenue to repay those war debts, the king decided to enforce various provisions of the Navigation Acts in early 1760-61 soon after his coronation, which directly affected American commerce. This decision led to the issuance of writs of assistance which empowered customs officials to search and seize colonial goods being shipped. James Otis defended the merchants of New England who were affected by the new writs, and he is credited with the patriots' cry for justice: "Taxation without Representation is Tyranny."

Soon others in Boston picked up the torch of freedom and continued the movement that Otis had started almost by accident, namely Samuel Adams, John Adams, and later the Lees of Virginia. Several years later, Otis's rallying cry was shortened to "No taxation without representation!" James Otis inadvertently planted the seeds of American discontent with British rule, but Samuel Adams watered and nourished them until they sprouted and sent down roots.

When most people hear the name "Samuel Adams" today, the first thought that comes to mind is the lager sold under his name. While he was a maltster (not a brewer), he should rightly be known as the "Father of the American Revolution," because without his efforts, it might not have occurred when and how it did. He wrote, spoke, and preached tirelessly in his quest to make America free from Britain's rule. But from the 1760s to the mid-1770s, Samuel Adams often worked alone in his quest for American rights and later, American independence.

Often Samuel Adams would preach to a deaf and apathetic audience, who would wake for a short time and then promptly go back to sleep. In the years when most of his fellow Bostonians (and fellow Americans) only wanted reforms with Great Britain, his vision was one of independence from very early on. After the Boston Massacre and the Boston Tea Party, the Colonies – especially the pulpits – debated and struggled over whether they should obey God or obey the king. After all, the Bible clearly said to honor the king (1 Peter 2:13-17) and submit to civil authorities (Romans 13). However, the civil authorities were treating the Colonies unjustly, and they believed that they had a right to speak out and make their grievances known.

Samuel Adams convinced many in Boston that God had a special plan for them – and for all America – when their forefathers settled New England. By invoking John Winthrop's dream of America being the "shining city on a hill" to shine the light of liberty to the rest of the world, Adams helped many see that independence was obedience to God, and while reforms with Britain might provide a temporary peace, they would not be fulfilling the special commission that their own forefathers had been given. The public conversion from reform to independence took several years and countless hours starting from the unrelenting zeal of one man, then a handful joined him, then entire churches, the city of Boston, the New England countryside, and then flowed throughout the Colonies.

Once the eyes of the Colonists had been opened and they realized just how badly their God-given, natural rights were being violated by their own government, they appealed to their Creator for assistance and then took action. The decision to write and then sign the Declaration of Independence was half the battle in restoring their inalienable rights, while actually securing those rights cost a heavy price in blood, sweat, and tears. As John Adams said years later upon reflecting on the Revolutionary period:

> *"The Revolution was effected before the War commenced. The Revolution was in the minds and hearts of the people; a change in their religious sentiments of their duties and obligations... This radical change in the principles, opinions, sentiments, and affections of the people, was the real American Revolution."*

If we are to reclaim our inalienable rights and restore our God-given republic, we must first firmly resolve to do so, and then appeal to our Creator to help us. There is no compromise between liberty and tyranny, and every generation of Americans must decide whether they want to be free and responsible for themselves or whether they want to be taken care of in exchange for state-servitude. We cannot have both.

What follows is the Declaration of Independence, which I highly encourage you to read in its entirety. The Declaration of Independence not only applied to that Founding generation two-hundred and thirty-seven years ago, but to every generation of Americans who wish to remain free. Many books either place the Declaration in the back or bury it in an Appendix, but it is far too important to ignore or skip – the Declaration is central to our battle against an ever-encroaching government, especially when it's our own.

As you read our Declaration of Independence, instead of reading it through the eyes of history as it was written by the Founders to the King of England, try reading it as though it were written to our own President, Congress, and the federal government today, to our very own King Uncle Sam. Contemplate the vast liberties that we have lost, and consider what our Founders would say and do if they were in our shoes today. Are we willing to face the facts that our own President and Congress has violated our sovereign rights just as grievously – if not more-so – than the King of England and the Parliament?

The Declaration of Independence is divided into seven parts, though some divide it into four, five, or six parts, depending on their point of view:

Part 1: The Introduction
Part 2: The Preamble
Part 3: The Indictment of George III
Part 4: The Denunciation of the British people
Part 5: The Declaring of Independence
Part 6: The Conclusion
Part 7: The Signatures

Again, as you read these timeless words, keep in mind that though the list of enumerated grievances were specific to King George and Parliament, similar grievances can just as easily be listed against our own President, Congress, and federal government today – especially with regards to the confiscation and redistribution of our wealth, health, property, and opportunity. Lastly, understand that these were not American citizens who issued this Declaration, but British subjects – against their own British government. Would we ever have the courage as American citizens to issue a similar Declaration against our own American government that has become tyrannical?

The Declaration of Independence

IN CONGRESS, JULY 4, 1776
The unanimous Declaration of the thirteen United States of America

When in the Course of human events it becomes necessary for one people to dissolve the political bands which have connected them with another and to assume among the powers of the earth, the separate and equal station to which the Laws of Nature and of Nature's God entitle them, a decent respect to the opinions of mankind requires that they should declare the causes which impel them to the separation.

We hold these truths to be self-evident, that all men are created equal, that they are endowed by their Creator with certain unalienable Rights, that among these are Life, Liberty and the pursuit of Happiness.

That to secure these rights, Governments are instituted among Men, deriving their just powers from the consent of the governed.

That whenever any Form of Government becomes destructive of these ends, it is the Right of the People to alter or to abolish it, and to institute new Government, laying its foundation on such principles and organizing its powers in such form, as to them shall seem most likely to effect their Safety and Happiness.

Prudence, indeed, will dictate that Governments long established should not be changed for light and transient causes; and accordingly all experience hath shown that mankind are more disposed to suffer, while evils are sufferable than to right themselves by abolishing the forms to which they are accustomed.

But when a long train of abuses and usurpations, pursuing invariably the same Object evinces a design to reduce them under absolute Despotism, it is their right, it is their duty, to throw off such Government, and to provide new Guards for their future security.

Such has been the patient sufferance of these Colonies; and such is now the necessity which constrains them to alter their former Systems of Government. The history of the present King [of Great Britain] is a history of repeated injuries and usurpations, all having in direct object the establishment of an absolute Tyranny over these States. To prove this, let Facts be submitted to a candid world.

He has refused his Assent to Laws, the most wholesome and necessary for the public good.

He has forbidden his Governors to pass Laws of immediate and pressing importance, unless suspended in their operation till his Assent should be obtained; and when so suspended, he has utterly neglected to attend to them.

He has refused to pass other Laws for the accommodation of large districts of people, unless those people would relinquish the right of Representation in the Legislature, a right inestimable to them and formidable to tyrants only.

He has called together legislative bodies at places unusual, uncomfortable, and distant from the depository of their Public Records, for the sole purpose of fatiguing them into compliance with his measures.

He has dissolved Representative Houses repeatedly, for opposing with manly firmness his invasions on the rights of the people.

He has refused for a long time, after such dissolutions, to cause others to be elected, whereby the Legislative Powers, incapable of Annihilation, have returned to the People at large for their exercise; the State remaining in the meantime exposed to all the dangers of invasion from without, and convulsions within.

He has endeavored to prevent the population of these States; for that purpose obstructing the Laws for Naturalization of Foreigners; refusing to pass others to encourage their migrations hither, and raising the conditions of new Appropriations of Lands.

He has obstructed the Administration of Justice by refusing his Assent to Laws for establishing Judiciary Powers.

He has made Judges dependent on his Will alone for the tenure of their offices, and the amount and payment of their salaries.

He has erected a multitude of New Offices, and sent hither swarms of Officers to harass our people and eat out their substance.

He has kept among us, in times of peace, Standing Armies without the Consent of our legislatures.

He has affected to render the Military independent of and superior to the Civil Power.

He has combined with others to subject us to a jurisdiction foreign to our constitution, and unacknowledged by our laws; giving his Assent to their Acts of pretended Legislation:

For quartering large bodies of armed troops among us:

For protecting them, by a mock Trial from punishment for any Murders which they should commit on the Inhabitants of these States:

For cutting off our Trade with all parts of the world:

For imposing Taxes on us without our Consent:

For depriving us in many cases, of the benefit of Trial by Jury:

For transporting us beyond Seas to be tried for pretended offences:

For abolishing the free System of English Laws in a neighboring Province, establishing therein an Arbitrary government, and enlarging its Boundaries so as to render it at once an example and fit instrument for introducing the same absolute rule into these Colonies

For taking away our Charters, abolishing our most valuable Laws and altering fundamentally the Forms of our Governments:

For suspending our own Legislatures, and declaring themselves invested with power to legislate for us in all cases whatsoever.

He has abdicated Government here, by declaring us out of his Protection and waging War against us.

He has plundered our seas, ravaged our coasts, burnt our towns, and destroyed the lives of our people.

He is at this time transporting large Armies of foreign Mercenaries to complete the works of death, desolation, and tyranny, already begun with circumstances of Cruelty & Perfidy scarcely paralleled in the most barbarous ages, and totally unworthy the Head of a civilized nation.

He has constrained our fellow Citizens taken Captive on the high Seas to bear Arms against their Country, to become the executioners of their friends and Brethren, or to fall themselves by their Hands.

He has excited domestic insurrections amongst us, and has endeavored to bring on the inhabitants of our frontiers, the merciless Indian Savages whose known rule of warfare, is an undistinguished destruction of all ages, sexes and conditions.

In every stage of these Oppressions We have Petitioned for Redress in the most humble terms: Our repeated Petitions have been answered only by repeated injury. A Prince, whose character is thus marked by every act which may define a Tyrant, is unfit to be the ruler of a free people.

Nor have We been wanting in attentions to our British brethren. We have warned them from time to time of attempts by their legislature to extend an unwarrantable jurisdiction over us. We have reminded them of the circumstances of our emigration and settlement here. We have appealed to their native justice and magnanimity, and we have conjured them by the ties of our common kindred to disavow these usurpations, which would inevitably interrupt our connections and correspondence. They too have been deaf to the voice of justice and of consanguinity. We must, therefore, acquiesce in the necessity, which denounces our Separation, and hold them, as we hold the rest of mankind, Enemies in War, in Peace Friends.

We, therefore, the Representatives of the United States of America, in General Congress, Assembled, appealing to the Supreme Judge of the world for the rectitude of our intentions, do, in the Name, and by Authority of the good People of these Colonies, solemnly publish and declare, That these united Colonies are, and of Right ought to be Free and Independent States, that they are Absolved from all Allegiance to the British Crown, and that all political connection between them and the State of Great Britain, is and ought to be totally dissolved; and that as Free and Independent States, they have full Power to levy War, conclude Peace, contract Alliances, establish Commerce, and to do all other Acts and Things which Independent States may of right do.

And for the support of this Declaration, with a firm reliance on the protection of Divine Providence, we mutually pledge to each other our Lives, our Fortunes, and our sacred Honor.

New Hampshire: Josiah Bartlett, William Whipple, Matthew Thornton

Massachusetts: John Hancock, Samuel Adams, John Adams, Robert Treat Paine, Elbridge Gerry

Rhode Island: Stephen Hopkins, William Ellery

Connecticut: Roger Sherman, Samuel Huntington, William Williams, Oliver Wolcott

New York: William Floyd, Philip Livingston, Francis Lewis, Lewis Morris

New Jersey: Richard Stockton, John Witherspoon, Francis Hopkinson, John Hart, Abraham Clark

Pennsylvania: Robert Morris, Benjamin Rush, Benjamin Franklin, John Morton, George Clymer, James Smith, George Taylor, James Wilson, George Ross

Delaware: Caesar Rodney, George Read, Thomas McKean

Maryland: Samuel Chase, William Paca, Thomas Stone, Charles Carroll of Carrollton

<u>Virginia:</u> George Wythe, Richard Henry Lee, Thomas Jefferson, Benjamin Harrison, Thomas Nelson, Jr., Francis Lightfoot Lee, Carter Braxton

<u>North Carolina:</u> William Hooper, Joseph Hewes, John Penn

<u>South Carolina:</u> Edward Rutledge, Thomas Heyward, Jr., Thomas Lynch, Jr., Arthur Middleton

<u>Georgia:</u> Button Gwinnett, Lyman Hall, George Walton

What was the real cost of signing the Declaration of Independence? Several lost everything they had worked all their lives for, while others were harassed, captured, and imprisoned. Would they have signed that piece of paper had they known what would happen to them? I believe they would – that's the type of men they were.

The question that we Americans today must ask ourselves is: "Are we willing to pay that same price for our liberty?"

The following article is one that often circulates on the Internet which summarizes the personal costs and sacrifices of the Signers of the Declaration of Independence.

"The Price They Paid"

Have you ever wondered what happened to the 56 men who signed the Declaration of Independence?

For the record, here's a portrait of the men who pledged "our lives, our fortunes and our sacred honor" for liberty many years ago.

Fifty-six men from each of the original 13 colonies signed the Declaration of Independence on July 4, 1776. Nine of the signers were immigrants, two were brothers and two were cousins. One was an orphan. The average age of a signer

238

was 45. Benjamin Franklin was the oldest delegate at 70. The youngest was Thomas Lynch Jr. of South Carolina at 27. Eighteen of the signers were merchants or businessmen, 14 were farmers, and four were doctors. Twenty-two were lawyers - although William Hooper of North Carolina was "disbarred" when he spoke out against the king - and nine were judges. Stephen Hopkins had been governor of Rhode Island. Forty-two signers had served in their colonial legislatures.

John Witherspoon of New Jersey was the only active clergyman to attend. (Indeed, he wore his pontificals to the sessions.) Almost all were Protestants. Charles Carroll of Maryland was the lone Roman Catholic.

Seven of the signers were educated at Harvard, four at Yale, four at William & Mary, and three at Princeton. Witherspoon was the president of Princeton, and George Wythe was a professor at William & Mary. His students included Declaration scribe Thomas Jefferson.

Seventeen signers fought in the American Revolution. Thomas Nelson was a colonel in the Second Virginia Regiment and then commanded Virginia military forces at the Battle of Yorktown. William Whipple served with the New Hampshire militia and was a commanding officer in the decisive Saratoga campaign. Oliver Wolcott led the Connecticut regiments sent for the defense of New York and commanded a brigade of militia that took part in the defeat of General Burgoyne. Caesar Rodney was a major general in the Delaware militia; John Hancock held the same rank in the Massachusetts militia.

The British captured five signers during the war. Edward Rutledge, Thomas Heyward, and Arthur Middleton were captured at the Battle of Charleston in 1780. George Walton was wounded and captured at the Battle of Savannah. Richard Stockton of New Jersey never recovered from his incarceration at the hands of British Loyalists. He died in 1781.

Thomas McKean of Delaware wrote John Adams that he was "hunted like a fox by the enemy - compelled to remove my family five times in a few months." Abraham Clark of New Jersey had two of his sons captured by the British during the war.

Eleven signers had their homes and property destroyed. Francis Lewis's New York home was razed and his wife taken prisoner. John Hart's farm and mills were destroyed when the British invaded New Jersey, and he died while fleeing capture. Carter Braxton and Nelson, both of Virginia, lent large sums of their personal fortunes to support the war effort but were never repaid.

Fifteen of the signers participated in their states' constitutional conventions, and six - Roger Sherman, Robert Morris, Franklin, George Clymer, James Wilson, and George Reed - signed the U.S. Constitution.

After the Revolution, 13 signers went on to become governors. Eighteen served in their state legislatures. Sixteen became state and federal judges. Seven became members of the U.S. House of Representatives. Six became U.S. senators. James Wilson and Samuel Chase became Supreme Court justices. Jefferson, Adams, and Elbridge Gerry each became vice president. Adams and Jefferson later became president.

Five signers played major roles in the establishment of colleges and universities: Franklin and the University of Pennsylvania; Jefferson and the University of Virginia; Benjamin Rush and Dickinson College; Lewis Morris and New York University; and George Walton and the University of Georgia.

Adams, Jefferson, and Carroll were the longest surviving signers. Adams and Jefferson both died on July 4, 1826, the 50th anniversary of the Declaration of Independence. Carroll was the last signer to die in 1832 at the age of 95.

240

While most of the facts in the patriotic article are accurate, there are several corrections to be made from TruthOrFiction.com (http://www.truthorfiction.com/rumors/p/patriots.htm):

First, none of the signers of the Declaration of Independence died in captivity. All but two, or possibly three, died natural deaths and the majority of them lived to advanced age and had adequate possessions if not wealth. Of the deaths, Thomas Lynch, Jr. was lost at sea on a recreational voyage, Button Gwinnett died from injuries in a duel with a political rival, and George Wythe was thought to have been poisoned by a man who wanted his estate, but the man was acquitted. At least four of the signers were captured by the British, but apparently because they were soldiers, not signers of the Declaration. We consulted seven sources about the signers and none contained accounts of what could be called torture, at least not that was directed toward any of them for being founding fathers. Two who were captured may have experienced some kind of torture because of the severity of their confinement, but that is conjecture. All were released and died natural deaths, although the health of some was affected by their imprisonment.

Quotes on the Declaration of Independence

"I always consider the settlement of America with reverence and wonder, as the opening of a grand scene and design in providence, for the illumination of the ignorant and the emancipation of the slavish part of mankind all over the earth." – John Adams

"That these united colonies are, and of right ought to be, free and independent states; that they are absolved from all allegiance to the British crown; and that all political connection

241

between them and the State of Great Britain is, and ought to be, totally dissolved." – Richard Henry Lee

"Idleness and pride tax with a heavier hand than kings and parliaments. If we can get rid of the former, we may easily bear the latter." – Benjamin Franklin

"Liberty cannot be preserved without a general knowledge among the people, who have a right...and a desire to know; but besides this, they have a right, an indisputable, unalienable, indefeasible, divine right to that most dreaded and envied kind of knowledge, I mean of the characters and conduct of their rulers." – John Adams

"While General Howe with a Large Armament is advancing towards N. York, our Congress resolved to declare the United Colonies free and Independent States. A Declaration for this Purpose, I expect, will this day pass Congress...It is gone so far that we must now be a free independent State, or a Conquered Country." – Abraham Clark

"I am well aware of the toil and blood and treasure it will cost us to maintain this declaration, and support and defend these states. Yet through all the gloom I see the rays of ravishing light and glory. I can see that the end is worth all the means. This is our day of deliverance." – John Adams

"Equal and exact justice to all men...freedom of religion, freedom of the press, freedom of person under the protection of the habeas corpus; and trial by juries impartially selected, these principles form the bright constellation which has gone before us." – Thomas Jefferson

"This was the object of the Declaration of Independence. Not to find out new principles, or new arguments, never before thought of, not merely to say things which had never been said

before; but to place before mankind the common sense of the subject, in terms so plain and firm as to command their assent, and to justify ourselves in the independent stand we are compelled to take. Neither aiming at originality of principle or sentiment, nor yet copied from any particular and previous writing, it was intended to be an expression of the American mind, and to give to that expression the proper tone and spirit called for by the occasion. All its authority rests then on the harmonizing sentiments of the day, whether expressed in conversation, in letters, printed essays, or in the elementary books of public right, as Aristotle, Cicero, Locke, Sidney, etc."
– Thomas Jefferson

"The Declaration of Independence [is the] declaratory charter of our rights, and of the rights of man." – Thomas Jefferson

"Do you recollect the pensive and awful silence which pervaded the house when we were called up, one after another, to the table of the President of Congress to subscribe what was believed by many at that time to be our own death warrants?" – Benjamin Rush

"We must all hang together, or most assuredly we shall all hang separately." – Benjamin Franklin

"Independence Day will be the most memorable Epocha, in the History of America. I am apt to believe that it will be celebrated, by succeeding Generations, as the great anniversary Festival. It ought to be commemorated, as the Day of Deliverance by solemn Acts of Devotion to God Almighty. It ought to be solemnized with Pomp and Parade, with Shows, Games, Sports, Guns, Bells, Bonfires and Illuminations from one End of this Continent to the other from this Time forward forever more." – John Adams

"All that I have, and all that I am, and all that I hope, in this life, I am now ready here to stake upon it; and I leave off as I begun, that live or die, survive or perish, I am for the Declaration. It is my living sentiment, and by the blessing of God it shall be my dying sentiment, Independence, now, and Independence forever!" – John Adams

"All honor to Jefferson – to the man who, in the concrete pressure of a struggle for national independence by a single people, had the coolness, forecast, and capacity to introduce into a merely revolutionary document, an abstract truth, applicable to all men and all times, and so to embalm it there, that to-day, and in all coming days, it shall be a rebuke and a stumbling-block to the very harbingers of re-appearing tyranny and oppression." – Abraham Lincoln

Our Firm Reliance on Providence

Today in our secular society, many historians, lawyers, and teachers smile (or even mock) the quaint notion of the Founders appealing to their Creator for assistance in protecting their rights, as if they were foolish to not only believe in God, but that He would somehow help them in their endeavors to secure their liberty. But the Founders certainly did believe in God and that He was with them in their proclamation of independence from Great Britain, and later in the war to defend their homes, families, and lives. Before, during, and long after the Revolutionary War, Americans gave God the credit for the securing of their liberties, because they knew they had not fought the war alone.

As a resolute Leftist and radical Progressive, it's only fitting that Barack Obama has left out "the Creator" from several of his quotes from the Declaration of Independence. On at least four different occasions Obama said, "We hold these truths to be self-evident, that all men are created equal, that each of us are endowed with certain inalienable rights, that among these

244

are life, liberty and the pursuit of happiness." Even a cursory examination of his reading demonstrates the fallacy of his intentional misquoting of the Preamble; if we have been created and endowed (given, granted) with certain inalienable rights, who gave us those rights? God? Providence? As a Leftist, he certainly doesn't believe that – to Obama and his fellow Marxists, the State is to be all-powerful in order to provide for the people.

The entire phrase of the Preamble is: "that they are endowed *by their Creator* with certain inalienable rights" – the very citing of Who gave us those rights is central to the Declaration. Knowing their God-given rights, our Founders declared that they were free to live under the dictates of their own consciences and not a tyrannical king and Parliament who refused to represent them and uphold their inalienable rights of life, liberty, and property. And considering who King George was and the forces at his disposal, the Founders knew that without God, they would not succeed in restoring and securing their liberties.

Again, our modern, secular historians mock the very notion that God even exists, let alone would bother to help a group of people to secure their freedoms. But what if the secularists are the ones who are naïve in their understanding of history – if not outright ignorant of what really happened during those days? George Washington and other Founders constantly beseeched God and relied upon Him to give them the victory, and often said so in their own words. They were often quite aware of how their own sins and shortcomings would affect whether God would help them or not.

What if God – or Providence, if you prefer – DID help Americans from the earliest days of our history because of their faith and reliance on Him? And if that is true, is God still helping America today?

Chapter 9 - The Constitution

"We have given you a Republic, if you can keep it." –
Benjamin Franklin

The United States Constitution is the oldest working constitution in the world today. Drafted in 1787 and put into effect in 1789, the Constitution has been incredibly stable and durable through the greatest era of change and challenges in the history of the world. When the Constitution was enacted, the basic steam engine was the height of technology. Today, we have the Internet, computers, automobiles, airplanes, nuclear bombs, cellphones, satellite technology, have landed on the moon, and have sent satellites to the planets and even outside our solar system. Through all the technological advancements, two horrific world wars, an extremely bloody civil war, the rise of communism, socialism, and fascism, the Constitution has stood strong – it has withstood the test of time.

But over the last several years, tyranny from within the very seat of government in our capital has arisen and now many Americans fear we are still living under the Constitution "in name only." Because of the hundreds of billions of dollars in bailouts, the vast power of the government bureaucracy, and the utter lawlessness of the Obama administration, Mark Levin has surmised that we are now living in a post-Constitutional era, in which the government simply ignores the limits placed upon it by the Constitution and essentially does whatever it wants.

However, the entire point of having a constitution – especially the U.S. Constitution – is to specifically limit and control the power of government at the national level. The Constitution was written to guarantee that the people of America would retain as many of their natural rights as possible and still have a functioning government to protect those rights.

246

The Articles of Confederation which had been enacted during the Revolutionary War had proven to be too weak and ineffective, and were actually endangering the peoples' rights because of the national debt, squabbling between the States, and lack of a national defense. The Preamble to the Constitution declares the sole purposes of why it was written:

> *We the People of the United States, in Order to form a more perfect Union, establish Justice, insure domestic Tranquility, provide for the common defence, promote the general Welfare, and secure the Blessings of Liberty to ourselves and our Posterity, do ordain and establish this Constitution for the United States of America.*

Barack Obama, Woodrow Wilson, and other Progressives decry that the Constitution is antiquated, outdated, and full of "negative liberties" – meaning that the Constitution describes what the government cannot do "to" you (negatively), but nothing about what the government can do "for" you (positively), such as providing healthcare and social-security. However, Obama and his fellow Progressives refuse to acknowledge the fact that in order for the government to provide a benefit to one group, they must first seize from others. Governments have no assets or income of their own except that which they take from the people, whether it be in the form of land, property, resources, or taxes.

There's a widely circulated cartoon in which Obama is holding a copy of the Constitution with James Madison sitting at his desk reviewing it, and Obama says, "Mr. Madison, I detected a flaw in your constitution. Nothing in it allows the government to confiscate wealth for redistribution." Madison glares back at him and responds, "That's not a flaw, sir, that's the point." Exactly – the Constitution was written specifically to protect American citizens from the redistributionist tendencies of government rulers, whether the confiscation is by the legislature, the executive, or the courts.

Before the midterm elections of 2010, Obama more or less worked within the bounds of the Constitution with regards to passing and enacting legislation. His party had unprecedented power since they controlled both the House of Representatives and also the Senate by a filibuster-proof majority. Additionally, the Democrat leaders of Congress held the same driving goal as Obama: to fundamentally transform the Republic of the United States of America. During that Congress, the healthcare system was nationalized, the Dodd-Frank banking bill was passed, along with a slew of other onerous bills.

But after getting walloped in the 2010 midterm elections in which the Republicans took over the House and cut down the filibuster-proof majority, Obama could no longer easily enact his legislation. However, because his party still controlled the Senate, most Republican bills were killed after passing the House, creating gridlock in the Congress. Seizing upon the public's frustration over the political haggling, Obama began denouncing Congress (for which the Senate was mostly responsible) and proclaimed that he would do all within his power to "get it done" in the name of helping the people.

While using executive power to slip around legislative gridlock may sound good, it's a complete abuse of power and a subversion of the Constitution. Our Constitution has two primary purposes: to adequately govern the people and the States, and to prevent tyranny from the Congress and the President, and also the people (i.e. democracy). The Founders were very concerned about the natural rights of everyone – from the powerful to the weak – and divided the powers of government granted by the people across three branches of government in order to create competition (and sometimes conflict) between the branches. If one or even two branches of government fell under corruption, the others would be able to use their specific, enumerated powers to protect the constitutional republic – at least until a future election when hopefully the people would elect more virtuous leadership.

Stability in government depends on minimizing the wild swings of public passions and the power of corrupt leaders. In fact, according to Federalist Papers #62-63, the reason why the Senate was organized with longer terms of tenure and equal representation for the States was to specifically slow down the legislative process and dampen the passions of the people for their own good – gridlock was the point! The Senate was designed to be a more deliberative body than the House, in which more experienced legislators (those chosen by their State legislatures) could revise and improve legislation that came from the House.

Tragically, the Founders could not foresee that the leadership of two branches of the government would one day work in tandem to subvert the very Constitution that their members had sworn to protect. With two branches marching in lockstep with one another, the pressure on the third branch of the government becomes enormous and without strong, virtuous leadership, the third branch often capitulates to the other two in order to protect their own power – if not to simply avoid a constitutional crisis. The surprise capitulation of John Roberts in the ruling of the constitutionality of ObamaCare in mid-2012 demonstrates what happens when gridlock in Washington fails and one branch of government is left supporting the Constitution.

Since losing the House of Representatives and the filibuster-proof majority in the Senate, Obama has not only passed his own legislation by Executive Order, he has begun ruling simply by fiat – no longer even bothering with Executive Orders. He directs one of his czars or federal department-heads to implement a new policy and they comply – regardless of whether they have that authority or not. Rule by fiat is the very definition of a tyrant and a complete breakdown of the Rule of Law. In the past, most presidents avoided such abuses of power because the threat of impeachment constantly loomed over them. But given the media and public outcry over the impeachment proceedings of Bill Clinton and the fact that a fellow radical controls the Senate, Obama has little fear of being impeached.

With no fear of Congress, Obama believes he can enact any policy he wants without accountability – all because he knows that Congress will not do their constitutional duty and enforce the Constitution and the Rule of Law. The breakdown in the Rule of Law in our nation is coming directly from the highest offices in our land by our own national shepherds. The elected men and women that we have entrusted with our power – who are supposed to be the very pillars of the law and protectors of the republic – are tearing it down with their own hands.

John Adams declared that the very foundation of the Constitution is the virtue of the citizenry, in that,

> *"The only foundation of a free Constitution, is pure virtue, and if this cannot be inspired into our people, in a greater measure than they have it now, they may change their rulers, and the forms of government, but they will not obtain a lasting liberty."*

Joseph Story, who served on the Supreme Court from 1811 to 1845, postulated that virtue at every level of society is necessary to not only enable the republic to function, but to exist. Republics fall when the virtue of the people – and then their representatives – falters and then fails.

> *"Republics are created by the virtue, public spirit, and intelligence of the citizens. They fall, when the wise are banished from the public councils, because they dare to be honest, and the profligate are rewarded, because they flatter the people, in order to betray them."*

If our constitutional republic is failing, it's because We the People have lost our virtues and have elected corrupt leaders who have lied to us and broken their oaths to uphold the Constitution. If we are to remain free and live under the guarantees of our Constitution, we must recover our morals and virtues and then expunge these corrupt caretakers from office as soon as possible. We also need to demand more accountability such as term-limits and personal liability for such abuses of power, if not hold our current crop of leaders personally responsible for their dereliction of duty.

Both the Declaration and Constitution acknowledge that it is the people who ultimately have the power, not one person or a small cadre of officials – and when government forgets that fact, rebellions and revolutions rise. Therefore, it was intended that under the Constitution, the will of the people would prevail in the end, even if several elections were required to do so. Until the people made their final decision about a certain law or policy, they could rely on the System of Checks and Balances to protect their liberties. However, there was one branch of government that the Founders did not apply enough checks to: the Supreme Court.

Not even fifteen years had passed after the Constitution was ratified did the Founders realize their flaw that the people had no clear way of overturning a Supreme Court decision. After Marbury v. Madison in which the Supreme Court seized the power of judicial review – deciding whether a law was constitutional or unconstitutional – the final authority on all laws and executive actions is decided by the Supreme Court, though they have no power to enforce their rulings. Both Madison and Jefferson recognized this flaw, though by then it was too late.

> *"The Constitution, on this hypothesis, is a mere thing of wax in the hands of the Judiciary, which they may twist and shape into any form they please."* – Thomas Jefferson

Tyranny and tyrants will always find the weakest link in a system and then exploit it for their own purposes, and though judicial review was established early in the republic, it wasn't until well into the Progressive Era that judicial activism became common. Today, some judges believe they have the authority to "legislate from the bench" and order the other branches of government to change or rewrite entire laws, while others they simply strike down on a whim.

When the Progressives began their long march through the institutions, one of the first pillars they attacked was the Constitution, the very bedrock of the Republic. The Progressives like Howard Lee McBain began to refer to the Constitution as a "living, breathing document," and therefore adaptable in meaning and interpretation as times and society changes. Since the Progressives would be thrown out (or arrested) if they openly declared that they wanted to do away with the constitutional limitations, they pursued a more subversive path in order to achieve the same results.

After the advent of the Progressive Era in the early 1900s, the tone of the amendments in the Constitution shifted – the very nature of the document began to be altered by the Progressives. The Constitution was changed into what the government could do "to" the people rather that what the government could not do; rather than limit the government, the Progressive amendments limited the people, the exact opposite reason the Constitution was written in the first place. With the passage of the Sixteenth Amendment, the federal government now has the direct power to seize property (income) from the people however it sees fit. The Seventeenth Amendment (Direct Election of Senators) effectively changed the republic into more of a democracy and the States lost most of their power within the federal government and the Senate. The Eighteenth Amendment (Prohibition) was a direct violation of the peoples' rights – regardless of how well-intentioned it may have been – and was thankfully repealed several years later.

Like the Declaration of Independence, the Constitution is far too important to stuff in the back of the book in an appendix – knowing the Constitution is central to protecting our liberties. The Constitution did not create self-government, it codified it. Self-government is up to us – but the Constitution does enable it to function effectively. We can unite behind it or ignore it as we have been doing for the last century. Today, the American republic stands on the edge of a precipice, and if we are to save the Republic, we must act immediately. If liberty fails in America, it will fail all over the globe.

The most critical amendment in the entire Constitution is not the First Amendment, but the Second Amendment – the Right to Bear Arms. The Second Amendment is what gives We the People "teeth"; without it, the rest of the Constitution is little more than words on paper. The recent Second Amendment infringements of Obama in the wake of the Sandy Hook Massacre (namely, the twenty-three Executive Orders) are not intended to make our schools or streets safer, as much as restricting the means of holding tyranny in check by the citizenry. The federal government can enact all the gun control laws they want and it will still do little to stop criminals who want to shed blood. Make no mistake, the Second Amendment is NOT about hunting or even personal self-defense – it's about preventing the federal government and the state governments from becoming tyrannical. The Constitution is a political document, the foremost binding contract between the people and their government, and the Second Amendment is the final check the citizenry has against their governments.

One of the primary reasons why the Constitutional Convention was called in 1787 was from the very real fear of defaulting on the national debt. Just like with personal/private credit, if a nation ruins their credit, no one will loan them money – especially when they need it the most, such as during a war or an invasion. A nation in debt is a nation in danger; and with our $16+ trillion debt today, America is in grave danger. Our Founders thought it to be a great evil to accumulate debt in one generation and then leave it behind for their children and grandchildren to deal with, but that's precisely what we have been doing for the last century, but especially for the last twelve years.

The U.S. Constitution was crafted to be a reliable, understandable contract between the people and their federal government. It contains 4,000 words in 11 pages and seven articles, all written at a democratic 9th-grade level. The Constitution is quite simple and brief, articulating the three branches of government and then spelling out the specific, enumerated powers in each branch, and how the branches "check and balance" one another to prevent tyranny.

In contrast to our Constitution, the European Constitution (and most federal legislation today) is a convoluted 855-page, 156,447-word masterpiece of bureaucratic legalese that was written at a post-graduate or even legal-scholar level. After only a few years, the European Constitution has proven to be so useless that the very European Union is on the verge of collapse!

Unlike the European Constitution which was written for lawyers and bureaucrats, the U.S. Constitution is for us – We the People – and was not only intended to be read by all, but to be understood by all. During the ratification process, several Founders were astounded – and of course pleased – to discover that the Constitution was being intelligently discussed and debated all over the country in the taverns, on the streets, and in the churches. Today however, most educated adults know nothing about the Constitution and have never even read it except for a brief overview in public school or college years ago. Given our ignorance of our own laws and Constitution, it's no wonder that our representatives no longer feel bound by it.

The U.S. Constitution is basically divided into twelve parts, defined by the Articles themselves and the other structures of the document:

Part 1: The Preamble
Part 2: Article I – The Legislative Branch
Part 3: Article II – The Executive Branch
Part 4: Article III – The Judicial Branch
Part 5: Article IV – The States

The CONSTITUTION of the United States of America

We the People of the United States, in Order to form a more perfect Union, establish Justice, insure domestic Tranquility, provide for the common defence, promote the general Welfare, and secure the Blessings of Liberty to ourselves and our Posterity, do ordain and establish this Constitution for the United States of America.

Article I – The Legislative Branch

Section 1 – The Legislature
All legislative Powers herein granted shall be vested in a Congress of the United States, which shall consist of a Senate and House of Representatives.

Section 2 – The House
The House of Representatives shall be composed of Members chosen every second Year by the People of the several States, and the Electors in each State shall have the Qualifications requisite for Electors of the most numerous Branch of the State Legislature.

No Person shall be a Representative who shall not have attained to the Age of twenty five Years, and been seven Years a Citizen of the United States, and who shall not, when elected, be an Inhabitant of that State in which he shall be chosen.

Representatives and direct Taxes shall be apportioned among the several States which may be included within this Union, according to their respective Numbers, which shall be determined by adding to the whole Number of free Persons, including those bound to Service for a Term of Years, and excluding Indians not taxed, three fifths of all other Persons [Modified by Amendment XIV]. The actual Enumeration shall be made within three Years after the first Meeting of the Congress of the United States, and within every subsequent Term of ten Years, in such Manner as they shall by Law direct. The Number of Representatives shall not exceed one for every thirty Thousand, but each State shall have at Least one Representative; and until such enumeration shall be made, the State of New Hampshire shall be entitled to chuse three, Massachusetts eight, Rhode-Island and Providence Plantations one, Connecticut five, New-York six, New Jersey four, Pennsylvania eight, Delaware one, Maryland six, Virginia ten, North Carolina five, South Carolina five, and Georgia three.

When vacancies happen in the Representation from any State, the Executive Authority thereof shall issue Writs of Election to fill such Vacancies.

The House of Representatives shall chuse their Speaker and other Officers; and shall have the sole Power of Impeachment.

Section 3 – The Senate
The Senate of the United States shall be composed of two Senators from each State, chosen by the Legislature thereof [Modified by Amendment XVII], for six Years; and each Senator shall have one Vote.

Immediately after they shall be assembled in Consequence of the first Election, they shall be divided as equally as may be into three Classes. The Seats of the Senators of the first Class shall be vacated at the Expiration of the second Year, of the second Class at the Expiration of the fourth Year, and of the third Class at the Expiration of the sixth Year, so that one third may be chosen every second Year; and if Vacancies happen by Resignation, or otherwise, during the Recess of the Legislature of any State, the Executive thereof may make temporary Appointments until the next Meeting of the Legislature, which shall then fill such Vacancies [Modified by Amendment XVII].

No Person shall be a Senator who shall not have attained to the Age of thirty Years, and been nine Years a Citizen of the United States, and who shall not, when elected, be an Inhabitant of that State for which he shall be chosen.

The Vice President of the United States shall be President of the Senate, but shall have no Vote, unless they be equally divided.

The Senate shall chuse their other Officers, and also a President pro tempore, in the Absence of the Vice President, or when he shall exercise the Office of President of the United States.

The Senate shall have the sole Power to try all Impeachments. When sitting for that Purpose, they shall be on Oath or Affirmation. When the President of the United States is tried, the Chief Justice shall preside: And no Person shall be convicted without the Concurrence of two thirds of the Members present.

Judgment in Cases of Impeachment shall not extend further than to removal from Office, and disqualification to hold and enjoy any Office of honor, Trust or Profit under the United

States: but the Party convicted shall nevertheless be liable and subject to Indictment, Trial, Judgment and Punishment, according to Law.

Section 4 – Elections, Meetings

The Times, Places and Manner of holding Elections for Senators and Representatives, shall be prescribed in each State by the Legislature thereof; but the Congress may at any time by Law make or alter such Regulations, except as to the Places of chusing Senators.

The Congress shall assemble at least once in every Year, and such Meeting shall be on the first Monday in December [Modified by Amendment XX], unless they shall by Law appoint a different Day.

Section 5 – Membership, Rules, Journals, Adjournment

Each House shall be the Judge of the Elections, Returns and Qualifications of its own Members, and a Majority of each shall constitute a Quorum to do Business; but a smaller Number may adjourn from day to day, and may be authorized to compel the Attendance of absent Members, in such Manner, and under such Penalties as each House may provide.

Each House may determine the Rules of its Proceedings, punish its Members for disorderly Behaviour, and, with the Concurrence of two thirds, expel a Member.

Each House shall keep a Journal of its Proceedings, and from time to time publish the same, excepting such Parts as may in their Judgment require Secrecy; and the Yeas and Nays of the Members of either House on any question shall, at the Desire of one fifth of those Present, be entered on the Journal.

Neither House, during the Session of Congress, shall, without the Consent of the other, adjourn for more than three days, nor to any other Place than that in which the two Houses shall be sitting.

Section 6 - Compensation

The Senators and Representatives shall receive a Compensation for their Services, to be ascertained by Law, and paid out of the Treasury of the United States. They shall in all Cases, except Treason, Felony and Breach of the Peace, be privileged from Arrest during their Attendance at the Session of their respective Houses, and in going to and returning from the same; and for any Speech or Debate in either House, they shall not be questioned in any other Place.

No Senator or Representative shall, during the Time for which he was elected, be appointed to any civil Office under the Authority of the United States, which shall have been created, or the Emoluments whereof shall have been encreased during such time; and no Person holding any Office under the United States, shall be a Member of either House during his Continuance in Office.

Section 7 – Revenue Bills, Legislative Process, Presidential Veto

All Bills for raising Revenue shall originate in the House of Representatives; but the Senate may propose or concur with Amendments as on other Bills.

Every Bill which shall have passed the House of Representatives and the Senate, shall, before it become a Law, be presented to the President of the United States;[2] If he approve he shall sign it, but if not he shall return it, with his Objections to that House in which it shall have originated, who shall enter the Objections at large on their Journal, and proceed to reconsider it. If after such Reconsideration two thirds of that House shall agree to pass the Bill, it shall be sent, together with the Objections, to the other House, by which it shall likewise be reconsidered, and if approved by two thirds of that House, it shall become a Law. But in all such Cases the Votes of both Houses shall be determined by yeas and Nays, and the Names of the Persons voting for and against the Bill shall be entered on the Journal of each House respectively. If any Bill shall not be returned by the President within ten Days (Sundays excepted) after it shall have been presented to him, the Same shall be a Law, in like Manner as if he had signed it, unless the Congress by their Adjournment prevent its Return, in which Case it shall not be a Law.

Every Order, Resolution, or Vote to which the Concurrence of the Senate and House of Representatives may be necessary (except on a question of Adjournment) shall be presented to the President of the United States; and before the Same shall take Effect, shall be approved by him, or being disapproved by him, shall be repassed by two thirds of the Senate and House of Representatives, according to the Rules and Limitations prescribed in the Case of a Bill.

Section 8 – Powers of Congress

The Congress shall have Power To lay and collect Taxes, Duties, Imposts and Excises, to pay the Debts and provide for the common Defence and general Welfare of the United States; but all Duties, Imposts and Excises shall be uniform throughout the United States;

To borrow Money on the credit of the United States;

To regulate Commerce with foreign Nations, and among the several States, and with the Indian Tribes;

To establish an uniform Rule of Naturalization, and uniform Laws on the subject of Bankruptcies throughout the United States;

To coin Money, regulate the Value thereof, and of foreign Coin, and fix the Standard of Weights and Measures;

To provide for the Punishment of counterfeiting the Securities and current Coin of the United States;

To establish Post Offices and post Roads;

To promote the Progress of Science and useful Arts, by securing for limited Times to Authors and Inventors the exclusive Right to their respective Writings and Discoveries;

To constitute Tribunals inferior to the supreme Court;

To define and punish Piracies and Felonies committed on the high Seas, and Offences against the Law of Nations;

To declare War, grant Letters of Marque and Reprisal, and make Rules concerning Captures on Land and Water;

To raise and support Armies, but no Appropriation of Money to that Use shall be for a longer Term than two Years;

To provide and maintain a Navy;

To make Rules for the Government and Regulation of the land and naval Forces;

To provide for calling forth the Militia to execute the Laws of the Union, suppress Insurrections and repel Invasions;

To provide for organizing, arming, and disciplining, the Militia, and for governing such Part of them as may be employed in the Service of the United States, reserving to the States respectively, the Appointment of the Officers, and the

Authority of training the Militia according to the discipline prescribed by Congress;

To exercise exclusive Legislation in all Cases whatsoever, over such District (not exceeding ten Miles square) as may, by Cession of particular States, and the Acceptance of Congress, become the Seat of the Government of the United States, and to exercise like Authority over all Places purchased by the Consent of the Legislature of the State in which the Same shall be, for the Erection of Forts, Magazines, Arsenals, dock-Yards, and other needful Buildings; – And

To make all Laws which shall be necessary and proper for carrying into Execution the foregoing Powers, and all other Powers vested by this Constitution in the Government of the United States, or in any Department or Officer thereof.

Section 9 – Limits on Congress
The Migration or Importation of such Persons as any of the States now existing shall think proper to admit, shall not be prohibited by the Congress prior to the Year one thousand eight hundred and eight, but a Tax or duty may be imposed on such Importation, not exceeding ten dollars for each Person.

The Privilege of the Writ of Habeas Corpus shall not be suspended, unless when in Cases of Rebellion or Invasion the public Safety may require it.

No Bill of Attainder or ex post facto Law shall be passed.

No Capitation, or other direct, Tax shall be laid, unless in Proportion to the Census or Enumeration herein before directed to be taken.

No Tax or Duty shall be laid on Articles exported from any State.

No Preference shall be given by any Regulation of Commerce or Revenue to the Ports of one State over those of another; nor shall Vessels bound to, or from, one State, be obliged to enter, clear, or pay Duties in another.

No Money shall be drawn from the Treasury, but in Consequence of Appropriations made by Law; and a regular Statement and Account of the Receipts and Expenditures of all public Money shall be published from time to time.

No Title of Nobility shall be granted by the United States: And no Person holding any Office of Profit or Trust under them, shall, without the Consent of the Congress, accept of any present, Emolument, Office, or Title, of any kind whatever, from any King, Prince, or foreign State.

Section 10 – Powers Prohibited of States
No State shall enter into any Treaty, Alliance, or Confederation; grant Letters of Marque and Reprisal; coin Money; emit Bills of Credit; make any Thing but gold and silver Coin a Tender in Payment of Debts; pass any Bill of Attainder, ex post facto Law, or Law impairing the Obligation of Contracts, or grant any Title of Nobility.

No State shall, without the Consent of the Congress, lay any Imposts or Duties on Imports or Exports, except what may be absolutely necessary for executing it's inspection Laws; and the net Produce of all Duties and Imposts, laid by any State on Imports or Exports, shall be for the Use of the Treasury of the United States; and all such Laws shall be subject to the Revision and Controul of the Congress.

No State shall, without the Consent of Congress, lay any Duty of Tonnage, keep Troops, or Ships of War in time of Peace, enter into any Agreement or Compact with another State, or with a foreign Power, or engage in War, unless actually invaded, or in such imminent Danger as will not admit of delay.

Article II – The Executive Branch

Section 1 – The President
The executive Power shall be vested in a President of the United States of America. He shall hold his Office during the Term of four Years, and, together with the Vice President, chosen for the same Term, be elected, as follows:

Each State shall appoint, in such Manner as the Legislature thereof may direct, a Number of Electors, equal to the whole Number of Senators and Representatives to which the State may be entitled in the Congress: but no Senator or Representative, or Person holding an Office of Trust or Profit under the United States, shall be appointed an Elector.

The Electors shall meet in their respective States, and vote by Ballot for two Persons, of whom one at least shall not be an Inhabitant of the same State with themselves. And they shall make a List of all the Persons voted for, and of the Number of Votes for each; which List they shall sign and certify, and transmit sealed to the Seat of the Government of the United States, directed to the President of the Senate. The President of the Senate shall, in the Presence of the Senate and House of Representatives, open all the Certificates, and the Votes shall then be counted. The Person having the greatest Number of Votes shall be the President, if such Number be a Majority of the whole Number of Electors appointed; and if there be more than one who have such Majority, and have an equal Number of Votes, then the House of Representatives shall immediately chuse by Ballot one of them for President; and if no Person have a Majority, then from the five highest on the List the said House shall in like Manner chuse the President. But in chusing the President, the Votes shall be taken by States, the Representation from each State having one Vote; a quorum for this Purpose shall consist of a Member or Members from two thirds of the States, and a Majority of all the States shall be necessary to a Choice. In every Case, after the Choice of the President, the Person having the greatest Number of Votes of the Electors shall be the Vice President. But if there should remain two or more who have equal Votes, the Senate shall chuse from them by Ballot the Vice President [Modified by Amendment XII].

The Congress may determine the Time of chusing the Electors, and the Day on which they shall give their Votes; which Day shall be the same throughout the United States.

No Person except a natural born Citizen, or a Citizen of the United States, at the time of the Adoption of this Constitution, shall be eligible to the Office of President; neither shall any Person be eligible to that Office who shall not have attained to the Age of thirty five Years, and been fourteen Years a Resident within the United States.

In Case of the Removal of the President from Office, or of his Death, Resignation, or Inability to discharge the Powers and Duties of the said Office, the Same shall devolve on the Vice President, and the Congress may by Law provide for the Case of Removal, Death, Resignation or Inability, both of the President and Vice President, declaring what Officer shall then act as President, and such Officer shall act accordingly, until the Disability be removed, or a President shall be elected [Modified by Amendment XXV].

The President shall, at stated Times, receive for his Services, a Compensation, which shall neither be increased nor diminished during the Period for which he shall have been elected, and he shall not receive within that Period any other Emolument from the United States, or any of them.

Before he enter on the Execution of his Office, he shall take the following Oath or Affirmation: – "I do solemnly swear (or affirm) that I will faithfully execute the Office of President of the United States, and will to the best of my Ability, preserve, protect and defend the Constitution of the United States [, so help me God]." [Added by George Washington upon his taking the First Oath of Office, and uttered by every president since].

Section 2 – Civilian Power over Military, Cabinet, Pardons, Appointments
The President shall be Commander in Chief of the Army and Navy of the United States, and of the Militia of the several States, when called into the actual Service of the United States; he may require the Opinion, in writing, of the principal Officer in each of the executive Departments, upon any Subject relating to the Duties of their respective Offices, and he shall have Power to grant Reprieves and Pardons for Offences against the United States, except in Cases of Impeachment.

He shall have Power, by and with the Advice and Consent of the Senate, to make Treaties, provided two thirds of the Senators present concur; and he shall nominate, and by and with the Advice and Consent of the Senate, shall appoint Ambassadors, other public Ministers and Consuls, Judges of the supreme Court, and all other Officers of the United States, whose Appointments are not herein otherwise provided for, and which shall be established by Law: but the Congress may by Law vest the Appointment of such inferior Officers, as they think proper, in the President alone, in the Courts of Law, or in the Heads of Departments.

The President shall have Power to fill up all Vacancies that may happen during the Recess of the Senate, by granting

Commissions which shall expire at the End of their next Session.

Section 3 – State of the Union, Convening Congress He shall from time to time give to the Congress Information of the State of the Union, and recommend to their Consideration such Measures as he shall judge necessary and expedient; he may, on extraordinary Occasions, convene both Houses, or either of them, and in Case of Disagreement between them, with Respect to the Time of Adjournment, he may adjourn them to such Time as he shall think proper; he shall receive Ambassadors and other public Ministers; he shall take Care that the Laws be faithfully executed, and shall Commission all the Officers of the United States.

Section 4 - Disqualification
The President, Vice President and all civil Officers of the United States, shall be removed from Office on Impeachment for, and Conviction of, Treason, Bribery, or other high Crimes and Misdemeanors.

Article III – The Judicial Branch

Section 1- Judicial Powers
The judicial Power of the United States shall be vested in one supreme Court, and in such inferior Courts as the Congress may from time to time ordain and establish. The Judges, both of the supreme and inferior Courts, shall hold their Offices during good Behaviour, and shall, at stated Times, receive for their Services a Compensation, which shall not be diminished during their Continuance in Office.

Section 2 – Trial by Jury, Original Jurisdiction, Jury Trials
The judicial Power shall extend to all Cases, in Law and Equity, arising under this Constitution, the Laws of the United

States, and Treaties made, or which shall be made, under their Authority; – to all Cases affecting Ambassadors, other public Ministers and Consuls; – to all Cases of admiralty and maritime Jurisdiction; – to Controversies to which the United States shall be a Party; – to Controversies between two or more States; – between a State and Citizens of another State [Modified by Amendment XI]; – between Citizens of different States; – between Citizens of the same State claiming Lands under Grants of different States, and between a State, or the Citizens thereof, and foreign States, Citizens or Subjects.

In all Cases affecting Ambassadors, other public Ministers and Consuls, and those in which a State shall be Party, the Supreme Court shall have original Jurisdiction. In all the other Cases before mentioned, the Supreme Court shall have appellate Jurisdiction, both as to Law and Fact, with such Exceptions, and under such Regulations as the Congress shall make.

The Trial of all Crimes, except in Cases of Impeachment, shall be by Jury; and such Trial shall be held in the State where the said Crimes shall have been committed; but when not committed within any State, the Trial shall be at such Place or Places as the Congress may by Law have directed.

Section 3 - Treason
Treason against the United States shall consist only in levying War against them, or in adhering to their Enemies, giving them Aid and Comfort. No Person shall be convicted of Treason unless on the Testimony of two Witnesses to the same overt Act, or on Confession in open Court.

The Congress shall have Power to declare the Punishment of Treason, but no Attainder of Treason shall work Corruption of Blood, or Forfeiture except during the Life of the Person attainted.

Article IV – The States

Section 1 – Each State to Honor all Others
Full Faith and Credit shall be given in each State to the public Acts, Records, and judicial Proceedings of every other State. And the Congress may by general Laws prescribe the Manner in which such Acts, Records and Proceedings shall be proved, and the Effect thereof.

Section 2 – State citizens, Extradition
The Citizens of each State shall be entitled to all Privileges and Immunities of Citizens in the several States.

A Person charged in any State with Treason, Felony, or other Crime, who shall flee from Justice, and be found in another State, shall on Demand of the executive Authority of the State from which he fled, be delivered up, to be removed to the State having Jurisdiction of the Crime.

No Person held to Service or Labour in one State, under the Laws thereof, escaping into another, shall, in Consequence of any Law or Regulation therein, be discharged from such Service or Labour, but shall be delivered up on Claim of the Party to whom such Service or Labour may be due [Modified by Amendment XIII].

Section 3 – New States
New States may be admitted by the Congress into this Union; but no new State shall be formed or erected within the Jurisdiction of any other State; nor any State be formed by the Junction of two or more States, or Parts of States, without the Consent of the Legislatures of the States concerned as well as of the Congress.

The Congress shall have Power to dispose of and make all needful Rules and Regulations respecting the Territory or other Property belonging to the United States; and nothing in this Constitution shall be so construed as to Prejudice any Claims of the United States, or of any particular State.

Section 4 – Republican Government

The United States shall guarantee to every State in this Union a Republican Form of Government, and shall protect each of them against Invasion; and on Application of the Legislature, or of the Executive (when the Legislature cannot be convened), against domestic Violence.

Article V - Amendment

The Congress, whenever two thirds of both Houses shall deem it necessary, shall propose Amendments to this Constitution, or, on the Application of the Legislatures of two thirds of the several States, shall call a Convention for proposing Amendments, which, in either Case, shall be valid to all Intents and Purposes, as Part of this Constitution, when ratified by the Legislatures of three fourths of the several States, or by Conventions in three fourths thereof, as the one or the other Mode of Ratification may be proposed by the Congress; Provided that no Amendment which may be made prior to the Year One thousand eight hundred and eight shall in any Manner affect the first and fourth Clauses in the Ninth Section of the first Article; and that no State, without its Consent, shall be deprived of its equal Suffrage in the Senate.

Article VI – Debts, Supremacy, Oaths

All Debts contracted and Engagements entered into, before the Adoption of this Constitution, shall be as valid against the

United States under this Constitution, as under the Confederation.

This Constitution, and the Laws of the United States which shall be made in Pursuance thereof; and all Treaties made, or which shall be made, under the Authority of the United States, shall be the supreme Law of the Land; and the Judges in every State shall be bound thereby, any Thing in the Constitution or Laws of any State to the Contrary notwithstanding.

The Senators and Representatives before mentioned, and the Members of the several State Legislatures, and all executive and judicial Officers, both of the United States and of the several States, shall be bound by Oath or Affirmation, to support this Constitution; but no religious Test shall ever be required as a Qualification to any Office or public Trust under the United States.

Article VII – Ratification

The Ratification of the Conventions of nine States, shall be sufficient for the Establishment of this Constitution between the States so ratifying the Same.

Done in Convention by the Unanimous Consent of the States present the Seventeenth Day of September in the Year of our Lord one thousand seven hundred and Eighty seven and of the Independence of the United States of America the Twelfth In witness whereof We have hereunto subscribed our Names,

Go. Washington - President and deputy from Virginia

New Hampshire: John Langdon, Nicholas Gilman

271

Massachusetts: Nathaniel Gorham, Rufus King

Connecticut: Wm Saml Johnson, Roger Sherman

New York: Alexander Hamilton

New Jersey: Wil Livingston, David Brearley, Wm Paterson, Jona. Dayton

Pennsylvania: B Franklin, Thomas Mifflin, Robt Morris, Geo. Clymer, Thos FitzSimons, Jared Ingersoll, James Wilson, Gouv Morris

Delaware: Geo. Read, Gunning Bedford jun, John Dickinson, Richard Bassett, Jaco. Broom

Maryland: James McHenry, Dan of St Tho Jenifer, Danl Carroll

Virginia: John Blair, James Madison Jr.

North Carolina: Wm Blount, Richd Dobbs Spaight, Hu Williamson

South Carolina: J. Rutledge, Charles Cotesworth Pinckney, Charles Pinckney, Pierce Butler

Georgia: William Few, Abr Baldwin

Attest: William Jackson, Secretary

In Convention Monday, September 17th, 1787.

Present,
The States of New Hampshire, Massachusetts, Connecticut, Mr. Hamilton from New York, New Jersey, Pennsylvania,

Delaware, Maryland, Virginia, North Carolina, South Carolina and Georgia.

Resolved,
That the preceeding Constitution be laid before the United States in Congress assembled, and that it is the Opinion of this Convention, that it should afterwards be submitted to a Convention of Delegates, chosen in each State by the People thereof, under the Recommendation of its Legislature, for their Assent and Ratification; and that each Convention assenting to, and ratifying the Same, should give Notice thereof to the United States in Congress assembled. Resolved, That it is the Opinion of this Convention, that as soon as the Conventions of nine States shall have ratified this Constitution, the United States in Congress assembled should fix a Day on which Electors should be appointed by the States which have ratified the same, and a Day on which the Electors should assemble to vote for the President, and the Time and Place for commencing Proceedings under this Constitution. That after such Publication the Electors should be appointed, and the Senators and Representatives elected: That the Electors should meet on the Day fixed for the Election of the President, and should transmit their Votes certified, signed, sealed and directed, as the Constitution requires, to the Secretary of the United States in Congress assembled, that the Senators and Representatives should convene at the Time and Place assigned; that the Senators should appoint a President of the Senate, for the sole purpose of receiving, opening and counting the Votes for President; and, that after he shall be chosen, the Congress, together with the President, should, without Delay, proceed to execute this Constitution.

By the Unanimous Order of the Convention

Go. WASHINGTON – President.
W. JACKSON Secretary.

The Bill of Rights

The conventions of a number of the States having at the time of their adopting the Constitution, expressed a desire, in order to prevent misconstruction or abuse of its powers, that further declaratory and restrictive clauses should be added.

Amendment I – Freedom of Religion, Press

Congress shall make no law respecting an establishment of religion, or prohibiting the free exercise thereof; or abridging the freedom of speech, or of the press; or the right of the people peaceably to assemble, and to petition the Government for a redress of grievances.

Amendment II – Right to Bear Arms

A well regulated Militia, being necessary to the security of a free State, the right of the people to keep and bear Arms, shall not be infringed.

Amendment III – Quartering of Soldiers

No Soldier shall, in time of peace be quartered in any house, without the consent of the Owner, nor in time of war, but in a manner to be prescribed by law.

Amendment IV - Search and Seizure

The right of the people to be secure in their persons, houses, papers, and effects, against unreasonable searches and seizures, shall not be violated, and no Warrants shall issue, but upon probable cause, supported by Oath or affirmation, and particularly describing the place to be searched, and the persons or things to be seized.

Amendment V - Trial and Punishment, Compensation for Takings

No person shall be held to answer for a capital, or otherwise infamous crime, unless on a presentment or indictment of a Grand Jury, except in cases arising in the land or naval forces, or in the Militia, when in actual service in time of War or public danger; nor shall any person be subject for the same offence to be twice put in jeopardy of life or limb; nor shall be compelled in any criminal case to be a witness against himself, nor be deprived of life, liberty, or property, without due process of law; nor shall private property be taken for public use, without just compensation.

Amendment VI - Right to Speedy Trial, Confrontation of Witnesses

In all criminal prosecutions, the accused shall enjoy the right to a speedy and public trial, by an impartial jury of the State and district wherein the crime shall have been committed, which district shall have been previously ascertained by law, and to be informed of the nature and cause of the accusation; to be confronted with the witnesses against him; to have compulsory process for obtaining witnesses in his favor, and to have the Assistance of Counsel for his defence.

Amendment VII - Trial by Jury in Civil Cases

In Suits at common law, where the value in controversy shall exceed twenty dollars, the right of trial by jury shall be preserved, and no fact tried by a jury, shall be otherwise re-examined in any Court of the United States, than according to the rules of the common law.

Amendment VIII - Cruel and Unusual Punishment
Excessive bail shall not be required, nor excessive fines imposed, nor cruel and unusual punishments inflicted.

Amendment IX - Construction of Constitution
The enumeration in the Constitution, of certain rights, shall not be construed to deny or disparage others retained by the people.

Amendment X - Powers of the States and People
The powers not delegated to the United States by the Constitution, nor prohibited by it to the States, are reserved to the States respectively, or to the people.

Additional Amendments to the Constitution

ARTICLES in addition to, and Amendment of, the Constitution of the United States of America, proposed by Congress, and ratified by the Legislatures of the several States, pursuant to the fifth Article of the original Constitution.

Amendment XI - Judicial Limits
[Proposed 1794; Ratified 1798]
The Judicial power of the United States shall not be construed to extend to any suit in law or equity, commenced or prosecuted against one of the United States by Citizens of another State, or by Citizens or Subjects of any Foreign State.

Amendment XII - Choosing the President, Vice-President
[Proposed 1803; Ratified 1804]

The Electors shall meet in their respective states, and vote by ballot for President and Vice-President, one of whom, at least, shall not be an inhabitant of the same state with themselves; they shall name in their ballots the person voted for as President, and in distinct ballots the person voted for as Vice-President, and they shall make distinct lists of all persons voted for as President, and of all persons voted for as Vice-President, and of the number of votes for each, which lists they shall sign and certify, and transmit sealed to the seat of the government of the United States, directed to the President of the Senate; – The President of the Senate shall, in the presence of the Senate and House of Representatives, open all the certificates and the votes shall then be counted; – The person having the greatest number of votes for President, shall be the President, if such number be a majority of the whole number of Electors appointed; and if no person have such majority, then from the persons having the highest numbers not exceeding three on the list of those voted for as President, the House of Representatives shall choose immediately, by ballot, the President. But in choosing the President, the votes shall be taken by states, the representation from each state having one vote; a quorum for this purpose shall consist of a member or members from two-thirds of the states, and a majority of all the states shall be necessary to a choice. And if the House of Representatives shall not choose a President whenever the right of choice shall devolve upon them, before the fourth day of March next following, then the Vice-President shall act as President, as in the case of the death or other constitutional disability of the President. – The person having the greatest number of votes as Vice-President, shall be the Vice-President, if such number be a majority of the whole number of Electors appointed, and if no person have a majority, then from the two highest numbers on the list, the Senate shall choose the Vice-President; a quorum for the purpose shall consist of two-thirds of the whole number of Senators, and a majority of the whole number shall be necessary to a choice. But no person constitutionally ineligible to the office of President shall be eligible to that of Vice-President of the United States.

Amendment XIII - Slavery Abolished
[Proposed 1865; Ratified 1865]
Section 1. Neither slavery nor involuntary servitude, except as a punishment for crime whereof the party shall have been duly convicted, shall exist within the United States, or any place subject to their jurisdiction.

Section 2. Congress shall have power to enforce this article by appropriate legislation.

Amendment XIV - Citizenship Rights
[Proposed 1866; Allegedly ratified 1868. See Fourteenth Amendment Law Library for argument it was not ratified.]
Section 1. All persons born or naturalized in the United States, and subject to the jurisdiction thereof, are citizens of the United States and of the State wherein they reside. No State shall make or enforce any law which shall abridge the privileges or immunities of citizens of the United States; nor shall any State deprive any person of life, liberty, or property, without due process of law; nor deny to any person within its jurisdiction the equal protection of the laws.

Section 2. Representatives shall be apportioned among the several States according to their respective numbers, counting the whole number of persons in each State, excluding Indians not taxed. But when the right to vote at any election for the choice of electors for President and Vice President of the United States, Representatives in Congress, the Executive and Judicial officers of a State, or the members of the Legislature thereof, is denied to any of the male inhabitants of such State, being twenty-one years of age, and citizens of the United States, or in any way abridged, except for participation in rebellion, or other crime, the basis of representation therein shall be reduced in the proportion which the number of such male citizens shall bear to the whole number of male citizens twenty-one years of age in such State.

Section 3. No person shall be a Senator or Representative in Congress, or elector of President and Vice President, or hold any office, civil or military, under the United States, or under any State, who, having previously taken an oath, as a member of Congress, or as an officer of the United States, or as a member of any State legislature, or as an executive or judicial officer of any State, to support the Constitution of the United States, shall have engaged in insurrection or rebellion against the same, or given aid or comfort to the enemies thereof. But Congress may by a vote of two-thirds of each House, remove such disability.

Section 4. The validity of the public debt of the United States, authorized by law, including debts incurred for payment of pensions and bounties for services in suppressing insurrection or rebellion, shall not be questioned. But neither the United States nor any State shall assume or pay any debt or obligation incurred in aid of insurrection or rebellion against the United States, or any claim for the loss or emancipation of any slave; but all such debts, obligations and claims shall be held illegal and void.

Section 5. The Congress shall have power to enforce, by appropriate legislation, the provisions of this article.

Amendment XV - Race No Bar to Vote
[Proposed 1869; Ratified 1870]

Section 1. The right of citizens of the United States to vote shall not be denied or abridged by the United States or by any State on account of race, color, or previous condition of servitude.

Section 2. The Congress shall have power to enforce this article by appropriate legislation.

Amendment XVI - Status of Income Tax Clarified
[Proposed 1909; Questionably Ratified 1913]
The Congress shall have power to lay and collect taxes on incomes, from whatever source derived, without apportionment among the several States, and without regard to any census or enumeration.

Amendment XVII - Senators Elected by Popular Vote
[Proposed 1912; Ratified 1913; Possibly Unconstitutional (See Article V, Clause 3 of the Constitution)]
The Senate of the United States shall be composed of two Senators from each State, elected by the people thereof, for six years; and each Senator shall have one vote. The electors in each State shall have the qualifications requisite for electors of the most numerous branch of the State legislatures.

When vacancies happen in the representation of any State in the Senate, the executive authority of such State shall issue writs of election to fill such vacancies: Provided, That the legislature of any State may empower the executive thereof to make temporary appointments until the people fill the vacancies by election as the legislature may direct.

This amendment shall not be so construed as to affect the election or term of any Senator chosen before it becomes valid as part of the Constitution.

Amendment XVIII - Liquor Abolished

[Proposed 1917; Ratified 1919; Repealed 1933 (See Amendment XXI, Section 1)]

Section 1. After one year from the ratification of this article the manufacture, sale, or transportation of intoxicating liquors within, the importation thereof into, or the exportation thereof from the United States and all territory subject to the jurisdiction thereof for beverage purposes is hereby prohibited.

Section 2. The Congress and the several States shall have concurrent power to enforce this article by appropriate legislation.

Section 3. This article shall be inoperative unless it shall have been ratified as an amendment to the Constitution by the legislatures of the several States, as provided in the Constitution, within seven years from the date of the submission hereof to the States by the Congress.

Amendment XIX - Women's Suffrage

[Proposed 1919; Ratified 1920]

The right of citizens of the United States to vote shall not be denied or abridged by the United States or by any State on account of sex.

Congress shall have power to enforce this article by appropriate legislation.

Amendment XX - Presidential, Congressional Terms

[Proposed 1932; Ratified 1933]

Section 1. The terms of the President and Vice President shall end at noon on the 20th day of January, and the terms of

Senators and Representatives at noon on the 3d day of January, of the years in which such terms would have ended if this article had not been ratified; and the terms of their successors shall then begin.

Section 2. The Congress shall assemble at least once in every year, and such meeting shall begin at noon on the 3d day of January, unless they shall by law appoint a different day.

Section 3. If, at the time fixed for the beginning of the term of the President, the President elect shall have died, the Vice President elect shall become President. If a President shall not have been chosen before the time fixed for the beginning of his term, or if the President elect shall have failed to qualify, then the Vice President elect shall act as President until a President shall have qualified; and the Congress may by law provide for the case wherein neither a President elect nor a Vice President elect shall have qualified, declaring who shall then act as President, or the manner in which one who is to act shall be selected, and such person shall act accordingly until a President or Vice President shall have qualified.

Section 4. The Congress may by law provide for the case of the death of any of the persons from whom the House of Representatives may choose a President whenever the right of choice shall have devolved upon them, and for the case of the death of any of the persons from whom the Senate may choose a Vice President whenever the right of choice shall have devolved upon them.

Section 5. Sections 1 and 2 shall take effect on the 15th day of October following the ratification of this article.

Section 6. This article shall be inoperative unless it shall have been ratified as an amendment to the Constitution by the legislatures of three-fourths of the several States within seven years from the date of its submission.

Amendment XXI – Repeal of Prohibition

[Proposed 1933; Ratified 1933]
Section 1. The eighteenth article of amendment to the Constitution of the United States is hereby repealed.

Section 2. The transportation or importation into any State, Territory, or possession of the United States for delivery or use therein of intoxicating liquors, in violation of the laws thereof, is hereby prohibited.

Section 3. This article shall be inoperative unless it shall have been ratified as an amendment to the Constitution by conventions in the several States, as provided in the Constitution, within seven years from the date of the submission hereof to the States by the Congress.

Amendment XXII - Presidential Term-limits

[Proposed 1947; Ratified 1951]
Section 1. No person shall be elected to the office of the President more than twice, and no person who has held the office of President, or acted as President, for more than two years of a term to which some other person was elected President shall be elected to the office of the President more than once. But this Article shall not apply to any person holding the office of President when this Article was proposed by the Congress, and shall not prevent any person who may be holding the office of President, or acting as President, during the term within which this Article becomes operative from holding the office of President or acting as President during the remainder of such term.

<u>Section 2.</u> This article shall be inoperative unless it shall have been ratified as an amendment to the Constitution by the legislatures of three-fourths of the several States within seven years from the date of its submission to the States by the Congress.

Amendment XXIII - Presidential Vote for District of Columbia
[Proposed 1960; Ratified 1961]
<u>Section 1.</u> The District constituting the seat of Government of the United States shall appoint in such manner as the Congress may direct:

A number of electors of President and Vice President equal to the whole number of Senators and Representatives in Congress to which the District would be entitled if it were a State, but in no event more than the least populous State; they shall be in addition to those appointed by the States, but they shall be considered, for the purposes of the election of President and Vice President, to be electors appointed by a State; and they shall meet in the District and perform such duties as provided by the twelfth article of amendment.

<u>Section 2.</u> The Congress shall have power to enforce this article by appropriate legislation.

Amendment XXIV - Poll Tax Barred
[Proposed 1962; Ratified 1964]
<u>Section 1.</u> The right of citizens of the United States to vote in any primary or other election for President or Vice President, for electors for President or Vice President, or for Senator or Representative in Congress, shall not be denied or abridged by the United States or any State by reason of failure to pay any poll tax or other tax.

Section 2. The Congress shall have power to enforce this article by appropriate legislation.

Amendment XXV - Presidential Disability and Succession
[Proposed 1965; Ratified 1967]
Section 1. In case of the removal of the President from office or of his death or resignation, the Vice President shall become President.

Section 2. Whenever there is a vacancy in the office of the Vice President, the President shall nominate a Vice President who shall take office upon confirmation by a majority vote of both Houses of Congress.

Section 3. Whenever the President transmits to the President pro tempore of the Senate and the Speaker of the House of Representatives his written declaration that he is unable to discharge the powers and duties of his office, and until he transmits to them a written declaration to the contrary, such powers and duties shall be discharged by the Vice President as Acting President.

Section 4. Whenever the Vice President and a majority of either the principal officers of the executive departments or of such other body as Congress may by law provide, transmit to the President pro tempore of the Senate and the Speaker of the House of Representatives their written declaration that the President is unable to discharge the powers and duties of his office, the Vice President shall immediately assume the powers and duties of the office as Acting President.

Thereafter, when the President transmits to the President pro tempore of the Senate and the Speaker of the House of Representatives his written declaration that no inability exists,

285

he shall resume the powers and duties of his office unless the Vice President and a majority of either the principal officers of the executive department or of such other body as Congress may by law provide, transmit within four days to the President pro tempore of the Senate and the Speaker of the House of Representatives their written declaration that the President is unable to discharge the powers and duties of his office. Thereupon Congress shall decide the issue, assembling within forty-eight hours for that purpose if not in session. If the Congress, within twenty-one days after receipt of the latter written declaration, or, if Congress is not in session, within twenty-one days after Congress is required to assemble, determines by two-thirds vote of both Houses that the President is unable to discharge the powers and duties of his office, the Vice President shall continue to discharge the same as Acting President; otherwise, the President shall resume the powers and duties of his office.

Amendment XXVI - Voting Age Set to 18 Years
[Proposed 1971; Ratified 1971]
Section 1. The right of citizens of the United States, who are eighteen years of age or older, to vote shall not be denied or abridged by the United States or by any State on account of age.

Section 2. The Congress shall have power to enforce this article by appropriate legislation.

Amendment XXVII - Limiting Changes to Congressional Pay
[Proposed 1789; Ratified 1992; Second of Twelve Articles comprising the Bill of Rights]
No law, varying the compensation for the services of the Senators and Representatives, shall take effect, until an election of Representatives shall have intervened.

Quotes from the Founders

"Hold on, my friends, to the Constitution and to the Republic for which it stands. Miracles do not cluster, and what has happened once in 6000 years, may not happen again. Hold on to the Constitution, for if the American Constitution should fail, there will be anarchy throughout the world." – Daniel Webster

"The Constitution of the United States is the result of the collected wisdom of our country." – Thomas Jefferson

"The number of individuals employed under the Constitution of the United States will be much smaller than the number employed under the particular states. There will consequently be less of personal influence on the side of the former than of the latter." – James Madison

"If men of wisdom and knowledge, of moderation and temperance, of patience, fortitude and perseverance, of sobriety and true republican simplicity of manners, of zeal for the honour of the Supreme Being and the welfare of the commonwealth; if men possessed of these other excellent qualities are chosen to fill the seats of government, we may expect that our affairs will rest on a solid and permanent foundation." – Samuel Adams

"In the formation of our constitution the wisdom of all ages is collected – the legislators of antiquity are consulted, as well as the opinions and interests of the millions who are concerned. It short, it is an empire of reason." – Noah Webster

"In the next place, the state governments are, by the very theory of the constitution, essential constituent parts of the general government. They can exist without the latter, but the latter cannot exist without them." – Joseph Story

287

"Republics are created by the virtue, public spirit, and intelligence of the citizens. They fall, when the wise are banished from the public councils, because they dare to be honest, and the profligate are rewarded, because they flatter the people, in order to betray them." – Joseph Story

"The Constitution doesn't guarantee happiness, only the pursuit of it. You have to catch up with it yourself." – Benjamin Franklin

"Firearms are second only to the Constitution in importance; they are the peoples' liberty's teeth." – George Washington

"The Constitution is the guide which I never will abandon." – George Washington

"The Constitution preserves the advantage of being armed which Americans possess over the people of almost every other nation where the governments are afraid to trust the people with arms." – James Madison

"The happy Union of these States is a wonder; their Constitution a miracle; their example the hope of Liberty throughout the world." – James Madison

"Our constitution was made only for a moral and religious people. It is wholly inadequate to the government of any other." John Adams

"The Constitution is not an instrument for the government to restrain the people, it is an instrument for the people to restrain the government." – Patrick Henry

Thoughts to Consider

One of the most tragic forces in every society is moral decay, especially after a society has been stable and prosperous for an extended period of time. Within a generation or two after a society or nation is founded, it begins falling away from its founding principles; it's occurred in nearly every nation regardless of how strict and how careful the founders were, and America has proven to be no exception to this law of decay. However, the moral decay has been accelerating over the last fifty years, and now America appears to be at the breaking point.

If the Rule of Law is to be reestablished and the Constitution is to be restored to its rightful place in America, then the restoration needs to begin with us in ourselves, our homes, our communities, and quickly propagate upwards to the people in elected office. Our current Congress, President, and courts don't defy the Constitution as much as just ignore it through policies, executive orders, and even legislation. To many of them, the Constitution is just another old piece of paper that is quaint, but worthless.

In the Old Testament, there was a story about a young king who found his nation to be in a similar state of moral, spiritual, and societal decay: King Josiah (2 Kings 22-23). Upon taking the throne, he ordered the priests to open the Temple and begin restoring it. While they were cleaning it out, they found a scroll of the Law – the Torah – and immediately took it to the king. The Torah, the Jewish "constitution" hadn't been read, much less followed, in centuries. As soon as King Josiah read the Law and saw how far his nation had fallen away from their constitution and principles, he tore his robes, proclaimed a fast, and then had everyone come to Jerusalem to hear the words of the Law, repent of their wicked ways, and return to their founding principles.

Today in the early Twenty-First Century, America needs to do the same thing: we need to immediately repent and return to our founding principles and embrace the virtues and ideas established by our Founders. And as for our president, our representatives, and our public servants, they should be the first to repent and return to following the Constitution with all their hearts, because they have been entrusted with it and have sworn an oath to uphold it (so help them, God)! Our Founding Fathers built this country after leaving the failed, tyrannical nations of Europe and came here to build a free nation based upon individual liberty and personal virtues. If we become enslaved, it will be our fault in not repenting – not theirs!

In Deuteronomy 31, Moses (Israel's equivalent to George Washington) commanded that the entire Law be read to the people at the end of every sabbatical year – every seven years. The Jewish holidays are more or less their catechism to ensure the Law permeates not only their daily lives, but their entire nation. The people were to also contemplate and discuss the Law on a regular basis, as well as diligently teach it to their children.

We in America must do likewise – we must begin reading the Declaration of Independence and the Constitution on a regular basis and discuss it. In our families and our schools, both should be read at least once a year without exception. We must teach our history and our founding principles and documents to our children and our families, before we lose them like the Jews lost their Torah before the Babylonian Captivity.

One of the requirements of holding any public office should be to read the Declaration of Independence and the Constitution every year and of course, before taking the oath of office by any federal official. Nationally, we should have our founding documents read publicly on our holidays – that's not too much to ask in exchange for the vast liberties we have been given by our forefathers.

Chapter 10 - The Invisible Hand

"I have lived, Sir, a long time, and the longer I live, the more convincing proofs I see of this truth – that God governs the affairs of men. And if a sparrow cannot fall to the ground without His notice, is it probable that an empire can rise without His aid?" – Benjamin Franklin

America is a special nation – and not only is it special, it's extraordinarily exceptional in every sense of the word. From the earliest days of its settlement, the very word "America" imparted hope, optimism, and the dream of a new life and new opportunities – and liberty.

As G.K. Chesterton once quipped, "America is the only nation in the world that is founded on a creed." This creed was first penned by Thomas Jefferson and is known throughout our nation even today as the Preamble of the Declaration of Independence:

"We hold these truths to be self-evident, that all men are created equal, that they are endowed by their Creator with certain unalienable rights, that among these are life, liberty and the pursuit of happiness."

The American Creed – along with the rest of the Declaration of Independence – declares that Americans believe that our Creator (the Judeo-Christian God) gave all people on the earth certain natural rights that no government or society has the authority to take away, namely our very lives, our individual freedoms, and our free pursuit of happiness. The rest of the Declaration goes on to describe that when our natural, inalienable rights are repeatedly violated without cause and without redress, We the People have the right to throw off the

291

shackles of that tyrannical government and institute new government that will not trample our rights.

Until the Declaration of Independence, kings and governments felt they had the complete authority to do whatever they wanted to their people, that the people existed merely to be subjects, serfs, or slaves of the State. The American Creed declared that the very opposite is true: the State exists for the benefit of the people, not the people for the benefit of the State. After all, which came first in history: various groups of people who settled a strange land and formed a government to keep order and protect their freedoms, or a government that founded a new land and then brought in all their subjects? In nearly every nation on earth, it has been the former, not the latter, from the very dawn of recorded history, but especially in the New World.

Given the stunning departure from the prevailing mindset of government and natural rights at the time, from where did Jefferson, Franklin, Adams, and the rest of the delegates of the Continental Congress obtain their revolutionary ideas about natural rights? Mostly, the writings of John Locke and Thomas Hobbes served as the philosophical and political foundation for the independence movement. However, even those ideas came from a much earlier, more widely-known source: the Bible. From the earliest days of the Colonies, the Bible was the primary foundation upon which the Pilgrims and the Puritans built their societies, devout Christians who wanted to follow the Word of God and His Laws rather than a king, a Parliament, and especially a state-controlled Church.

America's Puritan Foundations

The Puritan sect in Great Britain began as movement to reform the Church of England. As the Protestant movement rapidly spread through Europe and Bibles became more widely available, thousands of Christians began to see just how apostate the state-churches had become. The Bishops and other clergy had become servants of the State and often served for their own personal gain. The Puritans wanted to reform what they viewed as a corrupt church and make it follow the New Testament model more closely rather than the state-church entity of Rome.

As persecution set in under Queen Elizabeth and then King James, a small group of Puritans concluded that the Church of England was unable to be reformed and split off from the rest of the movement – separating themselves into an independent, ecclesiastical body. They became known as the Separatists and were soon persecuted more than their fellow Puritans because they held the radical opinion that no human king or queen should wield authority over the Church. If anyone could first lay claim to the idea of the "Separation of Church and State," it was the Separatists, and they paid dearly for it. Several years later, they separated even further, to about three thousand miles out of reach of the Queen and the Church of England. The Separatists are better known as the Pilgrims, and when they settled Plymouth, they brought their ideas of separating the church from the state with them.

Within ten years after the founding of Plymouth, King Charles arose in England who empowered the Church to effectively crush the Puritan movement once and for all. By that time, word of the growing success of the Separatists in the New World was circulating, and the Puritans made the decision to leave their homeland and reform the Church from the other side of the Atlantic. They petitioned the king for a charter and in 1630, the Puritans began a mass-migration to the New World. Over the next ten years, more than twenty thousand people migrated from England into the Massachusetts Bay Colony, and New England was established.

Throughout the early difficult years of settlement and the mass-immigration to New England, the Puritan's purpose and vision remained: to clearly demonstrate to their mother country how a society could function when based upon the Bible rather than a state-run church or a power-hungry king. In New

England, though there were elders and church-leadership, there was no nobility and everyone was expected to work hard, serve one another, and follow the dictates of their conscience as set forth in the Bible. Soon New England was flourishing while their neighbors in Jamestown – who wanted to replicate English society in the New World – were starving and making a nuisance of themselves to the natives around them. The migrants who served one another and worked together succeeded and quickly built a self-sufficient colony, while those in Virginia could not and had to be frequently resupplied from England for the next thirty years.

The Puritans in New England soon saw themselves as a sort of New Israel and New Jerusalem – a shining city on a hill (a phrase from the New Testament and coined by John Winthrop). Their New Jerusalem was intended to show the rest of the world the way to have a peaceful, free, moral society, where people were free to worship God without fear from the king, the State, or even the state-church. And while the Puritan congregational elders governed New England, they did so for the good of their fledgling colonies rather than for accumulation of power or personal gain. The Law of Christ - loving your neighbor as yourself – wasn't just a simple creed to the Puritans, but the principle they sought to live by.

In Puritan New England, there was initially no such connotation as the separation of church and state, because they were one in the same. However, the difference was that when society is based upon "loving your neighbor as yourself" and everyone is following the Ten Commandments, there will be very little crime, especially when people willingly submit to the authorities (the elders) for their own good. Since the Puritans were nearly obsessive about controlling their own individual behavior, there was little need for strong government – and self-government arose. The root of all self-government is the government of yourself, your family, and expecting others to do the same. But in the rare cases when there was a crime, the Puritans looked to the Bible to arrive at their punishments, often

294

excommunicating or banishing the criminals. Capital crimes were very few and far between, but there were several hangings for cases of adultery or murder. By our standards today, they seem backwards and cruel, but our crime rates are much, much higher than those of the Puritans, aren't they? Perhaps instead of condemning the Puritans for being intolerant, perhaps it is we who have become too tolerant of immorality and the crime it leads to.

One of the greatest truths that the Puritans and the Pilgrims (who were later absorbed into the Massachusetts Bay Colony) extracted from the Bible was the idea that without widespread self-control and personal virtue, liberty and self-government cannot exist. The Puritans were able to create the first self-governing, functioning society built upon the Judeo-Christian principles of the Golden Rule and the Ten Commandments. As the Puritans lived out their religion in their everyday lives, their model of a congregational society took root and spread, though it gradually dampened as more people began choosing their own faiths. Puritanism had greatly diminished by the beginning of the Eighteenth Century, but many of its ideals and standards remained in New England society and politics. The ideas of self-government and liberty through virtue remain today, nearly four hundred years after Puritan New England, though these principles have been under assault for the last several decades.

Since the beginning of the Progressive Era, the Puritans have been excoriated and maligned for their notions of rigorous self-control and obsessing over sin. The Salem Witch Trials have been blown out of proportion to nullify the multitude and magnitude of accomplishments that the Puritans achieved. Like the Pilgrims, these early Americans regularly petitioned God on their behalf and believed that He was starting something new in them, a nation built upon the Rule of Law and the Law of Christ (loving one another) rather than the fallible Laws of Man which always lead to tyranny. A century after Puritan New England waned, their legacy of self-government and liberty through Judeo-Christian standards and personal virtue remained strong, which eventually caused the Colonists to declare their right to self-government and permanently break with England.

Even fifty years after the Revolutionary War, the link between Christianity and American self-government remained strong. John Quincy Adams declared that from the beginning, Americans "connected in one indissoluble band the principles of civil government with the principles of Christianity." When Alexis de Tocqueville toured America in the 1830s, he observed that "America is the place where the Christian religion has kept the greatest power over men's souls; and nothing better demonstrates how useful and natural it is to man, since the country where it now has the widest sway is both the most enlightened and the freest."

Was America a better nation and our people generally happier when we were predominately a Judeo-Christian nation and had a solid moral foundation? Most certainly so, even all the way to the early 1960s, though crime had gradually been rising, especially during the days of Prohibition (which was another Progressive movement). When Alexis de Tocqueville visited America, he was astonished at the lack of crime, prisons, and even strife in American society. Why? Because people were still generally living according to the Bible and the personal principles of self-government and liberty were still strong, even 150 years after the end of Puritan New England.

Blessings and Curses

As the Puritans began to build New Israel, the world's first Judeo-Christian society, they were acutely aware that God had a unique plan for them – like ancient Israel, they would be a "light unto the nations." However, the Puritans very clearly understood from the Bible that the success of the plan or the fulfillment of the vision depended on their obedience to God. Through passages like Deuteronomy 28 and Leviticus 26, the Puritans understood how to recognize when they were truly following God's will or not by the various events occurring in their society – whether they were being blessed or struggling under trials.

When the native tribes around them would rise up and terrorize them or when there was a drought or even the specter of famine, the Puritans immediately repented of their sins, humbled themselves, and sought God through prayer and fasting. Often soon after they humbled themselves, the trial would come to an end and they would be spared, whether it was through a change in the weather like a long, gentle rain just before their crops were burned up or a sudden cease in the Indian attacks. When they were blessed, the Puritans gave God all the credit for their blessings, and when they were hampered by trials, they repented and sought after God.

Through many occurrences of this cycle of "blessings and curses," their belief that God governs in the affairs of men became even more of a reality. Even today, many Americans are still aware that our national, ecclesiastical, and personal behavior matter to God and that He still blesses us when we are doing right but curses us when we are doing wrong – or He simply removes His blessings and protections. And while those notions are mocked and derided by our secular culture, our schools, and even many of our churches today, that doesn't make those blessings and curses any less of a reality.

Near the end of Moses' ministry, forty years after bringing Israel out of Egypt and leading them through their wanderings in the wilderness, he reiterated their recent history to their children and recited the Law, as well as God's blessings for their obedience but also His curses on them for prolonged disobedience. If the Israelites completely broke their covenant with God, He swore to cast them out of the new land He was giving them and would scatter them to all the nations of the earth. But in His great mercy – as well as to keep His promises to Abraham, Isaac, and Jacob – He promised to regather them in the latter days and bring them back into the land and restore them as a nation. And the entire world has been watching God's restoration of the Jews to their homeland of Israel over the last century.

Through the interactions between not only God and Israel, but God and America, it can be concluded that the promises of blessings that God made to Israel can also be applied to any nation that makes a covenant with God. Several of His blessings on an obedient nation are that they will be blessed with fertile fields, plenty of grain, water and livestock, good leadership, victory in warfare, lack of illnesses and plenty of healthy children, and that they will be lenders to other nations and not debtors.

However, if a nation partakes in the blessings for obedience, they must also partake in the curses for disobedience. These curses involve droughts, famines, illnesses, loss of food, livestock, water, loss of children, loss of confidence, loss of victories in war, wicked leadership, and that they will become debtors and enslaved to other nations. Especially in warfare, they would be defeated regardless of how strong they were because God is responsible for the victory, and He had turned against them.

From the long history of the Israelites in the Bible, when they were obedient and God was with them, the Israelites were filled with courage and optimism, and even when severely outnumbered, they would win. During King David's reign, Israel became strong and blessed, and then during his son Solomon's time, they became incredibly prosperous. But at the latter end of Solomon's reign, they turned away from God and the nation was divided into Israel in the north and Judah in the south.

For the rest of their history, Israel and Judah were at war and would only return to God for brief periods of time. As both nations disregarded their covenant with God and turned to idolatry, they were consumed by fear, uncertainty, and were defeated regardless of how powerful they were. Sometimes God would even allow wicked rulers to come into power in order to drive the people to repentance, but as time went on even that didn't humble the people. Eventually, even God Himself turned against them and brought in the Assyrians and Babylonians to repeatedly punish the Israelites before finally casting them out of the land and exiling them to other nations.

Though the history of America has been only a fraction of Israel's, our nation appears to be following the same pattern that ancient Israel did: from a special, spiritual calling to being founded upon liberty and the Rule of Law, followed by cycles of disobedience, punishment, and revival, and then great prosperity followed by idolatry and the breaking of the covenant with God – and then national destruction. Over the last few decades, America has increasingly turned away from God, but like Israel in her latter days, we remained prosperous by His mercy.

Consider the tragic story of New England – it was settled by people of faith who were once extremely reliant upon Providence for their survival. By God's blessings, He used them to light the lamp of liberty that led to America's independence. For the next century, He continued to bless New England and caused them to shine the light of the Gospel and plant churches all over the nation. The Second Great Awakening from New England is why much of the foundation of the Midwest was Christian – it wasn't the South that was planting churches, but those from New England and other regions that earlier New Englanders settled. Their virtue and the struggle against slavery drove them to spread the Gospel across the entire continent.

But look at New England today – most of their churches are spiritually dead and more closely resemble the church-museums of Europe than living organisms. Not only have the churches of New England died, they were among the first to embrace textual criticism of the Bible and the mixing of liberalism and Progressivism with the Church. And by their former great reputation and the once-Christian institutions of higher-learning (like Princeton, Harvard, Yale, etc.), they have corrupted much of the country with Progressivism and are culpable for many of the evils that have spread throughout America. Consequently, the lampstand that once blazed from New England has been removed as with the Church of Ephesus in Revelation 2:5 – *"Remember therefore from where you have fallen; repent and do the first works, or else I will come to you quickly and remove your lampstand from its place – unless you repent."* The Church of Sardis in Revelation 3 is also highly applicable to those churches throughout America which were once living but are now dying – or dead.

Over the last several years, it's becoming increasingly clear that God has turned away from us and is removing His protection and blessings from our land. Through the horrible events of September 11th, the rampant murders and school-shootings, the rise of radical Islam and our involvement in war after war, and lastly the Financial Crisis of 2008 and the prolonged recession, our nation is tottering on the brink of collapse. Could it be that as a result of our pride and disobedience, He has allowed wicked, corrupt men and women to rule over us, He has removed His Hand of protection by allowing our enemies to break through our defenses, and in only a few years, allowed America to be changed from the world's foremost lender to the world's foremost debtor. Like the evil kings that were allowed to seize the throne of ancient Israel, could it be that Barack Obama was elevated into high office for the purposes of punishing and humbling our pride, in order that America be brought to repentance? God doesn't want anyone to perish (2 Peter 3:9), and if an extended time of trial is what is required to wake America up and lead her to repentance, then that's He will do.

Consider the story about King Ahab from 1 Kings 22:19-23, in which God allowed a fallen angel/demon to deceive the king in order to punish the nation of Israel because of their idolatry and wickedness. Few pastors speak of this because it appears to portray God as allowing or even condoning evil, but He's not – He's allowing the king and people to be tested to see if they will be deceived by a lying spirit. According to the Bible, all nations and their rulers are under His control, and He directs them as

300

He pleases (Proverbs 21:1, Daniel 2:21, 4:17). After all, the demon could have remained silent, the false prophets could've spoken the truth, or king could've ignored the bad advice. But none of them did.

> *Then Micaiah said [to the king], "Therefore hear the word of the Lord: I saw the Lord sitting on His throne, and all the host of heaven standing by, on His right hand and on His left. And the Lord said, 'Who will persuade Ahab to go up, that he may fall at Ramoth Gilead?' So one spoke in this manner, and another spoke in that manner. Then a spirit came forward and stood before the Lord, and said, 'I will persuade him.' The Lord said to him, 'In what way?' So he said, 'I will go out and be a lying spirit in the mouth of all his prophets.' And the Lord said, 'You shall persuade him, and also prevail. Go out and do so.' Therefore look! The Lord has put a lying spirit in the mouth of all these prophets of yours, and the Lord has declared disaster against you."*

Given that America elected – and then re-elected – a man who they knew little about and who had many extremely questionable associations, what if the unthinkable has happened: that Obama is God's instrument of punishment on our nation that has departed from Him? What if God has turned away from America because of our personal, ecclesiastical, and national sins? Today, America has become not only a constant participant in the things that God hates, but the primary exporter of immorality, violence, and perversity to the rest of the world! As far as morality is concerned, America is the problem in the world through our media, our entertainment, and our banking system that is only making the world's problems worse, not better. We should be exporting Bibles not bombs, missionaries not missiles, and building churches not strip-clubs.

After a steady diet of secularism and Progressivism over the last century, most Americans have forgotten the innumerable ways that God has helped America in her darkest hours. Not only did the Puritans and the early settlers understand how dependent they really were upon God, but our Founding Fathers knew that as well. Over and over during the Revolution, George Washington, the Continental Congress, and the churches throughout the nation beseeched God to help them in their Cause. Even the Constitutional Convention was fraught with heated arguments and nearly failed until the Framers began praying before every session and whenever they reached an impasse. Often soon after praying, a new idea was presented and a compromise was reached.

Something that early Americans and our Founders understood – that we have tragically forgotten – is that if we want God to protect us and help our nation, then we need to follow His precepts and commandments, namely to obey the Ten Commandments and serve one another.

The question of whether or not God has visibly moved in the history of America has already been answered in the fact that the United States of America not only became a nation, but the strongest and most prosperous nation in the history of the world. But since our history books have been heavily revised to exclude all mention of God and His works in our nation, some of the many accounts of how He has provided for us need to be recounted. Of all the nations in the history of the world (with the exception of Israel), there has been no other nation in which God has so visibly displayed His Providence.

The question that should at least give us pause to consider – if not cause us to fall on our faces – is that if God has so greatly blessed us when America followed Him, how terrible will our calamities be if we continue to disobey Him and break His commandments?

The Early Settlements

By their very survival, the early settlements in the New World demonstrated what sort of inhabitants and foundation that God intended for America. Though the Pilgrims were fewer, weaker, and poorer than their counterparts at Roanoke and Jamestown, they not only survived but flourished. The same proved to be true later with the Puritans who followed them soon afterwards. While the treasure-hunters and gold-seekers of Jamestown and other settlements languished under disease, starvation, and Indian attacks, those who came to America for freedom and worship flourished.

When the Pilgrims first landed at Plymouth, they were astounded to find not only fertile soil and drinkable fresh water supplies nearby, but that a significant portion of the land had already been cleared and was ready for planting. Their first year in Plymouth was horrific, with nearly half the settlers dying from disease and malnourishment; but the rest refused to leave because they knew that God would provide for them – somehow. In the following spring after their arrival, an Indian named Samoset walked right into their camp and spoke perfect English. A short time later, he brought another native named Squanto to their camp who had been a former inhabitant of the area. Squanto had been captured by the English years earlier and taken to England, where he had been educated and learned the English language. After he returned to America, he had found that his entire tribe of the Patuxet (one of the most fearsome tribes in the region) had been wiped out by a series of mysterious plagues (possibly smallpox). Squanto took it upon himself to take the Pilgrims under his wing and taught them how to grow corn and other crops, how to hunt and fish, and how to barter with the other nearby tribes.

Ten years after the Pilgrims landed in Plymouth in 1620, their Puritan brothers and sisters back in England fell under terrible persecution from the king and the Church of England, and decided to migrate to the New World. During the infamous era of pirates and terrible storms on the Atlantic, of the 198 Puritan ships that crossed over to the New World, only one was lost. From 1630 to 1640, over 20,000 Puritans migrated to New England, though some did return to England in the early years. Leaders like John Winthrop, John Cotton, and Thomas Hooker steeled the faith of the early settlers and within a matter of years, the new colonies were self-sufficient. While Jamestown continued to experience mortality rates exceeding 75% and had to be resupplied and repopulated for the first thirty years, New England was flourishing and growing after the first decade.

Time and time again in those early years in New England, the settlers saw the Hand of God moving among them. Sometimes they would be on the brink of starvation and then a ship stocked with new settlers – as well as much-needed supplies – would arrive at the last minute. Other times they would be experiencing a terrible drought which relented a day or two after a time of colony-wide prayer and fasting was proclaimed. Indian attacks were sometimes averted or diminished by the weather, the sudden threat of another nearby tribe, or even the sudden discovery of an impending attack that caused the settlers to flee or defend themselves. The acts of God were so numerous in those early years that Cotton Mather chronicled them in his book, "Magnalia Christi Americana" which was widely circulated throughout New England.

Another startling act of God on behalf of the Puritans in Massachusetts occurred in 1685. After Puritan New England had been well-established, the Crown and the Church of England began desiring to assert their authority over the colony. In 1683, King Charles II demanded the Massachusetts Bay Colony to hand over their charter so they would become a proper British colony with little independence both in their government and their worship. Once the Puritans received word of the order, they promptly refused to surrender their charter. King Charles was furious and decided to send Percy Kirk and 5,000 troops to Massachusetts to seize the charter and put down what he viewed as a rebellion against the Crown.

Word of the king's decision got back to Massachusetts in early 1685, and upon hearing the news, Increase Mather fasted and prayed. Once he was finished praying, he felt certain that God had assured him that Massachusetts would be delivered from the king and his soldiers. Two months later, the Puritans received word that King Charles had died of apoplexy – and that Kirk and the army would no longer be sent to Massachusetts. Mather worked back the date of the king's death and found it to be the very same day he had spent in prayer and fasting.

Also worthy of note is that slavery was first introduced at Jamestown during those early years, the very institution that would later spread throughout the Colonies and plague the country for centuries afterwards. Who knows how much pain, suffering, and bloodshed could have been avoided had slavery never been introduced at Jamestown.

The Colonies

After the Colonies were established and were steadily growing, the fervor of faith that had flowed throughout New England grew stale and began to diminish. As with ancient Israel, each succeeding generation in the "Promised Land" forgot what God had done for their forefathers and took His Providence for granted. But then in the early Eighteenth Century, God began moving again not only in New England, but throughout all the Colonies, rousing the people and awakening them to a new vision and purpose He had for the New World: the Great Awakening.

The Great Awakening began with a handful of preachers such as George Whitfield and Jonathan Edwards which not only led to tens of thousands of personal conversions and recommitments to Christianity, but also produced the spiritual foundation of independence. The critical importance of the Great Awakening is completely ignored in our secular public education system, and few today realize that the calls for independence and then the Revolutionary War were first preceded by the Great Awakening, a long period of spiritual revival that lasted nearly forty years. As the fires of the Great Awakening blazed through the Colonies, the old religious barriers between denominations, regions, and the Colonies were torn down and multitudes of new churches were planted. But even then, no one really understood what was happening or that the Great Awakening would one day eventually produce a new nation.

The generation that experienced the Great Awakening firsthand wasn't the generation that founded our nation, but their children's generation. The restored lives and new families from the Great Awakening produced men like Patrick Henry, Samuel Adams, John Adams, George Washington, Thomas Jefferson, and countless others who soon heard the call of freedom and proclaimed America's independence from Great Britain.

The Revolutionary War

Following on the heels of the Great Awakening, the fires of independence in the hearts and minds of Americans began to be stoked by men like Samuel Adams and Patrick Henry. Though the British army did most of the heavy-lifting of the French and Indian War, the long, widespread war on the frontier gave Americans the confidence that they could fight and win their independence, or at least defend themselves. The battles taught a small number of Americans the art of warfare and military strategy, as well as drawing out future Revolutionary military leaders such as George Washington, Ethan Allen, and Horatio Gates.

The French and Indian War also created the enormous debt for the British Crown that would soon ignite the fuse of the Boston Massacre, the Boston Tea Party, and later the Revolutionary War. But even the doubling of the national debt of Britain didn't have to end in her fighting her own Colonies; after all, they spent even more money in order to contain the Colonies and keep them part of the British Empire against their will. The British could have simply let the Colonies go and then taxed the imports and exports to pay their war debts rather than hire tens of thousands of mercenaries to fight their own countrymen. Could it be that God was moving in the British

Crown and Parliament as well, but to harden their hearts in order to bring about the Revolution? In America, the long war served to forge the new army and a new nation. If a nation cannot win their independence and sovereignty in the first place, they often cannot defend it later.

The actions of the obstinate King George and the prideful Parliament provoked the Colonists to action just after their spiritual courage had been bolstered by the decades of the Great Awakening. What began as "No taxation without representation!" soon gave way to "Give me liberty or give me death!" After that point had been reached, American independence was the only solution; they would not tolerate subjugation under the British Crown any longer. But in Boston, there was another rallying cry that seldom makes the history books of today: "No king but King Jesus!"

When the Revolution finally began, many Americans were still on the fence of whether they should follow Boston and the rest of New England into seeking their independence. After all, most Americans were very familiar with the Bible (especially after the Great Awakening), and everyone knew the verses that spoke of obeying civil authorities and even honoring the king and his soldiers. However, the American churches and the people eventually concluded that God had separated them from their motherland for a special purpose: to spread the Gospel to the New World and settle a new land which would be ruled not by a king, but by the Bible and the Rule of Law.

Soon after the Revolution started, the Colonists noted peculiar events in the weather and also the actions of the British commanders that seemed to parallel those they had read about in the Bible. It sounds laughable to our secularized ears and knowledge of history, but those who were eye-witnesses to the events not only recounted them for others, but would often write them down for others to read about later.

Early in the war when the British were quartered in Boston under General Howe (the spring of 1775), George Washington fortified Dorchester Heights which overlooked the harbor. That night when several thousand Continental soldiers were building up the earthworks, terrible winds and swells roared into Boston Harbor that prevented the British from responding. The next morning, the British were shocked that the Americans had fortified the high ground so quickly and completely that they evacuated Boston in order to save the ships they had stationed in Boston Harbor.

Five months later, the same General Howe landed 15,000 troops on Long Island and trapped Washington's army. After being thoroughly routed, it appeared that the Continental Army would be destroyed and the Revolution would soon be over. However, the day after their humiliating defeat, there was a terrible rain that made it impossible to fight; the Americans could either retreat or surrender, and the rain made retreat impossible. Later that evening, Washington ordered an evacuation, but the weather still wouldn't cooperate – until just before midnight when the winds suddenly changed direction and a heavy fog settled over Long Island. The thick fog was between the British and the American camps which prevented the British army from even seeing, much less stopping the silent American retreat. When the fog cleared the next morning and the British emerged to finish them off, the entire American army had disappeared in the dead of night. A similar fog-aided retreat occurred when the Continental Army was cornered in the Brooklyn Heights and barely escaped over the East River, which was completely controlled by the British Navy.

Another famous Washington movement aided by the weather was at the Crossing of the Delaware. During the attack on Trenton, there was a violent snowstorm blowing directly at the backs of the Americans and into the faces of the British. The American troops surprised the blinded British troops and scored a much-needed victory. After the snow melted, General Cornwallis marched his troops through muddy roads in order to trap Washington near Trenton and surround him the following morning. However, that night, the weather changed again and the ground quickly froze, enabling Washington to quickly move his troops out of the British trap. The Americans left so quickly and quietly that they didn't even bother to put out their campfires, and they moved around the entire British army unnoticed. But in the morning when the British entered the American camp, the ground quickly thawed, forcing them to slog through the mud once again. Meanwhile, Washington was on the other side of their lines and was already winning the Battle of Princeton.

In the Siege of Yorktown (the last battle of the Revolution), the weather also played a providential role in aiding the American efforts. Cornwallis was bottled up in the fort and was looking for a way to escape across the York River. The British Navy stationed in the Chesapeake was strangely delayed and Cornwallis had been relying upon them to help him escape, but the French had cut him off. The night that Washington's men began digging the trenches around the fort, the night became very dark and a gentle rain muffled the sound of their digging. When Cornwallis attempted to flee the fort to escape, the weather suddenly turned from a gentle rain to a violent storm that drove the British barges downriver and scattered his men. The next day, unable to fight and unable to retreat, Cornwallis surrendered to the tune of "The World Turned Upside Down."

The Early Republic

During the War of 1812 (which lasted until 1815), the new republic of the United States of America was almost destroyed. The British had been increasingly aggressive towards American ships, often capturing merchant vessels and pressing American sailors into service in the British Navy. The United States declared war on Great Britain and invaded Canada, burning the Parliament House in York (Toronto) to the ground. Though heavily occupied in Europe with war against Napoleon, the British retaliated by invading the United States. In 1814, the British sacked Washington D.C. and burned the White House, the Capitol Building, and other government buildings.

President James Madison proclaimed a National Day of Prayer in 1812 and 1813, though the war only worsened. In late August of 1814, when the British were burning the capital, ominous clouds rolled in and a bizarre tornado appeared and stopped the British efforts due to flying debris from the tornado. A number of roofs and chimneys also fell on top of the British troops, causing them to flee in disarray. A British historian recorded that more British soldiers were killed by the tornado that tore through Washington D.C. than from the American troops defending the capital.

As the British fled, the winds of the tornado gave way to rain which soon extinguished the fires, saving the White House and the rest of the city. On September 1st after the British had fled, James Madison issued a National Proclamation that credited Heaven (God) with saving the capital. That same year, Madison proclaimed a National Day of Public Humiliation, Fasting & Prayer on November 16, 1814. Five months later, Madison proclaimed a National Day of Thanksgiving & Devout Acknowledgment to God" on March 4, 1815, two weeks after the war ended.

Another miracle of the War of 1812 occurred after the peace treaty was signed in 1815 at the Battle of New Orleans. The British were preparing to attack the city, by which they would be able to control the mouth of the Mississippi River. Andrew Jackson and his group of Tennessee and Kentucky riflemen (along with some Indians, Creoles, and pirates), miraculously defended the city and drove the British away. In the Battle of New Orleans, only thirteen Americans were killed as opposed to the 2,000 British troops killed, which included the decimation of the Scottish Highlanders (Britain's most elite unit).

The Civil War

In contrast to the Revolutionary War and the War of 1812, there appears to be few occurrences in which God moved during the Civil War, or at least few occurrences which were recorded. The secession of the South and the proceeding Civil War were the culmination of over fifty years of heated debates, necessary compromises, and fevered emotions between the North and the South that finally exploded in all its terrible fury. When the smoke cleared after the Civil War, between 620,000 and 750,000 soldiers had been killed, along with thousands more from starvation, disease, etc.

Thomas Jefferson had an idea of the terrible cost of the eventual conflict caused by the institution of slavery when he said, "I tremble for my country when I reflect that God is just; that his justice cannot sleep forever." Even today in the age of modern warfare, the Civil War remains the bloodiest war in American history, claiming nearly as many American lives as all the other wars combined – including WWI and WWII, which claimed about 522,000 lives.

Slavery was a terrible national sin which may forever stain America; even a century after the slaves had been freed, the country almost erupted in a civil war again in the 1960s. If not for Martin Luther King, Jr. and other black leaders who pushed for civil rights through peaceful protests rather than violence, the country was spared much bloodshed. However, as soon as they obtained their civil rights, the black communities fell under the hypnotic trance of the welfare state which has all but destroyed their families and self-reliance.

Liberal minority leaders today continually keep their own people enslaved to the welfare plantation through a steady diet of victimhood and a sense of entitlement which appeals to their emotions and anger, but never really helps them become self-reliant and independent. The liberal leaders have been making empty promises to their minority base for the last fifty years, but their conditions continually worsen, not improve. The modern Civil Rights Movement is more about strengthening the liberal establishment and electing Progressive politicians than truly helping blacks and other minorities, but most refuse to even consider that reality.

At the time of the Revolutionary War, slavery was legal in the majority of the States – even in the North. However, the North gradually freed their slaves and abolished slavery by the mid-Nineteenth Century. Slavery was on the decline until the 1820s when the cotton gin was invented and cotton became the primary cash crop in the South. Then slavery exploded, not only becoming more widespread in the South but much more brutal. As the number of slaves increased, the more fearful their masters grew of violent revolts, and the harder they worked their slaves – and the more brutal the slave-masters became. Ironically, the slave-masters and many white Southerners were ruined by the institution of slavery and became as enslaved to it as those they held captive; when slavery finally ended, many fell into poverty because they had few practical skills to provide for themselves because the slaves had done most of the work for them.

In hindsight, it would have been much better for America – and especially the South – if they had abolished slavery when many of the Founders had wanted to: during the American Revolution. The Civil War ripped the entire nation apart, and while it hurt the North, it destroyed the South and set them back decades. But alas, hindsight is nearly always 20/20.

For the first two years of the Civil War, slavery was a secondary issue, while preserving the Confederacy or the Union was the primary motivation behind the war. It wasn't until the abolition of slavery became the focus of the war that the North began to prevail. On March 30, 1863, Abraham Lincoln issued a proclamation expressing the idea that the Civil War was a Divine punishment upon America for her sins. He designated April 30, 1863 as a day of fasting and prayer in the hope that God would restore the Union and bring peace to the country. Lincoln said, "...it is the duty of nations as well as of men, to own their dependence upon the overruling power of God, to confess their sins and transgressions, in humble sorrow, yet with assured hope that genuine repentance will lead to mercy and pardon; and to recognize the sublime truth, announced in the Holy Scriptures and proven by all history, that those nations only are blessed whose God is the Lord."

Several weeks after the proclamation, Robert E. Lee came to the conclusion that instead of fighting a defensive, guerilla-type war as they had been for the last two years (and succeeding), the Confederacy needed to invade the North and force them to stop the war. This invasion resulted in the horrible Battle of Gettysburg which devastated the Confederate Army. On July 1-3, 1863, the tide of the Civil War turned and resulted in 46,000 Union casualties but 51,000 Confederate casualties, in addition to killing, wounding, or capturing one-third of all the Confederate officers. The Confederacy never recovered from their terrible losses at Gettysburg.

Could God have hardened the hearts on both sides of the slavery conflict in the years leading up to the Civil War in order to forever end slavery and punish America for our national sins? Could He have also moved in the mind of Robert E. Lee, Abraham Lincoln, and their officers in order to turn the Civil War from a war about States' Rights to a war about slavery?

The Civil War may have formally ended at the Appomattox Courthouse, but it concluded with the assassination of Abraham Lincoln and later the period of Reconstruction. The way the Civil War ended and how Reconstruction was enacted left a legacy of hatred, bigotry, segregation, and racism that America has yet to fully overcome. The bloody Civil War that tore America apart and left deep scars on her has more than paid for her national sins.

The Modern Era

Some of the most dramatic examples of recent Divine intervention occurred during WWII, in which the very future of Western civilization was at stake. In May of 1940, over a period of two short weeks, the Germans had broken through the French lines, defeated the Belgians, and had pinned the British army at Dunkirk. The British army was on the verge of destruction, yet with certain victory at hand, Hitler suddenly halted the German offensive only twenty miles from Dunkirk because he was afraid that they were overexposed and could not be adequately resupplied.

While Hitler hesitated, a sudden thunderstorm grounded the German planes which allowed the Allied troops to set up a defense perimeter around Dunkirk. Immediately following a National Day of Prayer led by King George VI for their trapped army at Dunkirk, the British began a nine-day evacuation of Dunkirk over the typically rough and unpredictable English Channel. During those nine days, the sea on the Channel was as smooth as glass, greatly aiding the British retreat. But the day after the evacuation ended, the English Channel resumed with terrible swells and breakers that prevented the Germans from following them. Through that act of Divine intervention, more than 330,000 British soldiers were saved, which was almost the entire British army.

Two and a half years later, when the Allies began to liberate North Africa and Europe, an armada of 650 ships sailed undetected from England to North Africa by both the German Air Force and their U-boats for nearly two weeks. The day before the landing at Casablanca, the fifteen-foot waves prevented the Allies from landing – but the next morning the sea became calm and the landings proceeded in the midst of suddenly favorable weather.

On July 10, 1943 during the invasion of Sicily, General Eisenhower prayed over the armada and as the ships sailed out of sight, left them in the hands of God. But soon after the ships departed, terrible winds blew in and hampered the Allied invasion. Because of the weather, the Sicilians relaxed their defenses and the Allies were finally able to land successfully. Hours later, just before the attack was to commence, the winds suddenly died down and the raging seas stopped – and the invasion completely surprised the Sicilians and led to their defeat.

A similar abrupt change in the weather occurred on D-Day during the invasion of Normandy, in which Eisenhower purposely launched the invasion in bad weather. Due to the storms and the poor weather, the Germans had decided that no invasion would transpire. But on the morning of June 6, 1944, a short break in the bad weather occurred and the winds and seas became calm – along with the skies briefly clearing. The abrupt change in weather allowed the Allied planes to see and attack the Germans and the landings quickly commenced, catching the Germans off-guard.

In 1952 on the anniversary of D-Day, Eisenhower commented that, "This day eight years ago, I made the most agonizing decision of my life… the consequences of that decision could not have been foreseen by anyone. If there were nothing else in my life to prove the existence of an almighty and merciful God, the events of the next twenty-four hours did it. The greatest break in a terrible outlay of weather occurred the next day and allowed that great invasion to proceed, with losses far below those we had anticipated."

The Decision that Changed America

On June 17, 1963, America's highest court in the nation – the Supreme Court of the United States – declared that America was now independent of God and threw off the "shackles" of our Judeo-Christian heritage. America was now free to officially become a secular state like all the other nations, especially like those of enlightened Europe. In the case of "Abington School District v. Schempp," reading the Bible in public schools was ruled unconstitutional by Hugo Black and the Supreme Court.

Before that fateful decision, life had been improving in America year after year since the end of the Great Depression and WWII. Divorce-rates, dropout-rates, out-of-wedlock pregnancies, SAT scores, murder-rates, and other crime-rates had been steadily declining for years. America was getting better and better – until 1963. Then those same rates not only ceased improving, they exploded in the opposite direction!

It was as if some great Invisible Hand had been removed from America, and all the evil and chaos that had been restrained for years was allowed to deluge the nation. Immediately following the Supreme Court decision came the assassination of JFK, the escalation in Vietnam, the Great Society, the race-riots, the assassinations of RFK and Martin Luther King, Jr., and the massive anti-war protests that produced the radical Progressives which are now occupying many of our institutions, including the White House. Many of our youths who had been raised to hate communism and Marxism suddenly embraced it and sought to destroy the very nation which had given them everything. Overnight we went from optimism to pessimism, from respect for authority to rebellion, from light to darkness, and from order to chaos. Most of the problems plaguing America today are a direct result of the "fruit" produced during the 1960s.

Could it be that in 1963, God removed His Hand of protection over America – and not because He was being spiteful or capricious, but simply because we asked Him to? Could it be that by merely removing His Hand of protection from us, America quickly degenerated at the personal level, the family level, the community level, and at the national level? Unless due to a national crisis, the cultures of most countries slowly change over a period of years – in America during the 1960s, it seemed to happen in a matter of weeks or months. After 1963, the next generation in the universities suddenly, almost collectively decided to rebel against everything they had been taught and raised to believe.

Liberty and morality are intricately, tightly interwoven in the DNA of our hearts; when either side is torn off, it either dies or easily binds with a substitute that becomes inherently corrupt. When liberty is separated from morality, it degenerates into licentiousness or radical individualism. When morality is separated from liberty, it turns into legalism or authoritarianism.

316

In times of prosperity, pride rises and it becomes so easy to deceive ourselves and think that our prosperity is due to our own greatness, our own brilliance, and our own efforts rather than being the blessings of Providence.

September 11th and the Harbinger

From the preceding examples and accounts, God (or Providence, if you prefer) moved to help America numerous times in our history, though His actions were always precipitated by our churches, statesmen, and most of our nation humbling themselves and seeking Him in prayer and fasting. When faced with calamity and impossible odds, our presidents, governors, and pastors would proclaim a time of prayer and fasting to God that He might have mercy upon us and heal our land.

America has been incredibly blessed by God, and in times past, nearly all Americans acknowledged that fact. Even today, multitudes of Americans still acknowledge the Source of our blessings. However the difference between modern Americans and past generations is that they acknowledged that their sins were responsible for their punishment, while Americans today (by and large) do not. Our hearts have grown cold to Him, and it seems we pray more for His continued blessings and comforts without us bothering to repent and change how we're living. Our repentance and humiliation is often very temporary and superficial; we repent until the calamity has passed and then go right back to our former habits.

When the terrible events of September 11th, 2001 occurred and America was shaken, people filled the churches for weeks afterwards, humbling themselves and seeking God in the midst of our crisis. But did September 11th drive America to repentance? Not so you'd notice – the abortion clinics remained open and continued to slaughter over one million innocent children a year. Did we renounce our gluttony, covetousness, or adulterous ways? Did Americans take a break from their

317

shopping, excessive drinking, and pornography? No – yet we sought God's protection anyway, as if we thought He would continue to bless us without us having to genuinely turn from our sins.

The "wakeup call" of September 11th failed in part because our Christian, politically-correct president (George W. Bush) never told us to repent, but rather to go shopping and continue with our lives as if nothing had happened. But worse than that, when the people returned to the churches in droves, too many of the pastors and staff apparently had no clue as to what to do when people actually came seeking real answers – they couldn't and didn't teach the Word of God when people needed to hear it the most.

One of the surprise best-selling novels of 2012 was called "The Harbinger" by Jonathan Cahn. The premise of this fact-wrapped-in-fiction book is that God removed His wall or hedge of protection from America and allowed the terrorist attacks in order to get our attention, to drive us to repentance. But when we didn't repent, He then allowed other judgments to strike our nation such as Hurricane Katrina that devastated New Orleans and also the Financial Crisis of 2008.

What if these events are not meant to merely punish us but to get our attention and lead us to repentance? From the Old Testament history concerning God's interactions with Israel and other nations, if He cannot get their attention by one way, He continues to use other methods until either the nation repents or He reaches His limit with them. In Israel's history, that breaking point occurred when the nation became completely deaf and unrepentant to God, when they would slaughter the very men that God sent to speak to the people, as well as mercilessly slaughter their own offspring through child-sacrifices.

Another milestone that triggers God to move against a nation is when those in authority become incapable of telling the truth and when they devise evil continually, all the time. When a government becomes completely incapable of looking after its own people and the entire society breaks down, God often removes that government and places others in power to restore order. And given the blatant dishonesty, irresponsibility, theft, disregard for marriage and the family, the murdering of millions of innocent children (along with other sins), America and its leaders are dangerously close to bringing about God's judgment upon our land – if it hasn't already begun.

On January 17, 1994, the Northridge earthquake struck the San Fernando Valley. At the time, the Internet was just beginning to attract attention, and this particular earthquake hit the pornography industry very hard. The pornography industry was centered in and around Northridge and every major studio and distribution center was hit during the quake. Soon afterwards, the Internet boomed and the pornography industry exploded; now pornography from America is instantly distributed all over the world. What if the Northridge earthquake was both a judgment and a warning to America to get rid of that vile industry before the Internet went mainstream?

In mid-2012, on the same day that the Supreme Court announced their ruling on ObamaCare (June 28, 2012), a bizarre thunderstorm formation called a 'derecho' formed in west Chicago and zipped directly eastward before striking Washington D.C. Large portions of the capital and suburbs lost electricity, communications, and fell into a state of emergency. Washington's blackout lasted through the entire July 4th holiday. Could it be that God was trying to tell America something?

Later in 2012, only one week before the presidential election, Hurricane Sandy became a superstorm and ripped into the East Coast. The huge hurricane's diameter was over one thousand miles wide and stretched from Florida to New England, with the eye tearing through New Jersey before passing into Pennsylvania. Seven days before the election, electricity was cut to Lower Manhattan and the New York Stock Exchange was closed for half the week. The subways of New York City flooded after the city experienced the worst storm-surge since 1821. Again, could it be that God was trying to tell America something?

Of all the government policies enacted over the last century, ObamaCare will be the most transformative. Because the healthcare system has been effectively nationalized, it will change the entire relationship between American citizens and their government, and dependency will be cemented in place. If ObamaCare is not repealed, Americans will lose most of their personal freedoms over their own bodies; when government controls the healthcare system, they can control everything else.

The recent Drought of 2012 destroyed vast amounts of corn, wheat, soybeans, and other crops – corn yields were down about 13% from the previous year. There are those who liken this national drought to those which foreshadowed the Dust Bowl of the 1930s. On his "Thru the Bible" radio show in the 1960s, Dr. J. Vernon McGee said that "It was God who sent the Depression to my country," and that "If we had repented and had heard God at that time, we would never have had to fight in WWII. We would not have been in warfare in Korea, and then in Vietnam." What calamities lie in store for us because we have turned a deaf ear towards God and have refused to repent and seek Him, even after all the warnings He has been sending us?

At the beginning of the 2012 Drought, several Western states experienced the worst wildfires in their history. But were there any proclamations of prayer and fasting from our governors? Only one issued a call for their citizens to seek God's help: Governor Rick Perry of Texas. How many Colorado, Wyoming, and New Mexico pastors, governors, or other politicians called upon the people to pray for their states as they burned? Very few. The other governors remained silent as their states burned.

When Rick Perry did call for a day of prayer and fasting, his pleas were met with ridicule from all levels of the media, and most people ignored him. To top it off, Rick Perry was sued by several atheist and agnostic groups, as well as being attacked by the ACLU. When the next "natural disaster" occurs, will any governors even bother to suggest that people turn to God on behalf of their state? The governors of New Jersey, New York, and Pennsylvania didn't even mention God or prayer after their states were ravaged by the superstorm Hurricane Sandy.

It seems that Americans no longer tolerate calls for repentance and seeking God during terrible times. Has America become completely deaf to His methods of getting our attention, or are our hearts hardened beyond softening? If that is where we stand, then America may not be around much longer. Ancient Israel, the Roman Empire, and a host of many other once-great nations can testify to that reality.

Chapter 11 - Restoring our Faith

"It cannot be emphasized too clearly and too often that this nation was founded, not by religionists, but by Christians; not on religion, but on the gospel of Jesus Christ. For this very reason, peoples of other faiths have been afforded asylum, prosperity, and freedom of worship here." – Patrick Henry

The integrity of all democratic and republican forms of government relies upon the personal virtues and morals of their people. When personal virtues decline or even collapse, the society strengthens the police and government to attempt to keep the former degree of order. In the voting booths and then the general society, the decline usually takes longer to become evident as people increasingly vote more public benefits for themselves from the government's treasury. Soon political opportunists arise and take advantage of the faltering virtues in order to "save the society" – with themselves in control, of course. Within a matter of years or decades (depending on the form of government and the character of the people), the new society resembles very little of its former self.

Without a standard, solid set of virtues shared by the people and their leaders alike, democratic forms of government seldom form on their own. There must be a moral standard at the beginning of a society or there will be chaos and the society with either never form or will not last very long, much like trying to build a house with differing standards of measurements. If the carpenters, lumberyard, and other laborers/suppliers can't agree on the standard length of an inch, foot, or yard, the house probably won't be built; and if by some unlikely chance it is, the house won't be standing long.

Throughout history, most governments are formed around a powerful leader or conqueror and the people have very little say in the government that rules over them or even the laws which constrain them. As their power grows, most leaders become filled with pride and seek to cement their power and glory at the expense of the people. The occasions in which a powerful military leader willingly lays aside his own power are very few in history, yet in America, the occasion occurs every four or eight years since our Constitution was ratified over two hundred years ago. Every election in America can be viewed as a peaceful revolution, in which the people either retain or cast out their current government.

In America, that model of a civilian-leader came directly from the example set by George Washington, both after the Revolutionary War and after his first two terms as President. After the Revolution, he was so praised and beloved by the people and the military that many wanted to make him a king – but he adamantly refused and resigned from public service. Later after serving two terms in office, knowing that he was setting the example for all future presidents to follow, he declined to seek a third term. He and others feared that if presidents served more than eight years in high office, the desire to become some form of king or dictator would become too great and the republic would be transformed into a monarchy or empire like those in Europe.

Of all the Founding Fathers, George Washington best exemplifies virtue, both in war and in peace. Many of the Founding Fathers were renowned for their moral character and virtue, and so were the countless other people who chose them as their representatives. Moral, virtuous people do not select immoral leaders with which to trust their power, sovereignty, or voice, especially when it matters most. The corollary also holds true: immoral people do not select virtuous leaders to represent them, which would threaten their immorality. If our political offices are filled with immorality and crony capitalism, then what does that say about us who put those people into office?

Self-government begins with government of self – our human frailties, emotions, behavior, strengths, and weaknesses

– and without widespread personal self-government, local and national self-government cannot exist. Do Americans even want self-government today, which would necessarily include being virtuous? Do Americans want a society in which they take care of themselves or do they want to entrust their lives, liberties, and pursuits of happiness to someone else – even those they elect?

Where did that generation of Founding Fathers and the early American republic get their virtues and moral standards from? How did America lose her moral standards which had once been rock-solid? If modern America is lacking most of even its former basic values of civility, justice, and personal morality, is it possible for us to somehow renew those founding virtues and spread them throughout our faltering nation once again?

America's Faltering Faith

If the core of any republic or democracy is the personal virtues of its citizens, then the core of personal virtues is faith, typically faith in the Creator or the Supreme Being. There are variances to this generality in history, but the notion that Something or Someone greater than ourselves plays a central role in every culture, whether that entity be God, other gods, the king, or even the State. Depending on the particular gods of a society, this faith is often replaced by a fear of offending the king, the State, or the gods.

A startling insight into human behavior, thought, and worldview is that "We become like the gods we worship." This tendency doesn't just apply to individuals, but to entire societies, cultures, states, nations, and regions. If the gods of a land are violent, incestuous, or capricious, the people that worship such gods will become violent, sexually immoral, and untrustworthy. But if their gods are noble, virtuous, and courageous, the society will tend to take on those characteristics as well. We become like the gods we worship.

The gods who were first worshipped in America by the Indians were mostly animistic, violent, and capricious, though the legends and myths varied widely from tribe to tribe. When the Pilgrims, Puritans, and other Europeans came to America, their God was much different. And while most of the groups merely paid lip-service to the Gospel and sought after gold, land, wealth, or power, the Pilgrims and Puritans came to America to both spread the Gospel and build that "shining city on a hill" which they hoped would reform the Church of England.

The Puritans tightly coupled their Judeo-Christian beliefs with their civil institutions, particularly their schools, meetinghouses, and courts. The Puritans and their offshoots not only believed that all men are equal under God, they lived it. As the Puritans settled and spread throughout New England, their well-ordered institutions spread to other Colonies, with some modifications. The strictness of the Puritans was also tempered over time, and by the beginning of the 1700s, Puritanism was dying out – but the civil institutions they had created remained strong in the Colonies.

The First Great Awakening revitalized the spiritual condition of the Colonies and gave them the courage and reasoning to fight for their independence and then write the Constitution. Soon the pioneers began streaming west, first going past the Appalachians and then on towards the Mississippi. The Second Great Awakening spread the Gospel throughout the Republic and then spawned the abolitionist movement that led to the Civil War. Following the war, the pioneers resumed their westward push, taking their faith with them. Often portions of congregations would migrate together, and then build a church/schoolhouse soon after settling in their final location. Throughout the settling of America, churches were steadily planted and the Gospel was spread – along with the basic forms of civil government that the Puritans had laid down over two centuries earlier.

With the close of the Nineteenth Century, the frontier days had ended and people began spreading out within the States. With the exception of Alaska and Hawaii, the United States was complete. But soon after the Civil War, theological liberalism via the German Enlightenment crossed the Atlantic and began making inroads into the various denominations on the East Coast, particularly the more liberal denominations hungry for "new thinking." One denomination after another fell under the spell of the German Enlightenment, and soon the meanings of Biblical passages which had always been clear in the churches suddenly came into question, and along with it, the Bible's authority.

As the Bible was increasingly supplanted in American society, the moral fabric of the nation began to weaken. And though seminaries sprang up to correct the growing apostasy in the pulpits and the churches, the spread of theological liberalism continued. Soon, the apostates were aided by their embracing of the Theory of Evolution, which only increased the apostasy and liberalism in the various denominations. Now instead of being regarded as the Source of Truth, the Bible was just another religious book full of myths, legends, pithy proverbs, and tall-tales.

Though numerous denominations had already dethroned the Bible and undermined Scriptural authority from the pulpits, the American society was much slower to change, with the Ten Commandments and prayer still being a part of school, and often present on plaques and statues on public property. But since the Scopes Trial and the rulings of the Hugo Black Court, the ACLU and other lawyers' unions have successfully stripped America of its Judeo-Christian heritage, along with the instrumental role that the Bible and Scriptural authority plays in maintaining order in society.

When prayer and the Bible were finally cast out of school in 1963, the overthrow of Scriptural authority in America was complete. Within a matter of months, authority throughout the entire American society was called into question and a spirit of rebellion ensued. Almost overnight, the generation who had been given everything in the 1950s wanted to destroy everything their parents, grandparents, and forefathers had created. Eventually, the fires of rebellion burned out with the ending of the Vietnam War, but the spirit of rebellion against authority – especially Scriptural authority – remains.

The subversion of America's Judeo-Christian foundations did not occur all at once, but happened gradually – year after year, decade after decade, and generation after generation. Today, rather than being a manual for virtues, life, and an orderly, moral, just society, the Bible is increasingly viewed as an antiquated religious book, and most recently has been rendered a book of hate, racism, and bigotry because it contradicts the loosening, depraved values of our secular culture. The ultimate loosening of moral values in a culture is moral relativism, in which everyone determines what is right and wrong according to their own individual dictates, or as what the Bible describes as "doing what is right in their own eyes."

A society built upon the shifting sands of moral relativism simply cannot tolerate moral absolutes, especially those it disagrees with. But such societies with ever-changing (much less collapsing) moral standards rarely last very long in the grand scheme of history, any more than a house repaired or remodeled with different measurement standards will not last. From its earliest days when its foundation was the Bible, America resembled a strong house built upon the rock – but today has become more and more unstable since it replaced its foundation of moral absolutes with those of moral relativism.

The Root of America's Problems

At the root of all America's problems – and all other nations throughout all history – is the sin of its individual people. Yes, America's pulpits and churches went astray, but where were their congregations? In sound churches, if the pastor starts spouting heresy, the elders, the congregation, or the parent-organization will reprimand then replace the pastor with one of more-sound preaching and teaching. Apostate pastors typically have little effect unless their congregations are apathetic, spiritually-starved, or also apostate themselves.

Proverbs 14:34 declares, "Righteousness exalts a nation, but sin is a reproach to any people." No nation – regardless of the soundness of its foundations and the morals and courage of its ancestors – can skirt that spiritual law. When men abandon their families or a couple has a child out of wedlock, the government is often looked to in order to provide assistance for the mother and child. Government takes on the role of the 'father' or 'provider' rather than the man and therefore must grow to assume its new responsibilities and expenses.

The welfare policies of the federal government since the time of the Great Society have all but destroyed poorer minority families, especially those living in the inner-cities. If Uncle Sam offers to pay unmarried women more money a month than her boyfriend makes, then why would it make sense for her to marry him? And when more money is offered for each out-of-wedlock child, then isn't that simply encouraging her to have more children and never marry? And as the children grow and mature in that environment, how can they break the cycle of poverty and dependency when that's all they've ever known?

Compared to today's constant crises, America's problems had been insignificant when most people self-governed, self-controlled, and self-regulated themselves with a healthy reverence for the Ten Commandments and the Golden Rule. But with the weakening of the churches and the overstepping of the courts in the last century, those same Ten Commandments aren't even allowed to be displayed in the public square, whether the people want them there or not. The very antidote for the poison infecting our nation has been outlawed.

If self-restraint and basic morals cannot be posted in the public square nor taught in the classroom, how can any child be expected to consistently learn them outside their home, much less put them into everyday practice when they're teenagers and then later adults? Most parents still cite the Golden Rule in some form ("Treat others the way you want to be treated"), but there's no authority greater than their own that they can point to. For most kids, "Because I said so!" is hardly any authority at all, especially when the popular culture abhors authority of any kind.

James Madison declared, "We have staked the whole future of American civilization, not upon the power of government, far from it. We've staked the future of all our political institutions upon our capacity to sustain ourselves according to the Ten Commandments of God." Decades later, Noah Webster said, "All the miseries and evils which men suffer from vice, crime, ambition, injustice, oppression, slavery and war, proceed from their despising or neglecting the precepts contained in the Bible."

Today, when those very same Ten Commandments cannot be taught in our schools, displayed on our monuments, nor even uttered by our teachers, what sort of future will we and our descendants have other than in tyranny and bondage? For the first half of the nation's history, the Bible was the primary textbook used to teach reading, history, philosophy, and wisdom. The Bible formed the very cornerstone of American society – yet today cannot even be brought into a public school without nearly causing a lockdown. We all have a choice: submit ourselves to the unchanging laws of God or to the ever-changing, often tyrannical laws of man.

When we as individuals refuse to govern ourselves, we essentially cede our rights of self-governance to the State, such as when we break the law. And this is what has been happening at every level of Western society since Scriptural authority was tossed out the window – person by person, family by family, city by city, state by state, and in country after country.

The current upheavals in the American society can be further boiled down to the conflict between those who hold to the nation's foundations based upon the Creator versus those who want to change the foundations to be based upon those of Man.

In the end, it comes down to which value system the nation holds in higher regards: the rights of the Individual (as granted to all by the Creator) or the rights of the State (as granted by other people or a group).

The Influence of the Theory of Evolution

The Creation versus Evolution Debate is not an abstract, trivial religious argument – it's at the very foundation of our societal problems in America and the West today. Are all men created equal by their Creator, or are some "more equal" than others as determined by Random Chance? Under Creationism, we are all made "in God's image" and therefore should treat one another as equals. But under Evolution, if one group declares another group to be under-evolved or even apes who merely look like humans, that group has little ethical problems with completely exterminating that inferior group like vermin. Adolph Hitler was able to convince himself and much of his nation that he was actually helping the process of Evolution along by wiping out the Jews and the other groups he deemed to be inferior and parasitic.

It cannot be emphasized too clearly or too often that the Creation vs. Evolution debate is not merely a religious issue, but a cultural issue. In the Bible, Romans 1 declares that cultures which reject the Creator are given over to depraved, reprobate minds and perverse sexual appetites – which is evidenced in Israel's history, in dozens of ancient cultures, and throughout the West and America today. People debate whether homosexuality is acquired from a culture or is genetic – the answer is that it's likely both. As a culture increasingly rejects the Creator, He gives them over to degeneracy, and it becomes increasing depraved and filled with insatiable appetites. This isn't to explicitly judge or condemn people who are born with such appetites as much as the culture which has produced them. And not only do such cultures become increasingly sexually depraved, but they lose common sense, compassion, and respect for life, particularly innocent human life.

With the rise of atheism and secularism over the last century or two, it's become popular to criticize religious wars for claiming the lives of tens of millions of people over the centuries. Meanwhile, they neglect the fact that the secular, socialist, and communist governments slaughtered over 120 million people in the last century ALONE. Very few wars were solely religious because of the intertwining of religion and the state, as in most of the ancient empires, the Crusades and Muslim wars, etc. Until the last two hundred years, a nation's religion and their government were usually joined at the hip.

No society, culture, or nation can remain secular for very long because humans are innately spiritual creatures, and as such, we simply must worship something, no matter how ridiculous it may be (especially from another's point of view). Even atheists worship something: the nonexistence of God or another Supreme Being. Their religion of no-God is just as strongly felt and believed as every other religion in the world. However, atheists have even less evidence of the nonexistence of God than others have that He exists because of the complexity of the Creation. It's almost as if God wants us to seek after Him by faith in His revealed Word and His attributes that He has spread throughout the universe – and not simply by what we can see, feel, hear, touch, and smell around us.

Under the secular (or pagan) worldview which is based upon some form of Evolution or mythology, the State is almost always divine or all-powerful, with unlimited authority. Because the "gods" entrusted the king or the State to rule the people in their place, the king or the State becomes the object of worship and soon results in tyranny. And Evolution isn't much different, except that Random Chance anointed the "fittest" to rule. This pagan form of government, the "divine" rulership of kings, and the authority of the State by virtue of their gods has ruled all governments of the world for all history – except for the handful of occasions in which a nation was based upon the

331

model of authority and individual rights as espoused in the Bible.

The Biblical worldview declares that all people have natural rights that come from God (or the Creator) and that to protect and secure those natural rights, governments are instituted among men. Consequently, when governments violate those rights, the people have a right to either demand justice or throw off that government and devise another one in order to secure their rights. Therefore, the authority of the State is limited and granted by the people, and is best protected under either a republic or a limited democracy.

The only two nations which have directly derived their government, authority, and legitimacy from the Bible are ancient Israel and the United States of America. In ancient Israel, the virtues of the people waned as they fell into idolatry, then they were repeatedly enslaved and then re-liberated, until they finally lost faith in their own form of self-government and eventually begged God to give them a king "like all the other nations." Tragically, America appears to be following the same pattern: as the people fell away from their spiritual roots, their virtue waned and they wanted a secular, Progressive form of government "like all the other nations." But like all governments based upon secularism or paganism, this will only result in tyranny – as it has with our current president and administration.

At the core of all forms of modern tyranny lies the Theory of Evolution, which provides the necessary "origins" foundational component required for all philosophies and religions. If all men are "created equal" and our rights come from the Creator, then no one man or group of men has the authority to rule over others or take those rights away (without consequences). But under Evolution, the overriding principle is "Survival of the Fittest," which provides the moral justification that more powerful people can rule over the weaker or the inferior, subordinate ones. At the very heart of the Theory of Evolution lies sin and rebellion, in which man is trying to rationalize his true fallen condition away – that men can one day become gods themselves.

In all our modern secular, public schools and universities, the Theory of Evolution is not only taught and espoused, but its teachings are strictly enforced, with no alternate origins theories allowed even a cursory examination. Under traditional education, all theories should be examined, and let the students decide which one makes the most sense to them and be able/required to explain why. But such exploration and examination is not allowed in public schools and universities today, for fear that their secular theory of origins might be undermined. The evolutionary underpinnings of a society are critical if Statism, Secularism, and Progressivism are to flourish and maintain their control.

When a nation falls away from their religious values, it's often through the very institutions which were constructed to protect and propagate those values in the first place. First, the very notion of sin and a fallen-state of man is trivialized and then mocked, initially by the intellectuals and then by the popular culture. Then large groups of people join in and eventually even the pillars of society change their attitudes towards sin, immorality, and wickedness until immorality is good and morality is mocked as prudishness, being uptight, or Neanderthal.

In America today, even many of our churches ridicule the idea of man being fallen, sinful, condemned to Hell, and in desperate need of a Savior. Why? Because they embrace some form of Progressivism and an Evolutionary theory of origins (such as Theistic Evolution), which undercuts their own foundations. Some churches even teach that there are many paths to God, and wide is the road that leads to Heaven, because a loving God wouldn't want anyone to be condemned for eternity, would He? Today, even in many American churches, committing the sin of adultery and breaking your marriage vows is now excused as just "having a momentary lapse of judgment" or even "following your heart."

Whenever a nation tears down their foundations, allows their institutions to be perverted or corrupted, or the people simply grow tired of their long-held traditions, radicals and revolutionaries rise to overthrow the society for their own purposes. In the Bolshevik Revolution, the Communists arose and overthrew the Czar of Russia in order to institute a "pure" communist form of government and society. However, in order to do that, the communists had to destroy the society first – along with millions of people who didn't agree with them – before they could rebuild the society along Marxist principles.

Barack Obama's deep, revolutionary roots are betrayed when he conveniently leaves out "by our Creator" from the Preamble of the Declaration of Independence. Secularism and Creationism can walk hand-in-hand as much as darkness and light – there is no common ground between them; either one is true and the other is false. If our rights come from the Creator, no president has the right to subvert our freedoms and transform America into something we didn't want, let alone vote for.

Like every other president who raised his right hand and swore an oath of office, Obama was commissioned to uphold America's laws, traditions, and Constitution, not change or transform them into those of his choosing. And like every other president, Obama is responsible for maintaining and preserving the foundations of this republic to the best of his ability.

America – The Nation Founded on Faith

Before we can set out to restore America's crumbling foundations, we must first understand how they were constructed in the first place. We must learn about the builders and examine their original designs, and why they built the civil institutions the way they did.

The first successful colonies in North America were built by the Puritans, who fled the rising persecution of King Charles and the Church of England beginning in the late 1620s. From 1630 to 1640, over 20,000 Puritans migrated from England to the Massachusetts Bay Colony and soon created permanent, thriving settlements in the New World. Under the leadership of John Winthrop who saw the New World they were creating as a "shining city on a hill," by which England, Europe, and the other nations of the world would clearly see and know the right way to build and maintain their own societies.

What the Puritans believed had a direct, tangible impact on how they built their society and how they kept civil order. Unlike the corrupted Church of England they had fled, the Puritans believed that they as "light-bearers" were responsible for the redeeming of a wild, untamed land. They believed and lived according to a form of covenant theology, in which they were saved by a "Covenant of Grace" but that they maintained their faith by a "Covenant of Works." Under this theology, they were saved by grace as the New Testament declares, but they mixed in Old Testament ideas in that they had to maintain a "Covenant of Works" in order to keep God's blessing upon them and their new land.

The widespread adherence to such a theology will lead to a solid, orderly society in which everyone was very careful to self-govern themselves and look out for their neighbors, along with their children, grandchildren, and others in their community. Adults treated all the youths and children of the community as if they were their own, being careful to discipline and correct them. Being your "brother's keeper" was something they took very seriously, not just something they paid lip-service to.

Another view of what the Puritans believed and how they lived out their faith can be represented by the symbol of the Cross. The long, vertical beam of the Cross represented their most-important relationship: between themselves and God. The shorter, horizontal beam represented their relationship with one another, with all of them being under the headship of Christ. In order for their faith to be maintained and function properly, both aspects of the relationship had to be upheld.

Because of their solid beliefs in the Bible, the Ten Commandments, the Rule of Law, strong families, thriftiness, Yankee-ingenuity, self-control, curiosity, high regard for education, industriousness, solid work-ethic, and congregational communities centered around a church, the Puritans turned the raw, harsh wilderness into thriving colonies in a matter of years, while those in Jamestown and other settlements took decades to stabilize and become self-sufficient. In Puritan New England, most everyone looked out for one another – living out the Golden Rule to its fullest extent possible. These foundations that were laid down by the Puritans and those who modeled their civil societies after them were more or less kept until the mid-Twentieth Century.

The first generation of the Puritans hungered for the Word of God and incorporated it into the very fabric of their society at its earliest stages, and built it up from there. The first Puritans were quite mature in their faith, and because of their knowledge of the Bible and their persecution in England, they intimately understood that liberty and Christianity went hand-in-hand, and that liberty was impossible without it. Without widespread personal self-control and self-governance, true liberty in society cannot exist – and without personal faith in Christ Who enables them to live out the Golden Rule in their daily lives, such self-control and self-governance cannot be manifested in their daily lives.

However, as the Puritans grew and spread into the New World, they gradually lost the spirit of their faith and it became legalistic. They began living very outwardly pious lives, even if they were sinning privately. Since they knew their neighbors were always watching them for signs of them breaking their covenant (which could threaten the entire society), they became hyper-sensitive and nosy about everyone else around them. Their system of works rather than grace led to legalism, and then hypocrisy. From this religious environment sprang the Salem Witch Trials and the various modern stereotypes of the Puritans.

Because of the harsh outward legalism, fear, and hypocrisy, within two generations the Puritans began to decline. The children of the latter generations in the late 1600s rebelled against the harsh religious authority and wanted nothing to do with it. But the framework of the civil institutions that the Puritans created remained strong and spread throughout New England and the other colonies.

For most of American history, the Puritans were highly regarded until the Twentieth Century when the revisionists began rewriting history and vilified them as religious monsters. No one denies that the Puritans made some mistakes and that their society turned into a theocracy, but they and their children had the sense to reform it without much bloodshed. Once they woke up from the haze of zeal and fervor of the Salem Witch Trials, they were shocked and grieved over what had happened and began making reforms.

The Puritans not only built New England, but provided the model for hardworking, pioneering, orderly societies which covenanted together, which settled the rest of America and built the land we know and love today. Sadly, modern historians have blown the religious sins of the Puritans far out of proportion while their incredible accomplishments have been all but ignored. Often the same scholars who are most critical of the Puritans are those who also laud the morals and fairness of Marxism, communism, and socialism while ignoring the tens of millions who were slaughtered. The handful of people the Puritans hung for witchcraft is incomparable to the tens of millions of innocents slaughtered under Marxism.

Those who set out to overthrow a country always start by attacking the history and foundations, followed by corrupting the civil institutions such as the universities, courts, and government. Then they step back and let the weakened nation collapse under its own weight. The secularists attacked the Puritans first, then they attacked the integrity of the Founding Fathers, then they infiltrated the universities, the media, the seminaries, and then the various branches of government. After decades of their influence, America – by way of her corrupted institutions – is on the verge of collapse. The three centuries of stable foundations that began with the Puritans has been thoroughly corrupted in the last several decades by the secularists and Progressives.

The Puritans rightly understood that cultural decline is caused by spiritual decline, and that cultural battles are outward manifestations of deeper spiritual battles, which could only be fought with prayer and fasting. The central focus of the Puritan faith was their families and their strong, teaching churches and schools that taught the entire Bible rather than cherry-pick their way through it or teach without it.

Today in America, most churches no longer teach the "whole counsel of God," but go for the politically-correct, easy faith, and the loving-but-not-wrathful-God messages. Some churches in America today even completely neglect the Old Testament because God seems so harsh and angry, as opposed to the God of the New Testament. Consequently, many Christians today have a very shallow understanding of God and no longer revere Him and His hatred of sin like most Christians used to. Jonathan Edwards would have a very difficult time preaching his infamous sermon, "Sinners in the Hands of an Angry God" in most of America's pulpits today, though that sermon is credited with lighting the first fires of the Great Awakening.

The first Puritans tried to live out their faith in their everyday lives and constructed churches, monuments, universities, legislatures, courts, markets, and numerous other institutions around Biblical teachings to lay the foundations of America. They not only taught and lived out their values, they reinforced those values in their schools, businesses, literature, and societies – not just in their homes and churches. And since those first years, multitudes of Christians which followed after them continued to build on those foundations. Today, we have mere drops of the Biblical teachings, virtues, and moral values that the Puritans showered the Colonies in week after week, month after month, and year after year.

Until the middle of the last century, the vast majority of churches in America resounded with consistent Biblical teaching and moral clarity, and they played a vital role in stirring the hearts and minds of the country. When the Great Awakening began, many of the churches which had grown cold and stale resisted the fire, until many of them were converted and joined together to fan the spiritual flames. The pulpits of the Colonies helped convince the populace to support independence and the righteousness of the Cause, and bolstered the fledgling nation's spirit throughout the long war. Many of those same churches later stirred the States to rise up against the evils of slavery and continue with the Civil War, even when it was going badly.

It was the pastors who drove the Colonies to independence and then later spurred on the abolition movement that ended slavery. How many pastors and Christians participated in the Underground Railroad despite the federal government's edicts? Were they concerned with not upsetting the government at the time, even though the federal government strongly supported slavery? Of course not, but they knew their rights and refused to be silenced. They knew they had to obey God rather than men (Acts 5:29). But where are our pulpits today? Surely there's no lack of societal evils and other subjects to preach about – so why have so many of our pulpits fallen silent? Worse, why are so many of our churches advocating for the very things that the Bible calls abominations (such as abortion, gay-relations, etc.)? Could it be that they're afraid of losing membership and contributions, and also their tax-exempt status from the federal government? Not only that, their own congregations no longer tolerate sound teachings (2 Timothy 4:3), and simply leave if they don't like the message, the music, or the externals.

The reason why America is spiritually bankrupt today is because our pulpits and pastors have been compromised and no longer preach the undiluted Word of God. Far too many churches have the externals of religion but not the internals – the outward trappings of Christianity but not the spirit. But it's not only the fault of the pastors, but the people who seem to have little respect for Biblical teaching, Scriptural authority, or even Judeo-Christian traditions. A side-effect of living in a free, democratic society is that democracy – "the rule of the people" – eventually infects and undermines the Church, especially when society turns against authority in general. The liberal denominations have become so morally confused and corrupted that they freely embrace homosexual marriage, openly-gay pastors, and even abortion, though those are all declared to be wicked or abominations in the Bible.

How tragic it is today that America's brilliant beacons of light and liberty on the East Coast that stirred the nation to independence and then the abolition of slavery are now mired in darkness and servitude to theological liberalism and Progressivism. And because of our corrupted seminaries, politically-correct pastors, apathetic congregations, and fuzzy Biblical teaching, now entire denominations have fallen under the spell of the popular culture and moral relativism.

Israel is our Example

In examining America's moral, spiritual, and cultural decline – and how to avoid her looming collapse – there are several nations and empires in history we can study. If we can learn from their examples, there's a chance that we can turn this country around and head back in the right direction. The two nations that best model the road of decline that America is taking is the Roman Empire and the ancient nation of Israel. Spiritually, America most closely parallels Israel, since they were founded upon the Jewish Scriptures and worshipped the same God. America parallels ancient Rome in her basic republican form of government, the Rule of Law, and some of the other civil institutions.

Since the root of America's problems are spiritual rather than civil or organizational, we can learn the most from studying Israel's history and decline. When the Puritans founded New England, they envisioned themselves to be the spiritual New Israel, being called out from a foreign land, crossing the mighty waters, and settling in a fertile land flowing with "milk and honey." During the later Indian attacks, they saw God's Hand of correction as in the Book of Judges where He was calling His people to repentance and a renewing of the covenant between them. The covenant theology held by the Puritans only reinforced many of their ideas and views that they were not only resettled like ancient Israel had been, they were to carry on the flame of the One True God and be a light unto the rest of the nations.

The parallels between ancient Israel and modern America didn't just cease with the decline of the Puritans, and later Christians throughout American history recognized the continued parallels in our Revolutionary War and then again in our Civil War. Both nations were freed from wicked, cruel kings and were founded upon faith in God and the Rule of Law. Both nations were given exceptional opportunities and became courageous, powerful, and prosperous. And then once they became prosperous, both became self-reliant and fell into moral and spiritual decline. Halfway through their history, both separated into a northern kingdom and a southern kingdom, and then went through a period of civil war.

As nations prosper materially, they consistently lose their moral standards and virtues – they rise, prosper, become apathetic, and then fall. Some then rise again, while many simply migrate to other nations or evaporate into the silence of history. In Israel's history, after becoming enormously prosperous under the united kingdom of David and Solomon, the nation broke apart and then experienced several centuries of prosperity and spiritual decline. Eventually however, the Northern Kingdom (the House of Israel) and then the Southern Kingdom (the House of Judah) reached a point in which the people would no longer even listen to those God sent to them, much less humble themselves – even when good, God-fearing kings were in power. Finally, God saw that the Israelites were completely consumed with evil and thought only of evil continually all the time, and God was forced to judge them by sending their barbaric enemies to invade the land and send them into captivity.

After the trials of WWI, the Great Depression and then WWII, America began to prosper like never before in her history. But the more we prospered, the more we took those blessings for granted and became filled with pride. Suddenly, instead of America's prosperity being a result of God's blessings, we came to believe that we had done all these things by our courage, wisdom, intellect, ingenuity, and economic prowess. We became not only wealthy, but the wealthiest nation in the history of the world – and in our pride, we pulled further and further away from God and our humble beginnings. But since the turn of this century, God has been allowing tragedy after tragedy to strike America, in the hopes of waking us up before He is forced to judge us like ancient Israel and other nations throughout history. Like Israel thousands of years ago, America has lost her soul.

With America closely paralleling Israel's spiritual history, we must study and learn from their spiritual story as soon as possible in order to turn our nation away from certain destruction. Curiously enough, the Jewish population of the world today is almost evenly split between America and Israel at about 42% each. The remaining percentage is scattered throughout various pockets in Europe, South America, and the rest of the world. An in-depth study of ancient Israel's decline and their numerous parallels to modern America can be found in a book I wrote in 2010 called, "On the Precipice - Hosea speaks to America."

The Book of Hosea has a unique message in the Old Testament, in that God pours out His heart to His people who have deeply offended and betrayed Him over a long period of time. The tone and prose in the book shift back and forth between God's fury and grief, anger and sadness, love and heartache. Through the pen of Hosea, God alternates between a scorned, betrayed husband and a loving, grieving Father. Another Old Testament book which reveals the deep heart of God is the Book of Jeremiah (along with Lamentations), though it was written to the Southern Kingdom of Judah over a century after the Northern Kingdom of Israel had already been exiled.

Today in America, many Christians, pastors, and churches tend to shy away from studying the Old Testament books, especially those of the Minor Prophets. Why? Because those books tend to portray God as being very angry, jealous, and judgmental. Many people are uncomfortable with the Old Testament books because they don't fit with their mental image of God, or even that which the churches have taught. But God is not defined by us or by what we want Him to be – God is Who He Is, and God is known to us only by what He has revealed in the Bible and to a lesser extent, what He has revealed in His Creation (Romans 1:20).

After years of hearing about God as only a "God of Love," it's difficult for many Americans to reconcile the message and tone of these Old Testament books with their preconceived notions and Sunday School caricatures of God. Therefore, people or even pastors throw out numerous excuses for ignoring these books such as "Those books were written for a different people in a different time or in a different Dispensation." Another excuse is "They lived under the Law but we live under Grace." Yet it's through such moments of discomfort and challenges that our perceptions are altered, and often even our behavior. It's mostly during the challenges and difficulties in life that real, lasting growth and spiritual maturity occurs.

In most American churches before Progressivism and liberal theology took hold, the pastors preached from both the Old Testament and the New Testament, and people generally had a balanced view of God. If people are taught only the Old Testament view, they tend to become legalistic and the society becomes harsh, rigid, and cold. If people are taught only the New Testament view, they tend to become licentious and the society soon falls into disorder and even wickedness, because all their sins are forgiven whenever they ask. That's why America was different than other Christian nations of Europe – because they embraced the whole picture of God and they had both a solemn, healthy reverence for Him and His hatred of sin, and also His unfathomable grace. The Puritans and most of the churches of America were Christian churches with a Judeo-Christian theology and primarily followed the Bible as opposed to other churches which had been altered over the centuries by the clergy, traditions, and religion.

As a result of America's uniquely Judeo-Christian heritage, we have been blessed far more than ancient Israel. America was founded by people of faith who sacrificed everything they had to seek after God and His plan for the New World, Who then opened up their nation to bring in people from other faiths from all over the world. But we have forgotten one of the fundamental truths that our Founders knew with certainty: from whom much is given, much will be required (Luke 12:47-48). Because of the faith of her Founders, America has been given much in terms of courage, heritage, liberty, health, abundance, and prosperity. And because of those blessings, much will be required of America.

But we've been taking those blessings for granted for far too long, and we seldom even express our gratitude any more. Like Israel, we've been richly blessed and have become self-reliant to the point that we think all these things have been done by our own efforts, rather than by God's blessings. The ultimate tragedy of history may be unfolding before our very eyes: when a nation founded on the Bible that took on the role of New Israel fails to learn from Israel's history. And if America was blessed much more than ancient Israel, will our fall be that much greater as well?

America was not only given nearly every conceivable opportunity to grow and prosper, she was also endowed with many wise forefathers who extensively wrote in order to pass on their wisdom and personal experiences to their posterity. They didn't just write volume after volume for their own benefit, but for ours. One of the greatest fears of our Founders was that their posterity would forget or disregard their sacrifice and the foundations they had so carefully, painstakingly laid with their very blood, sweat, and tears.

Today in America, we have a choice: we can continue to be carried on by the currents of secularism, Progressivism, popular culture, ignorance, and apathy and then one day soon find ourselves flying over a cliff into complete societal and economic collapse – or we can stop our downward spiral and turn back to our spiritual, societal, and national roots and set out to restore this nation that so many have loved, fought, and died for.

America's Day of Reckoning?

Since the 1990s, America has been experiencing an extended series of natural disasters ranging from hundreds of tornadoes, devastating hurricanes, unusual earthquakes, deep financial instability and foolish, dangerous policies by our political leadership. In the past, most Americans would've seen these events for what they are: chastisements from God intended to get our attention, to wake us up and recognize what is really happening. But today when a governor proclaims a day of fasting to seek God and plead for Divine Providence (as earlier governors did), he is mocked and derided as a religious fanatic. We have strayed so far from God that He is no longer even alive to most of us. Nietzsche had it half-right when he brazenly declared, "God is dead" – but the Living God is only dead to those who refuse to see Him. Indeed, God is dead only to those who are perishing (1 Corinthians 1:18-25).

Is the God of the Bible an "angry God of Wrath"? From a cursory reading of the Scriptures, one could certainly form that impression – but they would be greatly mistaken. God held His peace through centuries of betrayal before He was forced to punish the nation of Israel, even though He sent prophet after prophet to rebuke and correct her. God does not delight in

345

judgment and damnation, but in repentance (Ezekiel 18:23). Repentance is simply turning from your current path – in a religious context, it's turning from evil to good, from pride to humility, from faithlessness to faith, and from unbelief to belief.

How many times has God reached out to America through "natural" disasters, books, churches, preachers, leaders, and her people? More times than we have any idea of. But what makes modern America different than past generations is that she's increasing turning a deaf-ear to those warnings, even though they're becoming louder, clearer, and more frequent.

What's the cause of so many of America's problems today? The lack of knowledge of the Lord and the Scriptures, even though most homes still have a Bible in them. American teens and schools were quite stable – if not gradually improving – up until 1962 when prayer was effectively removed from our public school system (David Barton, "America: To Pray or Not to Pray"). After that event, America morally and spiritually fell off the cliff and has been worsening ever since. What quickly followed the Supreme Court's decision was the assassination of President Kennedy, the race-riots, Vietnam, the rebellions of the Sixties, the rapid spread of Communism, and the casting aside of the Gold Standard. If America would not have cast God out of the schools, would those same events have even occurred or transpired the way they did?

Stability and confidence did not return to the United States until we had a Christian president who was faithful to the nation's foundings and tried to uphold the Founders' vision of limited government: Ronald Reagan. Now we have a radical Progressive president (Barack Obama) who is actively trying to undo the "Reagan Revolution" and the nation is once-again filled with indecision, instability, and rising lawlessness not seen since the Sixties and Seventies.

Nations get the leaders they deserve and in that regard, modern America is no different than ancient Israel. How can we reverse the decline of America and restore common-sense leadership to our nation? By immersing ourselves in the knowledge of the Lord, humbling ourselves and repenting, and obeying His Word. Spiritual restoration always precedes personal restoration, which in turn precedes societal and then national restoration.

The tireless ministries of the handful of men in the First Great Awakening of the 1730s through the 1760s resulted in multitudes of people – often entire households and towns – coming to repentance and being saved. That generation in turn produced the early Founding Fathers who rose up and cast off the chains of the British Empire and then formed the new nation of the United States of America.

One generation of ordinary people faithfully teaching their children the knowledge of the Lord laid the foundations for the greatest nation the world has ever known. One generation. Does our generation have the courage, fortitude, and sensibility to humble ourselves and teach our children as the Founders' parents did, or will we shrug our shoulders and continue selfishly on our way and leave them and our country to its decline into the abyss?

When the Islamic terrorist attacks of September 11th occurred, America immediately afterwards experienced a very short, fleeting spiritual revival. For the first time in years, our churches were once again filled and the political haggling and instability ceased. The nation came together in the wake of an incredible, horrible attack that cut to the heart of our nation.

But the busyness and concerns of modern life soon pushed those thoughts of seeking after God out of the minds of most Americans and life more or less returned to normal. We were awakened from our spiritual slumber for a brief moment, yawned, and then promptly went back to sleep. Our own repentance was no better than ancient Israel's in the face of disaster: a morning cloud, a fleeting wisp of hope that quickly evaporated (Hosea 6:1-6).

For the next seven years, we continued on with our normal lives as if nothing bad was happening, as if nothing was wrong. Yes, we were fighting the wars in Iraq and Afghanistan and ridding the world of terrorism, but we weren't attacking the root of Islamic terrorism as much as pruning the extreme branches. Meanwhile, the tree not only continues to grow, but is watered, fertilized, and nourished by our own labors through our oil and gas revenues and our self-defeating energy policies.

Then came Hurricane Katrina, the spike in gasoline prices, the sub-prime mortgage crisis, and then the Financial Crisis of 2008. But did we see what was really happening and repent, or did we continue on our merry way? Not only did we refuse to repent, we then elected a man into the highest office of the land who we knew very little about, though his background and associations were highly suspect. We knew Barack Obama was hiding much of his history (his birth-certificate, his high-school and college transcripts, his state-Senate papers, his medical records, etc.), but we elected him anyway. And then even after a disastrous four years of his presidency, we re-elected him.

Now as we enter into the next four years of this president, we are paying the price for our foolishness with the longest, most meager "recovery" since the Great Depression, over $6 trillion in new debt, massive new regulations, higher taxes on the horizon, and a disastrous nationalized healthcare system.

The only real good news that has come from Obama being president is that average Americans have begun waking up to our bankrupt spiritual, societal, and economic conditions and are shaking off their years of apathy and ignorance. But simply waking up and realizing that we have enormous problems is not enough – we must do something about these problems, and fast.

If America is to be saved, we must return to our founding principles and transform this country from the inside out – starting with ourselves.

Where Do We Begin?

If you are reading this book, then you likely have a deep love for America and your heart is breaking for her in her current dismal state of decline. But America's decline didn't start overnight and will not likely be reversed overnight.

As an observer of American civilization, it's sometimes hard to notice how far we've declined if we only look back at the last few years, or even the last decade. But as one goes back further – even by sampling popular culture – it's obvious to see that our nation's spirit is being methodically being ripped apart from the inside. Twenty years ago, the cultural rot was well-underway but was nowhere near the levels of today. Going back further, such as fifty, seventy, or even one hundred years, our rapid decline is appalling.

The pillars of our society which once held us together are not only crumbling and falling apart, but are systematically being torn down by the very people who should be upholding them. Our public servants have turned themselves into our masters, and there seems to be little recourse or accountability on their behalf. Tragically, America appears to be following in the footsteps of all the once-great nations and empires like Great Britain, Rome, and Greece.

Why? Because of us – her people – because of our sin. Moral, law-abiding, free people don't need more government, they need less. Just look at our popular culture and entertainments, the movies we watch and the music we listen to. Take a few moments and consider how far we've fallen away from our roots. We've given up building our civilization and our society and passing on our values to the next generation. We daily sacrifice the future for the fleeting comforts, thrills, and entertainments of the present. Again, if you want to see where a nation is headed, just look at the next generation.

The solution to America's problems is not in our leaders, our media, and certainly not our capital – the solution lies with us: her people. America will be saved only by average citizens who love their country and are willing to sacrifice their own immediate comforts for the sake of raising and guiding the next generation. People like you and me.

Since most of the civilization and so many of our institutions are corrupted, how then can the decline be reversed? If you study Israel's history in the Scriptures, you'll discover that it starts in the home, with everyday people like us. The highpoint of Israel's history – the days of King David and his son Solomon – followed some of the worst low-points in her history: the days of the Judges. Those days were characterized by brutality, bloodshed, idolatry, violence, widespread corruption, tyranny, and anarchy. And like modern America, ancient Israel was plagued by moral relativism in that "everyone did what was right in their own eyes." (Judges 17:6)

How did that ancient corrupted nation produce great men such as David and his Mighty Men? The short answer is that it didn't – God did. God was the one who moved in the hearts of His people and caused them to raise up their children to fear God and obey His commandments. There were no institutions or schools to do it for them – they did it themselves and they started with their children at home.

Reversing America's decline starts in our hearts and the hearts of our children and presses outwards. It starts with average men and women who refuse to lie down and surrender to the corruption in our culture, but rise up with courage and stand for what's good, true, and right. It starts with parents who not only refuse to allow their children to be infected with popular entertainment, media, and philosophies but who also teach them to recognize what is good and what is evil, and to cling to what is right.

It's hard to turn a family around and even harder to turn a nation from her natural path towards decline. But with God's help and grace, we can do it. We must first humble ourselves and acknowledge our sins, and then we must obey Him and His Word.

If America is to be saved from a catastrophic collapse, we'll likely know it long before our politicians, economists, and media experts do. If we see a spiritual revival taking hold and a genuine return to our national roots, then perhaps the country will be saved. But if we continue on the way we have these last fifty years, then the United States of America as we have known it probably will be lost.

There is what appears to be a promise of restoration for a wayward nation in the Old Testament. Though it was given explicitly to Israel at the time, the story of Jonah and the repentance of Nineveh shows that this promise can be applied to any nation that repents from their evil ways and turns to God. That promise is found in 2 Chronicles 7:

If My people who are called by My name will humble themselves, and pray and seek My face, and turn from their wicked ways, then I will hear from heaven, and will forgive their sin and heal their land. – 2 Chronicles 7:14

Where does the Third Great Awakening begin? With us – in our prayer closets, around our dinner tables, in our churches, with our social media, in our classrooms, and then in our public squares. Some are saying that the Third Great Awakening has already begun, since the previous Awakenings weren't perceived or even recognized until years afterwards.

Though fixing America's spiritual issues is almost as daunting as attacking our $16+ trillion national debt, we must understand that we're not alone – and with God, all things are possible. Restoring and saving America begins with each one of us in our personal, daily lives. As we are individually restored, we then spread the process to those around us, first in our families, then in our churches, and then in our growing spheres of influence throughout the nation – and then the world. But it all starts with us as individuals who are willing to humble ourselves, submit to God, and do what is right.

The three practical steps of restoration are: Repentance, Revival, and Reform. First, we must Repent of our sins and turn from our wicked ways to God. Then we must feed on His Word and let it penetrate every area of our lives, Reviving our spirit and allowing God to transform us from the inside-out. Lastly,

351

we must make tangible, lasting Reforms in our lives and surroundings to support the Revival.

Repentance: let each of us confess our sins, acknowledging our apathy and turn back to God
Revival: let us spread the Gospel once again and renew the dying spirit of our families, our communities, and our nation
Reform: let us take action and cement the revival/new-spirit through reforming our churches, schools, states, and government

These same three steps (Repentance, Revival, and Reform) can be applied to our failing families, our dying churches, our crumbling communities, and also our cities, states, and nation. The process is the same, though the audience varies and is on different scales. As we are personally restored, we must then take the revival to the next level: to our churches.

As Christians, we in the congregations need to hold our pastors/staff accountable to preaching the whole message of the Bible (not just the easy parts) and spiritually feed us the way we need to be fed. Like Joshua, our spiritual leaders need to be strong and courageous and not hesitate from speaking out about the rampant sin and wickedness engulfing our culture, along with naming names and calling out our cultural and political leaders at every level of our society for what they say and believe, and how they comport themselves.

Likewise, the pastors need to hold their congregations accountable by not just attending church and a handful of people doing all the work, but getting involved and doing something to spread the Gospel. The beauty of the church is not in the grand buildings we see around us, but in the people from every "tongue, tribe, and nation" (and background and social-class) worshiping God and working together as one body in order to spread the Gospel and build the Kingdom. Christians are not supposed to "go" to church – Christians are supposed to

BE the Church, and that means being stirred up and often thrown out of our comfort zones.

America's churches hold the key to revival across the nation, but those in our churches begin with us. Dive into the Bible and make it a part of your daily life. Build a relationship with God just as you would with your spouse, family, and friends. If you do not attend church, find one that reveres the Bible and then get involved with it. Faith builds upon faith, and surrounding yourself with like-minded believers is part of the personal Reforms.

For most of America's history, John 3:16 was the best known and most often quoted verse, but in America today, it's Matthew 7:1 – "Judge not lest ye be judged." That's the attitude of not only an unrepentant people, but those who are actively refusing to repent. Such an attitude indicates they do not want to be judged or condemned in order that they may continue in their sin. When someone wields that verse, they're essentially screaming "Let me do whatever I want, whenever I want, and with whoever I want!" at you in a pious, lofty sort of way.

First and foremost, pastors and churches need to return to expounding the Bible and teaching it from the pulpits. Every verse of the Bible was put there for a reason, and it's a pastor's duty to teach the "entire counsel of God" – even if the people don't want to hear it (Acts 20:27). Pastors are to preach, expound, and explain – and the congregation is to digest it and then put it to use in their daily lives as they go out into the world. A pastor's primary duty is to know and wield the Word of God to help their flock grow to maturity, not to manage every single church item or task. Even Moses had to delegate responsibilities, like all good leaders do.

Secondly, our church music and style of worship matters – a lot. In most contemporary churches today, there is a great deal of emotions and energy, but often a complete lack of reverence, holiness, and sacredness – especially when everyone is wearing street-clothes (including the pastor). Understand that those aren't necessarily wrong and no one should be excluded for wearing such (of course), but the congregational attire and style of music does make a big difference. Churches don't have to be mortuaries, but they should probably not emulate secular rock-concerts either. The entire atmosphere within a church should be one that exudes a sacred, safe, solid place where people can draw closer to God. More often than not, our external environment influences how we think, feel, and especially worship – and for that reason alone, worship should be peaceful, wholesome, reverent, and conducive for helping people grow and mature in their faith.

Go into the average contemporary church today and what will you typically find? A multi-media stage featuring a praise-band that often bears uncanny similarities to a secular rock band. But look at what is missing from most contemporary services:

Where are the altar-calls ringing out for the unsaved to come to the Lord and be saved?

Where are the hymns of past generations that held such deep meaning for so many believers?

Where are the cries from the pulpits to put aside our wicked ways and repent of our sins?

Where is the clear, undiluted teaching of the Scriptures that once resounded from our churches?

Where is the beauty, reverence, and sense of holiness that once pervaded our sanctuaries?

In most of our churches today, these foundational elements are simply no longer present – there is either a deafening silence or the booming noise of modern music (with Christian lyrics at times). So many of our churches seem more concerned with making the people comfortable and keeping them entertained during the worship service than immersing them in the Word of God and bringing them to repentance and maturity. Multitudes of churches have stopped teaching the undiluted Word of God

354

in favor of topical studies heavily mixed with the contemporary "wisdom" and the opinions of worldly experts.

When we sing the modern praise songs rather than the hymns of our parents and grandparents and we feel our hearts rise, are we having an emotional response to the music or something greater and deeper? Are we being moved in the "flesh" or in the "spirit"? How often does our Sunday worship carry over into the week and the rest of our lives? Is our worship of the Living God only confined to the measly hour or two we give Him on Sunday mornings?

The purpose of church assemblies is to reverently worship God, grow in the knowledge of the Lord via the Word, and mature in the faith – not to be entertained. But as more time and effort is spent trying to make the Sunday service more attractive to seekers or to make the people comfortable and stay put in the cushy chairs, the less time remains for Biblical teaching. How much can really be taught in a twenty-minute or even a fifteen-minute sermon?

Most old-time preachers were just getting warmed up at that point and would often preach for at least an hour. Even our secular elementary schools spend forty-five minutes teaching each subject. Yet a forty-five minute sermon for adults would not be tolerated in most churches today. The American people cannot tolerate being bored, after all. Again, our churches are infested with the "rule of the people" rather than the Rule of the King. Where in the Bible do we find any pastors or prophets toning down their messages or polling the congregation to see what will "sell" or not?

The main thrust of the worship service should be for growing and maturing the people, and that can only happen with an in-depth exposition of the Word of God. Topical studies have their place, but the main service should be used for feeding the people straight from the Bible. Rather than worrying about whether some newcomers or seekers completely understand the message or not, we should be worried about whether the congregation is being fed and maturing. God promises that "His

Word will not return void," (Isaiah 55:11) but too many of our church leaders are so worried about catching and holding newcomers that they spiritually starve the rest of the congregation.

It's not the church's main purpose (as a corporate entity) to go out and bring new people into the church, but to feed the people already in their care. If the church exerts all their efforts toward bringing in seekers, there isn't much left for maturing their own people. Also, when the people aren't growing in their faith, they tend to let the church organization do most of the work of the Great Commission for them. The people tend to become spiritually apathetic and lethargic and fail to grow and mature.

But when the people are spiritually fed and mature in Christ, they are then adequately equipped to go forth and care for the poor, the sick, and of course, spread the Gospel. The people in the churches must become filled with the knowledge of the Lord before they can take it to their families, neighborhoods, places of employment, and so forth. But on a large scale, that is no longer occurring in most American churches – the people are no longer being fed more than spiritual "milk" (or perhaps "yogurt"), and maturity takes longer and longer, if it even occurs at all. Therefore, is it any wonder that the knowledge of God is growing faint throughout our land?

How about our churches in America set aside the four-piece bands, the extravagant multimedia presentations, and the half-time sermons and get back to the basics of singing a couple hymns and spend the bulk of the service immersing the people in the Word of God? How about we step out in faith and preach the Word again and leave the church growth up to God? When we stand before Him someday, is He going to pull out a rap-sheet on us and knock off points because we didn't draw large crowds or bring millions into the Kingdom? No – He'll simply be checking for whether we were faithful for the opportunities, gifts, and talents He gave us, and how we put them to use on His behalf (Matthew 25:14-30; Luke 19:12-28).

356

If we want to understand why our inner-cities are full of poverty and crime, we have to look no further than our churches. Where are they? Why do they pull back and relocate away from problem-areas with the rest of the suburbs? The Church has been called to do the opposite, and the early settlers of America did just that: they invaded the darkness of the frontier with the light of the Gospel. The Church is the only hope for our slums, not government handouts and entitlement programs. If the churches of yesteryear behaved the way that most modern churches do today, much of the West would've never been settled.

We should be flooding the inner-cities with the message of Christ and providing real help to those in need, such as food, clothes, counseling, literacy-classes, job-training, and other forms of charity. Instead of spending hundreds of thousands of dollars on those new buildings that are often half-empty, the Church should be creating or supporting inner-city churches – or planting their own like they would in a foreign country halfway around the world. Storing up treasures in Heaven doesn't mean building more extravagant church facilities, but reaching lost souls who need saving, and helping real people who are trapped and hurting.

America was founded by not merely groups of individuals working together – it was founded by churches of people who had covenanted together to settle a new land that would be built on faith. We must do likewise.

The Faith of Our Founding Fathers

Since the beginning of Progressivism, the faith and beliefs of our Founding Fathers have been called into question by liberal scholars and historians who sought to reshape America into something it was not. By denigrating or even vilifying our Founders, they caused people to not look to the wisdom of great men like George Washington, Thomas Jefferson, John Adams, Patrick Henry, Ben Franklin, and countless others who shaped

357

our nation. Once a nation's heroes are trampled underfoot, the rest of the foundation can be called into question and the nation can more easily be torn away from its roots and "fundamentally transformed."

America's Founders cherished their faith and God-given freedoms more than life itself, and they proved it over and over by their sacrifice. Yet today, those same men and women are often painted as greedy, rebellious, power-hungry slave-owners instead of men of faith, conscience, and integrity. If we are to believe these revisionist historians, then America's founding wasn't all that special – and possibly even criminal. In that light, America's current era under the boot of Progressivism and secularism doesn't look that bad, does it?

But what if the Founders were Christians and did establish a nation founded on faith? Then America's current days are not only tragic, but should outrage all American citizens of faith about what is happening to our country.

Was America ever really a Christian nation? Modern scholars may protest that we never were, declaring the nation's Founding Fathers to be mostly Deists and such. But rather than brazenly declaring "we know better now," perhaps we should read what a few of the Founders actually said about what they both believed and felt with respect to God, faith, and liberty.

"We've staked our future on our ability to follow the Ten Commandments with all of our heart." – James Madison

"Without morals a republic cannot subsist any length of time; they therefore who are decrying the Christian religion, whose morality is so sublime and pure (and) which insures to the good eternal happiness, are undermining the solid foundation of morals, the best security for the duration of free governments." – Charles Carroll, signer of the Declaration of Independence.

"We have no government armed with power capable of contending with human passions unbridled by morality and religion. Avarice, ambition, revenge, or gallantry, would break the strongest cords of our Constitution as a whale goes through a net. Our Constitution was made only for a moral and religious people. It is wholly inadequate to the government of any other."
– John Adams

"I have lived, Sir, a long time, and the longer I live, the more convincing proofs I see of this truth–that God governs the affairs of men. And if a sparrow cannot fall to the ground without His notice, is it probable that an empire can rise without His aid?" – Benjamin Franklin

"In the beginning of the contest with Britain, when we were sensible of danger, we had daily prayers in this room for Divine protection. Our prayers, Sir, were heard, and they were graciously answered... do we imagine we no longer need His assistance?" – Benjamin Franklin, at the Constitutional Convention, Thursday June 28, 1787

"Freedom is not a gift bestowed upon us by other men, but a right that belongs to us by the laws of God and nature." – Benjamin Franklin

"Man will ultimately be governed by God or by tyrants." – Benjamin Franklin. In Benjamin Franklin's 1749 plan of education for public schools in Pennsylvania, he insisted that schools teach "the excellency of the Christian religion above all others, ancient or modern."

"For my own part, I sincerely esteem it [the Constitution] a system which without the finger of God, never could have been suggested and agreed upon by such a diversity of interests." – Alexander Hamilton, in 1787 after the Constitutional Convention

"I have carefully examined the evidences of the Christian religion, and if I was sitting as a juror upon its authenticity I would unhesitatingly give my verdict in its favor. I can prove its truth as clearly as any proposition ever submitted to the mind of man." – Alexander Hamilton

"It cannot be emphasized too clearly and too often that this nation was founded, not by religionists, but by Christians; not on religion, but on the gospel of Jesus Christ. For this very reason, peoples of other faiths have been afforded asylum, prosperity, and freedom of worship here." – Patrick Henry, in his speech to the House of Burgesses in May 1765.

"Providence has given to our people the choice of their rulers, and it is the duty, as well as the privilege and interest of our Christian nation to select and prefer Christians for their rulers." – John Jay

"Of all the systems of morality, ancient or modern which have come under my observation, none appears to me so pure as that of Jesus." – Thomas Jefferson

"The God who gave us life gave us liberty. And can the liberties of a nation be thought secure when we have removed their only firm basis, a conviction in the minds of the people that these liberties are a gift from God? That they are not to be violated but with His wrath? Indeed I tremble for my country when I reflect that God is just, and that His justice cannot sleep forever." – Thomas Jefferson

"We have staked the whole future of American civilization, not upon the power of government, far from it. We've staked the future of all our political institutions upon our capacity...to sustain ourselves according to the Ten Commandments of

God." – James Madison, to the General Assembly of the State of Virginia in 1778.

"If we abide by the principles taught in the Bible, our country will go on prospering and to prosper; but if we and our posterity neglect its instruction and authority, no man can tell how sudden a catastrophe may overwhelm us and bury all our glory in profound obscurity." – Daniel Webster

"Finally, let us not forget the religious character of our origin. Our fathers were brought hither by their high veneration for the Christian religion. They journeyed by its light, and labored in its hope. They sought to incorporate its principles with the elements of their society, and to diffuse its influence through all their institutions, civil, political, or literary." – Daniel Webster

"The duties of men are summarily comprised in the Ten Commandments, consisting of two tables; one comprehending the duties which we owe immediately to God – the other, the duties we owe to our fellow men." – Noah Webster

"In my view, the Christian religion is the most important and one of the first things in which all children, under a free government ought to be instructed...No truth is more evident to my mind than that the Christian religion must be the basis of any government intended to secure the rights and privileges of a free people." – Noah Webster, in the preface to his American Dictionary of the English Language of 1828.

"Let it be impressed on your mind that God commands you to choose for rulers just men who will rule in the fear of God [Exodus 18:21]. . . . If the citizens neglect their duty and place unprincipled men in office, the government will soon be corrupted . . . If our government fails to secure public prosperity and happiness, it must be because the citizens neglect the

Divine commands, and elect bad men to make and administer the laws." – Noah Webster, in 'The History of the United States'.

"In the beginning of the contest with Britain, when we were sensible of danger, we had daily prayers in this room for Divine protection. Our prayers, Sir, were heard, and they were graciously answered... Do we imagine we no longer need His assistance?" – Benjamin Franklin

"All the miseries and evils which men suffer from vice, crime, ambition, injustice, oppression, slavery and war, proceed from their despising or neglecting the precepts contained in the Bible." – Noah Webster

"The Bible was America's basic textbook in all fields." – Noah Webster

"Education is useless without the Bible." – Noah Webster

"The name of American, which belongs to you, in your national capacity, must always exalt the just pride of Patriotism, more than any appellation derived from local discriminations. With slight shades of difference, you have the same religion... Reason and experience both forbid us to expect, that national morality can prevail in exclusion of religious principle..." – George Washington in his Farewell Address to the nation.

"It is impossible to rightly govern the world without God and Bible." – George Washington

"What students would learn in American schools above all is the religion of Jesus Christ." – George Washington, in his speech to the Delaware Indian Chiefs on May 12, 1779.

"To the distinguished character of patriot, it should be our highest glory to add the more distinguished character of Christian." – George Washington, at Valley Forge on May 2, 1778.

And finally during his inauguration, George Washington, the Father of our Country, took the oath as prescribed by the Constitution but also added several religious components to that first inaugural ceremony: before taking his oath of office, he summoned a Bible upon which to take the oath, added the words "So help me God!" to the end of the oath, and then leaned over and kissed the Bible.

"When the people are virtuous, they cannot be subdued. But when they lose their virtue they'll be ready to surrender their liberties to the first external or internal invader." – Samuel Adams

Chapter 12 - Restoring our Foundations

"The only foundation for a useful education in a republic is to be laid in religion. Without this there can be no virtue, and without virtue there can be no liberty, and liberty is the object and life of all republican governments." – Benjamin Rush, Signer of the Declaration of Independence

The United States of America is one of the youngest nations in the world, yet it has been the most prosperous, the most decent, and the freest in all of history. But as quickly as America arose, she can just as quickly fall apart and fade away. And after a century of self-destructive Progressivism and twelve years of incredibly irresponsible borrowing, spending, and terrible mismanagement, America is rapidly declining.

Earlier in her history when America faced uncertain times, spiritual revivals broke out which bolstered the people and gave them not only a renewed spirit, but the courage to press forward in the midst of terrible circumstances and enormous challenges. Each spiritual revival of the nation not only changed that generation, but the course of our history.

Would the American Revolution or the Civil War have broken out had there not been the preceding spiritual revivals? Would we still be subjects of the British had we never been spiritually stirred by the First Great Awakening and been filled with the courage and determination to declare and then fight for our independence? What if the Second Great Awakening had never occurred? Would slavery still exist in half the country if we had remained apathetic to the plight of millions of people in our own land?

When we look back at our forefathers, we marvel at their courage, their determination, and their perseverance. But they were no different than us – they were just ordinary men and

364

women who chose to do what was right, regardless of the difficulties they faced. Though our circumstances are different, they had the same fears, the same excuses for apathy, and the same discouragements. But in spite of those huge challenges and obstacles, they forged a new nation that was based upon the principles of liberty and justice for all.

In our own day, we stand on the edge of a great precipice, just like our forefathers once did. We too have a choice: we can stand up and fight for our nation and our God-given rights, or we can shrug our shoulders, shrink back from the battles ahead, and tremble quietly behind closed doors.

We can lament that these challenges have come in our days, but so does everyone who's faced with such difficulties – our only responsibility is to meet those challenges head-on and fight the good fight. We can accept the challenge of restoring our nation or we can surrender America to Europe's fate: a slow, painful death through cultural and political suicide. We have a choice – and part of that choice is to never give up, never surrender, and never despair, regardless of how dark our days become.

One story from the early days of the American Revolution exemplifies the attitude we must have if we are to preserve and restore our nation. After the fires of patriotism had died down following the Boston Massacre, James Warren began to lose heart when town after town in Massachusetts refused to respond to their pleas to continue the Cause against Great Britain. Despondent, he wrote to Samuel Adams saying of their fellow citizens, "They are dead and the dead cannot be raised without a miracle." Adams promptly responded: "Nil desperandum – Never Despair. That should be a motto for you, me, and all liberty-loving people! All are not dead, and where there is a spark of patriotic fire, we will rekindle it."

After a few months, they certainly did rekindle that patriotic fire, almost single-handedly. But what if Adams and Warren had given up the cause of liberty because the people continued to slumber in their apathy? Fortunately for us and the rest of their posterity, they didn't – and like those early patriots, we must never give up and never despair either.

America's Foundations

Just as every house must have a firm, solid foundation upon which to stand, so must every nation if it is to endure. And the elemental foundations of every nation are common virtues, common laws, common traditions, and typically a common language.

When the United States was only a fledgling confederation of English colonies, upon what was this foundation constructed? What forged those various and diverse peoples into a single nation? From the first colonies established on the shores of the East Coast and Massachusetts Bay, the consistent ambition of the colonists was to establish a land in which the Christian religion could be freely practiced and the spread of the Gospel would be unrestrained and undiluted by others. Later, many more colonists came to breathe the refreshing air of the personal liberty and freedom the Colonies offered to all who came to the shores of the New World.

For the next one hundred and fifty years after the colonists began streaming into America, the Colonies remained loyal to Great Britain. And though there were grumblings from time to time, they remained on peaceful terms with their mother country. But early in the 1750s, something began to change. A cultural shift began to occur.

Before any visible, outward shift is manifested in a nation or society, an invisible yet profound spiritual shift must occur first. The spiritual shift which occurred twice in America's early history was the Great Awakening, which spurred America into the Revolutionary War and then again in the Second Great Awakening, which culminated in the Civil War. In the previous century, there were two more spiritual shifts: that of evolutionary philosophy and its immediate offspring, secular humanism. These two latter shifts pushed the character of

America back towards that of Europe and away from her Founders, who had rejected and abandoned European philosophy, thought, and society to start a new country: a free country based upon God and the Rule of Law, not the Rule of Man.

In the first Great Awakening of the 1740s through the 1760s, the Gospel and the teachings of the Bible rang throughout the Colonies. People in the tens of thousands heard the Good News and repented and were spiritually reborn. Homes were renewed, parents were changed, families were altered, and children were raised with the wisdom of the knowledge of the Bible and what God expected of a decent, orderly society and a free people who wished to remain free.

The spiritual heritage produced by the Great Awakening eventually led to the cry for independence from an ever-encroaching British King and Parliament indifferent to the Colonies. The King, Parliament, and the British people began to consider the Colonists to be their subjects rather than their fellow citizens. And when this new spiritual heritage had matured in America, it led to the Revolutionary War and then later gave birth to the Constitution.

The Second Great Awakening of the 1800s to the 1840s eventually propelled the nation into the Civil War, the most divisive, bloodiest war America has ever experienced. Brothers fought against brothers, families against families, and neighbors against neighbors. And yet the country endured, recovered, and then prospered, unlike most nations that are overtaken by civil war.

The third spiritual change in America was more gradual and subtle, which began in the 1870s in the universities and then migrated to the secondary schools and eventually into the primary schools: the replacement of our Judeo-Christian religious heritage with secular humanism. By neglecting and disregarding our religious moorings, America became untethered and has been floundering on the sea of secularism since the 1960s.

However, the societal upheavals of the 1960s were produced by the spiritual apathy and hypocrisy in the 1950s, as well as the false teaching and the philosophy that if we are prospering, we must be in God's favor, or at least be heading down the right road as a nation. However, the wealthier America became, the more we came to rely on our prosperity as our measure of success as opposed to the measure of our character and virtue.

Character is formed in the crucible of trials and suffering – the "Greatest Generation" had character-development forced upon them by the Great Depression and WWII. But their children and the subsequent generations had no such trials, and look how our national character has declined with each generation. No generation wants to go through economic hardships or through war, but those events do test that generation and either produce greatness or insignificance. Perhaps one of the reasons why the protest groups and revolutionaries in the Sixties arose was because they felt insignificant compared to their parents' generation – and they wanted to gain glory, purpose, and significance for themselves.

James Madison declared, "We have staked the whole future of American civilization, not upon the power of government, far from it. We've staked the future of all our political institutions upon our capacity…to sustain ourselves according to the Ten Commandments of God." Also, Noah Webster said, "All the miseries and evils which men suffer from vice, crime, ambition, injustice, oppression, slavery and war, proceed from their despising or neglecting the precepts contained in the Bible."

When most people self-governed and self-regulated themselves according to the Judeo-Christian religion, America's problems had been insignificant. But with the overstepping of the Courts, the most basic of those values, namely the Ten Commandments, aren't even allowed to be displayed in the public square, whether the people want them there or not. When timeless principles of law and order, self-restraint, and basic morals cannot be posted in the public square nor taught in the classroom, how can any child be expected to consistently learn them outside their home, much less put them into everyday practice when they're teenagers and then later adults? Today's children get most of their values from the television, the Internet, and their peers instead of their families, churches, and schools.

Some Judeo-Christian values are still basically taught in our society, but they have been steadily declining. Many people still know what the Golden Rule is ("Treat others the way you want to be treated"), but that's only the weaker half of the Greatest Commandment, which is "You shall love the Lord your God with all your heart, mind, soul, and strength." (Mark 12:29-31) Without the Greatest Commandment, the Golden Rule is weakened and often easily tossed aside.

If America's homes, families, communities, and institutions are to be saved and restored, then we must return to our Judeo-Christian heritage, and that doesn't mean just posting the Ten Commandments in our classrooms or reciting a Pledge. Many look around and think, "It's not that bad," but could it be that we've been living on borrowed time? We need to re-internalize Judeo-Christian values and regularly practice them in our daily lives, as well as pass them on to our children and the next generation.

If we really want to restore sanity to our country, our civilization, and our culture, we need to take the long-term approach like the Left did sixty years ago: "the long march through the institutions." The political Left began infecting the entertainment industry and made liberalism "cool" in movies, television, and music and portrayed their opponents as old, out-of-touch, and paranoid. As their ranks swelled during the anti-war movement, they swept through the universities. When the dust of the Sixties finally settled, they were holding key positions in the universities, which produce all the teachers, pastors, media, entertainers, communicators, lawyers, scientists, and politicians – and then it was only a matter of time before they took over all the other civil institutions.

One bright spot in our current gloomy future is that conservatives have many opportunities ahead of us, the reason being that as an ideology, liberalism is on its last legs – it's morally, fiscally, and intellectually bankrupt and has an unprecedented record of failure everywhere it's implemented. Unfortunately, the Left is currently in power and deeply entrenched in our civil, cultural, and political institutions. However, most of those institutions are highly dependent upon centralized power and our debt-ridden financial structures. When the dollar collapses, it'll bring down the welfare state, big government, and most of the other institutions the Left has taken over. Sooner or later, the government – like every other bankrupt household which has trashed its credit – will be forced to return to fiscal sanity and common sense, though it will probably be very, very painful.

One reason why the early Pilgrim and Puritan settlers succeeded in building a virtuous, moral society was because of their reverence for covenants. They primarily had a covenant with God and a covenant with one another: each had to fulfill their obligations if they expected others to fulfill theirs. Adults held one another accountable for character, morality, and virtue, and childrearing was viewed as the responsibility of both the family and the community, rather than the family alone. The churches, schools, and the rest of the community were expected to reinforce the moral standards taught in the churches and practiced by the families.

Part of the reason American society has broken down is because those moral standards are no longer reinforced outside the family, if not often undermined by our schools and the popular culture. As a result, the families have broken down and with them, the American society.

To be clear, restoring our Judeo-Christian heritage doesn't mean a return to Puritanism – it means a return to the two-fold covenant and the building of strong families and spiritually investing in the next generation. Strong families build strong communities, and strong communities build strong nations.

370

Character and Virtue

To the younger generation of Americans and far too many others, character and virtue fell by the wayside in the 1960s with the youth-movement and the counter-culture. However, character and especially virtue in America had been declining for most of the Twentieth Century as a result of the decline of Judeo-Christianity and the rise of secularism. As moral relativism set in, there appeared to be little need for character, much less virtue.

The foundation of any form of government – but especially a constitutional republic based upon self-government – is the character of its citizens. Yet look around – are most of the people we see in the media, our public institutions, and especially our government of good character? Tragically, far too many are not; they are easily bribed, manipulated, and those in power often say or do whatever it takes to remain in power. A nation founded on the principles of self-government begins with the governing of one's self: personal character.

What is meant by "character"? Character is practicing in private what you preach in public. Character is doing what's right regardless of the cost, inconvenience, and consequences. Character is demonstrated by putting others ahead of yourself, self-sacrifice, hard-work, honesty, generosity, perseverance, and virtue. Character means making tough decisions and then sticking by them.

Along with character, there must be virtue, since they walk hand-in-hand and are different sides of the same coin. The most basic definition of virtue is "moral excellence, goodness, righteousness." It's impossible to have good character without virtue, and impossible to have virtue without character. Like character, virtue must be continually aspired to, taught, reinforced, and practiced in everyday life. In our popular culture today, the entire notion of virtue is often portrayed as being old-fashioned and antiquated, but virtue is not dependent on

371

technology or even one's standard of living. People can be just as moral and decent with plenty as they can with little – it's about where their "heart is" rather than how much they have.

Both character and virtue require a moral standard, and in traditional America, that meant Judeo-Christian values, such as trusting in God, treating others the way you wish to be treated, and being honest and hard-working. Proverbs 14:34 declares that "Righteousness exalts a nation, but sin is a reproach to any people." For most of America's history, our standard of righteousness and goodness came from the regular, consistent teaching of the Bible and Judeo-Christian values. Did everyone adhere to them? Certainly not, but at least there was a moral standard and code of behavior which everyone was expected to abide by and aspire to.

But with the rise of secularism and Progressivism which requires it, the moral standard has increasingly been lowered and even abandoned – after all, a culture cannot have a moral standard if no one can agree on those standards. Imagine the disaster that would result if all the carpenters, plumbers, and framers tried to build a house but couldn't agree to standard units of measurement. Chaos would ensue, and even if they somehow managed to build that house, it wouldn't stand for very long. Yet that is what has happened to America over the last century – we have thrown out the Judeo-Christian standards and refuse to agree on another moral standard. To make matters worse, one of the pillars of secularism is the complete absence of moral standards in favor of moral relativism.

As a result of America's abandonment of moral standards, is it any wonder our families, churches, communities, and nation have broken down? Character builds nations, but immorality – and the disregarding of moral standards of behavior – tears them down.

Since the 1990s, it's become fashionable among the political class (most of which is highly Progressive and secular) to legalize destructive personal vices but heavily tax and regulate them in the hopes of discouraging their use or at least obtaining

372

tax revenue from those who continue to indulge in their vices. This practice of legalizing vices in order to regulate and tax first began with tobacco and cigarettes, then moved on to gambling, and today marijuana. After marijuana, prostitution will likely be pushed for legalization – after all, it's the woman's body (or man's) and only consenting adults are involved, right? Who are you to say what I can or cannot do with my body?

Using personal vices such as gambling, smoking, drugs, and prostitution to grow the state instead of legitimate businesses not only demonstrates the degeneracy of our society, but reinforces the lack of moral standards and self-destructive behaviors. It's like saying, "Let us do evil so that good may result!" Will legalizing marijuana, gambling, prostitution or any of these other vices that are detrimental to a person's character, their families, and their communities really help our nation? Of course not – debauchery always produces more debauchery and eventually self-destruction. There might be a short-term increase in tax-revenue and decrease in police expenditures, but long-term those vices destroy the lives of the abusers, their families, and their communities.

Over the last few elections, the issues that have attracted the most attention aren't about responsible governance but petty, vice issues like tobacco, gambling, gay-marriage, and pot-legalization. How laughable (and pathetic) is it that we think that legalizing vices or legitimizing immorality will somehow magically improve our nation? What does it say about our nation when our financial system is in shambles, regulations and taxes are out of control, and our liberties are being trampled, but the two issues that really bring out the vote are pot-legalization and gay-marriage?

What does it say about a city, state, or nation that builds itself upon immorality? What does it say about us when our healthcare system is funded by tobacco, alcohol, and now marijuana taxes, which only cause more health-problems and dependency? What does it say about us when our schools are funded by lottery tickets and casinos which prey upon financially irresponsible people? What does it say about us when taxes on alcohol are used to fund anti-alcohol agencies and regulation or even healthcare? Also, what happens if those vices that our Progressive politicians are trying to punish are ever given up? More tax revenue will need to be raised to cover the revenue shortfall, and those taxes will hurt those of us who are already struggling under our tax-burden as it is.

Fixing America begins with individual Americans returning to following the Judeo-Christian moral standards and practicing them in their daily lives, and then teaching them to the next generation and those around them. Instilling character and virtue back into the heart of our nation is far more important than our petty political squabbles, our education system, and even our economic problems.

Healing the heart of America begins with healing our own.

Charity and Community

Americans have historically been a very generous people. Even though our GDP has steadily increased (until recently), charitable giving has remained relatively steady to GDP (slightly below 2%); the more America has prospered, the more we have given – even in difficult economic times. Relative to GDP, Americans give more than twice as much (1.67%) as the next most generous countries: the UK at 0.73% and Canada at 0.72%.

However, though our giving has remained steady, often our charity either is not given to where it's most needed or it simply doesn't go far enough in helping those in need. The true purpose of charity is to help others in need, not to build monuments to ourselves, like foundations, bigger churches, memorials, etc. It's been proven that the charity which reaches the people who need it the most often helps grow the economy because it helps the needy personally recover. If more of the charitable giving was spent on programs to help lift others out of poverty and get them on their feet, fewer people would need to rely on state and federal welfare programs, which rarely help any recover.

One of the problems of the Industrial Age of the last two centuries was that enormous amounts of wealth was created very quickly, but too little of it was given away to help the poor. The principle "To whom much is given, much will be required," especially concerns charity. As a result of the huge (and growing) wealth-gap between the rich and the poor, political opportunists used class warfare tactics to tax the rich in order to redistribute a portion of their wealth to the poor in exchange for the more numerous votes of the struggling underclass.

These opportunists and the political philosophy of Progressivism and Socialism may not have risen to power if the wealthier people had been more charitable. And this isn't merely being more charitable in giving, but being more charitable in the sense of higher wages, better working conditions, etc. Also, when these new taxes did arise, the politicians created tax-shelters such as foundations and trusts in which the rich would donate their money to have it remain under their control, yet not be taxed as income. The more clever philanthropists created foundations and university programs which trained students to use their patented products and methodologies in order to increase their profits.

For example, the founders of some pharmaceutical companies would contribute to foundations that would award grants, scholarships, and other donations to universities, provided that they would teach what the foundations recommended. The foundations would then recommend certain treatments and drugs (often from their parent pharmaceutical companies) for various diagnoses. In this way, the foundations became a way for companies to not only shelter their taxable income, but also grow their future revenue.

Yet despite the billions given annually to foundations, the vast bulk of charitable giving in America comes from individuals. From the National Philanthropic Trust, the largest source of charitable giving comes from individuals, at $217.79

billion in 2011, or 73% of total giving, followed by foundations ($41.67 billion/14%), bequests ($24.41 billion/8%), and corporations ($14.55 billion/5%). In 2011, nearly $300 billion was given by American individuals and corporations.

One of the more disturbing aspects of Barack Obama's tax-reform plans was to reduce or eliminate the tax-deduction for charitable giving on our income tax returns. Part of the reason America is so charitable is because donations are tax-deductible, and most Americans would rather see their hard-earned money be given away to a cause or charity that they choose rather than to the government, where it's frequently wasted or spent on programs they may not agree with.

Why Obama would want to discourage charitable giving – particularly during difficult economic times when charity is most needed – is open to speculation, but the simple answer is that as a radical Progressive, he likely believes that welfare should come solely from the government, and private charity is reducing the Progressives' ability to redistribute money. In the minds of most Progressives, all money belongs to the government in the first place, and personal income is merely what the government allows you to keep.

During difficult times, Americans are usually able to rely upon one another and work together as families and communities for the benefit of everyone. Charity doesn't just help those who are on the receiving end, but also those on the giving end – giving and helping others makes people feel better, as well as draws people together in stronger bonds. Personal and community giving is good for everyone, and can help rebuild communities and societies that are turning inward and falling apart.

The giving-spirit of Americans must be fostered and encouraged throughout society rather than squelched or burdened by our tax code and our politicians.

Civility and Manners

One of the more visible manifestations of good character and personal virtues is public civility and manners, which have been declining since the 1960s with the rise of radical feminism, the Sexual Revolution, and the foolish counter-cultural philosophy of "never trusting anyone over thirty."

Most manners are rooted in the idea of putting others ahead of yourself (sacrifice) and refraining from offensive language and crude behavior. Just because we feel something in a particular moment and want to insult or retort, that doesn't mean we should; self-government begins with self-control and restricting our behavior regardless of our feelings which are often very temporary. Children used to be taught manners and civility at a young age so they wouldn't act like brutes when they were older – today many adults act like brutes because they were never taught any differently, and now that's the popular way to behave.

In the feelings-based culture that arose with the youth-movement in the 1960s and 1970s, basic manners and civility – particularly with the flippant use of curse words and other foul language – have taken a nose-dive in American culture. The popularization of rap, hip-hop, and street-talk and the loosening of profanity restrictions have caused foul language to become so widely accepted that many of our young people have difficulty speaking coherent sentences without lacing them with profanity.

Along with tossing out basic civility, the youth-movement that arose with the Baby Boomer generation collectively rebelled against most forms of authority in their quest to create a new world of peace, tolerance, openness, and free-love. If you have no respect for authority, then why should you be civil? "If it feels good do it" might feel right or even seem right at the moment, but it's incredibly shortsighted and usually doesn't consider the much longer-lasting, often permanent consequences of those feelings. Again, controlling your

377

temporary feelings and passions is the most basic form of self-government.

Like character and virtue, civility and manners must be taught from a very young age and reinforced throughout life, as well as be reinforced by our families, schools, communities, employers, media-outlets, and politicians. Swearing and coarse language might seem cool when you're thirteen, but it's not so cool when you're thirty – it only shows others that you haven't learned to control your language, temper, and words yet. In public – particularly in the media and politics – civility needs to be relearned and restandardized; there is no excuse for a public speaker or politician who cannot carry on a civil conversation without resorting to interruptions, personal insults and attacks, swearing, and inappropriate displays of emotion. Your speech is a window into your heart, and if little more than foul language is coming out of your mouth, then what will those around you think is inside you?

Another aspect of manners, civility, and self-control is personal modesty as well as decency, which applies to both boys and girls as well as men and women. Just as using foul language betrays a lack of self-control and immaturity, so does wearing overly-revealing clothing (for girls/women) and saggy-pants that show one's underwear (for boys/men). In particular, immodest clothing has no place in offices, businesses, schools, and of course, churches and synagogues. If there's one place where females especially should dress modestly (or at least not immodestly), it's in religious settings. Far too often today, it's difficult to tell whether the young women have confused the church with the nightclub (or brothel). The image you project on the outside is the only one that most people will see, so we must consider what image we wish to present to those around us.

Lastly, a higher form of civility is one that can be used to influence another who is being rude, angry, or argumentative. Love covers a multitude of sins (1 Peter 4:8), and by not only controlling your emotions but listening and then responding

378

with love and understanding can help change the other person for the better. Ironically, the primary person who's changed when you control your emotions is *you*! One of the Judeo-Christian virtues is to bless others when they curse you, and to love your enemies (Matthew 5:44). Responding with quiet civility (or better yet, love) will often dump water on the flames of anger and hate (Proverbs 25:21-22); after all, it's hard to remain upset with someone who's not feeding your anger by responding to it in kind.

Anger and incivility can be overcome by love, service, and charity. Again, it's very difficult to continue in your anger or even hate when your adversary is doing good to/for you! What would America look like if more of us actually "loved our neighbors as ourselves" instead of merely paying it lip-service?

Family and Marriage

Strong nations start with strong communities, strong communities start with strong families, and strong families start with strong marriages. If the heart of a nation could be examined, it would start with the families and the marriages. The foundational unit of every nation is the family, and what is the state of the average family in America today? Broken, confused, angry, anxious, and distressed. Why are so many of our families broken and in shambles? Because so many of our marriages are broken, falling down, and being torn apart. As of 2011, America has the highest divorce rate in the world – even more than the secular, socialist states of Western Europe (though many simply don't bother getting married any longer).

If America is still a center-right or even a nominally "Christian" nation, then why are so many of our marriages and families in distress? The primary reason is because we've thrown away our Judeo-Christian values that emphasize the sanctity of commitment, which is exactly what marriage is: a sanctified commitment. A marriage is more than simply a social contract between two people, it's supposed to be a sanctified, holy union of two very different creatures – one man and one woman – for life until "death do them part." The Judeo-Christian model of marriage is the formation of one new "person" out of two different people, which then produce children who are evidence of that new, special union. Marriage can even be considered a more basic form of the "e pluribus unum" pillar of the American Trinity: e duo unum – "out of two, one."

Because of "no-fault" divorce, the hyper-sexualization of our culture, the trivializing of marriage (and commitments in general), and the idea of "if it feels good do it," marriages have been under attack since the 1960s and 1970s. A major component of personal character is sticking to our commitments and having the integrity to keep our promises regardless of our feelings and circumstances. Again, character means keeping your word and often putting others ahead of yourself and your own desires.

If you're stuck in a bad/unhappy marriage, remember that you made a commitment (especially if you have dependents). Try to repair your marriage with prayer, repentance, and counseling – preferably religious-based counseling. Try to do everything you can to stick it out until the kids turn eighteen and can be on their own. If your marriage cannot be salvaged, then try to end it as peaceably as possible – for your families' sake if nothing else. Broken marriages produce broken families, which produce broken communities and then a broken nation – which is where we are today.

Another cause of the breakdown of marriages and homes in America is the "Great Society" welfare system of LBJ, which has effectively replaced the father and his income with the federal government and the welfare check. The single greatest cause of poverty and violence in America – especially in the black community – is the high absence rate of fathers and the lack of traditional homes. Good fathers provide stability and income to homes, but that interferes with the votes that are easily obtained from welfare recipients and others dependent on

380

the government and the Progressive politicians who thrive on it. After all, the less that people are dependent on corrupt politicians (or any politician), the less likely they are to vote for them to stay in power. The welfare state (and now healthcare) is not about welfare or helping anyone – it's about wielding power over others, pure and simple.

Same-sex marriage doesn't significantly contribute to poverty and crime (because it's still very rare in America) as much as it further degrades the traditional institution of marriage. But marriage isn't just about two people living under the same roof – it's about building society and propagating heritage and values. The traditional family that was once the bedrock of America is being attacked from two sides: the welfare state which profits/grows from destroying marriages, and also gay-marriage, which makes marriage more or less meaningless (if it isn't already), relegating a spouse to the status of "a slightly more permanent boyfriend or girlfriend." Has gay-marriage strengthened the institution of marriage where it is legal? Not at all – it's further damaged it as evidenced in Europe and other Western nations which have legalized gay-marriage. In those nations, marriage has become all but meaningless and has declined even further.

At the heart of the same-sex marriage issue, it isn't really about granting or denying someone a "right" as much as weakening or trivializing the primary building blocks of society. In the list of the "45 Communist Goals" referenced in Chapter 4, #26 and #40 are specific to promoting homosexuality and discrediting marriage/family – and gay-marriage is the union of those two goals. Now, if encouraging homosexuality and discrediting marriage and family (along with gay-marriage) aren't destructive to a society, then why are they in the list of communist goals in the first place?

Education and Learning

One of the primary pillars of secular philosophy and the Progressive movement is the idea that with enough education, every problem in society can be solved. Utopia, that magical, wonderful place with no anger, violence, war, crime, or even unhappiness, is just a short distance away if we all have enough education and higher-learning.

What the Progressives fail to admit is that education mainly affects the mind and not the heart, as proven over and over during the last century. Some of the world's best educated, most qualified minds in the world designed the concentration camps, the gas-chambers, and entire countries that resembled gulags and then systematically murdered tens of millions of innocent people. Secular education has little effect on the moral character of a person – but it does make it much easier to rationalize immorality and even condone immoral behavior, regardless of how horrible that behavior might be. Most of the Nazi organizers of the Holocaust were extremely cultured and well-educated, but still managed to murder over 12,000,000 innocent people. And yet the Progressives keep pushing for more education and more grand solutions, despite their unprecedented record of failure after failure. In their minds, the Secular Utopia ever remains just out of reach; if only the next generation could be freed from the shackles of tradition and religion that their parents corrupt them with!

Ironically, the more the secular humanists and Progressives attempt to solve humanity's "heart" problems with education, the worse society gets – as well as the worse education becomes. Since the Bible and religion were thrown out of schools in the early 1960s, education standards have steadily declined. A number of people in America believe that the public schools are intentionally "dumbing down" the students in order to make them more accepting of the secular-state, dependency, and our bloated nanny-state, cradle-to-grave federal government. If that's the case, then America is spiraling downward in a self-defeating cycle faster than most of us fear.

382

During the Cold War when the news of Sputnik became known, tougher education standards and curriculums were created to prepare the next generation of Americans to meet the new Soviet challenges head-on. However, the educators expelled God from the classroom, and along with Him, wisdom, respect for authority, order, and the love of learning. The more money we have spent on education and the harder we have pushed students, the worse the results seem to become. In order to mask how bad the public schools have declined, the SAT and ACT tests were rewritten and the college admission requirements lowered relative to the students' declining performance. As our educational standards have declined, so has the curriculum in most public schools, particularly when federal funding is linked to student performance. In order to keep the federal funds flowing into the schools, the requirements have been eased.

A simple way to measure how far the American education system has declined is to compare the textbooks of today to those before the American education system was federalized. Go to a library and find a history or math textbook written before 1960 (or even earlier) and note how the material is more difficult and requires more comprehension and the questions require more thought composition. Another test is to find an old newspaper and observe the higher language and reading-level of the text. Recall the earlier statistics of declining literacy rates and recall that the Federalist Papers were published in newspapers to convince the average citizens to adopt the new Constitution – now those same papers can barely be comprehended by college students!

Decades later after the expulsion of God from the classroom, our schools have experienced a continual, consistent decline in math, science, language, and reading standards. In fact, one commentator quipped that if these standards had been forced upon us by anyone other than ourselves, it would've been considered an act of war. The Bible says, "The beginning of wisdom is the fear (respect) of the Lord." (Proverbs 1:7) Could it be that the more our education system has been secularized and the less God has been respected, the more that wisdom – which causes a love of learning – has been disregarded? Could it be that children in American schools today don't have a learning problem as much as a "love of learning" problem?

At the beginning of the last century, most primary schools ended at the eighth grade, after which the young men and women began learning a trade through apprenticeships, trade-schools, or went on to higher education. This was the age of multitudes of inventions and numerous innovations that forever changed the face of America and the rest of the world. However, with the rise of secular humanism in the education system, the length of formal public education has been expanded at the expense of apprenticeships and practical work experience. Today, our young men and women begin working in their "trade" at least six years later (if not eight or even ten) than they did a century ago, solely because of the expanded years of public education.

Mark Twain's infamously said, "I've never let my school interfere with my education." There's a great amount of wisdom in his proverb – in modern America, school has been interfering with the education of our young people for decades. Where do most people acquire their knowledge today? Much of it is not from our schools any more – it's from the Internet, books, and learning from other people. Classrooms are an antiquated means of transferring knowledge to large groups of people in order to produce a certain standardized citizen: like creating widgets in a factory. But students are not identical, cookie-cutter widgets: they're individuals with their own talents, loves, dreams, goals, and aspirations.

Young people are naturally full of energy and a love of learning, but prolonged formal education often saps both that energy and that love. During their prime learning and creative years, our young people spend countless hours bored out of their minds learning facts and figures they'll rarely need that will be forgotten hours after the tests are finished. Stop and consider how much time, energy, money, and resources are wasted teaching young people subjects they don't want to learn, they'll never need nor use in their lives, while also destroying their natural curiosity and love of learning in the process. The first rule of education should be the same as that in non-socialized medicine: "First do no harm."

What if the boundless energy and motivation of our youths was encouraged to be put to good use again, like learning practical skills and new trades in our Information Age rather than wasting away in our classrooms for thirteen years of their lives (or eighteen if you include college)? Would our teenagers be so bored, restless, and rebellious if they were encouraged to be more responsible at a younger age? What if we really encouraged them to strive for their full potential and pursue the trades or skills that interest them instead of confining them to a factory-style, mass-production-oriented classroom for thirteen years of their lives?

How did earlier generations often accomplish so much at such a young age? Why did most of the great American inventors only have eighth-grade educations (if that)? Why were some of our presidents studying law at a mere fourteen years old? Could it be that we expect far too little of our children and actually strangle their potential by subjecting them to far too many years of formal education? In our ever-changing modern Information Age, people no longer work in the same factory or the same company for thirty years and then retire – most people even change careers several times over the course of their lives. Why waste those early years in a classroom when people could be exploring what interests them and developing their natural talents and abilities and then putting those skills to good use?

Kids are only as responsible as they are encouraged (or even allowed) to be. Rather than expecting little of our teenagers, we should be expecting more, challenging them more, and encouraging them to be responsible, productive, engaged citizens. Rather than idolizing youth and denigrating adulthood, we should be doing the opposite, and that means changing the culture and our antiquated, Industrial Age education system – or at least our individual segments of it.

Along with changing our attitudes and expectations of public education, we must also rethink the purpose and necessity of a university education. Every year, droves of college graduates attempt to enter the workforce and are turned away because they are either not qualified or because of the bad economy. Meanwhile, they've racked up thousands upon thousands of dollars in student loan debt that they have no viable means of repaying. And those who are able to find employment after college are often not even employed in their field of study. Since that's all too often the case, then what did they accomplish by going to college in the first place? As with high school, many receive an education that they'll never use, and are armed with knowledge that few employers even care about. However, that college education provided them with a diploma and boatloads of debt that will require ten to twenty years to pay off.

Over the last two decades, the costs of a university education have increased over 130% while net-income has declined (both relative to inflation). Today, the average college student graduates with over $23,000 in student loans. What's driving the tuition hikes? Partly supply-and-demand – everyone thinks they need a Bachelor's degree to land a decent job – but also federal education subsidies. As with other subsidized institutions, universities have figured out that the more federal student loan/grant money is available, the more they can raise their tuition rates. If the federal student-loan subsidies did not exist, students (and their parents) would be much more cost-conscious in their higher education decisions and colleges would have to lower their rates to compete. But as with every other market the federal government injects itself into to "help," prices are continually inflated to correspond with the rising subsidies.

But the debilitating costs of college education are only part of the problem facing the younger generations. The biggest problem with our universities is that they purposely tear down the values of the students and indoctrinate them with secular, Progressive thinking. Since the 1960s, young people go off to college with the values instilled in them by their parents, churches, and communities and then emerge with an entirely different set of values. That's evidence of indoctrination or even brainwashing by our higher education system.

Universities were founded to impart knowledge, wisdom, and search for the truth in a wide variety of subjects. But today, they are little more than ivory temples of secularism, socialism, and Marxism. Not only that, but colleges are increasingly teaching students only how to recite the mantras of Progressivism rather than pursuing the truth and rationally, logically examining the various sides of an issue. Universities are all too often filled with Leftist, Marxist professors who care little for the truth as much as churning out future little Marxists like themselves. And to make matters worse, the parents of the students gladly pay for it, sometimes even taking out second mortgages to foot the enormous costs of their children's education!

In both public schools and universities, too many parents have disconnected the consequences of sending their children to those institutions because of the schools' reputation and grandeur. Does it really matter how beautiful the school buildings are if the students' values, character, and minds are being destroyed – or if they're not really learning anything useful? In America today, it seems like most parents would rather send their kids to polished, brand-new schools in which the students learn very little instead of older, less elegant schools that push them hard to learn and grow.

Also in America, the more the State involves itself in the education of our children, the more the State seems to think that the children belong to them as opposed to the parents, and too many parents willingly agree and shirk their responsibilities to educate their children. To be clear, the education of their children is the parents' responsibility and theirs alone. Masses of well-educated people are beneficial to communities and the country, but their education is not nearly as important as their personal values, character, and virtues. Character builds and preserves nations, not education. And if our secular education system is the primary cause of the decline of our values and is detrimental to the character of our children, then it should be either reformed or even abandoned.

Today in America, because of the federalization, unionization, secularization, and the decline of our public school system, millions of parents are choosing to send their children to private schools, religious schools, or even homeschooling them. It's become increasingly obvious that the current education system cannot be reformed, so people are finally taking responsibility for their children and abandoning the failing system. The pressures and workload the education system is placing on our children is crushing them and destroying their love of learning, and as long as federal money is tied to test results, the current burdens will only increase. Today in America, kids aren't being allowed to be kids.

So far, the results of alternative education have been very encouraging, particularly with homeschooling. Children are retaining their parents' values, achieving better results on the standardized tests, and are actually allowed to enjoy their childhood while they can. If you can remove your children from public school and homeschool them, consider doing so – odds are they'll have far fewer problems when they're older.

Entertainment and Media

Another significant cause of America's cultural decline comes from our national addiction to entertainment and media. Hollywood and the entertainment empires have taken it upon themselves to not only determine what American cultural standards are, but what they should be. When Hollywood was confined mostly to movies, it was relatively harmless; however, after the television was invented and Hollywood had a constant presence in our lives and homes, it soon began influencing our values and changing them into theirs.

Television has been the most influential form of media in the world, far greater than radio, newspapers, and books. As a result of the tremendous market potential of advertising, competition for audience attention in television became enormous. Producers and writers continually "pushed the cultural envelope" in order to capture larger audiences for longer amounts of time – and therefore more advertising revenue – and soon television shows were filled with content that would've never been acceptable in our culture before.

The type and quantity of media that we allow into our homes has a tremendous influence upon our lives, our virtues, our families, and our relationships – perhaps even the biggest influence. And with a media that thrives off of extremism, violence, adultery, promiscuity, and sarcasm, is it any wonder that American culture has followed after what Hollywood has fed it? The modern media today all but sets the moral standard for society, and the average person has little say in the content that appears on television or in the movies – except by "voting" with their pocketbooks and changing the channel.

If we are unhappy with our depraved culture and abysmal moral standards, then it's up to us to change it in our individual homes, families, and personal lives. The first step is limiting how much of the depraved popular culture enters our homes and our lives. Rather than continue to begrudgingly fund Hollywood in the name of entertainment, simply "starve the beast" and refuse to fund it anymore. Don't pay for movies, watch television shows, MTV, or purchase other cable channels you don't agree with. Don't be afraid to walk out of movies and demand a refund (along with telling the theater why) when there's inappropriate material in movies – especially children's movies. Money is literally the only language Hollywood understands, so we must make our voices heard.

As parents, we have enormous control over what comes into the minds and hearts of our children and our homes. As parents, we have every right to monitor our children's media and Internet activities, because whatever enters into their senses will sooner or later enter their hearts. When we let various forms of media into our lives, imagine those characters sitting right next to us and our kids in the same room. Would we tolerate the words they say and their behavior in our homes? Most of them we would not – so why do we allow them into our homes via the television and the Internet?

Yes, restricting media is sometimes difficult, but so is life. Do we want our kids to become like the characters that they're watching or listening to? People become like the gods they worship, which is especially true with modern media which makes the current "stars" seem larger than life or even godlike at times. If we want to know why half the boys in America have their pants hanging off their butts, refer to girls as "bitches," and use language most adults would never even think of using twenty or thirty years ago, we have to look no further than MTV and the music that is popular today.

How do we turn around our culture? By starving the Hollywood-imposed popular culture of our cash, our attention, and our affection. This doesn't mean throwing out our televisions, laptops, and tablets – those are merely conduits for the media that we choose to consume. How about we replace the negative forms of media with positive forms, such as replacing sarcasm or disrespect with encouragement, violence with peace-making, and clean, moral-filled shows instead of crude, filthy shows? And that doesn't just go for the kids, but for us parents too – we must set the example that we expect them to live by. If there are certain shows you feel you simply can't live without, then how about installing a profanity filter on your television or gradually reduce your dependency on those shows? If you're addicted to a show you know that isn't good (like soap operas or reality-shows), try skipping an episode, then two, then four, and keep doubling the amount you skip until you're free. You might be surprised at how liberating it is not to be chained to a TV show.

If there's one sector the Progressives have a stranglehold on, it's the popular culture and the media. Most Republicans (moderates and conservatives alike) have yet to figure out how to effectively use the media to their advantage rather than cowering in fear from it. The media is merely a mechanism, a tool which can be a powerful weapon when utilized properly and effectively. Ronald Reagan was one of the few conservatives who could use the media to his advantage, often with good-natured humor.

Comedy in particular is one market that people from all walks of life enjoy and can be reached through. Today, the worldview of the next generation is largely shaped by late-night comedy because of their school, work-schedule, and friends. Most of the comedians today are on the Left, which only reinforces the more-liberal tendency of most teens and young adults. However, the Left is a treasure-trove of comedy (and disaster) and is ripe for conservative comedians and entertainers to illustrate the absurdity of Progressive policies and thinking. Remember, if we don't reach out to the next generation, then others will.

As people seeking to restore and build up our collapsing culture, it's up to us to create a safe-haven in our homes. In our media-saturated culture, we must be very alert to its influence and effects on our personal lives and our families – particularly our children who absorb much more than we often think they do.

History and Heritage

When a nation forgets its history and heritage, it quickly loses its identity. This is one reason why Progressives love to distort and rewrite history – because it causes people to question and doubt their heritage and heroes. Since the rise of Progressivism, America's heroes and Founding Fathers have been marginalized, denigrated, and even vilified in our universities and most recently, our public schools. Lately, very little room in our history books are given to them and their incredible accomplishments, in favor of providing additional room for the more recent history of the Progressive Era.

One of the worst history books which has become the standard in our universities is "A People's History of the United States" by Howard Zinn, a radical revisionist historian (as well as an active member of the Communist Party USA). In his own words, Zinn described himself as "something of an anarchist, something of a socialist. Maybe a democratic socialist." Zinn's book has done more to destroy patriotism and love for America in our younger generations than most of the other history books. If the Soviets had wanted to write a history book to be used in our schools and destroy students' respect and admiration for our Founding Fathers, it would've closely resembled Zinn's history book. So why is that book the standard history text in our universities?

In a 1998 interview, Zinn said he had set a "quiet revolution" as his goal for writing "A People's History." He clarified his statement further by saying, "Not a revolution in the classical sense of a seizure of power, but rather from people beginning to take power from within the institutions." The Left's revolution began in our universities, and since the products of our universities have moved on to infest every nook and cranny of our institutions, it's only natural that the Progressives would also rewrite American history to fit with their warped opinions of it – and to suit their own purposes in transforming the country.

Any textbook used in our universities and public schools should first and foremost tell the truth and provide an accurate, unbiased picture of history. Where commentary or opinion is warranted, perhaps the opposing argument or opinion should also be given. Our schools are intended – and expected – to educate students, to encourage them to seek out the truth, not indoctrinate them. Also, anti-American teachers and professors have no business teaching our students, particularly history and sociology. What are domestic terrorists like Bill Ayers and Bernadine Dohrn doing teaching in our universities and being paid to warp our students' minds and hearts? And those two only scratch the surface – it seems like the more radical a scholar is, the more he or she is revered in our modern secular universities.

Without the accurate teaching of history, a nation loses their identity and neglects their heritage. Such was the case in the Soviet Union where the joke was, "In the Soviet Union, the future is known; it's the past which is always changing." Joseph Story, an early American historian said, "Let the American youth never forget, that they possess a noble inheritance, bought by the toils, and sufferings, and blood of their ancestors; and capacity, if wisely improved, and faithfully guarded, of transmitting to their latest posterity all the substantial blessings of life, the peaceful enjoyment of liberty, property, religion, and independence." Younger generations of Americans are not only being made to forget our history, but are being taught a radical, perverted view of it.

Not only does our history curriculum need to be expunged of Progressive and radical revisionism, but it needs to be "brought alive" and not merely consist of dry statistics, names, dates, and facts. History consists of real people who lived in real times who accomplished real deeds. How about we start studying the books that many of them wrote, along with the books that influenced them and made them the men and women they came to be? How about mixing in some of the many writings of Ben Franklin, Samuel Adams, John Adams, Thomas Jefferson, and Abraham Lincoln? How about we listen to the people themselves in their own words instead of a historian's opinion and summation of them? And rather than expunge all reference of how religion influenced these people, how about the books just be honest and at least mention that religion played an important part of who these people were? How about we let these people speak for themselves for a change? But above all, history should be honest and accurate.

In addition to restoring our history curriculum, we also need to greatly increase the time spent on American history and reduce the amount of time spent on the study of other nations that aren't nearly as important nor relevant. How is it that many American students know more about Mexican history or African history than American history? A cursory study on African, Asian, and South American history is certainly useful for introducing students to those continents, but a study of American, European, and American State history should be taught over and over. If America is to continue as a nation, we must remember our history – and teach it to the next generation!

Parenting

As a result of our faltering families and broken marriages, parenting in modern America has become more unpredictable and unstable than ever. Many parents today treat their children more like their little best friends than young people who need to be given guidance, direction, and discipline. Because of divorce and the plethora of single-parent homes, parenting is often more difficult and stressful than ever before, because that one parent has to not only provide for their kids and maintain the home, but also play the role of both parents.

One of the worst aspects of the modern family is the limited, neglected role the fathers have with their children, particularly in the case of divorce. Both mothers and fathers are needed, but fathers are critical in the development of character, virtue, discipline, and courage as the children mature. Mothers are the most influential for character and virtue during the children's formative years, but fathers tend to be the biggest influence on kids as they enter adolescence and mature towards adulthood.

Because of the rampant materialism and bad economic times, it's easy for parents to misplace their priorities and work extra hours or take on additional jobs and responsibilities. It's one thing to put in extra hours to make ends meet, but quite another to work extra in order to afford more creature-comforts and material gratifications that can be delayed (or even done without). When the kids move out and we look back over our lives, most of us will wish we spent more time with them and less time working those extra hours for things we don't really need.

Another disease in our American homes is apathy, lethargy, or us paying more attention to our hobbies and entertainments than our children and spouse. For fathers and husbands, how about we turn off the television, set aside the Sports section, and put down the remote and the phone and connect with our wife and kids? What's happening in their lives? Do you know who their friends are, what their current interests and hobbies are? What are their hopes, fears, dreams, and aspirations? Disconnected and absent fathers are the primary source of so much confusion, anger, resentment, and identity problems in our young people today, particularly our young men.

And for mothers, is it really necessary to work a fulltime job outside the home? After taxes, daycare, and transportation, is it really worth your time, energy, and effort to try to be "supermom?" The most common ailment among American mothers today is exhaustion. Can the family get by without the expensive vacations and extra luxuries for the few years that the kids are being raised? When they leave home, will you regret missing most of their childhood because you were working and they were in daycare? Who is really raising your kids – their parents (you) or the daycare workers and then the primary school teachers? Of course, sometimes both parents need to work fulltime jobs to make ends meet – but that should be the exception rather than the rule.

Mothers are the glue of our families and fathers are the backbone. Our goal should be to produce decent, wise sons and virtuous, intelligent daughters who will hopefully raise the next generation rather than abort them. We can do better – we must do better!

As parents, it is us and us alone who are responsible for instilling character, virtue, and disciple at a young age in our children and then continuing until they leave our homes. Are our careers more important than the character of our kids? Decent societies begin with decent homes and strong families; the goal of parenting is to produce moral, well-adjusted young adults. And please don't confuse decent homes by meaning how fancy they may be. The exterior residence we call our homes isn't nearly as important as the family that dwells inside. In America today, we have far too many luxurious homes with bankrupt families inside, much like our brand-new school buildings being full of students who can barely read and write at their grade-level.

A parting word for many fathers is: "Why aren't you teaching respect for girls or women any longer?" Girls and women are to be cherished, respected, and honored, and not be merely used for carnal enjoyment and then discarded. If you are teaching respect for women and your sons aren't getting it, do you know what music they're listening to and what videos/movies they're watching? Who are their peers? Could it be that they're receiving mixed messages between you and other sources, and that you're losing the battle for shaping their character?

And for mothers, why aren't you teaching your daughters how to dress and behave modestly? Look at the way girls dressed before the mid-1990s and compare them to today. Why do most of the girls – as well as many of the women – in our schools, shopping malls, and even churches more closely resemble streetwalkers or prostitutes than ladies who have a healthy measure of self-respect? If you don't want boys or young men to treat your daughters like sex-objects, then they need to stop dressing like they are. Modesty and self-respect begins with mothers, and you should be setting the standards – not the clothing designers and department stores – for how your daughters dress. Yes, there will be arguments, debates, and fights over styles of dress, but their virtue and character are infinitely more important than following the latest styles which continue to be more and more immodest. Seriously, do you want your daughter to be known for their brains or their breasts?

In summary, parents are to impart their values, heritage, and wisdom to their children – not solely the schools, the churches, nor the communities. If we want to fix our country, we must invest in the next generation – the Progressives and degenerates in our popular culture certainly are. It's time we took responsibility for the precious gifts who have been entrusted to our care. It is parents, not schools, peers, or pop-culture who should be having the greatest influence in our children's lives. Lastly, it's okay if you're trying to do the right thing and your kids hate you for it (and tell you so); they'll likely thank you after they've grown up.

Public Assistance

An issue that goes hand-in-hand with charity is public assistance, or welfare. There are circumstances in which people or families fall on hard times and are unable to provide for or care for themselves, and therefore need help. Americans are a compassionate people, and we are often there to lend a hand through private charity, giving to shelters and kitchens, hospitals, and other institutions that help those in need. Throughout American history, welfare has been the responsibility of churches and other religious organizations, until secularism and Progressivism began usurping those duties.

As Progressivism evolved in America, opportunistic politicians realized they could create a permanent underclass of dependents through the state-run welfare system. The welfare policies of FDR often had some form of work-requirement for most forms of welfare, but LBJ's Great Society reforms effectively did away with those. As a result, a new demographic was created that could be easily manipulated to ensure guaranteed votes in each election.

When coupled with Social Security and Medicare, the number of Americans dependent upon some form of government assistance has skyrocketed, particularly as the population ages. And that dependent voting block typically votes Democrat, because they created those programs and have successfully vilified the Republican Party as wanting to mercilessly cut those entitlements. Today, regardless of the facts on entitlements, taxes, and spending, all the Progressives in the Democrat Party have to do to rally their dependent voter base is to "cry wolf" and threaten that the Republicans will cut public benefits or entitlements if they win the election – even though entitlements are never cut regardless of which party is in power. Politicians may often be inept, but most are not suicidal.

Permanent welfare and dependency on public assistance from generation to generation saps dreams, ambition, incentive, and life from the dependent class. In our inner-cities, tens of thousands of Americans are all but trapped in the public assistance programs, which are designed to keep them alive, but never lift them out of their poverty or dependent circumstances. Consider how many people have lived in public housing for generation after generation since the Great Society. The Great Society was supposed to lift the poor out of poverty, not keep them trapped in it.

Just before every election, the politicians make their rounds and promise to improve the living conditions of those on public assistance, but their lives rarely ever really improve. Let's be honest for a moment – many of our politicians care little for the poor, and more for their votes. If they did genuinely care about them, they would help lift them out of poverty instead of leaving them in squalor. These are our fellow Americans who are being taken advantage of year after year, and are treated just a little better than slaves living on a plantation. They may not have to work, but if they don't vote the way they're told to, their welfare checks and public assistance programs are threatened.

So what's the answer to breaking the cycle of dependency on public assistance and welfare? The federal welfare reforms of 1996 showed the way by linking work requirements to public assistance (though with exceptions for disability and other circumstances). By assisting and encouraging people who were able to work to find and keep jobs, the welfare reforms helped lift many people out of poverty and off the welfare rolls. In fact, the program cut child-poverty in half. The program worked very well from 1995 to 2012 when Barack Obama gutted the work-requirement by an Executive Order.

As Americans who favor limited government and self-determination, public assistance should be avoided at all costs – and be used only as a last resort. It used to be shameful to be on welfare, because it meant that not only could you not provide for yourself, but that you didn't have any friends, family, church, or community that were willing or able to help you. Today in America, going on welfare has almost become cool and is treated as the first option, with food-cards and debit cards even being advertised and handed out like candy.

It's no wonder that welfare spending has increased over 40% since Obama took office – he's recreating the permanent dependency class as a means of providing his party with easy, reliable votes. But while being on welfare may keep those who are dependent alive, it certainly doesn't improve their lives or encourage them to strive to get off of public assistance.

Race and Societal Divisions

In America since the days when slavery became a profitable institution, racism has existed – as it has in most other cultures of the world. And while there was a great deal of racism in America for much of our history, because of the efforts of Martin Luther King Jr. and other civil rights leaders of the 1960s, racism has greatly declined in America. One of the few good deeds that Hollywood did was break down many of the racial stereotypes and present portraits of equality and possibilities to strive for with shows like "The Cosby Show" and others.

However, a handful of political opportunists like Al Sharpton and Jesse Jackson discovered that America's struggle with racism could be used for their personal political and financial gain and created the "race industry." Though only pockets of true racism remain, these opportunists regularly condemn America for her racist past and demand reparations or more redistribution of wealth (managed by them, of course) in order to pay for those past sins. Nevermind that America overwhelmingly elected a black man as President only forty years after the Civil Rights Movement. In the minds of these race-opportunists, America will always be racist and never be absolved – and of course, must forever pay for her past sins.

Along with the race-baiters, there are other opportunists who seek to divide America into groups and classes and pit us against one another, usually for their political gain. The Occupy Wall Street movement is one of the most recent examples. Since before 2000, we've continually heard that the rich are getting richer and the poor are getting poorer. In fact, we've been hearing that for most of the last century, thanks to the Progressives who use it as one of their primary class warfare weapons. However, does raising taxes on the rich ever really help the poor or the middle class? No, the only ones who benefit from such class warfare tactics are the politicians and opportunists. The best way for the poor to "soak the rich" and take money from their pockets is to go work for them. And if the poor really want to make the rich pay, they should make every effort to climb the company-ladder and earn even more!

What would America look like today if we had refused to be pitted against one another for the benefit of others? What if we really followed the Judeo-Christian ideals as set forth in the Declaration of Independence and the Ten Commandments, that all men (and women) are created equal and are entitled to life, liberty, and the pursuit of happiness? What if some white men had refused to obey the racist laws of segregation and had given

400

Rosa Parks (and other black women) their seats on those public buses? What if white people had started using black restrooms/fountains and ended segregation themselves? Just because unjust laws are passed doesn't mean they should be obeyed – and in fact, they shouldn't!

To heal our societal divisions and render the class warfare tactics meaningless, we must show love and compassion to our fellow citizens, even if we don't agree with their views and opinions. For example, when radical homosexuals staged a "kiss-in" in front of the traditional-family-supporting Chik-fil-A restaurants, Chick-fil-A demonstrated love by offering water to the protestors rather than blocking them, suing them, or even retaliating against them. Chick-fil-A could've called the police and had them thrown off their property but did not, even though some of the public displays of affection were vulgar and could've cost them their customers and business.

Now contrast Chick-fil-A's response to the protesters with those of the Wall Street bankers and the Occupy Wall Street crowd. The bankers routinely mocked and derided the protesters, which only enraged them all the more and emboldened them. The bankers could've shown them love by leaving their grand towers of finance and gone down to pass out water, food, or even internship opportunities. But they didn't, and the protesters stayed around for months.

In all forms of societal division, the right way to respond is to show your "enemies" compassion, gentleness, and understanding. Counter-protest their angry protests and rallies by love, charity, and service. Showing genuine concern and caring often disarms all but the most hateful and irrational of adversaries. After all, it's very difficult to remain upset with someone if they're really trying to help you.

Religion and Values

Life is often difficult and challenging, and it's easy to look at the world around us and feel helpless or even hopeless, especially when evil seems to be increasing. Everyone, but children especially, need regular doses of common-sense, moral teaching. Our churches and synagogues used to provide these moral reinforcements, but with the rise of secularism, many people today derive their morals from whatever media and books they consume – most of which are secular or even anti-religious.

As a result of widespread secularism and declining numbers, too many churches either preach a watered-down, defective Gospel and semi-Biblical values, or they preach a feel-good, social message that is relative only to the culture. A multitude of other churches have become apostate and no longer hold to Biblical standards or Scripture at all.

Churches and synagogues are not supposed to be social clubs – they're supposed to be satellite offices of the Kingdom, safe embassies within a chaotic, sometimes hostile country (2 Corinthians 5). Regular exposure to moral teaching – preferably in a religious setting – is needed to counteract the steady diet of secular humanism. People become like the gods they worship, or put another way, "Where your treasure is, there your heart will be also." (Matthew 6:21) If people are constantly focused on their own creature comforts, materialism, and pursuit of power, then that's what they'll become: carnal and focused only on what's right in front of them. Children and teenagers are especially impressionable and susceptible to the influence of the media they consume: television, video games, music, movies, and other games, as well as their peers and other figures in authority.

Lastly, the teaching of Evolution in our schools and even its pseudo-scientific variant "Theistic Evolution" in some of our churches goes directly against the Judeo-Christian Scriptures. Evolution – the teaching that humans arose from lesser creatures (apes, monkeys, earthworms, pond-scum) inherently robs people of their meaning and intrinsic self-worth. If you believe that you're meaningless, then life is meaningless, so why should you try to improve the world or even try to live a decent moral life? Having a philosophy of life based upon Evolution gives people the justification to do whatever they want – good or evil – because there's no Higher Power to expect and demand otherwise.

As Aldous Huxley, the famous evolutionist admitted, "I had motives for not wanting the world to have meaning; consequently assumed it had none, and was able without any difficulty to find satisfying reasons for this assumption. The philosopher who finds no meaning in the world is not concerned exclusively with a problem in pure metaphysics; he is also concerned to prove there is no valid reason why he personally should not do as he wants to do. For myself, as no doubt for most of my contemporaries, the philosophy of meaninglessness was essentially an instrument of liberation. The liberation we desired was simultaneously liberation from a certain political and economic system and liberation from a certain system of morality. We objected to the morality because it interfered with our sexual freedom."

Business and Corporations

Small and medium-sized businesses are the backbone of the American economy, but have been taking a beating since the Great Recession began in mid-2008. Obama's massive amounts of new taxes and regulations have strangled small and medium-sized businesses and have put many out of business – permanently. Large companies and corporations have also been hurting, but they are better able to "weather the storm" and can use lobbyists to obtain waivers from the new regulations and can outsource or off-shore labor costs to reduce their expenses.

Since Barack Obama took office, crony capitalism has been thriving, particularly in the green-energy industry. This form of crony capitalism involves Obama and other government officials steering huge federal grants and loans to alternative energy companies whose chairmen, founders, or executives had contributed to his political campaigns. Since then, at least fourteen different solar companies have gone bankrupt, and all received federal money that likely won't be repaid. The Chicago Way has become the Washington Way.

In a constitutional republic based upon limited government and the free market, there should not even be a hint of crony capitalism in our political system. One way to limit crony capitalism is rather than try to prevent corporations, unions, and non-individuals from contributing to political campaigns, open the floodgates and remove the limits which only foster corruption. However, every dollar contributed must be publicly accounted for – people should know what politician received how much money and from who, without exception. Until recently, corporations were prevented from making political contributions, but the Supreme Court agreed with their arguments that unions and other groups had "free speech" and they did not.

Crony capitalism is but one problem plaguing American businesses – others are high energy costs, burdensome government regulations and compliance, insurance costs, competition with other nations with unfair labor advantages (like China), and legal costs (such as from frivolous lawsuits). Particularly damaging is the new top-down, central-planning mentality of the federal government, which thinks it has the right to inject itself into every facet of American society – our businesses, homes, schools, and churches. That's not limited government – that's authoritarian or even totalitarian government.

Unless laws are being broken, the federal government has no right under the Constitution to regulate business, just as it has no right to regulate churches or synagogues. Under the American system of federalism, States are to regulate businesses, and the federal government is to regulate the commerce between the States – and commerce is not business. Perhaps we need a policy of "Separation of Business and Government" and free the markets from the stranglehold of the federal government.

The Ten Commandments

America was founded to be a religious nation – though certainly not a theocracy – in which the Gospel could be freely proclaimed and people were able to worship as they saw fit. America was intended to be a land of religious liberty, in which no person's freedom of worship was restricted, provided they were not breaking the law. Throughout history, whenever religion and the government were joined, other religions or denominations would be persecuted. With such a wide variety of denominations and religions in America, the Framers of the Constitution made it neutral with respect to religion, so that no one denomination or religion could become the "established state religion."

This doesn't mean the government created by Constitution is secular as we define it today – it just means that it's neutral and is to treat all religions and religious individuals according to the same standard of justice: blindly and impartially. Secularism used to be defined as "no preferred religion," but modern secularism today is understood as being anti-religious or "no religion can be tolerated at all." And while the federal government was to be neutral toward religion, that certainly didn't mean the States had to be, especially since several States at the time had established State-religions and State-denominations.

Under the Constitution, the United States of America was never intended to be a secular nation, much less ruled by central-planners or political aristocrats dwelling in a capital far removed from the realities of the rest of the nation. Having a secular – or religiously-blind – government is entirely different from being a secular nation. But with the rise of secularism and its centers of power in our universities, the idea of secularism became redefined and the New Secularists sought to remove all trace of Christianity from America. The proponents of America's Judeo-Christian heritage have been in a spiritual and

405

cultural war against secular humanism for the last century when European ideas began being embraced in our churches and universities.

The primary reason our country has been falling apart is because we are in a spiritual civil war with those who wish to tear our nation away from its religious moorings. The last major purging of our Judeo-Christian roots from our public institutions was the forced removal of the Ten Commandments from our courts and public schools, the very places that Higher Authority must be cited in order to establish authority, recall our religious heritage, and maintain the Rule of Law.

At the base of our common law in the United States of America is the Ten Commandments, which are built upon both the Greatest Commandment ("You shall love the Lord your God with all your heart, soul, mind, and strength") and the Golden Rule ("You shall love your neighbor as yourself"). Since America began being settled in 1620 until well into the 1960s, the Ten Commandments formed the basis of our notion of self-government. After all, if everyone is following the Ten Commandments, there will be little need for the police, the courts, and strong governing authority. The more righteous and law-abiding a society is, the less government is required.

Essentially, the Ten Commandments were America's moral standard, and people were simply expected to know and obey them. Much of early American law built upon the Ten Commandments and then added more specific laws to address the various needs of particular people in particular areas. If our own courts and government has not only abandoned, but torn out the moral standard upon which American self-government was based, how can our form of self-government possibly continue?

James Madison, the primary author of the Constitution declared:

"We have staked the whole future of American civilization, not upon the power of government, far from it.

We've staked the future of all our political institutions upon our capacity...to sustain ourselves according to the Ten Commandments of God."

Unless the Ten Commandments once again become America's moral standard, she is doomed to moral and societal collapse. One cannot destroy the foundations of their house and expect the house to remain standing – at least not for very long.

The Ten Commandments are divided into two basic categories: the commandments between people and God and those between people and others. The first four commandments speak to the vertical relationship between mankind and God, while the other six comprise the horizontal relationship among mankind. Note that these Commandments cannot be separated from one another – we can't keep only the ones we choose and expect to have moral societies. Most certainly the first Four cannot be expunged, because they provide the entire basis, foundation, and authority for the next Six.

The Ten Commandments

1. I am the Lord your God. You shall have no other gods before Me.

2. You shall not make for yourself a carved image; you shall not bow down to them nor serve them.

3. You shall not take the name of the Lord your God in vain.

4. Remember the Sabbath day, to keep it holy. Six days you shall labor and do all your work, but the seventh day is the Sabbath of the Lord your God

5. Honor your father and your mother, so that your days may be long upon the land.

6. You shall not murder.

7. You shall not commit adultery.

8. You shall not steal.

9. You shall not bear false witness against your neighbor.

10. You shall not covet anything that is your neighbor's.

In the Bible (especially the Old Testament), God admonished the people to consider and talk about His Commandments all the time, to keep the spiritual things in the forefront of their consciousness rather than just being an afterthought (Deuteronomy 6, 11). In America today, we must do likewise if we want to save our unique Judeo-Christian nation – we must once again memorize and obey the Ten Commandments and familiarize ourselves with the Bible, and also study American history and the wisdom of our Founding Fathers. The Bible is roughly one-third law/wisdom, one-third prophecy, and one-third history. We must restore all three aspects of America's Judeo-Christian heritage in our lives, homes, and families if the America we love and hold dear is to survive.

If we are determined to restore America to her founding principles, let us make no mistake – it will not be easy. Also, it will take a great deal of time, perhaps even a generation, but it can be done – it has been before, but we must start today. America is one of the few nations on earth that was built from the ground up, and that's the only way to restore it: from the grass-roots. The restoration of America will not come from the government, nor from the Congress or the President – it can only come from us.

We built this country, but now it's falling apart. Let us set out to restore and revitalize it before it comes crashing down and is lost forever. We should try to always keep these four things before us: love of God, love of our families, love of our neighbors, and love of our country.

Chapter 13 - Restoring our National Spirit

"If you love wealth better than liberty, the tranquility of servitude better than the animating contest of freedom, go home from us in peace. We ask not your counsels or arms. Crouch down and lick the hands which feed you. May your chains set lightly upon you, and may posterity forget that you were our countrymen." – Samuel Adams

Just as her people are living, breathing organisms, so America is a living, breathing entity – all countries are. All nations have a period of youth where energy, idealism, courage, and spirit abounds and they grow – sometimes to greatness and sometimes not. All nations go through periods of increase and decrease, rise and decline. Over the course of history, many nations and empires have even died violent deaths by foreign powers, while others simply grow old and feeble, and eventually pass away with the quiet gasp of abandonment like a ghost town.

Today, much of the West is not only in decline, but is dying. The evil twins of Secularism and Socialism have robbed the Western nations of their dignity, heritage, values, and history. The rise of the European Union has done more to divide and denigrate the West than unite it – much of the West today is like a cancer-ridden, aging old man. Great Britain used to be called the "sick man of Europe," but today it's most of the continent. Hastening the death of the West is the rise of Islam, which opposes all things Western and European; however, for the first time in history, Islam is not invading Europe by the sword, but by their loose immigration policies, democracy, and welfare programs. With the looming failure of the EU, nationalism is on the rise, but so much of their history and heritage has been lost that the people have no idea of how to protect their way of life, much less restore their countries.

Where America differs from most other nations in the West (and the rest of the world) is that our times of decrease were typically viewed as temporary setbacks and were therefore brief. The Great Depression and the late 1970s were exceptions to this general attitude, when prolonged economic misery had dampened our outlook to the point that even our national spirit was filled with malaise. Then Ronald Reagan was elected to office and the attitude of the country dramatically improved – almost overnight. No longer was America this bungling, inept, uncertain, aging power but a young, energetic nation once again. Not since JFK had America been as optimistic as during the Reagan years, and those times of optimism lasted not only for his eight years in office, but for most of the three decades that followed his inauguration – until the Financial Crisis of 2008 when the U.S. fell into a deep recession that we are still climbing out of more than four years later.

Barack Obama's "science czar" John Holdren is quoted as saying, "We can't expect to be number one in everything indefinitely." While what he said is true in the context of history, those are hardly words that inspire the confidence needed to pull the country out of a recession. However, Holdren unknowingly provided an important insight into what he and his fellow advisers in the Obama administration consider their overall purpose to be: managing America's decline. With the "new normal" of 8+% unemployment, blatantly-corrupt leadership, trillion dollar deficits, and a military spread increasingly thin around the globe, it appears that the Obama administration is doing just that.

Since his surprising reelection, Obama has been pitting the federal government against the people in increasingly aggressive tones, particularly with gun-control in the wake of the Sandy Hook Massacre. Many are even fearing that he's planning and preparing for widespread martial law – especially if another economic calamity occurs. In early March of 2013,

410

the stock-markets finally returned to their previous record-highs before the Financial Crisis of 2008. However, the economy is still weak and unemployment is still very high – it's not that the overall economy is roaring at the moment as much as Wall Street and the banks, whose portfolios have been inflated by the Fed's trillions of dollars in quantitative easing.

What's really happening in early 2013 is that another huge financial bubble has been created, and sooner or later, it'll burst like the last one in 2007-2008. From Jim Cramer of CNBC, here's a comparison of where the economy is today and where it was the last time the NYSE reached these levels (14,164.5 DJIA):

Regular Gas Price: Then $2.75; Now $3.73
GDP Growth: Then +2.5%; Now +1.6%
Americans Unemployed (in Labor Force): Then 6.7 million; Now 13.2 million
Americans On Food Stamps: Then 26.9 million; Now 47.69 million
Size of Fed's Balance Sheet: Then $0.89 trillion; Now $3.01 trillion
US Debt as a Percentage of GDP: Then ~38%; Now 74.2%
US Deficit (LTM): Then $97 billion; Now $975.6 billion
Total US Debt Outstanding: Then $9.008 trillion; Now $16.43 trillion
US Household Debt: Then $13.5 trillion; Now $12.87 trillion
Labor Force Participation Rate: Then 65.8%; Now 63.6%
Consumer Confidence: Then 99.5; Now 69.6
S&P Rating of the US: Then AAA; Now AA+
VIX: Then 17.5%; Now 14%
10-Year Treasury Yield: Then 4.64%; Now 1.89%
EURUSD: Then 1.4145; Now 1.3050
Gold: Then $748; Now $1583
NYSE Average LTM Volume (per day): Then 1.3 billion shares; Now 545 million shares

411

While not entirely conclusive, these indicators point to a weak economy that's still very fragile – if gasoline prices skyrocket or the credit-markets collapse again, confidence will drop and the stock-market could quickly crash, creating another panic sell-off. Like many of the facts that the Obama administration produces, the numbers may look good, but the fundamentals simply don't support them.

Where is Our Patriotism?

In the spring of 2010, I went on a study-tour of Israel with Koinonia House (http://www.khouse.org) and visited the main tourist sites in the land, and also spent a half-day volunteering on a tank-base. Immediately upon arriving in Israel, I was struck by the stark differences in vibrancy, energy, patriotism, and sense of purpose between Israel and America. While many Americans seem to have resigned themselves to their fate of high-unemployment and inept leadership, the Israelis have not – even though they're plagued with the constant threat of terrorist attacks and nuclear annihilation by Iran. Though they may be frequently upset with their government, they still love their country and are quick to show it. Everywhere we went throughout the land, we saw Israeli flags proudly being displayed, often in surprising ways. Sometimes they were large banners draped from buildings and balconies, while other times they were simply stickers on the sides of homes and businesses. But they were there – and they were everywhere.

I distinctly remember thinking "Wouldn't it be great if Americans displayed the flag as often as the Israelis do!" With that thought in the back of my mind, when I returned to the States, I began looking for our flag everywhere I went – but most of the time I couldn't find it without really trying. In Israel, I could literally stand in any location, look around for a few seconds and spot an Israeli flag. In the United States, I had to hunt around to find our flag, which is usually confined to government buildings, handfuls of businesses, and private homes. The differences between the outward displays of patriotism between our two nations were very stark.

The public display of flags is the outward expression of the feelings of patriotism in a nation. What's one simple measure of how people feel about their country? Look for their flags. If they are everywhere, you can be reasonably certain that the people love their country and aren't afraid to show it. But if you have to go searching for their flags, there is something deeply troubling the nation's spirit.

Long before Obama was elected, the American spirit was troubled. It has been for much of the last century, but especially since the 1960s. When our enemies are upset about America's military or policies, one of the first things they do is publicly burn our flag and stomp on it. But in the 1960s, this became a common occurrence even here at home, not some obscure nation on the other side of the world.

Something deep within our nation is sick, or possibly even dying. We Americans used to be proud of our nation most of the time, despite her mistakes – and every nation makes them. Now that seems to be the exception rather than the rule. Now we feel brief, fleeting episodes of pride in our nation around the holidays or when we see or hear stories of our soldiers and their bravery. But the general feeling of pride in who we are as a people and what America stands for is gone, and no one seems to know how to get it back. At times, it seems as if half the country doesn't even want it back; that portion of the country seems to just want to take all they can get from the rest of us while they can get it, nevermind that the country is being ripped apart.

In times of uncertainty and especially distress, people look to their government for stability and leadership. And while our elected officials provided solid leadership in the past, that no longer seems to hold true today. Like our country, our politicians are deeply divided as to their visions for the nation. Many of our leaders in Washington not only refuse to do anything about our problems, but exacerbate the divisions and tensions in the country for their own personal political gain. It used to be that we all had about the same picture for America, but we differed in our ideas of how to get there. Now, we have completely different pictures of what we want America to be, with roughly a third of us wanting to stay the course and maintain our heritage of liberty and limited government, while the other third is demanding equality on every level and cradle-to-grave social programs (such as in Europe), with the last third being undecided or even apathetic.

Plagues on our National Spirit

Over the course of the last century, numerous infections to our national spirit have been allowed to grow and fester to the point where these infections have become cancerous tumors. If our national spirit is to be revived and restored, we must first identify the tumors plaguing America's heart, methodically cut them out, and then take steps to heal our nation.

Debasement by our Officials

Politics used to stop at the water's edge, but recent politicians – especially Barack Obama, his czars, and the more extreme members of his party – have been denigrating and betraying their country for political gain for years. Elected officials who trash the United States overseas should be immediately censured if not removed from chairmanships and even from office. If you don't like the country you're supposedly serving, then you have absolutely no business being in public office.

Another insult to America is Obama's chronic tendency to apologize for past or even present actions of the United States, along with the compulsion to bow to other foreign leaders (like the king of Saudi Arabia). American presidents and other officials – presumed to be Christians by the nature of the country they represent – should never bow to any king or foreign dignitary. Bowing means that you're debasing yourself before another person and in essence, declaring that they (and their country) are superior to you and yours. It's an abomination to see Barack Obama as President of the United States of America bowing before the king of Saudi Arabia or the prime minister of China/Japan. Presidents and Prime Ministers hold more or less the equivalent position – neither is obligated to bow to the other, unless both are bowing at the same time as a sign of mutual respect.

Can anyone in their right mind picture George Washington, Thomas Jefferson, Abraham Lincoln, Ronald Reagan, or even Bill Clinton bowing to another king? Did Jefferson bow and kiss Napoleon's boots when negotiating the Louisiana Purchase? He would've declared war on him before that ever happened! In the past, if any of our presidents had bowed before another king or foreign dignitary while they were president, the people and the Congress would've commenced impeachment proceedings before that president was even able to return to the country!

We Americans overthrow kings, dictators, and tyrants – we do not bow before them. But our current tenant in the White House doesn't seem to understand that.

Loose Borders and Broken Immigration

For at least the last two decades, our immigration and border policies have been a mess. The mainstream media has all but turned the illegal immigration problem into a civil rights problem, rather than a simple question of whether people immigrated here legally or not. Both political parties have ignored and neglected the immigration laws in the hopes of gaining political points with millions of potential new voters or other special-interest groups that lobby heavily.

Either the United States of America has real borders and immigration laws or it does not – and if it does not, then is America still a real nation or is it merely a place on the map?

415

Borders are the very essence of a nation's sovereignty, and if our federal government refuses to police its own borders, then the States, counties, and cities have an obligation to their people to step up and protect their own sovereignty. Maddeningly, the Obama administration has sued Arizona over their state-law that does just that: protect the State's borders because the federal government refuses to.

With the exception of the Native Americans who were here before the Europeans came, all Americans are immigrants. However, most of our ancestors immigrated here legally – they went through the legal immigration process at the time and became citizens. Immigration is of tremendous benefit to a nation because it continually brings in people with different skills, perspectives, and life-experiences into a nation, adding to the vast melting pot that is the United States of America.

And while others in the poorer nations in Central and South America may have valid reasons for wanting to immigrate to the United States, most people agree that they should do so legally, just like everyone else who wants to settle in America. Why should the people who immigrate legally have to spend upwards of $15,000 and years waiting for their green-cards when tens of thousands sneak across the border and are given all the same benefits and privileges for free – and then protected? Everyone can see that's unjust and unfair, and when illegal immigrants use roads, water, and other infrastructure they have not paid for, they're stealing from the citizens of the United States. Illegal is illegal, no matter how it's renamed or repainted.

In a twist of irony, American citizens are experiencing the same problem over immigration and border-control from the federal government as the natives they once pushed out in the Nineteenth Century. At that time, the Indians had made numerous treaties and solemn agreements with the federal government to protect the borders of their negotiated lands. However, the federal government couldn't (or wouldn't) enforce those treaties and tens of thousands of settlers from the

East violated the treaties because they knew the borders wouldn't be enforced. As a result, the Indians would either retaliate and try to enforce their borders themselves, or they would remove their tribes further West. Eventually, the pioneers pushed them out of all their lands. In the early Twenty-First Century, the border situation has been reversed – now the citizens are protesting the invasion of their lands by the "natives" and the federal government is once again ignoring their complaints about border security. Perhaps as we have done, so will be done to us (Obadiah 1:15).

First and foremost, the federal government needs to enforce the border laws already on the books. The Rule of Law applies not just to civil law, but to border laws too, doesn't it? And contrary to what our politicians say, the border problem really isn't that difficult – but the politicians want to delay and twist the issue for their own benefit in order that the problem isn't fixed and more illegal immigrants enter the country. One solution (after closing the borders) would be to offer a grace-period of six months for illegal immigrants to leave the country. After that, if you are here illegally, you will be fined and be deported; if you would like to stay in this country, then you will have to enter the legal immigration process like every other immigrant. Another way is to pressure Mexico to enforce their border laws, since their encouragement of illegal immigration into the United States is half the problem. In prior days, Americans would've solved the problem themselves instead of relying on the federal government.

Not only do we need to discourage illegal immigration through strong border policies and enforcing our own laws, we also need to make the legal immigration process much faster and cheaper, to both help and encourage more of the people who want to be here legally to do so. Simplifying the immigration process and enforcing the immigration and border laws will have the same effect as simplifying the tax code: millions of people will be drawn out of the shadows and participate in the legal immigration process.

417

As for sanctuary cities and states who offer in-state tuition for illegal immigrants and their children, Congress should also pass a law that makes condoning and rewarding such law-breaking illegal, in conjunction with closing the borders. Congress could also heavily tax (or just outlaw) the ability for illegal immigrants to send money back to their home-countries, as well as mandating that all employers use the eVerify system to check immigration status. Those are all legitimate forms of regulating interstate "commerce." The Congress can also threaten the Executive branch with impeachment if the border and immigration laws are not enforced – which is what they should have done years ago. Also, the refugee program needs to be examined and reformed, so that refugees who are relocated to America become part of the culture rather than simply replant their own cultures here and live on welfare at our expense. If refugees are going to be receiving government assistance that comes from our pocketbooks, then they should at least be encouraged to contribute to society and be put on a path to citizenship. Encourage them to adopt American values and mix them into the Melting Pot.

Showing that we mean business with enforcing our borders and reforming our immigration policies will either drive most of those who are here illegally back to their home-countries, or it will encourage them to become lawful citizens. America is either a sovereign nation of laws and defined borders or it is not.

Corrupt Leadership

In a democratic republic, we get the leadership we elect. Are we really proud of the various perverts, crooks, racists, and the community-agitators we have elected to office who have the responsibility of representing us? If you have children or grandchildren, would you trust those you have voted for to babysit for you? Would you trust them to chaperone your daughter, your son, or your grandchildren? Would you trust

418

them with your spouse or significant other? Tragically, the answer would have to be "No!" for many of those we have put into office.

Party politics always divides and polarizes a nation, as well as elevates people of poor character into high office – the very place they should not be. Further frustrations in politics are caused by the leadership being set against their own base. One of the main reasons the Progressives have been winning elections lately is because their Democrat Party leadership adheres to their base's ideals of socialism and centralized government. In contrast, the Republican Party is failing because their leadership refuses to adhere to their base's ideals of limited government and conservative values. If a house divided against itself cannot stand, then neither can a political party.

There are a growing number of Americans who are fed up with the both political parties and are beginning to unite under another platform of common interests such as low taxation, border and immigration control, and reduced regulation. The problem is that they have no alternative third party to fall into at this time, so they remain disenchanted in their respective parties. The Libertarian Party shows promise of drawing this voting bloc in, except they have a rather juvenile image to overcome, namely their cult-like reverence for Ron Paul and their pet issue of marijuana legalization. Liberty cannot exist without morality, and the Libertarian Party doesn't seem to understand that – yet. If the Libertarian Party could move past marijuana legalization and focus on a message of individual liberty and personal responsibility, they could present a real alternative to many who are disgusted with the two primary political parties.

Over the years, Americans became apathetic and lazy and began electing those who only brought back the most "pork" and goodies from the federal trough than actually representing their constituents and listening to the people, much less than doing what's best for the country. A representative democracy is only as strong as its representatives, and the representatives are only as good as the people who place them in office. If we're apathetic and refuse to vote or we vote for those who don't have the same values we do, then we will be poorly represented. If we vote for a slick-talking, manufactured politician instead of a man or woman of principles and personal discipline, then we'll get what we voted for: an empty suit who grows crony capitalism.

The widespread disconnect of personal values and voting has brought America to the place where she is now: on the verge of collapse. Elections matter, and refusing to take part in the political process because it's difficult, ugly, or depressing only gives us the government we have today. Too many people feel there is nothing that they as one person can do to fix the system, and that's simply untrue. We must band together and prevent those we entrust with public office from taking any more of our liberty, property, and sovereignty than they already have.

Enacting and enforcing term-limits and accountability for all elected officials would go a long way in fixing the problem of our representatives disconnecting themselves from their constituents. Senators should have the same term-limits as Presidents: two terms and no more. For Representatives, no more than four terms in office should be the rule, which would prevent them from accumulating too much power and influence in the Capitol and with the lobbyists.

As for accountability, tying budget deficits to our representatives' salary and even personal wealth will drive out those who are more likely to abuse their office and political power. For example, if Congress and the president refuse to pass a budget or they run a deficit, then they do not get paid – along with their staffs and specific areas of oversight (national-defense might be the exception). Perhaps splitting up the federal budget according to state or region and then holding the representatives of those districts accountable would force the mismanaged, ill-represented States from affecting the rest of the country. Power needs to be drained away from Washington D.C. and taken back by the States as quickly as possible.

Lastly, our Representatives and Senators should be required to publicly release their tax records every year while they're in office, several years prior to taking office, and also for the ten years following the time they left office. Our elected leaders (along with their friends and families) should never be personally benefiting from holding public office without accountability or transparency.

This is our country, and these are our representatives, senators, presidents, and every other public servant are OUR employees and are paid from OUR labors. They have no right to enrich themselves at our expense.

Voter Fraud and Contesting Elections

Since the flurry of lawsuits that enveloped the 2000 presidential election between Bush and Gore, it's now become common for the losing party to sue over the election results and demand recounts, especially when elections are close and suspicions of voter fraud abound. In the 2012 presidential election, voter fraud was even worse than in 2008, particularly in heavily urban, swing-state precincts.

The best way to restore integrity to our elections is by regularly cleaning out the voter registration rolls and making sure that people show valid photo-identification when they vote. If the registration rolls have thousands of fraudulent or invalid entries and no photo-identification is required, then the system is left wide open to voter fraud – and even voting by illegal immigrants. Over the last decade, legislation has been passed in several states requiring some form of photo-identification along with purging voter rolls of deceased people or fraudulent entries.

However, lobbyists and various civil rights groups (along with liberal, Progressive politicians) are trying to block that legislation on the grounds that some minorities might be disenfranchised because they are less likely to have driver's licenses. These arguments are usually baseless since some form of photo-identification is required when opening bank accounts, cashing checks, and countless other activities that require identity verification. Besides, if someone really wants to vote, they will comply with the rules and obtain some form of valid identification to ensure that they can vote. Noteworthy is the fact that in all the swing-states of 2012 where photo-ID was not required, Obama won amidst reports of massive voter fraud.

Along with requiring photo-identification and cleaning up the voter registration rolls, the ability to register and then vote on the same day should be outlawed. When registration occurs on the same day as voting, there's not enough time for the voter's residency to be validated. The minimum time allowed between registration and voting should be at least a month – again, if voting is that important to you, then you'll make sure that you register in time to vote.

Lastly, both parties need to have observers at every polling place and report any irregularities and illegal activities. Also, all polling places should be policed and monitored to ensure that the poll-watchers aren't kicked out and the ballot boxes tampered with as they were in Philadelphia in 2008 and 2012.

Violent Protests and Community Agitators

Another plague upon the spirit of America is the mass protests that often turn violent in our cities and their flagrant acts of anarchy and destruction. Even before the Occupy Wall Street protests spread to other large cities in the country, their true colors began to show. Their initial purpose was to protest what they viewed as the injustice of how rich the Top 1% were in comparison to the poverty and struggles of the other 99%. However, the OWS protests soon devolved into camps of debauchery and lawlessness and their message fell apart. The media did their best to paint the OWS protests as a response to the TEA Party protests, but there was simply no comparison. The TEA Party protests were very civil and peaceful, and much larger than the media would like to admit.

The United States of America was created by the efforts of those who tirelessly protested against the abuses of power and acts of tyranny by King George and the British army. There were only a few occasions where the protests turned violent, such as the Boston Massacre, storming the governor's mansion, and the tar-and-feathering of a Stamp Tax collector. Protest-groups such as the Sons of Liberty led by Samuel Adams were usually very peaceful, spreading their messages of liberty and independence by speeches, picketing, and pamphlets. Even during the Boston Tea Party when some of the trunks were damaged, the protesters reimbursed the captain for the damages. They could've easily burned the ships along with all their men onboard, but they didn't – they made their point as peacefully as possible and sent the king their message.

There are two basic types of protests: those made up of mobs which only seek to vent their anger and seize or destroy property, and those which are made up of regular people who are upset and want to send the authorities a civil, clear message. The latter is the model that the TEA (Taxed Enough Already) Parties encompass, which sprang up soon after Obama began pushing his healthcare reform bill. The TEA Parties were not highly organized like the OWS protests and haven't become violent once, and have been peaceful and convincing to those who are willing to listen. After several of their protests, rather than leaving behind a mess of litter and trash, they picked up after themselves and left the parks in a cleaner condition than what they had found them in. That is the very model of a peaceful, purposeful protest.

The protests which become violent and disorderly have no place in America, nor should those who organize and populate them. Whether such protesters are anarchists, radicals, or even teachers and professors, they should protest in a peaceful, orderly fashion in an attempt to get their message across. Violent, chaotic protests only serve to hurt their cause and distort the picture of America, as well as turn most of the informed public against them.

Before he sought public office, Barack Obama touted himself as a community organizer. A more accurate term would be a community agitator, because the tactics he practiced came straight from Saul Alinsky's book "Rules for Radicals." What such community organizers do is rile up a community and divide it up into groups, only to pit them against one another for their own personal or political gain. It's recently been learned that the local police in some of the cities were under pressure by the Obama administration to use kid-gloves on the OWS protesters – enabling them to become even more violent and riotous than they already were.

There is a time and place for protests, and of course, a civil means for protesting. We are all part of the same communities and the same country, and there is no excuse for the destruction of private or public property during any protest. We should be critical of evils and injustice, and speak out to make our voices be heard – but to improve the society and get redress for grievances, not tear it apart. We Americans are not anarchists, and no one who loves their country wants to see the continually-replayed footage of looters running wild and our cities burning.

Biased and Negative Mass-Media

Nothing can dampen one's spirit faster than turning on the news or picking up a newspaper these days. "If it bleeds, it leads!" seems to be the media's primary motto for decades. The media has discovered that the more horrific, violent, and bloody the news is, the better it sells. When people have a strong emotional reaction to something, they become more likely to purchase it. But what does such repetition of violence and bad news do to peoples' attitudes and the society? A steady diet of terrible, depressing news soon creates the very society that once provoked it to outrage!

The purpose of the media is (or at least used to be) to honestly inform the public of current events, and more space should be given to local and regional news rather than national and global news. Opinion has very little relation to raw news most of the time, and the two should be kept entirely separate, which is the purpose of a news section of the paper and an editorial section. Unbiased, objective reporting is what most Americans expect from their news sources, but is usually not what they are given.

Since the days of the Vietnam War and especially after Watergate, the purpose of the mainstream media has changed to mold and shape public opinion for their own goals rather than simply inform the public. Before the rise of talk-radio and the small outlet of conservative media, there was only one view of the news presented to the public, and the news providers claimed to be objective and unbiased. However, without any real competition, there was no good way to tell how objective the mainstream media actually was. If you're only getting one side of the story or argument, you're probably not getting the whole picture – and most of America wasn't until the mid-1990s. Now that there's genuine competition in the media, people are better-able to make informed decisions about news and politics for themselves. However, with such competition comes accusations of bias and conflict – but that's what happens in any competitive enterprise or industry. In reality, the news is just another product.

One simple way to improve your attitude and spirit is to limit your consumption of the news or even take a day or two off from it each week – especially Sunday mornings. Another way to deal with the news is to treat all sources as if they are biased, read opposing views/sources, and then make an informed decision for yourself. And though the news may be screaming, "The sky is falling! The sky is falling!" remember that they're in business to sell a product, and that product is the news.

Political Correctness and Abuse of Freedoms

Before the rise of the Progressive Era, the abuses of our natural rights were relatively few and far between. The very idea that the majority culture had to change itself in order to accommodate a particular person's (or a minority's) wishes was unimaginable. If someone was offended by another's display of patriotism or religious expression, that was their problem. People had the common sense and understanding to realize that everyone at one time or another is offended by something, and that everyone is entitled to their expressions as long as it didn't damage another person or their property.

Today, we've sacrificed much of our history, heritage, and even individual rights on the altar of political correctness. Now, our rich Judeo-Christian heritage has been all but stripped from our country, just because an activist group or even one person at times was offended. When someone from the ACLU becomes upset because of a graduation prayer or the simple sight of a Christmas tree or Nativity scene, the courts are quick to rule on the side of the one being offended, and that's if the offending group doesn't immediately cow-tow to the ACLU's demands. However, the same judicial system that requires the removal of all religious symbols when one person is offended then turns around and adamantly protects the First Amendment rights of that person to then go and burn the American flag – the foremost symbol of the country that protects their rights to free speech and expression.

At first, the double-standard was not so obvious, but shocking enough to the general populace that we didn't know how to properly respond. Most of us thought that such offenses and occurrences were so outrageous and ridiculous that they'd never spread throughout the country. But after fifty years of political correctness, far too much of the Land of the Free and Home of the Brave cowers in fear of offending someone and has been completely stripped of its religious heritage and many of its national symbols.

With great freedom comes great responsibility, especially when those freedoms are protected by the Rule of Law. For much too long, we have allowed the minority of people who hate this country's Judeo-Christian heritage to bully the rest of the nation around and force the majority to bow to their beliefs and their sensibilities. To that, we must emphatically declare, "NO MORE!"

As free people and citizens of the United States of America, we have every right to express our religion and history the way that we see fit. When those who are offended threaten a lawsuit if we don't bow to their wishes, we should inform them of our First Amendment rights and then promptly ignore them. If they take us to court and the court rules against us, then we must appeal or even not comply with the court-ruling that violates our rights. A court of men has no right to violate our natural, God-given rights, especially when those rights are enumerated and protected by the Supreme Law of the Land: the Constitution and the Bill of Rights.

We must no longer allow a tiny minority of malcontents to force us as the majority to surrender and suppress our beliefs. This is OUR country too, and it was founded by religious people, not atheists and secularists.

Victimhood Mentality

Following the Civil Rights Movement fifty years ago and the subsequent implementation of affirmative-action policies, it's become commonplace for entire groups of people to be portrayed as victims of society. Sometimes there are legitimate victims, but most people claiming such victimhood status today are not; they're simply trying to blame others or "the system" for their own problems.

Along with the group-victimhood mentality is the corruption and perversion of our legal system for greed and personal gain. In the past, people often avoided going to court because of the expense, time, and trouble of involving the legal system in their problems. Today, because of the huge sums awarded by juries, people sue corporations, businesses, doctors, and sometimes even their own neighbors in the hopes of winning millions of dollars. People used to go to court in order to get justice – today, too many people go to court in order to "win life's lottery."

Two of life's most important – and also most difficult – lessons that everyone should learn early on is: "Life is tough" and "Life is unfair." The sooner that each of us learns, accepts, and internalizes those truths, the freer and happier we'll be. Yes, life is messy and fraught with injustice and accidents; let us do our best to treat one another as neighbors instead of enemies. If an injustice or accident has occurred, we should try to resolve it among ourselves, without involving lawyers and the legal system.

A special word to liberal, angry, or "disenfranchised" black Americans: if you want to really feel like you belong in America, you must break free of this constant mentality of victimhood. Yes, many blacks were brought here against their will and cruelly enslaved by some of our ancestors, but Americans fought a terrible war over their treatment and the horrible institution of slavery. The ancestors of most Americans today had nothing to do with slavery, since many of them were still in Europe! Not only that, the North had tens of thousands of blacks who had always been free and had never felt the lash of a whip in their lives. If you're black and playing the victim, are you really even certain that your particular ancestors were slaves?

Martin Luther King, Jr. proclaimed his vision for not only black Americans in his "I Have a Dream" speech, but for all Americans, that we would judge one another by our merits and character rather than by the color of our skin. If we ever want to become a more unified, peaceful society, we need to become more colorblind and see people for who they are on the inside, rather than from what they look like on the outside. Where did King and many of the Civil Rights leaders get their notion of being colorblind from? The Bible, specifically in Acts 17:26 – "And He has made from one blood every nation of men to dwell on all the face of the earth, and has determined their pre-appointed times and the boundaries of their dwellings…"

When you play the victim and throw out the race-card, you're not making people more colorblind, you're making them more color-conscious. That dishonors not only Martin Luther King Jr.'s vision, but makes light of the horrible suffering of your own ancestors. How many of them hung on in the hopes of a better day and a brighter future for their children, especially during the Civil War? They had no choice in how they lived when they were in shackles, but you do – you are just as free as every other American! Learn to use the vast resources of America and unmatched generosity to put your liberty and privileges as Americans to work to improve yourselves! That's what so many of the former slaves aspired to once they were finally free.

One highly-recommended book is Booker T. Washington's autobiography. His personal story of his numerous struggles, obstacles, and desire to help blacks live free and prosperous lives is an inspiration to anyone, but especially black Americans. Those newly freed, former slaves utterly despised the victimhood mentality and fought it as much as they could. After all, they had been living at the mercy of the whites their entire lives, and many abhorred the idea of being dependent upon them again.

If your slave-ancestors saw how you're living today after being free for one hundred and fifty years, most would likely slap you upside the head. You're dwelling in one of the greatest, richest, and freest countries in the world – why are you squandering the incredible opportunities that are available to you, opportunities that your ancestors could barely dream of? Use your freedom to better yourself and make something of your life – no group should live in slavery today simply because their ancestors were once in shackles. When you're free but still living and acting like you're enslaved, you are not only desecrating the memory of those who fought the Civil War and the subsequent wars to keep you free, but you're desecrating the very memory of your own enslaved ancestors.

Hyphenated Americans

Over the last several decades in America, it's become politically-correct to refer to various groups and races of people within America by prefacing their region of origin before "American"; i.e., black people are "African-Americans." Soon after the various races and groups in America were divided and categorized, the idea of multiculturalism set in, which tossed out the Great Melting Pot and replaced it with the notion that all immigrants could not only retain their own customs, languages, and lifestyles – but should retain them and not assimilate into America. Not only that, but multiculturalism and political correctness working together ends up forcing Americans to change to accommodate the various sub-groups rather than those groups integrating into the existing American culture and adding their distinct culture/flavor to it.

Teddy Roosevelt said it best in 1915 when he stated, "The one absolutely certain way of bringing this nation to ruin, of preventing all possibility of its continuing to be a nation at all, would be to permit it to become a tangle of squabbling nationalities, an intricate knot of German-Americans, Irish-Americans, English- Americans, French-Americans, Scandinavian- Americans, or Italian-Americans, each preserving its separate nationality, each at heart feeling more sympathy with Europeans of that nationality than with the other citizens of the American Republic." Unfortunately, Roosevelt used Progressivism and the public education system to accomplish his goals (some of which were racially motivated).

Except for the native Americans who lived here before the Europeans first came to America's shores, every Americans' ancestors came from somewhere else. America has always been a nation of immigrants which have become one new nation under a common system of laws and general beliefs. The beauty and uniqueness of America is "e pluribus unum" – out of many, one!

Declining Church Involvement

Most of the previous plagues on America's spirit involve "externals," such as policies, laws, and circumstances that are affecting how Americans interact with one another and how the country functions (or misfunctions). However, beneath all those problems lurks a much more elemental plague: our dying Judeo-Christian institutions and their influence.

While most Americans today are probably just as spiritually-minded as they have been since our founding, much of the new spiritualism is more emotionally-based and mystical rather than being based in reason and everyday applications. The idea of absolute truth when comparing and evaluating religions has been thrown out and has been replaced with moral relativism, under which truth becomes changeable and therefore meaningless. When truth becomes relative, it ceases being truth.

The reason why America functioned so well for so long was because of our high regard for moral standards and the common-sense proverbs and truths of the Judeo-Christian religion. Mental illness, depression, and a host of other psychiatric conditions were relatively few when the people were receiving regular moral teaching, wisdom, and spiritual encouragement from the Bible and our churches. Whatever we dwell on, that we become – we become like whatever we worship.

Nearly simultaneously after WWII, congregations became bored and restless while the churches ceased teaching and proclaiming truth from the pulpits. In order to keep their membership and their churches "relevant," the more Progressive churches and denominations began teaching social and environmental messages rather than the Gospel and the rest of the Bible. In the past, they would water down or even misteach some of the Bible, but once they became little more than religious social clubs, they ceased even teaching that.

In the past when the people began to grow cold to the churches, the pastors would preach all the harder and tell the people the danger of wandering away from their spiritual roots. Sometimes they would return, or at least the remaining people in the congregation would remain. But the pastors stopped preaching and softened their message until it became devoid of all truth and consequences. They gradually stopped preaching about the reality of Hell and the consequences of wandering away from the faith because it was no longer popular in the culture. However, once Hell is no longer mentioned in church, there's no longer any reason to preach the Gospel – and therefore the church loses its entire purpose for existing. To be fair, it wasn't just the leaders who failed but their congregations because they no longer tolerated sound teaching (2 Timothy 4:3).

Churches are to be the salt and light of a culture; salt, in that it is to preserve, season, and improve life; and light in that it exposes the sin, darkness, and evil in a culture so it can be rooted out and destroyed before it drags the culture down with it. When the church in a society is functioning properly, the society improves because it's being regularly watered with Biblical truth and having its spirit refreshed. But when the church declines or dies out, soon the society does as well because it becomes spiritually famished, if not spiritually dead. If a culture, society, state, or nation is faltering, one only needs to look at the state of its churches and take its "spiritual temperature" to determine whether the culture is improving or declining.

Often, our churches may look new and shiny on the outside, but are spiritual dead or even apostate on the inside. At the root of America's faltering churches is their failure to expose the disease of sin so it can then be remedied. Whenever a church falls away into apostasy, it's either because it fails to address sin in the pulpit or the congregation, or it begins misusing the Bible and misteaching Biblical principles. Pastors need to keep themselves from sin and expose the sin of the people so it can then be addressed. For churches to be healed and brought back to life, sin must be exposed, corrected, and then the people need to be encouraged. The demise of the institution of the family and our culture comes directly from the churches which tolerate sin in their pulpits and either ignore or even encourage it in their congregations.

If we want the nation's spirit to improve, people need to seek out and get involved in Biblical churches and surround themselves with people who want to preserve and improve the country from the inside out.

Passing on our Heritage

One of the primary reasons the American Experiment has been failing over the last century is because of our negligence in passing down our American values, beliefs, history, and heritage to the next generation. When public schools became widespread, college attendance soared, more mothers began working outside the home than inside the home, and families began splitting up, we stopped passing on our unique American story to our children. And when our children are fed the revised version from our Progressive-based education system, they are not equipped to counter it – and usually even embrace it.

In the Bible, Deuteronomy 6 commands the people to diligently teach the Torah – the laws, history, and heritage of Israel – to their children and post the commandments on their doorposts and throughout their homes. But there were no special institutions or temples enacted or even suggested in order to pass on their story – it was primarily the responsibility of the families, then the communities and the priests. Within the home, it fell upon both parents (but especially the father) to teach the Law to their children and speak of it often in everyday life: when they wake up, when they lie down, when they eat, when they sit, when they walk. The more we speak to our children about our history and our values, the more they will absorb – particularly during childhood. Then when they are older, they will be more likely to follow in our footsteps and pass our values on to their children.

Since the end of WWII, too many American families have broken up due to divorce or spreading out across the country which hampers such passing on of our heritage. In earlier times, if the parents failed to communicate their values, grandparents and the extended family was typically closeby that could communicate them, or at least reinforce them. Then when those children raised in weakened families went off to college in droves during the 1960s, they came under the heavy influence of the numerous anti-American, pro-Marxist professors and societies that had taken root in the late 1950s. Almost overnight, the generation which had been given everything turned rebellious and sought to transform (and sometimes even overthrow) the very country that had given them so many tremendous privileges and opportunities.

The root cause of the turbulent Sixties was both the parents' failure to pass on their values and the failure of the children to fully absorb them. We must understand that if we don't diligently teach our children our values and history, someone else will. It's not the responsibility of the schools and universities to teach our children our heritage – it's ours! Schools are intended to educate the students, to provide them with raw knowledge and teach them "reading, writing, and arithmetic." And while churches and Sunday schools usually teach values and morals, they cannot compare to the teaching of character, virtue, and heritage that should be occurring in our homes over the course of our daily lives.

In the Bible, several national holidays (feast-days and holy-days) were decreed and mandated for all the people to keep every year, without exception. The purpose of these holidays were to pass on their history, their worship of God, their traditions, and gather together as families, communities, and as a nation. On these holidays, portions of the Law and their

434

history are read by everyone year after year, decade after decade, and generation after generation. Consequently, the Jewish people have survived in the face of incredible adversities and persecution for over three thousand years. How did they do this? By God's grace, promises, and their obedience in observing their holidays and passing on their history, heritage, and values to the next generation.

Some of the practical steps that we as Americans can take that will leave a lasting impression on our children and families are to mimic some of the elements of the Judeo-Christian religious holidays. Just like the Jewish people proudly and prominently display the Star of David, we as Americans can display the American flag outside our homes. Instead of bringing it out only on the Fourth of July, display it on most days of the year.

When the Jews observe the Passover – the day in which Israel was taken out of Egypt – they read the story of the Exodus. We Americans should do likewise and read our Declaration of Independence on every Fourth of July with our families and tell of the people and events of the American Revolution. Three months later on Constitution Day, we should also take it upon ourselves to read the Constitution in its entirety – including the Bill of Rights. Not only should this be done in our homes, but in the halls of Congress and the White House. If Israel is commanded to read the Law during the Feast of Weeks (the day when Moses was given the Law on Mount Sinai), then surely we can read the Constitution which is much shorter. Even today in Israel, the entire nation shuts down on Yom Kippur (the Day of Atonement) and observes a national moment of silence for two full minutes on Yom HaShoah in memory of the victims of the Holocaust, and then one full minute on Yom Hazikaron, their Memorial Day. Why cannot we do likewise? A few minutes of national silence to remember our veterans is the least we can do to honor those who gave us the freedoms we enjoy.

We are responsible for passing on our heritage to those who will come after us – our failure to adequately, consistently do so is a major reason why the United States is in the mess it's in. Talk about America and her Founding Fathers with your children often, even if they complain about it; no one else will be able to teach them like you. Yes, we've been negligent. Yes, we have failed many times in the past. So what? It's not our past failures that matter, but what we choose to do with today and with the future. The days of shirking our duties and responsibilities and leaving them to someone else are over. If America is to be restored and endure, it must start in our own homes with our own children, and then our grandchildren, families, friends, and neighbors.

Though the task of restoring our country may seem nearly impossible, much of the heavy-lifting has already been done for us by our Founders and those early generations. We Americans don't stand on the shoulders of giants who were born that way – we stand on the shoulders of ordinary men and women who became giants because they sacrificed greatly for their country!

Knowing our National Hymns and Songs

Songs, psalms, and hymns also play an important role in maintaining and restoring our country, as well as passing on our national heritage. Songs differ from poetry in that they propagate a spiritual and emotional element in the tune. The human spirit has always been highly influenced by music; when people are happy, they tend to listen to more upbeat music; when sad, they listen to more somber songs or melodies. Music can also change your mood, often with little effort. Listening to the opposite type of music than your mood can also even change your mood to match that of the music.

Hymns and psalms communicate history, theology, and the spirit of the writer and era in which they were written. Also, there's something special about how music helps the lyrics be remembered, typically with little or no effort. How many psalms or paragraphs in books have you memorized? Most people today memorize (or even can memorize) very few written passages. However, how many songs can you recite the words to – hundreds? Thousands? Consider how hearing just a short clip of a tune can make you instantly recall not only the entire melody, but most of the words as well. That is the power and purpose of songs, psalms, and hymns: to help you remember the tune and prose and take them to heart.

National hymns and patriotic songs tell of the glory, history, and important moments of a nation in a way that is easily remembered. Nearly everyone in America knows the first verse of our national anthem, "The Star Spangled Banner," though most of us have to sing it to recite the words. Songs connect timeless words with one's heart, lifting the spirit and drawing out deep, timeless courage from our soul. And while our Founders' deeds can be found in their private journals, letters, and history books, their spirit and courage are usually found in our national songs.

The following songs are a few of our most beloved national hymns. Aside from the first stanza of "The Star Spangled Banner," our national songs are seldom sung any more, but they should be on a regular basis. In the aftermath of September 11th, how wonderful it was to see our Congress stand on the steps of the Capitol and sing "God Bless America." On that terrible day and in those moments when our warring political parties set aside their great differences and publicly sang a national hymn together, it felt like the country was returning to her roots – we were all Americans once again instead of Democrats, Republicans, and independents. And though that spirit only lasted a few moments, we knew that we were all united in our grief – that we had all been wounded that day.

It may feel silly or awkward at first, but why not sing our national hymns with our families on those special holidays? After all, we used to in most of our churches, but that ceased after the modern pop-culture Christian music replaced the traditional hymns and melodies. You can also encourage your

church or community-center to host special services on
Veterans Day, Memorial Day, and Independence Day.

Most of the lyrics to these songs weren't written by famous
composers or poets, but by ordinary men and women who
deeply loved their country – men and women like us. As you
read these timeless words, consider the circumstances that drew
these great songs from the very souls of their writers, people
who had a profound love for this country and sacrificed so
much for the liberty, freedoms, and privileges that we still enjoy
today.

"My Country 'Tis of Thee"

In 1831, Samuel Francis Smith wrote the lyrics to "My
Country 'Tis of Thee" while enrolled at Andover Theological
Seminary. When a friend asked him to translate some the lyrics
from German songbooks, a melody in Muzio Clementi's
Symphony No. 3 caught his attention. Instead of translating the
lyrics for the song, Smith decided to write his own American
patriotic hymn to the melody. The song was first performed in
public on July 4, 1831, at a children's Independence Day
celebration in Boston, and the song was later published in 1832.
Several additional Abolitionist verses were added in 1843 by A.
G. Duncan, along with an extra verse to celebrate Washington's
Centennial and then several more verses by Henry van Dyke.

My country, 'tis of thee,
Sweet land of liberty,
Of thee I sing;
Land where my fathers died,
Land of the pilgrims' pride,
From ev'ry mountainside
Let freedom ring!

My native country, thee,
Land of the noble free,

438

Our American Awakening

Thy name I love;
I love thy rocks and rills,
Thy woods and templed hills;
My heart with rapture thrills,
Like that above.

Let music swell the breeze,
And ring from all the trees
Sweet freedom's song;
Let mortal tongues awake;
Let all that breathe partake;
Let rocks their silence break,
The sound prolong.

Our fathers' God to Thee,
Author of liberty,
To Thee we sing.
Long may our land be bright,
With freedom's holy light,
Protect us by Thy might,
Great God our King.

Our joyful hearts today,
Their grateful tribute pay,
Happy and free,
After our toils and fears,
After our blood and tears,
Strong with our hundred years,
O God, to Thee.

We love thine inland seas,
Thy groves and giant trees,
Thy rolling plains;
Thy rivers' mighty sweep,
Thy mystic canyons deep,
Thy mountains wild and steep,—

All thy domains.

Thy silver Eastern strands,
Thy Golden Gate that stands
Fronting the West;
Thy flowery Southland fair,
Thy North's sweet, crystal air:
O Land beyond compare,
We love thee best!

"America the Beautiful"

The lyrics to "America the Beautiful" were written by Katharine Lee Bates in 1893 after she had taken a train to Colorado Springs. After being inspired by several sights on her trip, she began writing the words into a poem. When she reached the summit of Pikes Peak, the words of the poem came to her, and she wrote them down after returning to her hotel room. Two years later, the poem was published in a magazine to commemorate the Fourth of July. It quickly caught the public's attention and a tune written by Samuel Ward in 1882 was combined with the lyrics and published together as a hymn in 1910.

Over the last century, there have been numerous efforts to designate "America the Beautiful" as a national hymn, to be used with or in place of our national anthem, "The Star-Spangled Banner," but none have succeeded yet.

O beautiful for spacious skies,
For amber waves of grain,
For purple mountain majesties
Above the fruited plain!

America! America!
God shed His grace on thee,
And crown thy good with brotherhood

440

Our American Awakening

From sea to shining sea!

O beautiful for pilgrim feet
Whose stern impassion'd stress
A thoroughfare for freedom beat
Across the wilderness

America! America!
God mend thine ev'ry flaw,
Confirm thy soul in self-control,
Thy liberty in law.

O beautiful for heroes prov'd
In liberating strife,
Who more than self their country lov'd,
And mercy more than life.

America! America!
May God thy gold refine
Till all success be nobleness,
And ev'ry gain divine.

O beautiful for patriot dream
That sees beyond the years
Thine alabaster cities gleam
Undimmed by human tears.

America! America!
God shed His grace on thee,
And crown thy good with brotherhood
From sea to shining sea.

"The Star-Spangled Banner"

On September 3, 1814, after Washington D.C. was burned, Francis Scott Key and John Stuart Skinner embarked on a

441

prisoner-exchanged mission and were taken aboard the HMS Tonnant. The prisoner-exchange succeeded, but then delayed after Key and Skinner overheard details of the plans for the British attack on Baltimore. They were held captive on the ship until after the battle and then released shortly afterwards.

During the night of the attack on Fort McHenry, Key witnessed the terrible bombardment firsthand and noticed that the fort's smaller "storm flag" continued to fly. But because of the smoke from the barrage and the storm, he would not know how the battle had turned out until dawn. When he looked for the flag the next morning, the smaller flag had been replaced with the much larger flag that Major George Armistead of Fort McHenry was infamous for flying. Through the perilous night, the star-spangled banner still streamed.

While still on the ship the day after the attack, Key wrote a poem he titled "Defence of Fort McHenry" on the back of a letter he had kept in his pocket. After they were released nearly two weeks later, the poem began to spread and was soon put to the tune "The Anacreontic Song," by English composer John Stafford Smith.

The song quickly became popular and was then reprinted in a number of newspapers throughout the United States. As the song gained in popularity, Thomas Carr of the Carr Music Store in Baltimore published the words and music together under the title "The Star-Spangled Banner."

The song continued to be enormously popular and by the early Twentieth Century, there were various versions of the song in circulation, and President Woodrow Wilson tasked the newly-created U.S. Bureau of Education with providing an official version. In 1916, Wilson decreed that "The Star-Spangled Banner" be played at military ceremonies and other similar occasions. Two years later, the song was played at the 1918 World Series, beginning the long tradition of playing the song before sporting events, though the song had been performed at games as early as 1897.

Our American Awakening

But even after "The Star-Spangled Banner" was standardized by Wilson's order, America still didn't adopt it as the national anthem. In 1931, John Philip Sousa wrote in favor of making the song our national anthem, stating that "It is the spirit of the music that inspires" as much as Key's "soul-stirring" words. On March 3, 1931, President Herbert Hoover adopted "The Star-Spangled Banner" as the national anthem of the United States.

O say can you see by the dawn's early light,
What so proudly we hailed at the twilight's last gleaming,
Whose broad stripes and bright stars through the perilous fight,
O'er the ramparts we watched, were so gallantly streaming?
And the rockets' red glare, the bombs bursting in air,
Gave proof through the night that our flag was still there;
O say does that star-spangled banner yet wave,
O'er the land of the free and the home of the brave?

On the shore dimly seen through the mists of the deep,
Where the foe's haughty host in dread silence reposes,
What is that which the breeze, o'er the towering steep,
As it fitfully blows, half conceals, half discloses?
Now it catches the gleam of the morning's first beam,
In full glory reflected now shines in the stream:
'Tis the star-spangled banner, O! long may it wave
O'er the land of the free and the home of the brave.

And where is that band who so vauntingly swore
That the havoc of war and the battle's confusion,
A home and a country, should leave us no more?
Their blood has washed out their foul footsteps' pollution.
No refuge could save the hireling and slave
From the terror of flight, or the gloom of the grave:
And the star-spangled banner in triumph doth wave,
O'er the land of the free and the home of the brave.

O thus be it ever, when freemen shall stand

Between their loved home and the war's desolation.
Blest with vict'ry and peace, may the Heav'n rescued land
  Praise the Power that hath made and preserved us a nation!
Then conquer we must, when our cause it is just,
  And this be our motto: "In God is our trust."
And the star-spangled banner in triumph shall wave
  O'er the land of the free and the home of the brave!

"God Bless the USA"

The most recent popular American "national song" is Lee Greenwood's song, "God Bless the USA" This song first appeared in the spring of 1984 and reached #7 on the Billboard magazine country charts soon after being released. Later that year, it was played at the 1984 Republican National Convention, but the song gained even greater notoriety during the 1991 Gulf War when it was played to boost morale among the troops.

The popularity of the song rose again ten years later after the September 11th attacks and again during the War of Iraq, and the song was re-recorded and re-released. Today, the song is popular at sporting events and often played at political conventions and TEA Party gatherings.

If tomorrow all the things were gone,
  I'd worked for all my life.
And I had to start again,
  With just my children and my wife.

I'd thank my lucky stars,
  To be livin' here today.
'Cause the flag still stands for freedom,
  And they can't take that away.

And I'm proud to be an American,
  Where at least I know I'm free.

444

Our American Awakening

And I won't forget the men who died,
Who gave that right to me.

And I gladly stand up,
Next to you and defend her still today.
'Cause there ain't no doubt I love this land,
God bless the USA.

From the lakes of Minnesota,
To the hills of Tennessee.
Across the plains of Texas,
From sea to shining sea.

From Detroit down to Houston,
And New York to L.A.
Well there's pride in every American heart,
And it's time we stand and say.

That I'm proud to be an American,
Where at least I know I'm free.
And I won't forget the men who died,
Who gave that right to me.

And I gladly stand up,
Next to you and defend her still today.
'Cause there ain't no doubt I love this land,
God bless the USA.

And I'm proud to be an American,
Where at least I know I'm free.
And I won't forget the men who died,
Who gave that right to me.

And I gladly stand up,
Next to you and defend her still today.
'Cause there ain't no doubt I love this land,

God bless the USA.

Maintaining our Spirit

America is more than just a place or a continent – it's an idea, and for centuries the very word "America" meant freedom, honor, and courage, the very ideas embodied in the American Trinity (individual liberty, belief in God, and "e pluribus unum"). We must restore that idea and her good name by how we live and how we honor her. And that doesn't necessarily mean doing something great or just celebrating our national holidays once or twice a year, but in how we live each and every day.

America wasn't built by winning great wars or by becoming fabulously prosperous. America became great by how her people lived in their day-to-day lives, by how they raised their children and passed on their values, and by how they served one another and treated others the way they themselves wanted to be treated. America was great before all the trappings of wealth and power by virtue of the goodness of her people and by their heritage of faith, honor, and love of country. America was a great nation because Americans were good people.

For far too long, we have been apathetic in our duties to pass on our values, our heritage, and our history to the next generation and to those around us. We have been cowed, bullied, and allowed our God-given rights to be trampled on by others who despise America and what she stands for. The time has come for us to stand up and declare, "NO MORE!" We are Americans and we are free – no one has the right to deny another speech and religious expression. And though they may try, we must and will defend our rights. We are Americans!

When others get upset and demand that you must not pray in public, that you can't display a Nativity scene on your own property, or even that you should not display the American flag, politely smile and inform them of your God-given, First Amendment rights: your freedom of speech and religious expression – and then ignore them. If needbe, let them take you to court, but never, ever surrender your rights and bow to their childish, tyrannical demands. That's why much of the American spirit has been crushed and trodden underfoot for the last fifty years – because too many good people have allowed themselves to be shouted down and bullied into submission. Too many of us have surrendered our rights because of an obstinate few.

However, while we're free to speak, worship, and display our patriotism, we shouldn't be obnoxious about our displays of patriotism and religious expression. We want to draw people in and stir their hearts, not drive them away! For example, it's one thing to display an American flag on your porch, but quite another to paint the flag over most of your house. The same with Nativity scenes – lighting up your neighborhood and blasting Christmas music over the entire block will likely do more harm than good.

Many Americans today are genuinely fearful about the demise of our country because of the unfathomable debt and the edicts emanating from our elected officials. But even if we lost everything – all our wealth, our homes, our military, our freedoms – there would still be an America as long as it lives on in our hearts, minds, and souls. And as long as it continues to live on there, it will always exist.

"God grants liberty only to those who love it, and are always ready to guard and defend it." – Daniel Webster

Chapter 14 - Restoring our Republic

"Do not blame Caesar, blame the people of Rome who have so enthusiastically acclaimed and adored him and rejoiced in their loss of freedom and danced in his path and given him triumphal processions. Blame the people who hail him when he speaks in the Forum of the new wonderful good society which shall now be Rome's, interpreted to mean more money, more ease, more security, and more living fatly at the expense of the industrious." – Marcus Tullius Cicero

During the Constitutional Convention in the summer of 1787, George Washington presided over the proceedings and always sat in an elegant chair that was crowned with the symbol of the sun peeking over the top with its rays streaming outward. This chair is still on display at Independence Hall in Philadelphia.

When the Constitution was finally drafted and the convention was drawing to a close, Benjamin Franklin remarked, "I have often looked at that picture behind the president without being able to tell whether it was a rising or setting sun. Now at length I have the happiness to know that it is indeed a rising, not a setting sun."

Later when the convention had ended, a woman outside called out to Franklin and asked, "Well, Doctor, what have we got, a republic or a monarchy?" to which he promptly answered, "We have given you a republic, if you can keep it."

The wisdom of Benjamin Franklin's words ring true just as much today as they did 226 years ago: we have a republic, if we can keep it – and today in the early Twenty-First Century, that's a big "if." Today in the United States, many Americans fear that the sun is setting on the Great Republic, and with good reason.

Our American Awakening

Every generation of America is responsible for keeping the republic of America alive and healthy. Each generation must strive to leave the republic in better shape than when they inherited it. Each generation of Americans must pass on the accumulated values, history, and heritage of the republic to the generation that follows after them. Every generation has a duty not only to protect the country that our ancestors fought, bled, and died for, but the very integrity of the republic that they sacrificed for.

History demonstrates that all republics and democracies tend to fizzle out and fade over time, with most lasting only about two hundred years. Most were not conquered by other nations as much as they imploded or were transformed from within. As the morals and standards of the citizenry of a republic falter, the integrity of the republic fades, and problems escalate to the point in which the people become highly receptive (if not demanding) of a strong, charismatic political leader to step in and solve the problems that their lack of virtue has created. However, since absolute power always corrupts absolutely, those political leaders typically refuse to relinquish their granted powers and return them to the republic – if the republic continues to exist at all.

In that regards, the American republic is no different than those which have preceded it, particularly the Roman Republic. In 2008, America selected a young, charismatic political leader while actually knowing very little about him – and not really caring. We were quick to fall under the grand, lofty rhetoric of Barack Obama without bothering to examine his records, most of which he had sealed from our eyes anyway. The Constitution is only as strong as those who we entrust it to, and when we elect leaders who disregard it or view it as an obstacle to their goals (such as "negative liberties"), WE end up being the ones who shred the contract of limited government between ourselves and the federal government. Rome chose the same path when Julius Caesar stormed onto the scene in the waning days of the Roman Republic and transformed it into the Roman

Empire. And within a matter of years, tyranny crept into the Empire and set it on the road to ruin. Eventually, the people in Rome were only concerned about "bread and circuses" – eating well and being entertained. But was that Caesar's fault? No – it was the people who supported him and refused to turn against him as he "fundamentally transformed" their own republic. Thankfully for us, Obama is no Caesar – although he still enjoys incredible support among both the pop-culture voters and the elite, ruling-class voters.

Though the Constitution is by no means perfect, it has more than stood the test of time and has been proven to be the best design of government between a people and their national government in the history of the world. The power of the Constitution lies in its limited, specific, enumerated powers, the separation of powers under three branches of government, its system of checks and balances, and its guarantee of individual rights. Because of its simple yet profound design, it enabled the creative powers of its people to be unleashed like no other nation in history.

However, though the United States of America has been unparalleled in terms of prosperity, freedom, and power, it's hard to cherish a Constitution like ours after always living under its shade. It's hard to comprehend just how precious liberty truly is unless tyranny has been personally experienced. When we take our Constitution and our liberties for granted, we not only do so at our peril, but at the peril of our children and grandchildren. Since the beginning of the Progressive Era, Americans have been experiencing more and more tyranny, though much of it has been "soft" and has not been nearly as noticeable in our daily lives – until recently. Following September 11th – but especially since the election of Barack Obama – Americans have been watching the soft tyranny of Progressivism steadily harden and become more intrusive in their daily lives.

By its very nature, the soft tyranny of Progressivism cannot last forever, and the speed and degree to which its tyranny

450

hardens is dependent upon the arms and diligence of the citizens. As our debts and liabilities have exploded under Barack Obama by his dramatic expansion of government and spending, the soft tyranny has rapidly hardened, though America is still in the early stages of the process. Under Bill Clinton, several federal agencies began arming themselves, and Obama has now expanded that to the point that even the Social Security Administration and the Department of Education are stockpiling weapons and ammunition. When non-defense federal agencies begin hoarding weapons and ammunition, the citizens have every right to be concerned and demand their immediate removal, because those weapons are intended to be used against them, not foreign threats.

Fortunately, since Obama took office in 2009, Americans have purchased massive quantities of firearms and ammunition like never before, out of the growing fear that self-defense will soon be outlawed or at least severely restricted. Most Americans who know history understand the sort of leader that Obama has the very-real potential to become: an authoritarian tyrant. Now more than ever before in American history, the people are highly suspicious – if not downright afraid – of their own federal government.

A popular quote often attributed to Thomas Jefferson is, "When governments fear the people, there is liberty. When the people fear the government, there is tyranny." As government expands, tyranny follows – and liberty always shrinks. If millions of Americans today are fearful of their government, then that's a good indication that tyranny is rising – and rising quickly.

Progressivism vs. Constitutionalism

One of the best mechanisms designed into the Constitution was the ability to amend the document. The Framers knew that the document wasn't perfect and had the foresight that all nations change over time, and that occasions would likely arise in which the document would need to be modified in order to meet the needs of the republic at that time. However, they purposefully made the process of amending the Constitution difficult so as to provide stability and assurance that the Constitution would not (and could not) be changed on a whim by the people or the States.

Over the course of American history, the Constitution has only been amended twenty-seven times, with ten of those encompassing the Bill of Rights that was ratified immediately after the Constitution took effect. The amendments which followed were usually far and few in between, being proposed only after a constitutional crisis such as in 1803. Three other periods in which the Constitution was amended with two or more amendments were in the 1860s after the Civil War, in the early 1900s when the Progressive Era became popular, and lastly in the 1960s during the Civil Rights Movement.

Most amendments involved guaranteeing the rights of certain groups of citizens who had been disenfranchised across several states, while others added clarifications to existing articles of the Constitution, such as the Twenty-Second Amendment and the Twenty-Third Amendment (Presidential Term-limits and the Presidential Vote for the District of Columbia). Two amendments should have never been made: Prohibition (the Eighteenth) and its subsequent repeal (the Twenty-First), because they had nothing to do with the structure or process of government, nor the rights of the people. The catastrophe of Prohibition exemplifies the failures of Progressivism and how it leads to crime, violence, and tyranny.

Only two amendments have fundamentally altered the relationship between the American people and their government: the Sixteenth Amendment (the Income Tax) and the Seventeenth Amendment (Direct Election of Senators). Both amendments were proposed and ratified during the Progressive Era, when socialist democracies became popular and republics were thought to be outmoded, outdated forms of government. Amendments were only intended to add or modify the details of the existing articles of the Constitution, not fundamentally change the very structure of the government already established in the document.

Prior to the Sixteenth Amendment (the Income Tax), the federal government primarily interacted with the States rather than directly with the people – as it was intended to. The federal government collected revenue primarily by tariffs and duties from the States – consumption taxes on imports that came from outside the country. The Founders knew full well that good government means limited government, and the best way to limit the size and scope of government is to limit the amount of revenue that flows into the Treasury. By limiting federal revenue to consumption taxes and the ability to borrow by selling bonds, government growth was dependent upon the prosperity of the economy. When the economy was prosperous and people were importing more luxury items, federal revenue increased. Conversely, when times were difficult, government revenue contracted as fewer luxury items were imported and fewer tariffs were collected.

The first federal income tax was instituted by Abraham Lincoln during the Civil War, which the Treasury was having a difficult time financing because it lacked the widespread support of the North and the massive tariff-revenue from the Southern ports. In the years before the Civil War, the South contributed 87% of the federal revenues, which evaporated when the Southern States seceded. When the Treasury couldn't sell war-bonds quickly enough to finance the war, Lincoln instituted the federal income tax (thanks to the support of the Radical Republicans) to provide a stable flow of revenue to the Treasury. Soon money began flowing into the Treasury again, and the revenue was no longer so dependent upon the economic conditions of the country. After the war ended, the federal income tax was repealed, but the foundation had been laid for the Sixteenth Amendment – the financial engine of Progressivism.

Without a regular, steady flow of money into the Treasury, Progressive policies cannot be financed unless massive amounts of money can be borrowed – or printed. The Federal Reserve System coupled with the progressive federal income tax has given the Progressives all the cash they needed to implement their goals of turning America's constitutional republic into a Western socialist democracy. But one obstacle remained in their path: the Senate. Since the Senate was composed of legislators who's primary purpose was to protect the interests of their State (rather than solely their nation), the structure or composition of the Senate had to be changed.

Unlike Constitutionalism, Progressivism is ever-changing. As soon as the Progressives achieve one goal in their march towards "Utopia," they feel compelled to create a new "struggle," the reason being that if they ever finally do succeed in creating their utopia, they will no longer be needed. Since direct democracy gives Progressives more power to enact their laws and policies, the constitutional republic – primarily protected by the Senate – needed to become a democracy. The quickest way for that to occur in the minds of the Progressives was to turn the Senate into simply another House of Representatives, which represented the people instead of their States. This was the thinking behind the Seventeenth Amendment – the Direct Election of Senators.

With the ratification of the Seventeenth Amendment, the fundamental structure of the Legislative branch was changed, and the United States government was altered from being a republic into a democracy. After the amendments of Prohibition (the Eighteenth) and Women's Suffrage (the Nineteenth), the Progressives had made all the "constitutional" alterations necessary in order to enact the rest of their agenda on their road to Utopia. But after a century of Progressive legislation and policies, is America a better nation today than it was before the Progressive Era? Do we have more liberty now? Do we have less crime and more justice in our society? Do we have more genuine wealth today? Do most Americans feel optimistic about the future and good about their country after a century of Progressivism? If we're getting closer to the Progressive Utopia, then why are so many people unhappy and why is America unraveling?

The time has come for Americans to decide whether the United States becomes a full-fledged socialist democracy (like the ones which are imploding in Europe), or return to being a constitutional republic based on limited government managed by common-sense statesmen rather than professional politicians.

Restoring the Constitution

If America is to return to being a constitutional republic rather than becoming more of a socialist democracy, then there are several actions which must be taken immediately in order to restore the Constitution and the federal government it rules to its rightful place in our society.

First and foremost, the Constitution must be taught year after year, to generation after generation throughout America. The document is not difficult to read and is intended to be read and understood by everyone – after all, the Constitution is the defining contract between the American citizens and their federal government. Most Americans can understand it without needing a lawyer (or a politician) to explain it to them, much less a constitutional scholar. The Constitution is only as powerful as it's revered by the people, and it's been neglected for far too many years by the people, the lawyers, the schools, and certainly by the politicians. The Constitution must be taught by parents, grandparents, aunts and uncles, in our churches, in our community centers – everywhere, instead of just for a few days in high school.

Along with teaching the Constitution, the concepts of federalism must also be revisited and taught. Our Constitution and the republic it created is a federal form of government, not a national government (much to the dismay of the

Progressives). The central idea in a federal government is that the States are confederating, or mutually giving up a small portion of their sovereignty and rights in order to benefit the entire union. A national government exists exclusively for the nation (and often the capital), while a federal government exists for both the union and the States which comprise it.

Next in importance to the First, Second, and Fourth Amendments in the Bill of Rights is the Tenth Amendment, which defines the entire relationship between the federal government and the States. It could be argued that the Tenth Amendment is more important than all the others, since Thomas Jefferson even said that "The Tenth Amendment is the foundation of the Constitution." Like the Tenth Commandment ("Thou shall not covet"), the Tenth Amendment is the broad "catch-all" amendment which underpins the entire Constitution:

> *Tenth Amendment: "The powers not delegated to the United States by the Constitution, nor prohibited by it to the States, are reserved to the States respectively, or to the people."*

As the power of the federal government has grown, the Tenth Amendment has fallen by the wayside as it is a direct impediment to federal power. The federal government was intended to be very small in size, limited in power, and have very few responsibilities, namely, only those enumerated in the Constitution. If we really returned to being a constitutional republic, there's no reason why the federal government couldn't be run by 10,000 employees or less (200 per State), rather than the roughly 2,850,000+ federal employees we have today. In the aftermath of September 11th, a continuity plan was put together by the Bush Administration that identified 250 critical positions needed to keep the federal government functioning in the event of a catastrophic event. If only 250 people are needed to keep the government going, then what do we need the other 99.99% for? Many of the federal agencies duplicate those that already exist in most of the States anyway, such as the EPA, HHS, Department of Education, etc.

If Americans are serious about returning to limited government, then the number of federal employees needs to be dramatically cut as soon as possible. As part of that dramatic reduction process, all the unconstitutional departments, agencies, executive orders, and legislation needs to be evaluated and cut, or at least severely reduced in size and scope. As the federal government draws closer to collapse under the weight of itself and the exploding national debt, these cuts will have to be made sooner or later.

National Reforms

At the top of the list of national reforms which must be implemented in order to return to a limited, constitutional government in the United States is putting an end to the central bank – the Federal Reserve. Politicians are too easily tempted by the magic money that the Fed can create at the click of a button. As long as that money is available, the politicians will find a way to spend it. The United States survived a terrible civil war, rebounded into prosperity, and then spread over the entire continent without a central bank. One of the Federal Reserve's primary duties is to contain inflation, but by controlling the money supply and the interest rates, the central bank is the primary culprit in creating inflation.

Ending the Federal Reserve's monopoly on our monetary system is only half the solution to stabilizing America's money supply – the other half is returning to the Gold Standard. In fact, any standard would be better than what we have today, which is no standard at all. Since its founding, the United States of America had one of the most stable currencies in the world because of our strong reliance on the Gold Standard – until 1971 when Richard Nixon completely removed it. The American dollar used to be referred to "as good as gold" and "the almighty dollar" because of its renowned stability and

457

guaranteed conversion to gold or silver. Until the Gold Standard is re-enacted, the financial stability of the United States will always be dependent upon the whims of our central bank, the Congress, or the President. But is that our money or theirs? It's ours!

Whoever controls the money supply of a nation effectively controls the entire economy and government of that country. The Founders understood that principle and specifically left the control of the money supply to Congress, and not anyone else (Article 1, Section 8). Also worthy of notice is that the Constitution specifically says the "coining" of money, not the "printing" of money. The Founders hated paper money because it was too easily manipulated and counterfeited, as well as highly prone to instability and inflation. Paper money is nothing more than banknotes and IOUs – the only reason why our dollars have any value today is because of what our banks, businesses, and citizens have agreed upon through everyday commerce. But when the Fed dumps trillions of new dollars into the economy, it's literally stealing from us by devaluing our currency through inflation.

Next to the monetary reforms, the current federal progressive income tax system needs to be thrown away and replaced with either a flat income tax or consumption taxes. Income taxes are punitive in nature, such that the harder people work, the more they're punished for their labors – especially under a progressive income tax system. The federal income tax system was created specifically to provide a stable, steady stream of revenue into the Treasury which would be spent by the Progressive Era politicians in Congress. The government of the United States was very limited in size and scope until the Sixteenth Amendment was ratified and the federal income tax was instituted – but since then, it has exploded into an unbelievable mass of duplication, bureaucracy, and intrusion.

Money is the mother's milk of politics and government, and if we want to reduce the corruption in our politics and the influence of politicians in our daily lives, then we need to drain as much money away from our federal government as possible. For most of America's history, the federal government was funded exclusively by tariffs and bonds, and served the citizenry quite well. Money (or rather, the love of money) is also the root of all kinds of evil (1 Timothy 6:10), and when those in government are awash in money, they begin devising ways to keep that money and those votes rolling in. Good, self-limiting government seeks to reinforce good citizenship, character, and virtue in society, while corrupt government thrives on dependent citizens, crime, and immorality in order to increase their influence and power.

One of the schemes that politicians use to get elected (and stay elected) is through class warfare and special-interest group politics. By dividing the society and then conquering the various individual groups, they can often cement their support much easier than by trying to win an undivided electorate. Since the start of the Progressive Era, the group most often demonized by the Progressives was the wealthy, who are often referred to as the "rich," the "Top 1%," or those who "don't pay their fair share" – even though they pay a far greater percentage and amount of their personal income than everyone else under the progressive income tax system.

According to the IRS, the Top 1% (those who earned more than $380,000 in 2008) paid more than 38% of all the federal income tax revenues. The Top 10% (who made $114,000 or more) paid 70% of all income taxes. The Top 50% ($33,000 or more) paid slightly more than 97% of all federal income taxes. The lower 50% paid less than 3%, and most of those actually received income tax refunds from the earned income tax credit and other credits! Only the Progressive federal government has figured out a way to issue refunds to people who have paid little or no income taxes. This is pure wealth redistribution: "From each according to his means, to each according to his needs" – with the federal government taking out its "fair share" in the process.

459

There are three basic requirements to any tax system: fairness, efficiency, and simplicity. When the Soviet Union collapsed in 1991, their progressive income tax system also collapsed. What did the former communists (i.e. Progressives) replace it with? A simple, flat income tax of 13% which was collected without a huge, complicated bureaucracy of thousands of tax agents and tens of thousands of accountants trying to comply with the tax laws. After Iraq was liberated, the United States imposed a similar tax scheme on the country: a flat 15% income tax. As a result of the low, efficient, simplified tax system, both economies began quickly recovering and the government continued collecting revenue. Today, Russia has a negligible national debt of $196 billion (12.8% of GDP, $1,370 per person). In contrast, America's national debt is $16,454 billion (105.6% of GDP, $52,320 per person).

Now, if such a simple tax system can work wonders in collapsed or destroyed economies and help them quickly recover, then why can't we do the same here in the United States? One of the primary reasons the Obama economy has been so sluggish (or downright miserable, depending on your perspective) is because businesses and investors are unsure of their tax liabilities due to all the new laws and regulations (and new healthcare expenses), along with the frequent bickering and threatened expiration of the "Bush Tax Cuts" of 2001. If businesses can't accurately estimate their tax liability for the next few years, they're less likely to make long-term investments, purchase new equipment, or hire more employees (or give decent raises). Fortunately, the "fiscal cliff" negotiations in early 2013 cemented most of those lower rates in place, as well as finally indexing the Alternative Minimum Tax to inflation.

Whenever Progressives rail about "tax cuts for the rich," they're presuming that it's their money (or the government's) in the first place instead of those who have earned it. Who goes to work and earns that paycheck every day, us or Uncle Sam? And whose name is on those paychecks, ours or Uncle Sam's? Since

FDR began the practice of the IRS automatically withholding taxes from our paychecks rather than waiting for us to write them a check, the Progressives seem to act like it's all their money in the first place and our net income is the amount they're letting us keep. Also, the Reagan tax reforms (based upon the Laffer Curve) proved that lower taxes and a simplified tax code actually cause tax revenues to increase – which doubled while he was in office even though the tax rates were much lower. In the federal government today, we do not have a tax or revenue problem – we have a spending problem. A BIG spending problem.

In order to bring in additional revenue, the federal government could sell a small portion of its massive land holdings (650 million acres – nearly 30% of all U.S. land) or sell its own resources to pay down the national debt and reduce the burden on the taxpayers. There's no reason why the government couldn't do either of those or even a combination of both to quickly cut the $1.3 trillion/year deficits and have a balanced budget – or at least more of a balanced budget.

During the mid-1970s, the Congress adopted a new budgeting procedure called "baseline-budgeting," which helps them more easily create a budget for the next year. In baseline-budgeting, the overall budget is automatically increased by an average of 6-7% each year, with the various departments and programs growing by a certain percentage of that portion based upon various CBO projections. Before baseline-budgeting, Congress used zero-based budgeting, in which a department or program would get no money unless it requested a specific amount – and justified it based upon their prior and projected expenditures. After baseline-budgeting was enacted, the various federal agencies and programs no longer had to compete with one another for their portion of the budget because it would automatically be increased each year, regardless of waste, duplicity, inefficiency, or effectiveness.

This accounting change which removed the burdensome, boring (and quarrelsome) task of creating a budget every year

461

from the Congress has led to trillions of dollars in waste because there's no longer any fiscal accountability in the federal government. If you're in any management position of the federal government, why be efficient if you know your budget will increase regardless of your performance? As with the creation of the Federal Reserve System, the Congress delegated their duties to another agency so there would be less hassle and personal accountability. Consequently, the size and scope of the federal government – along with the national debt – has been skyrocketing ever since baseline-budgeting was implemented.

When budget cuts are mentioned in Congress and the Progressives start screaming about catastrophic cuts, they are usually not talking about actual cuts to the funds that department, agency, or program will be given, but from the amount slated in the baseline-budget. For example, if a program has a baseline-budget increase of 7% and Congress decides to cut that by 4%, the Progressives and the media decry the "draconian" cuts. But in reality, only the projected increase has been cut – the program's budget was still increased by 3%. And so it continues, year after year, decade after decade, with the federal government growing larger and larger and requiring more and more money because of baseline-budgeting. Washington doesn't have a revenue problem as much as a spending problem – regardless of their revenue or the economy, baseline-budgeting demands that more money be spent.

If Congress and the rest of the federal government really want to get serious about their spending, one of their first reforms will be to eliminate baseline-budgeting and return to zero-based budgeting, which will force their departments and programs to cut waste and compete with one another for those precious federal budget dollars. The bloat and deficits at the federal level could be dramatically reduced by that simple accounting change alone. But until that occurs, we can be certain that the federal government is not serious about returning to fiscal responsibility, regardless of their wailing and caterwauling about draconian, catastrophic budget cuts.

Last, but certainly not least, the United States needs to decide and articulate exactly what America's international involvement is. We say we don't want to be the "World's Policeman" but then go ahead and assume the role anyway, but rarely consistently. In the name of fighting terrorism, the United States repeatedly violates foreign airspace and the sovereignty of other nations such as Pakistan, Somalia, Yemen with drone attacks and has deployed Special Forces troops to more than 75 countries, as well as initiating a war in Libya while continuing the wars in Iraq and Afghanistan – all under the supposedly anti-war president Barack Obama.

Americans are a peace-loving people, but we are always ready to come to the defense of our country. However, with the exception of September 11th and the Cuban Missile Crisis, there's been no real national defense threat since WWII. We do not like having to fight foreign wars, especially when we are not allowed to be victorious. Until the Korean War (and WWI to some extent), we were dragged kicking and screaming into foreign wars; now we are constantly fighting them with little or no clear objectives. Many Americans worry when the defense budget is threatened to be cut, even though our entire military budget is greater than the next fourteen largest nations combined (China, Russia, United Kingdom, France, Japan, Saudi Arabia, India, Germany, Brazil, Italy, South Korea, Australia, Canada, and Turkey)! National defense has become another way for both parties – but the Republican Party in particular – to justify spending billions upon billions of dollars we don't have, just like the Democrat Party does with entitlements and welfare.

In his farewell address in 1796, George Washington warned us to beware of foreign entanglements; it would be nice to return to a time when were only entangled in foreign problems instead of drowning in them. We need to return to securing our own hemisphere or even just our own borders rather than be scattered all over the globe. Many nations resent our constant military presence and never compensate us in the name of trade or payment, such as South Korea, Japan, and Germany. WWII ended almost 70 years ago, the Korean War ended 60 years ago, and the Cold War ended over 20 years ago. Why do we need to station tens of thousands of troops in places that haven't seen war for decades?

Bring the troops home and completely overhaul our foreign policy (which should involve gutting the State Department), particularly with regards to the United Nations which has become a haven for anti-Western dictators. While the idea of an international forum and community of nations is laudable, it clearly does not work – there are more wars and suffering on the earth than ever before. If we want to improve America's image around the world, then maybe we need to stop being the eternally nosy neighbor and mind our own business for awhile. And for goodness sake, let's stop this nonsense of sending billions of dollars in foreign aid to countries that hate America. Far too many of our hard-earned tax-dollars are going straight to the very people who want to destroy us!

Americans are well-armed and if another nation tries to invade us, they'll have "We the People" to deal with behind every tree, car, and building. Our federal (and State) tyrants would do well to keep that in mind as well should they attempt to violate our Second Amendment rights.

Federal and State Reforms

If America is to return to being a constitutional republic rather than a socialist democracy, we need to return to federalism as it was originally designed. Before the Civil War, America was referred to as "*these* United States," denoting a union of many sovereign states confederated under a federal system of government. But after the Civil War, the reference was changed to "*the* United States," which means a national government rather than a federal government.

Federalism is a political structure in which a group of states are bound together by covenant as in a confederacy with a governing, representative head. Federalism in America is a system of government in which sovereignty is constitutionally divided between the central government and the States, whereby the power is shared and divided between the national and state governments. James Madison defined the model of American federalism in Federalist Paper #45 that "The powers delegated by the proposed Constitution to the federal government are few and defined." Accompanying that statement is the Tenth Amendment in the Bill of Rights, which declares that "The powers not delegated to the United States by the Constitution, nor prohibited by it to the States, are reserved to the States respectively, or to the people."

During the ratification process of the Constitution, the Anti-federalists primarily opposed the Constitution (though not specifically the entire federal system) because in their opinion, it created a federal government which was too centralized, too strong, and would be prone to tyranny over time – and that's precisely what has happened. Many of the accumulated problems and federal bureaucracy are a direct result of too much nationalism and not enough federalism, if not a downright ignorance of the Constitution and abuse of power by the federal government. The Civil War showed the States what would happen if one or more States dared to refuse to obey the federal government or nullify a federal law that would hurt their State(s) or violate their sovereignty.

Until recently with the passage of the healthcare law, the word "nullification" was confined mostly to history books, but now it's been making a comeback. Madison and Jefferson – as well as other Founders – believed that nullification was entirely appropriate at times and was guaranteed by the Tenth Amendment. However, Andrew Jackson's threat of federal force against South Carolina over the Tariff of 1828 caused them to back down and only further made their resentment of the federal government continue to boil. It's arguable that secession – if not the Civil War – could've been avoided if a nullification amendment would've been proposed and ratified

465

that would give the States explicit freedom to nullify certain federal laws that they didn't agree with. Given the federal government's penchant for over-reaching and tendency to trample States' rights, adding an explicit nullification amendment to the Constitution would go a long way towards restoring federalism in *these* United States of America.

For most of the problems and quarrels plaguing our nation today, letting the States handle them is the most appropriate solution, particularly with education, energy, healthcare, environmental stewardship, gay-marriage, abortion, airport/traffic security, and even the larger entitlements such as Medicare and Social Security. Some of the federal/state reforms will need to occur almost simultaneously, such as tort reform and healthcare reform, because they are co-dependent on one another. But certainly the "one size fits all" notion of government in America today was never intended by our Founders because it leads to divisions within the country, inefficiency, and the accumulation (and abuse) of too much power in the hands of people far removed from those they are supposed to be serving. When left to the States, there is more accountability, as well as competition between the States to have the best, most efficient systems. Under a national system, there's very little competition or accountability, which is why we have so many problems with our federal government today.

Two issues that will require a creative solution between the federal government and the States are the issues of border security and identity verification, such as photo-identification for voting. Border security is primarily a federal responsibility, but both the Bush and Obama administrations have been negligent (if not treasonous). Not only that, but when Arizona passed their own border-security legislation to compensate for the federal negligence, the Obama administration sued them! First and foremost, the federal government should be enforcing the border and the immigration laws already on the books. However, if the federal border patrol is negligent, the border States have every right – under the general principles of

466

sovereignty – to police their own borders. It's the same as if the police on your block would refuse to arrest people who kept breaking into your house and harassing your family – you have every right to defend your life, liberty, and property against any form of foreign invasion.

The use of photo-identification and some form of secure identification mechanism (instead of a simple nine-digit Social Security Number) would help tremendously in preventing voter fraud and identity theft. The Progressives have been vehemently fighting state legislation that requires a valid form of photo-identification to vote on the premise that it would discriminate against minority and lower-income voters, even though it's required to open bank accounts, cash paychecks, buy tickets, and do many other typical things in our society – including registering to vote. If a photo-ID is required to register to vote, then why wouldn't it also be required to vote? Which is more important: registering to vote or actually voting? The real reason why the Progressives oppose photo-identification laws is because it would prevent most forms of voter fraud – and everyone knows it.

Legislative Branch Reforms

Though Congress is highly unpopular today, most of their bad press is caused by their own negligence, extreme partisanship, and personal conflicts of interest. Most of the reforms needed in the Legislative Branch involve simply cleaning out the professional politicians who have been in office far too long for their own good – much less their constituents'. The Legislative Branch needs to reassert itself – particularly when one party controls both the Executive and the Legislative Branches. More onerous, tyrannical legislation has been passed into law under one-party control than at any other times and it often makes little difference which party is in power. When either party wins both the Executive and

467

Legislative branches, they usually try to cement that power as much and as quickly as possible.

First and foremost, we must enact and enforce strong measures of accountability for the Legislative Branch and their support staff – namely term-limits and strict conflicts of interest rules. The idea that our public servants can personally profit from their time of service is outrageous, as is the full-pay for life that some of the senior members of Congress receive. Public service primarily means service for the benefit of the public, not for the benefit of our politicians' pocketbooks.

A term-limits amendment for Congress and all other elected officials should be ratified and enforced as soon as possible. Because of the power and influence of their office, far too many of our representatives become disconnected from their constituents over time and become petty rulers rather than our representatives. Senators should have the same term-limits as presidents: two six-year terms and no more. For Representatives, no more than four terms in office should be the rule, which would prevent them from accumulating too much power and influence in the Capitol and with the lobbyists.

Another problem which has become increasingly common in Congress is their propensity for writing absurdly long, complex bills full of legalese that few even take the time to read, let alone attempt to understand and debate. With complexity comes fragility – and many loopholes. A national healthcare law over 2,400 pages and an immigration reform bill over 1,500 pages aren't pieces of legislation as much as disasters waiting to happen! If our Founders could write an 11-page Constitution that defines most of the government and can be read and understood by most of the citizenry, then certainly Congress can write a simpler piece of legislation that most people with high-school educations can read and understand. Good legislation is simple, clear, and concise; complex legislation that's impossible for anyone other than legal scholars to understand is purposely written in such a manner to confuse – if not obscure other components within the legislation. As we say in software,

"Keep It Simple, Stupid" (Will Rogers would love that motto, particularly with how it applies to Congress).

As for accountability, tying budget deficits to our representatives' salary and even personal wealth will drive out those who are more likely to abuse their office and power. For example, if Congress and the president refuse to pass a budget or they run a deficit, then they do not get paid – along with their staffs and areas of oversight – including national defense. Perhaps splitting up the federal budget according to state or region and then holding the representatives of those districts accountable would force the mismanaged, ill-represented States from affecting the rest of the country.

Our Representatives and Senators – and every other elected and appointed official – must be required to publicly release their tax records every year while they're in office, several years prior to taking office, and also for the ten years following the time they left office. Profiteering must be rooted out and expunged from the political system in order to restore the public trust. Again, our public servants should never be personally benefiting from holding public office without accountability or transparency – if such profiteering occurs, the violators should pay the amount back fourfold (just to throw out a number) as well as spend the same length of the time they served in office in federal prison. Slapping the wrists of our corrupt politicians clearly doesn't work – they need to fear and respect the laws like everyone else, and because they hold high office, they must be held to a higher standard.

Lastly, both the House and the Senate need to return to their enumerated powers and responsibilities – as well as not shirking them either. Under the utterly partisan leadership of Harry Reid, the Senate has neglected its constitutional duty in keeping the Executive Branch accountable, and has even neglected its role in confirming appointees in the name of efficiency. The Senate has two primary responsibilities: to vote/negotiate on legislation and confirm appointments made by the Executive Branch. The Senate has been negligent on both responsibilities, as well as refusing to pass a budget since April 29, 2009 – nearly Obama's entire time in office.

When there's no budget, there's no accountability nor even hint of restraint and responsibility on the part of the politicians in Washington. Without a budget, the government will simply keep borrowing and spending money through resolution after resolution as the need arises. If every household needs a defined budget to responsibly manage their finances, then so does our multi-trillion-dollar federal government. How about we demand that a balanced budget amendment is passed (with specific limits on spending and borrowing), and if Congress cannot pass a budget for a given year, the previous budget automatically remains in effect – but with no increases in spending nor the ability to pass resolutions enabling them to spend more money. Spending money is the only language that too many of our politicians understand, and they must be the first to return to virtue and responsible governing.

Last but not least, the size and scope of the federal government must be greatly reduced. After decades of new departments and duplicitous agencies that continually grow larger and more powerful, a vast unelected bureaucracy has been created at the federal level, which seems to intrude more and more into our daily lives. Americans instinctively bristle and rebel at such bureaucratic attempts to control their lives. This is one of the main reasons so many of us are upset at the actions of our federal government these days, because they seem to think they know how to run our lives better than we do, and are forcing us to conform to their values on every level of our society, even down to the very type of light-bulbs that can be bought and sold. When a cadre of unelected officials has the power to control what we can buy or sell, that's not liberty – that's tyranny.

Executive Branch Reforms

The last two presidents – George W. Bush and Barack Obama – have done enormous damage the office of the Presidency and the Executive Branch through their overspending (as enabled by Congress), their use of unconfirmed advisors (czars), their use of war powers, and their over-use of Executive Orders. Much of what the Republicans rail against Obama for was set forth by Bush, though Obama took them to the next level, particularly the use of unmanned drones in attacking terrorists, consolidating power under Executive Orders, and retaining dozens of czars.

Executive Orders were first used by George Washington during his first term for the purposes of delegating authority and executing the duties of his office. However, subsequent presidents have widely abused the use of Executive Orders, with FDR being the worst. Lincoln issued the Emancipation Proclamation via Executive Order, which supposedly freed the slaves of the Confederacy, though it was never enforced until after the Civil War had ended. FDR signed 3,522 Executive Orders while in office, which created dozens of government agencies with limited accountability, and even arbitrarily set the gold price according to his personal affinity for the number "21." However, Obama has used Executive Orders to accumulate and consolidate vast "emergency powers," such as direct control over all communications, all shipping, all food resources, all banking resources, etc. As of March 2013, Obama has only signed 147 Executive Orders, but has offered over 900 (according to Dr. Warren Beatty of the "American Thinker").

The following is the total number of Executive Orders according to president – notice how the numbers jump during the Progressive Era beginning with Teddy Roosevelt through Harry Truman, with FDR almost doubling Woodrow Wilson's number of 1,803 in his four terms in office (3,522 orders total).

George Washington: 8
John Adams: 1

Thomas Jefferson: 4
James Madison: 1
James Monroe: 1
John Quincy Adams: 3
Andrew Jackson: 12
Martin van Buren: 10
William Henry Harrison: 0
John Tyler: 17
James K. Polk: 18
Zachary Taylor: 5
Millard Fillmore: 12
Franklin Pierce: 35
James Buchanan: 16
Abraham Lincoln: 48
Andrew Johnson: 79
Ulysses S. Grant: 217
Rutherford B. Hayes: 92
James Garfield: 6
Chester Arthur: 96
Grover Cleveland: 253
Benjamin Harrison: 143
William McKinley: 185
Theodore Roosevelt: 1,081
William Howard Taft: 724
Woodrow Wilson: 1,803
Warren G. Harding: 522
Calvin Coolidge: 1,203
Herbert Hoover: 968
Franklin D. Roosevelt: 3,522
Harry S. Truman: 907
Dwight D. Eisenhower: 484
John F. Kennedy: 214
Lyndon B. Johnson: 325
Richard Nixon: 346
Gerald R. Ford: 169
Jimmy Carter: 320

Ronald Reagan: 381
George Bush: 166
William J. Clinton: 364
George W. Bush: 291
Barack Obama: 147+

If we continue to allow presidents to use Executive Orders to execute the responsibilities of their office, then some basic rules and guidelines need to be implemented to prevent the President from becoming a dictator. First, every Executive Order must have both an explicit expiration date, along with a congressional and judicial review date. If the Executive Order expires without being reviewed, it immediately becomes null and void rather than law. If the Congress or the Supreme Court finds any Executive Order to be unconstitutional, the Executive Order also immediately becomes null and void. Also, all Executive Orders passed by a president should automatically expire when that president leaves office. As for all the existing Executive Orders, they should be cancelled when the new rules take effect. The Constitution is very clear in that all laws emanate from the Legislative Branch, not the Executive Branch or the Judicial Branch.

Along with restricting the power and scope of Executive Orders, the practice of using "czars" or personal advisors for the President needs to end immediately. Everyone surrounding the President – especially his advisors – need to be explicitly appointed by the President and confirmed by the Senate without exception. Anyone who is whispering in the President's ear (with the exception of his family) should go through the confirmation process. That's the entire purpose of the Cabinet: to assist the President in executing the duties of his office. If any President refuses to formally appoint his advisors, then he should be impeached – pure and simple. Everyone who holds high office or advises others in high office needs to be transparent and accountable. No one in a constitutional republic is above the law – especially not the President.

Judicial Branch Reforms

What the Left and the Progressives often fail to accomplish through the Legislative and Executive Branches of government, they nearly always succeed in the Judiciary. The overreaching Judiciary – not the Congress or the President – has given America legalized-abortion, the banning of prayer in our taxpayer-funded schools, and the removal of the Ten Commandments in the public square. The current issues before the courts today are gay-marriage, wrongful birth lawsuits, marijuana legalization, and nearly any other frivolous lawsuit imaginable.

The greatest constitutional threat to the United States has typically not been from the Congress nor the President, but from those in the Judiciary, which has the power to rule on any topic that comes before them, from electric cars to Nativity scenes to the national healthcare law and even presidential elections. How is it today that Christmas decorations are declared as being too religious for the public square while Ramadan, Hanukah, or even Kwanza displays are deemed as simply adding more diversity and flavor to the culture? Such rulings most often come from unaccountable judges, not elected legislatures.

The simplest, most sweeping ways the secularists strip America of her religious and traditional heritage is through the courts. The Supreme Court, the federal courts, and the State courts increasingly decide which laws are constitutional, which candidate actually won an election, and which wars and military actions are appropriate and/or legitimate. Judicial activism ("ruling from the bench") threatens the very foundations of our constitutional republic because these judges can simply make up new laws or directives on a whim with no accountability or oversight – or redress.

Once appointed, judges at any level have few restraints on their power, not to mention the power of judicial review in the

474

federal courts – being able to declare any law as unconstitutional, regardless of the peoples' wishes. Even more astounding, recently several State courts have issued orders to the Legislative and Executive branches to create laws and/or policies to fit their rulings. And because no legislature or governor wants to retaliate and create a "constitutional crisis," the power of the courts continues to expand. Again, the corrupted media typically sides against the politicians who threaten their power and place in the State.

The weakest link in the Constitution has always been the Judicial Branch, in which there is no explicit check-and-balance on the Judiciary other than appointment by the President then confirmation by the Senate, and the organization of the appellate court system by the Congress. Thomas Jefferson and James Madison both recognized this fatal flaw in the Constitution when Marbury v. Madison was decided and both spoke out against the Court. Jefferson later declared, "The Constitution, on this hypothesis, is a mere thing of wax in the hands of the Judiciary, which they may twist and shape into any form they please." And over the years, the Judicial Branch has done precisely that.

The addition of a simple, straightforward amendment would restore the constitutional balance of power between the three branches of government and restrain the Judiciary to its proper bounds:

"The decision of any federal court may be overturned by a two-thirds majority vote in both the House and the Senate and the consent of the President. Any federal court justice may be removed from office by a two-thirds majority vote of the Senate and the consent of the President."

The United States from its inception is a constitutional republic and is ruled both directly and indirectly by the people, not unaccountable judges. A judge only has the authority to decide whether the case before them is based upon the written law, not to decide the validity of the law itself. The legislatures create the laws, and the judges test the laws as they relate to the people. If and when a law is bad, it's up to the people via their legislatures – not the appointed judges – to remedy the law.

How much different would our American society look today if such a critical check and balance existed in the Constitution? Would we have abortion rights? Possibly, but only in the States in which the people voted to have it be so. Would we be able to read the Ten Commandments in our public squares? Probably in a handful of states and cities. Would our children be allowed to say a short prayer before graduations and football games? Most likely. America would look much more like our Founders had envisioned, and how it functioned before the Progressive Era.

Without the amendment to restore the proper checks upon the Judiciary, in the future it may not matter who the Presidents or the governors are, nor the Congressmen we elect, nor the laws our elected representatives pass. The Nine in Black and their appellate counterparts will have final – and completely constitutional – authority. Often the Supreme Court rulings don't directly affect the people as much as inflame their passions, such as with the Dred Scott Decision (which declared that slaves were property, not citizens), Roe v. Wade (legalization of abortion), and Korematsu v. United States (which allowed the federal government to place citizens in internment camps during a time of war).

Reforming the Judicial Branch ties directly in with the strengthening of the Tenth Amendment and the restoration of federalism to the federal government. Under federalism, the cultural-dividing issues such as abortion, gay-marriage, marijuana-legalization, assisted-suicide, and other moral/societal issues are left up to the States and would affect only those specific States. America is still very diverse, and pressing everyone into one set of morals has only divided this nation and created all sorts of cultural wars and battles. If California wants to legalize gay-marriage or assisted-suicide, then that's their prerogative – but why should their values be forced upon the rest of the nation by the federal courts? Liberal States wouldn't like it if the conservative States passed laws they abhorred that were impressed upon them any more than the conservative States like liberal laws they are forced to comply with.

As with most of the other problems in our current federal government, the federal courts need to be stripped of much of their power and returned to their proper role of limited authority under the Constitution.

Turning Reforms into Realities

Many of the reforms set forth in this chapter may seem to be little more than pipe-dreams, but they are what needs to be done if the republic of the United States of America is to be preserved and restored. Because of our last two presidents and the various Progressive entitlements finally reaching their apex, the national debt will have more than tripled from 2000 to 2015.

Congressman Paul Ryan has recently introduced a new budget plan which attempts to save the entitlement programs that far too many Americans have become dependent on. The plan calls for balancing the budget within ten years, which is too long to be realistic. Even Barack Obama promised to cut the deficit in half in only four years, though he made absolutely no attempt to cut his previous outrageous deficits and only continued his borrowing-and-spending spree.

Any budget plan that takes longer than four or even eight years to balance the budget is not aggressive enough, because the politicians will not abide by any spending restrictions as soon as they find an excuse not to. The federal budget needs to be ripped apart and completely stripped down to its bare minimum if the republic is to be saved. The time for gradual entitlement reforms expired in 2000 when our national debt was under $6 trillion – we are now at the point of needing to slash-and-burn to save the republic and our way of life, but

Washington simply continues to not only ignore the crisis, but worsen it through their overspending and incompetence.

Sooner or later, the federal government will return to common-sense budgeting and governance, though the path our elected officials have placed us on will involve a lot of pain and suffering for the entire country. No nation can borrow even a fraction of what we do without terrible consequences, and the longer we delay in paying down our debt, the worse the pain and suffering will be for us, our children, and even our grandchildren.

During the Revolutionary War, Thomas Paine echoed the sentiments of most Americans in that Founding generation, as well as those which had settled the Colonies: "If trouble must come, let it come in my day, that my child may have peace." Is it better for us to suffer the consequences now or continue delaying them for our posterity, despite the fact that the consequences will be infinitely worse? Do any of us want our children to suffer more than what we ourselves are willing to suffer?

At this point in our history, new patriots must rise and take their stand for the republic, or it will inevitably collapse or continue to be fundamentally transformed into a tyranny. Early in our history, Samuel Adams said, "If ever time should come, when vain and aspiring men shall possess the highest seats in Government, our country will stand in need of its experienced patriots to prevent its ruin." That time is now – not tomorrow, next month, or next year. Every election matters, and we are in the mess that we're in because we've lost our virtues, forgotten our spiritual and national heritage, ignored the wisdom of our Founding Fathers, and neglected our Constitution.

In the past, people were taught that it's not polite to talk about religion or politics. However, that's all the Progressives talk and think about – especially politics. Because we and former generations felt that being polite was more important than standing up for our values and heritage, the Left and the Progressives have taken control of the media, the education system, our political system, and most of our culture. We didn't want this war, but it's been forced upon us nevertheless; the question is whether we will fight for our principles or continue to surrender.

Politics is exhausting and frequently discouraging – we are not only embroiled in a cultural war, but in a war of ideas and a war of values, a war for the very heart and soul of America. Our Founders weren't thrilled with political battles either, and theirs were often worse than the ones we're fighting. At least we can point back to them and cite their experiences and wisdom; they, however, had to devise and formulate the ideas of self-government and limited government on their own.

> *"I must study politics and war that my sons may have liberty to study mathematics and philosophy. My sons ought to study mathematics and philosophy, geography, natural history and naval architecture, navigation, commerce and agriculture, in order to give their children a right to study painting, poetry, music, architecture, statuary, tapestry, and porcelain."* – John Adams

Thomas Jefferson once said, "Rebellion to tyrants is obedience to God." Shall we continue to obey those who have set themselves over us and abuse their power? We have a moral obligation to ignore or disobey evil laws and policies that trample our natural rights, such as the national healthcare law. We are Americans and bow to no one except our God. Our Constitution and Declaration of Independence guarantees us life, liberty, and the pursuit of happiness – but it's up to us to claim those guarantees and rights. We have been entrusted with this republic founded on the Ten Commandments and the Rule of Law, and have been ordained to govern ourselves, not to be enslaved to a king, a president, a congress, or a court.

If we are to restore our republic, we must return to federalism and use the Constitution as our standard for the federal government, especially with regards to the Tenth

Amendment. We must root out all the tentacles of Progressivism and replace them with personal and community charity, individual responsibility, and self-governance. This process will not be easy – it will take year after year, election after election, and generation after generation. The Progressives have been working for over one hundred years to transform the American republic into a socialist democracy; it very well may take another century to restore it to its foundations if the United States hasn't collapsed by then. A more reasonable restoration should take between thirty to forty years, roughly the peak period of influence in a generation.

With all these reforms – even if the reforms were foolproof – they won't become realities unless many people get involved and actively push them. Often, getting involved appears much more daunting or even frightening than it really is. To get started, pick a political or social issue that personally appeals to you – one that you can get fired up about – and then seek out like-minded groups or individuals. Quite often a movement starts with only one or two people who are enthusiastic and committed about turning their goals into realities. Participate in groups, join organizations, attend events, and make your voice heard (or just lend others support). If no groups or events exist nearby, then start them yourself. Also, the Internet and social-media provide incredible ways to connect with others who share your opinions and enthusiasm. You'll be surprised to find how many people have the same views as you do – especially in politics – but don't speak out because they feel isolated and alone, particularly when they're vastly out-numbered in their area.

When the majority refuses to speak and all that's heard is the boisterous, rancorous minority, the politicians and policy-makers often craft their legislation and policies accordingly. And soon that majority wakes up to a community, state, or even country that they no longer recognize. When the majority of Americans fell silent in the 1950s and 1960s, those who chose to speak (the youth movement) became seen as the new

480

majority and changed the country – in many cases for the worse. Perhaps if most Americans had not become apathetic towards politics and the cultural changes then, America would not be in the national upheavals it's in now.

The restoration of American principles and ideals will not be easy, and those in power will not relinquish their power willingly nor quietly. They can harass us, silence us, persecute us, imprison us, but in the end we will win because their cause is evil whereas ours is just. Consider that the tiny minority of the Progressives and the secularists have successfully turned America from her Judeo-Christian principles into a secular society in only the last generation or two. How did they do it? By being committed, relentless, and boisterous. However, they stand resolutely against God and Judeo-Christian principles which encourage perseverance, faith, and staying the course. It's shameful that the secularists have more patience or even courage than we do – especially those of us who are people of faith.

Some of the practical methods that the Progressives used to change America into a secular state can likewise be used to restore her Judeo-Christian values. The Progressives are highly organized and adept at appealing to peoples' emotions to get their messages through. Conservatives can use the same mechanisms with moral values, economic principles, and even abortion. For example, one way we might better draw others to the pro-life side – especially the black mothers and children who are being targeted by the Progressives – is to couch the anti-abortion/pro-life argument in the same terms as the old abolition movement. If people can relate the horrors of abortion to the horrors of slavery, they will link the abolition of abortion to the abolition of slavery, and therefore be more apt to move against abortion. In every advertisement, the relationship between abolishing abortion to abolishing slavery should be clearly made until abortion is abolished. Both institutions are horribly evil and inhumane, and ironically both were protected by the most vocal supporters of the Democratic/Progressive Party.

Since they were in the minority for so long, the Progressives learned to maximize their influence and formulate strategies that work. They are years ahead of the conservatives and libertarians in organizing and reaching the next generation. If conservatives are to ever get their message out, they must organize and focus! Instead of having a handful of big organizations with broad purposes, they should break them up into smaller, single-issue groups and then go hammer away at the opposition from many different sides. For decades, the Left and the Progressives have been able to inflate their perceived influence by having multitudes of organizations, though not necessarily many foot-soldiers – and we can do the same. That's basic strategy when fighting a war: making your opponent think you're much more powerful than you really are.

Throughout our struggle to restore the American Republic, we must not lose heart and we must not abandon our faith – regardless of the immediate setbacks and lack of results. Genuine faith always bears fruit, though often it may not be seen until years or decades later. We should accept the reality that we may not see America revived in our days, but we should continue to try to restore her anyway. Perhaps we are to be like the stepping stones of the Pilgrims: laying down our lives and our comforts for the sake of our children, that they may walk safely across our backs and live in a free nation under God once again.

If you care about your country, now is the time to get involved and make your voice not only heard, but resonate throughout America.

Chapter 15 - What Lies Ahead for America?

"The God who gave us life gave us liberty. Can the liberties of a nation be thought secure when we have removed their only firm basis, a conviction in the minds of the people that these liberties are a gift from God? That they are not to be violated but with His wrath? Indeed I tremble for my country when I reflect that God is just, and that His justice cannot sleep forever." – Thomas Jefferson

Over the last several years since the Great Recession began and Barack Obama was elected to office, many people have been asking questions that were unthinkable only a decade ago, such as "Is America on the brink of a complete societal and economic collapse?," and even "Is it too late to save America?"

When we look around at our nation today, on the surface those questions almost seem preposterous. After all, isn't America the wealthiest nation in the world? Not only that, but isn't America one of the smartest, most decent nations on the earth? America is still all about baseball, hot dogs, and apple pie, right? On some level, those stereotypes still hold true, but just under the surface, our nation appears to be speeding towards collapse.

On the outside, we appear to be rich because of our towering cities, grand hotels, new cars, and our incredible capital – but most of that wealth is financed through mind-boggling amounts of personal, state, and national debt.

On the outside, we appear to be highly educated because of our sparkling new schools and pristine universities – but our schools continue to produce students who have no love of learning, know little of our nation's history, and sometimes cannot even read or write.

On the outside, we appear to be moral because of all the churches that still dot the landscape – but too many of those same churches are either empty inside, spiritually dead, or even apostate and teach the very values that destroy societies rather than build and sustain them.

On the outside, we appear to have perfect, loving homes because of our luxurious houses and manicured lawns – but inside our families are in distress and suffering from divorce, infidelity, abuse, and lack of authority, discipline, and intimacy.

Over the last fifty years, America has become a shell of her former self, looking wonderful and perfect on the outside, but inside she is crumbling and falling apart. America had been incredibly prosperous throughout much of her history, but none more-so than for the twenty-five years that stretched from early in Ronald Reagan's term in the Oval Office until Barack Obama took office in 2009. For over a quarter century – even in the midst of uncertain times – America remained prosperous. Though our recessions during that time period were difficult, they were usually brief, averaging eighteen months.

During those years of prosperity, both our public and private debt skyrocketed; the more we earned, the more we borrowed because of our great credit rating – we were good for it. Not only did our government go on a spending spree, but most of our households did as well. We became accustomed to buying nearly anything we wanted whenever we wanted, regardless of whether we could really afford it or not. After all, tomorrow would be better than today, right? We assumed our homes would always increase in value, we would get raises year after year if we worked hard, and even if we lost our jobs, we could simply get another one and our extravagant lifestyles could continue.

But the Great Recession that began in 2008/2007 has been dragging on for years now, and there appears to be no real end in sight to the bad economy and high unemployment. The stock market is sizzling at the moment but mostly from artificially-low interest rates and the endless currency injections from the

Fed. We currently have an administration in the White House that seems content to preside over America's decline rather than lead us out of it. The Congress and the White House have been gridlocked for more than two years, and the debt and regulations continue to skyrocket. Our embassies burn, our ambassadors and troops are abandoned, our credit rating drops, and the fiddling from the White House only continues.

Since Barack Obama took office, the government will have increased the national debt by more than $6 trillion dollars (as of March, 2013). The old joke used to be "Don't worry if you don't know how much a billion is, Congress doesn't ether!" Now that could be said of a trillion (a thousand billion or a million million). Though the House of Representatives has been relatively faithful in passing a serious budget, the Senate under Harry Reid has refused to even look at it, preferring instead to continue operating through a series of spending resolutions financed by more borrowing – using the Fed's credit-card for every program under the sun. If the average American family needs a budget to stay on track with their day-to-day finances, then surely doesn't the government? For our Senate to refuse to even create a budget is not only negligent, but even treasonous given our debt problems!

Under Barack Obama, the federal government borrowed more in his first two years in office than we did in our first two hundred! Not only that, but Obama was able to pass his expensive healthcare reform legislation which effectively nationalized one-sixth of the American economy, which further increases our mammoth liabilities and economic instability. The bill was promoted as the solution to repairing the healthcare system and reducing costs, but it was more about control of the healthcare system than improving healthcare. Once the government controls the healthcare system of a nation, the people will continue to vote for more and more taxes and entitlements under the premise of maintaining and improving the system.

But Obama's attacks on America's foundations don't just involve nationalizing the healthcare system and exploding the national debt – since the midterm elections of 2010 when the Republicans were swept back into office, he has been ruling by a series of executive orders and policies through his cadre of unconfirmed, unvetted, unconstitutional czars. The constitutional system of Checks and Balances and Separation of Powers only works when the branches of government are playing by the rules and willing to enforce the checks of the Constitution on the other branches.

If Congress was working properly, Barack Obama would've been impeached after his first two years in office, let alone pass the national healthcare legislation.

If the Supreme Court and the federal courts were working properly, ObamaCare would've been thrown out of court within the first few hours, let alone going through the appellate process before being found constitutional by the highest court in the land. One wonders when the last time the Justices even read the Constitution and the Bill of Rights given their ruling.

But because of the rising tyranny of Barack Obama and his czars, the exploding national debt, the erosion of our constitutional rights, and because the economy continues to languish, many Americans are finally waking up to our grim reality. After all, you can only hit the snooze button so many times before the alarm clock finally breaks. For the first time in their lives, Americans are reading and studying the Constitution outside the classroom, paying attention to politics, and are talking about Medicare, Social Security, and taxes. Americans are starting to toss out the traditional tax-and-spend politicians and are finally demanding accountability from those in elected office. We the People are fed up with our representatives and we're letting them know it.

But are Barack Obama and our frequently self-serving political parties to blame for America's financial mess? For many of our immediate problems, yes – but for our long-term problems, no – those have been building for decades. For the last one hundred years, many Americans had the idea that because there were so many rich people in the country and that the government had access to so much money, they could simply take more from the rich to give to the poor. Somehow, we were able to convince ourselves that taking from one citizen to give to another wasn't stealing. But it is, and deep down, everyone knows it – even if we don't like to admit it. While it may not seem fair that some have much more money than others, that's life – life is unfair. That's life in a free country, where we're free to succeed, yet also free to fail.

For most of America's history, a sense of optimism, hope, and purpose filled the nation – primarily because it was a free country. During the darkest days of the American Revolution, the Civil War, and even the Great Depression, there was still a sense that though the country was battered and bruised, she would emerge stronger and brighter than before. Even after the long Great Depression, even though the closed businesses and vacant homes could still be seen throughout our land, there were still innumerable opportunities that existed if one applied themselves and worked hard. That was the American Dream: that your future was what you made of it by dreaming big and working hard.

The United Police State of America

But now that American Dream is being threatened like never before because the threat is coming from the highest offices of our land. Today in America, our hopes and dreams not only seem to be fading, they seem as if they are being crushed by the very people and institutions we have entrusted to keep and protect our society. Rich, fertile lands, forests, and resources are declared to be off-limits by unnamed bureaucrats in our regulatory agencies thousands of miles away. Farmers are not allowed to water their own fields or clear their own lands because of some trivial species of mouse, squirrel, or owl on their property. Property rights which were always considered sacred and unalienable are not at all anymore.

In our airports, free citizens are treated like suspects, regularly being subjected to humiliating inspections while others have their personal property rummaged through as if they were smuggling the worst forms of illegal contraband imaginable rather than simple deodorant and shampoo. Overhead in our cities, on our farms, and on our roads, we are watched by millions of traffic-cameras and now fleets of unmanned drones – all without warrant or warning. When we buy or sell anything, our financial transactions are monitored, analyzed, and stored away in massive databases which can then be used against us if we break one of the countless laws or regulations we have no knowledge of.

When the Soviet Union collapsed and the Iron Curtain fell in 1991, the free-world breathed a sigh of relief. The constant, looming threat of a horrific nuclear exchange appeared to be finally over and we were still alive. Washington and Moscow would never launch nuclear weapons against each other – the fifty-year Cold War was over, and America had won. But then came the Islamic terrorist attacks of September 11th, 2001 and the cries for increased security in our homeland to prevent such attacks from ever occurring again. Now America increasingly feels like the Soviet Union, though without the gulags – yet.

Tyrants always need some form of military or police power to remain in authority, and Barack Obama and the radical Progressives are no different. And while the Constitution does not explicitly forbid the president from establishing a standing army, the funding for any army must be authorized by the Congress (Article I, Section 8) and be renewed every two years. However, the idea of a standing army did not sit well with the Founders and the people, and it was one of the primary accusations they made against King George III in the Declaration of Independence. The National Guard system in America is responsible for keeping order within the States above and beyond the responsibilities of local police and state

488

troopers. The purpose of the United States military is to protect the nation from exterior threats, not internal threats.

Unfortunately for the Progressives, Barack Obama, his Cabinet, and his supporters are extremely unpopular with the military. So instead of raising a civilian army – as he suggested he wanted to do during his campaign of 2008 – Obama has simply armed and fortified several government agencies under his control. The militarization of the government agencies actually began under Bill Clinton, with George W. Bush creating the Department of Homeland Security which consolidated several federal agencies into one. Again, Barack Obama has followed in his predecessors' unconstitutional footsteps in heavily arming numerous federal agencies such as the FAA, the IRS, the Department of Energy, the Postal Service, the Social Security Administration, and even the Department of Education and the Bureau of Printing and Engraving. But why arm these non-military federal agencies?

If the U.S. military – under the control of the President – is responsible for defending the United States against exterior threats, then who are these armed federal agencies defending against? Obviously, it can only be US – the American citizens. These armed federal agencies constitute an illegal standing army under the control of the President of the sort that has never been tolerated before in American history: a de-facto national police force that sees the citizens as their threats rather than their masters.

In late 2012, the federal government announced it was purchasing 1.2 billion rounds of ammunition; since then, it has been increased to 1.6 billion rounds, along with 2,700 light-armored tanks. Understand that this order was placed by the DHS, not the DOD, meaning that this ammunition is not intended for external threats, but internal threats. There are several possibilities why such a huge requisition has been made is that the federal government is purposefully trying to create a shortage of ammunition, or they are preparing for widespread civil unrest which would likely result from a massive economic collapse. Either way, the announcement does not bode well for law-abiding American citizens. Ironically, soon after the orders were placed, the Obama administration and the Progressives unleashed sweeping new gun-control legislation designed to restrain the citizenry.

An informed, armed, and watchful citizenry is the only restraint the American people ultimately have against tyranny – foreign or domestic. The primary deterrent to Japanese and even Soviet invasion in the United States was their understanding that tens of millions of American citizens were armed and the consequences of an invasion would be utterly disastrous. The Progressive politicians can pass whatever legislation they want, but self-defense in any form is not only a Constitutional right, but a fundamental human right. Regardless of what occurs, Americans must NOT be disarmed; otherwise, there will be no defense for Christians, Jews, and any other minority who craves individual liberty (especially with the rise of Islam throughout the West).

In the past, Americans allowed the FBI, CIA, and other federal police institutions to exist in order to combat interstate crime, the violent mafia, and communism during the Cold War. However, few Americans ever thought that radical Progressives who despise the Constitution would be elected (and re-elected) to office and fill the federal government with likeminded radicalized public servants. What happens when large-blocks of law-abiding citizens become the enemy of the State because the State has been thoroughly corrupted? Apart from the military which is overseen by Congress and directed by the President, the federal government has no constitutional mandate for these armed agencies.

If our liberties are to be restored, these federal agencies should be disarmed and weakened immediately, if not disbanded. If the terrible day comes when the federal government turns against the citizenry and makes the unconstitutional demand that we turn in our guns, then we must rise up to defend our inalienable rights just as our Founding

Fathers did. As mentioned in Chapter 4, one of Saul Alinsky's rules was that "The action is in the reaction," meaning that you must figure out how you want your adversary to react and then plan a strategy that will provoke that reaction. If Obama is purposefully trying to provoke a mass-revolt by his unconstitutional Executive Orders and overreaching, we must be very careful and not allow ourselves to fall into that trap. We must assume a defensive posture until we have no choice but to fight back to protect our homes, families, and liberties.

Such times of chaos not only enable the "homeland security" and the police to behave immorally and tyrannically, but the people too. If and when the chaos begins, the officials who are perpetuating their tyranny upon a peaceful, law-abiding citizenry have far more to fear than we do, because we vastly outnumber them by at least 30,000 to 1 (assuming there will be about 10,000 tyrants and those under their command) – and we are still very well-armed. This is why we must never, EVER hand over our weapons, because when we do, we will have no defense against any tyrant – even one duly elected by the people. Keep in mind that everything Adolph Hitler did from 1933-1945, he did legally (and no, there is currently no real basis for comparing Obama to Hitler except in his rhetoric). Would the Holocaust have occurred if Hitler had not disarmed the citizenry first? But even if the worst occurs, when the dust settles, those tyrants will be hunted down and brought to justice, just like the Nazis were after WWII.

The Crushing National Debt

Since Barack Obama became the Democrat presidential candidate in 2008, gun and ammunition sales have been skyrocketing, with the total number of guns in America having almost doubled in the last four years alone. There's a reason why the firearms industry has named Obama "the Greatest Gun Salesman in America": people are scared of the federal government, pure and simple. Because of his socialist policies, his radical czars, and the federal government's desire to regulate everything – including firearms – people are buying guns and ammunition like crazy in case those weapons are suddenly outlawed.

But it's not only the radicals, Progressives, and even communists that Obama has appointed to high-office that have caused an uproar in America, it's his massive stimulus programs, the nationalization of healthcare, the mountains of new and costly regulations, and the trillion-dollar annual deficits. Current projections now indicate that by 2025, the annual deficits will surpass 100% of GDP; by 2037, the annual deficits will be 200% of GDP. There's a genuine, palpable fear that by Obama's brazen, reckless spending that he's purposefully trying to "break the bank" in order to destroy the free-market system of the United States of America and permanently institute centralized, top-down control of the entire economy. And they might be right.

In his writings of how to transform democracies into authoritarian states, Karl Marx observed that "Democracy is a form of government that cannot long survive, for as soon as the people learn that they have a voice in the fiscal policies of the government, they will move to vote for themselves all the money in the treasury, and bankrupt the nation." Others have made the same observation over the years, but theirs were dire warnings rather than the purposeful instruments of destruction as espoused by Marx.

Since Obama became president, welfare and dependency on government benefits and programs have skyrocketed, and Obama has only encouraged such dependency when he should be doing the exact opposite. At least when FDR was president, people had to work for most of their benefits – but Obama recently struck similar work-requirements from the 1996 welfare law (again by fiat, not by the Rule of Law through Congress). If it seems like Obama is trying to turn America into a gigantic European-style welfare state, perhaps it's because he is!

But while the American welfare state is being expanded, the European welfare state is collapsing under its own weight and decay. Everyone can see that socialism and government dependency is an utter failure, yet Obama and the Left still shout "Forward!" Could there be another more sinister purpose for the transformation of American into a massive welfare state?

John Adams, Signer of the Declaration of Independence, co-author of the Constitution, and Second President declared, "There are two ways to enslave a nation. One is by the sword. The other is by debt." Since America is still too strong and well-armed to be conquered by the former, the radical Progressives of our era have decided to "fundamentally transform" America through massive deficit-spending and exploding national debt. The borrower is slave to the lender (Proverbs 22:7), and that holds true for nations just as it does for individuals, families, and companies.

If America cannot be conquered by the sword (which has always rallied the nation to arms), then it may be conquered by the enormous debts that have been incurred over the last twelve years. When George W. Bush incurred $5+ trillion in new debt, Barack Obama called it "irresponsible" and "unpatriotic" – but after taking office, Obama has borrowed the same amount of money but in half the time! If Bush's borrowing and spending was irresponsible and unpatriotic, then what can be said of Obama's spending? It's more than irresponsible and unpatriotic – could it possibly be purposeful or even treasonous?

How is it that America, which is arguably the most technological, prosperous country on the planet, has one of the most inefficient, wasteful governments? Rather than becoming more efficient and more cost-effective, our federal government is fraught with waste, duplication, and a glut of employees, managers, and bureaucracy it doesn't need. But it's not only stumbling along in a bungling fashion, it's increasing its size, scope, and power at a breathtaking pace. The federal government has turned into the very sort of tyrannical body that our Founders rebelled against.

The Rise and Fall of the West

Oswald Spengler, an early Twentieth Century German historian and philosopher, formulated a cyclical theory of the rise and decline of civilizations, which are documented in his books, "The Decline of the West." He related entire nations and empires to biological organisms: they are born, they rise and grow strong, then they deteriorate and finally die. Then out of their ashes, new nations are born and the process repeats itself.

According to Spengler's theory about how nations and empires decline, first the spirit weakens and dies – the religion and character that once gave energy to the civilization becomes rigid, and traditions that were once cherished become mundane and meaningless. National purpose wanes and people turn to accumulating possessions, pleasures, and land to fill the void (materialism).

Next, the soul of the nation dies: corruption in the government, the education-system, and the religious-system flourishes, leadership and the respect for authority rapidly deteriorates and lawlessness explodes. The nation is turned into a hollow, empty shadow of its former self with no character, no life, and no purpose. The streets and homes are filled with chaos and everything seems to be falling apart or coming unglued.

In the final stage, the body of the nation dies. Either another nation conquers it, the original nation collapses upon itself and is reconstituted as a different nation (or fragments into multiple nations), or the people simply abandon it en-masse and migrate somewhere else to start over. Throughout the West, we see this cycle at various states, but most nations are on the decline, especially those of Western Europe.

While America is languishing, Europe is having even bigger problems, as their banking system which was tied to ours has also begun to collapse. Many of the nations which make up the

European Union have been socialist democracies since WWII, and now they are suffering the consequences of being little more than welfare states. Several of those nations have guaranteed lifetime unemployment benefits, which essentially pay people never to go back to work. With these conditions in mind, many fear that the entire West will suffer a catastrophic financial collapse which will make the Great Depression look like a bump in the road.

Europe's spirit died when it cast aside Christianity over a century ago, while its soul was critically wounded in WWI and then finally died in WWII and the Holocaust. America's own spirit died shortly afterwards, and its soul died when JFK was assassinated. Europe has now entered the middle of the last stage and is in transition to physical death, while America has just entered the final stage in the last several years but is rapidly catching up to Europe.

While Europe's civilization is declining, Islam inside most European countries is rising, which is further pushing it away from Western values and principles. If birth-rates and cultural trends continue, most of Europe will look very similar to the Middle East in only a few more decades. Nature abhors a vacuum, and this principle holds true for religion just as it does in nature. The spiritual vacuum created by secularism must be filled with "something" and if Christianity and Judaism are highly discouraged by the educational system and the culture, then the culture will turn to the next available religion with the most energy.

In Europe, the spiritual vacuum created by secularism is being filled with Islam – even though historic Western principles and institutions which were born in Europe are completely at odds with most of Islamic law, teaching, and culture. In the long-run, Islam will always win over secularism, because people can't believe in nothing – religion is part of our very nature. It could very well be that the rise of Islam and other forms of totalitarianism and authoritarianism is God's current punishment against a nation or culture that embraces secularism

495

and expunges Judeo-Christian values. If Europe wants to be saved from the new Dark Ages, it should embrace Judeo-Christian values that build civilizations, rather than secularism and Islam which tears them down. We can either submit to the light yoke of Judeo-Christian values or bow our necks to the heavy boot and sharp sword of Islam. We have a choice – for now.

Because of rampant political correctness which subverts traditional Judeo-Christian values in favor of secular humanism, Islam is rising in America just as it is in Europe. If and when Christianity is purged from America, Islam will fill the void and then the battle will be between Islam and the Humanists. But the Humanists will lose because people MUST believe in something, and usually something greater than themselves. Most religions believe in a higher power or "god" of some sort, but Humanism in its various forms does not – Humanism believes in humans. Following that war, the religious battle will likely come full-circle back to Judeo-Christian values versus Islamic values. If we in America want to see where we are quickly heading, we only need to watch Europe, particularly Great Britain.

A broader battle than even Judeo-Christianity versus Islam is between individual rights versus the rights of the totalitarian State; after all, the two go hand-in-hand. The predominant religion in a nation usually forms the basis of its national philosophy and character, which in turn produce its civil institutions and government. America was not founded merely for religious freedom, but specifically to be a Judeo-Christian nation founded on individual liberty – and the limited government set forth in our Constitution reflected that philosophy and our religion. Only Judaism and Christianity emphasize individual liberty, whereas most other religions do not – they emphasize collectivism, socialism, and various forms of totalitarianism. Just as an individual's beliefs determine their philosophy and then their behavior, so does the religion of a nation.

Is it really too late for America to turn around and walk away from the precipice? I believe that there is still time to turn around and return to our founding principles, to correct our nation's course and right our trajectory. Many observers of America believe that we were on the cusp of a spiritual revival in the wake of September 11th, but it failed because our media and politicians were afraid of losing power, and because our freshly-filled churches couldn't adequately provide answers to people who were suddenly overcome with fear and uncertainty. The good news is that there are still millions of God-fearing people throughout America, and we still have a rudimentary moral compass, broken and damaged as it may be. Most of us still just want to be left alone and live our lives, raise our families, and work hard as best we can. When disaster strikes, we still heavily donate money, supplies, and time to help those in need, though we could use that money ourselves.

The heart of America has not yet grown cold, but it has been cooling for many years. We have not yet digressed as deeply into societal collapse as Great Britain and much of Europe have, though we seem to be quickly following in their footsteps. Like the dying church of Sardis in Revelation 3, we must "be watchful, and strengthen the things which remain, that are ready to die."

Also, we should keep these times in perspective – this is the third model of government America has had: first, the Colonial Charters under Great Britain, followed by the weak, problematic government under the Articles of Confederation, and since 1787, the constitutional republic we're familiar with. The Progressive Era early in the last century corrupted our republic into more of a socialist democracy, though the transformation has been relatively slow and gradual, at least until the last few years. The average democracy/republic lasts about two hundred years, and unless we return to our founding principles, we too shall find the great American republic thrown into the dustbin of history.

The Cycle of Democracy

Is America really on the verge of economic and societal collapse? With the recent stock-market recovery, many would argue that we are not. However, America cannot continue spending over $1 trillion dollars more per year than it raises in revenue – it simply can't. The last four years have proven beyond a doubt that Keynes' economic theories about deficits and stimulus are utter failures. If America is to survive, we all need to learn to live within our means as quickly as possible – especially the federal government.

Alexander Tyler, a Scottish historian at the time of the American Revolution, observed that the average age of the world's greatest civilizations from the beginning of history has been about two-hundred years, and that during those two-hundred year lifespans, nations always progress through the sequence known as the "Cycle of Democracy":

1. From Bondage to Spiritual Faith;
2. From Spiritual Faith to great Courage;
3. From Courage to Liberty;
4. From Liberty to Abundance;
5. From Abundance to Complacency;
6. From Complacency to Apathy;
7. From Apathy to Dependence;
8. From Dependence back into Bondage.

America has proven to be no exception to this cycle, for we too have gone from bondage in England, Europe, and numerous other nations, to liberty and great abundance. But sometime in the middle of the last century (after WWII), America moved into the Complacency stage. After the Cold War ended in the early 1990s, we moved into the Apathy stage, in which most Americans simply no longer cared where the country was going as long as we were prosperous, unemployment was low, and consumer goods were cheap – even if we were buying them from Red China at the expense of our own companies and employees.

But with the Financial Crisis of 2008 and the long Great Recession that followed, America has moved into the Dependency stage. Unemployment benefits have been extended to an astounding ninety-nine weeks – nearly two years! In addition to the overextended unemployment benefits which have been found to be fraught with mismanagement and fraud to the tune of over $14 billion per year, the food-stamp program has more than doubled (from $30 billion to $72 billion), with nearly twice as many dependents as in 2007 (from 26 million to 45 million and rising).

In America as of early-2013, one out of every seven people are dependent on the government for food-stamps, and one out of every five are dependent upon the government for survival. Coupled with Social Security, Medicare/Medicaid, and other various entitlement programs, now 49% of all Americans are receiving some form of government entitlement. Not only that, but now 50% of all Americans do not pay any federal income tax to sustain those benefits – and many are simply drawing from the Treasury without contributing. These huge entitlements are obviously unsustainable and are driving the country towards an unprecedented economic disaster, and this is even before the new national healthcare law has been fully implemented.

The massive entitlements were being sustained by huge loans from China and Japan, but even those are drying up, so the Federal Reserve has been printing and loaning the trillions of dollars in new debt to the U.S. Treasury. The borrowing from the Federal Reserve only ensures a more insidious form of enslavement than borrowing from a foreign power: inflation. Currency inflation bleeds the value of the money that people earn and save in their retirement and savings accounts. Through the inflationary/monetary policies of the Federal Reserve – especially after Richard Nixon took the dollar off the Gold Standard, the U.S. dollar has lost over 80% of its value since

1971. This only increases economic instability and dependency on the part of the people.

The health of the economy and the amount of dependency determines how long the Dependency stage lasts. If there is a significantly higher proportion of producers to dependents, the Dependency stage can continue almost indefinitely. But when the proportion diminishes to the point at which only a handful of producers are supporting each dependent, the Dependency stage draws to a close. When the producers equals the dependents – and especially when there are fewer producers than dependents – the Bondage stage emerges, in which more and more of the producers' income is used to finance the dependents. Eventually the point is reached where the producers become the dependents – and then the system collapses.

In America, we are speeding into the Bondage stage because dependency is now highly encouraged by our government in order to "fundamentally transform" the nation so that high dependency is forever cemented in place. But make no mistake: eventually, the national debt that our government has rung up over the last two decades will have to be repaid – either by massive tax increases (serfdom or enslavement), property confiscation, or inflation (or hyperinflation). The borrower is always slave to the lender, and the more money that has been borrowed, the heavier those chains of bondage will become.

What lies ahead for America as we move further into the Twenty-First Century? Soft-tyranny that is quickly hardening through high taxes and onerous regulations, and then soon serfdom – economic slavery, at least for a while. Taxes on the rich will continue to increase until they leave the country or completely stop investing in companies and financial markets. That's the danger of class warfare – that one group of people is degraded, insulted, and almost criminalized, while the rest of the country becomes dependent upon their taxes for their benefits and even survival. As Margaret Thatcher once quipped, "The problem with socialism is that eventually you run out of other people's money." America is at that point today, but we keep printing, borrowing, and then spending that money we don't have. How long can we possibly continue to base our government, our economy, and our lives on money created out of thin air?

When the wealth of the vilified rich dries up, the tax burden will only increase but with no one to foot the bill – so those in the thinning middle-class will have their taxes dramatically increased, until that source of revenue dries up also, as more and more people decide that they can "earn" more by being on government welfare than working. We're approaching that point now, in which a welfare-recipient's benefits/income is worth more than they can earn from a full-time minimum-wage job. When that's the case, why would they want to work when they can earn more in government benefits than by being productive citizens?

Any society based upon wealth-redistribution eventually collapses because it reaches a tipping point in which there's simply nothing left to redistribute. And if our current fiscal policies don't change soon, we will find out precisely where that tipping point is.

Rough Roads Ahead

As has been the case for the last century or so, European trends foreshadow what likely lies ahead for America. The socialist economies of Europe such as Greece, Italy, Spain, Portugal, and Ireland are completely bankrupt and are on the brink of collapse. But France and the United Kingdom are following closely on their heels and they show no evidence of changing course. Only Germany's economy and currency has been keeping the Euro afloat, and with it, their economies. But not for long.

Currently, Germany is footing much of the bill for Europe's extravagant welfare programs, but soon the German people will come to their senses and refuse to be enslaved through high-taxes just to pay for the generous welfare benefits of the rest of

Europe. When that ends, either the U.S. or the Federal Reserve will likely step in and bail them out, if China doesn't jump in first (though that seems increasingly unlikely). Such "too big to fail" interventions only prolong and deepen the financial problems, just as they have for the last decade, but especially after the Financial Crisis of 2008.

Regardless of Europe's deepening crisis, the fundamental problems of socialism and wealth-redistribution in America remain. Even if Americans and our elected officials came to their senses today and returned to sensible spending, budgeting, and taxation, the $10 trillion debt from the last thirteen years would still remain – which we will have to make the huge interest payments on, along with those of the previous $6 trillion. By 2030 (though likely much sooner), the U.S. government will have to borrow/print money just to make the interest payments on the national debt!

It could very well be that the United States as a government-entity will collapse under the weight of her own debts and the unsustainably of her own policies, but "We the People" will continue on – though the adjustment will likely be quite difficult. But many of us are still rugged individualists and when tough times come, we will rise to the challenge. These days in the Great Recession could very well be preparing us for darker, more turbulent years ahead. Americans aren't really faced with the threat of foreign invasion as most other unstable countries are, but we are more likely to be enslaved to our national debt and our foreign creditors through massive tax increases. Some say we already are enslaved to our foreign creditors and the Federal Reserve – we just don't recognize it as such.

When the financial situation becomes entirely unsustainable, the United States government and the economy could go "supernova" and America will be thrown into a brief era of hyperinflation in order to cut down our financial obligations and balance the books. Most governments which have similar crushing liabilities do go that route. Years of chaos and terrible economic times follow, but eventually the people adjust and things settle down. Our currency and economy are largely based on confidence, and at this point in our history, we have little confidence in either one because of our over-regulating, over-spending federal government. Americans have an advantage in both those areas in that many of us are armed and will defend ourselves, and that millions of us are still very independent and will find a way to keep our families fed and safe.

Another possible path for America is like that of Russia after the collapse of the Soviet Union. When the communist government abruptly collapsed, the people suddenly had to earn money and learn how to function for themselves after decades of having every aspect of their lives dictated to them. The powerful mafia and black-markets suddenly arose, since the government was in a shambles and could no longer keep them in check. But the government still needed income and soon formed partnerships with the mafia. After several years of hyperinflation, the people learned how to function in a freer/capitalist society, but the corruption between the government and mafia remained. However, the Russian path seems unlikely for America because most Americans still obey the law and hate corruption and dishonesty in our public officials. We still try to function within the boundaries of the law and when laws become onerous, we try to change them rather than ignore or blatantly break them.

The best alternative for America in the coming years is to look to our immediate neighbor to the north: Canada. In the 1990s, Canada faced an alarming future of massive deficits and national debt, huge entitlement obligations, a stagnant, declining economy, and was saddled with inefficient, wasteful government bureaucracies. But when their representatives and officials came to the awful realization that their policies would have dire consequences that could no longer be delayed, they dramatically slashed government spending and the bureaucracies, privatizing many of their government services and agencies.

As each department/agency was privatized, the employees became tax-revenue providers (taxpayers) instead of tax-revenue consumers (dependents). Not only that, but Canada reformed many of their entitlement programs to be more sensible, such as increasing the retirement age, tightening their welfare and unemployment programs, and cutting taxes. Also, the Canadian federal government began slashing regulation and their own responsibilities and left those up to the provinces, further reducing their expenses and obligations.

Canada not only stopped their runaway borrowing and deficit-spending, they also began paying down their national debt and had paid off nearly a quarter of it before the Great Recession hit and their economy temporarily declined. But because of low taxes and sensible fiscal policies, Canada was not nearly as affected by the Financial Crisis of 2008 and their economy has been recovering much faster than that of the United States.

America has two choices: collapse or reform.

Two Paths for America

At this point in American history, there are two paths that we as a country can take – there is no third option. We can continue rushing down the road of Progressivism and enter the dark night of European socialism like most of the West, or we can return to the tried-and-true principles of Americanism that founded this nation and led it to greatness. We can continue entertaining ourselves to death, or we can turn from our petty entertainments and immoral indulgences. We can either continue borrowing and spending money we don't have on luxuries we don't need, or we can return to common-sense, limited government and sacrifice some of our creature-comforts for our children and grandchildren.

The looming financial catastrophe is only an indication of deeper problems in our nation, such as widespread instant gratification, living for today with little concern for tomorrow, mass-narcissism, lack of purpose or motivation, and the denial of tomorrow's consequences for today's decisions. After four years of the Great Recession, many in our nation are dispirited at the economic and moral decline, especially those who have played by the rules and saved hard for their future, only to see it evaporate because of the financial crisis, inflation, and stagnant economy. Some even wonder what's the point of trying to find work or struggling to stay in business when it seems that the government is encouraging dependency and millions of able-bodied people not to work.

The pillars of our society which once held us together are not only crumbling and falling apart, but are systematically being torn down by the very people who should be upholding them, like our elected officials, teachers, lawyers, the media, and other cultural leaders. Our public servants have turned themselves into our masters, and there seems to be little recourse or accountability on their behalf. Tragically, America appears to be following in the footsteps of all the once-great nations and empires like Great Britain, Rome, and Greece. In many places throughout our land, the "shining city on a hill" that Ronald Reagan once saw have been turned into filthy, violent slums.

Before the election of Barack Obama, many of the worst policies came directly from our capital, but after he took office, the size and scope of the terrible regulations and policies from Washington have only increased. By the stroke of a pen, the Secretary of the Interior illegally shut down energy production in the Gulf of Mexico and has refused to allow it to resume. No one gave him that authority – he just seized it and used the power of the Executive Branch to force the oil companies to comply. Even after the federal courts rebuked him and decreed he had no such authority, Ken Salazar simply reissued another mandate that they would have to fight all over again. A similar situation has occurred in the coal industry, which has been all but shut down by the new EPA regulations. How can it be that a cadre of unelected bureaucrats in our capital city can wield such power over the entire nation and directly affect our businesses, energy prices, food prices, and our own personal lives? Those in the capital now seem to be acting as if they control the entire country and care only about how it affects them and not us. That's certainly not how most Americans think it should be.

Will the entire nation go down with our capital? That appears doubtful; a significant portion of Americans today recognize the source of most of our problems: Washington D.C. After two centuries of entrenched institutions, departments, and bureaucracy with few reforms, too much power has been accumulated in too many hands in the federal government, and people are sick of it (according to many of the polls). The various departments of the federal government have sufficiently insulated themselves from much accountability because the money always seems to be there. And with more and more sweeping edicts emanating from Washington, the capital is becoming a stench in the nostrils of millions of Americans.

The days of most Americans wanting bigger and better government are ending, but the Progressive politicians, the public sector unions, the mainstream media, and the entrenched bureaucrats haven't gotten that message through their heads yet. Though the "Sequester" has begun to take effect, it's merely cut 2.4%-3% from the annual 6-7% rate of growth – the government will still grow by 3%+ and the Progressives are screaming as if it were cut by 30%! If they caterwaul like this now over such tiny cuts (in growth, no less), how will they react when the big cuts are forced upon them by economic circumstances due to their own fiscal mischief and Progressive policies? After the Financial Crisis of 2008, Americans have scaled back their spending, but the federal government has exploded their spending when they should be scaling back as well. The first rule of deficits is like the first rule of holes: stop digging! In the government's case, it's to stop spending.

Americans used to revile communism and socialism, but now we have all but embraced it under the label of Progressivism – to our demise. If America is to be saved, we must reject it, return to our founding principles, and purge all

506

trace of it from America. If we do not change course in both our culture and our fiscal policies immediately, our collapse will be painful, spectacular, and far worse than any before or any after us.

If the Collapse is imminent, how do we prepare? As the Collapse draws closer, we must organize by families, churches, neighborhoods and become self-sufficient again. We cannot just stock up on food and essentials and expect to weather the storm by ourselves. If we don't quickly organize, the evils that occur in the midst of such chaos will only explode, especially if the crisis becomes desperate. We must be alert and understand that when the Rule of Law collapses, the police will not be able to protect us. Looters, rapists, murderers, and other criminals must be quickly, severely brought to justice rather than be allowed to run rampant while we wait for the police (who will be too busy to respond). This is yet another reason why We the People must all stay adequately-armed and prepared.

A Third Great Awakening?

As for the United States of America itself, though the federal government may collapse, we still have our state and local governments which can effectively keep our local infrastructure and day-to-day lives going. It could be that we turn into a Balkanized country, in which groups of neighboring states form their own federal systems if the one in Washington no longer functions. It could also be that some states simply stop obeying the federal government without formally seceding, thus avoiding another horrible civil war.

The absolute worst thing that could happen – that we should all pray does NOT happen – is that any of our presidents or elected officials are assassinated. America does not change presidents or "fix" elections by shooting their leaders – that's the sign of lawlessness, radicals, communists, and other tyranny. Assassinations wound the very heart and soul of a nation, and God does not excuse such bloodshed. When citizens begin assassinating the leaders they don't agree with, the end is near for that nation. Once political assassinations start, it's very difficult to get them to stop – for good or bad leaders.

For the first time in decades, millions of Americans are reading the Constitution and are realizing just how far we've strayed from its precepts. The rising cry of federal abuses of the Tenth Amendment ("The powers not delegated to the United States by the Constitution, nor prohibited by it to the States, are reserved to the States respectively, or to the people.") are encouraging, though it was probably the first amendment to be abused or ignored after the Constitution was ratified. All governments tend to grow and overstep their bounds, even a well-designed, limited federal government such as ours.

It's difficult to picture another Civil War on America's horizon, mainly because those boundaries were fairly well-defined between the North and the South, and it really was two different countries fighting one another: the South for her independence (and to keep slavery) and the North to keep the Union together. Slavery was the fire that made the entire pot boil over and forced the two countries to resolve their differences. It's more likely that the conflict looming before us will be primarily between the federal government and groups of States. It's not a good sign when the federal government and the States begin suing one another, especially when the people often hold more affection for their State than the federal government.

For those of us who are Christians, we should also recognize these times we're living in for what they are: the End of the Age. We may not be the last generation before the End Times begin, but we may be one of those living just before it. In these uncertain times, we are called to hold fast to Him and His Word (Hebrews 10, Revelation 3), keep watch for His Coming, and encourage one another all the more as we see that Day approaching (Hebrews 10:25).

If America is to be saved from a catastrophic financial and societal collapse, we will likely know it long before our

508

politicians, economists, and experts do. If we see a spiritual
revival taking hold and a return to our Judeo-Christian roots, I
believe the country will be saved. But if we continue on the way
we have these last fifty years, then the United States of America
as we have known it probably will be lost.

As long as there are those of us who love our country and
bitterly cling to our American heritage (along with our Bibles
and guns), there will always be hope for our country. When our
Founders declared their independence from Great Britain, they
knew they had a righteous cause – and so do we in defending
and restoring our country. They were enormously outgunned
and outnumbered, but they fought anyway because they knew it
was the right thing to do. I believe that same spirit still lives in
America, and it is growing. The vast majority of people in the
country don't want a new form of government, they simply
want the foolishness and corruption expelled from the system.
Most Americans want politicians who will tell them the truth –
no matter how terrible and depressing it may be.

In the context of history, America's current cultural war
could be thought of as another great battle for freedom –
America's Struggle Against Communism. Though America
defeated the Soviet Union, we never completely defeated
communism. Much like the proverbial ring in "Lord of the
Rings," we had a chance to destroy communism forever, but we
chose not to – we chose to use it for our own political purposes,
it corrupted us, and now it threatens to engulf the world once
again, with its throne firmly set in Washington D.C.

If viewed in that context, then Barack Obama is merely the
latest emissary of communism, albeit the most powerful
Progressive that America has ever known. But even after
Obama leaves office, the institutions that produced him are still
as corrupted as ever and will continue to produce more tyrants
until the Marxist ideas that feed them are replaced with those of
liberty.

In the years before the British rose up against America, God sent the Great Awakening to prepare our ancestors for their struggle against the tyrannical King George.

In the years before the Civil War, God sent the Second Great Awakening, which stirred the hearts of Americans once again and destroyed our original national sin: slavery.

Could it be that God is today sending the Third Great Awakening to finally destroy communism, secularism, or even abortion, which has murdered more people on the face of the earth than all the other wars put together?

The Greatest Miracle

While completing the first manuscript of this book, it dawned on me that two days after the Inauguration on January 22, 2013, it will be the 40th anniversary of Roe v. Wade. Over the course of the forty years of abortion in America, more than 55 million innocents have been slaughtered and thrown into dumpsters, incinerators, or dismembered in the name of "convenience" and "freedom."

In the Bible, "40" is figuratively the number of probation or testing – the Flood lasted for forty days, Israel wandered in the wilderness for forty years, and forty years passed from the time Jesus preached against the Temple until it was destroyed. Will the Third Great Awakening begin on the fortieth anniversary of Roe v. Wade and finally end it? Or will God conclude that America has failed the test and be judged for the horrible bloodshed of the innocent?

Until abortion is outlawed and the horrible evil of that institution is atoned for, I fear that there may be no hope for America. Perhaps He is waiting for America as a nation to put the debate to rest and at least decide on the legality (or illegality) of abortion as a law passed by our Congress and President instead of being ruled on by our Supreme Court. And depending on our decision, will God use our enemies to judge us like He used Israel's horrible/cruel enemies to judge her?

510

Will God use the Iranians or the North Koreans and their nuclear weapons against us? The Book of Obadiah (v15) states, "As you have done, it shall be done to you; your reprisal shall return upon your own head." Will that be applied to America, especially since we have been the only nation in the world to use nuclear weapons against another nation?

Even the rationalist Thomas Jefferson understood that God will judge America for her sins, and the bloody Civil War was His judgment against us for slavery, our greed, and our pride. If the Civil War was how God poured out His wrath upon us for slavery, how much greater will His wrath be against us for our slaughter of over 55 million innocent children? Do we somehow think that He won't or that He has changed His mind about His hatred of murder, much less the murder of the innocent?

There are many miracles in the Bible, particularly in the Old Testament and the Gospels. However, perhaps the greatest miracle in the Old Testament is overlooked by the vast majority of Bible students, preachers, and scholars. The most fascinating part of this miracle was that it didn't involve any strange signs or wonders like burning bushes, chariots of fire, or even bringing the dead back to life.

The greatest miracle in the Bible is in the Book of Jonah, but it didn't involve being swallowed by a great fish or even surviving such an ordeal – but a nation which was on the brink of not only self-destruction, but Divine judgment. The real miracle of the story actually occurred after Jonah was spat out by the fish and finally obeyed God to go preach to Nineveh. As soon as he arrived in the great city, he began preaching a message of complete and utter destruction upon the wicked city. Jonah's message was simple, and there wasn't even a "repent or else" condition (Jonah 3:1-10):

> *Now the word of the Lord came to Jonah the second time, saying, "Arise, go to Nineveh, that great city, and preach to it the message that I tell you." So Jonah arose and went to*

511

Nineveh, according to the word of the Lord. Now Nineveh was an exceedingly great city, a three-day journey in extent. And Jonah began to enter the city on the first day's walk. Then he cried out and said, "Yet forty days, and Nineveh shall be overthrown!"

So the people of Nineveh believed God, proclaimed a fast, and put on sackcloth, from the greatest to the least of them. Then word came to the king of Nineveh; and he arose from his throne and laid aside his robe, covered himself with sackcloth and sat in ashes. And he caused it to be proclaimed and published throughout Nineveh by the decree of the king and his nobles, saying,

*"Let neither man nor beast, herd nor flock, taste anything; do not let them eat, or drink water. 8 But let man and beast be covered with sackcloth, and cry mightily to God; yes, let every one turn from his evil way and from the violence that is in his hands. **Who can tell if God will turn and relent, and turn away from His fierce anger, so that we may not perish?"***

Then God saw their works, that they turned from their evil way; and God relented from the disaster that He had said He would bring upon them, and He did not do it.

The city of Nineveh, the capital city of the Assyrian Empire, was one of the greatest cities of the ancient world, and encased within fifty-foot thick, thirty-foot high walls that circled the city for about ten miles. The population of Nineveh is estimated to be between 600,000 and one million people, with 120,000 children according to Jonah 4. At the height of its power, the very word "Assyrian" or "Nineveh" would strike complete terror in the hearts of people because of their terrible cruelty. In the ancient world, it was usually far better to die than be caught alive by the Assyrians.

The Assyrians were renowned for inventing ways of making their victims suffer, which often involved skinning or flaying them alive, impaling them on stakes, nailing them to trees, cutting off various limbs and other body parts, and even "opening the bellies" of pregnant women in front of their husbands before putting the men to death. When deporting captives, the Assyrians would strip their prisoners completely naked, put large fishhooks through their jaws or eyelids and then march them away. And these grisly examples aren't even the worst forms of torture the Assyrians invented – and often documented on their monuments, walls, and steles.

When Jonah began preaching to Nineveh, the people heard his message and then immediately began to repent – men, women, and children. No one told them to – they just did it. Finally, the king received word of Jonah's message and humbled himself by leaving his throne, putting on sackcloth and sitting in ashes, the Middle Eastern sign of terrible mourning and debasement. Not only that, he issued a decree throughout the city for everyone (including the animals) to do likewise and not even eat or drink, in the remote, desperate hopes that God would see their genuine repentance and spare them from His wrath. He reasoned that if God was warning them though this strange, outspoken prophet, that there was a chance – or even the sliver of a chance – that God would be merciful to them and stay their execution. And He did! The greatest miracle of all the Old Testament is that the godless, horrible people of Nineveh heard the Word of God, humbled themselves, and repented of their wicked ways – nearly a million people from the least to the greatest.

What happened in Nineveh that caused God to withhold His judgment? The Assyrians had a massive, complete spiritual awakening – a Great Awakening – and they humbled themselves as quickly as they could. They knew that they had committed great sins that had not gone unnoticed, and when Jonah appeared and began speaking, they were conscious-stricken and repented in dust and ashes from the king on down to the lowest of their people – including their animals.

If a prophet such as Jonah entered ANY of America's cities today – including our capital, Washington D.C., the most powerful city in the world – would any of those cities repent? Who knows? It's likely that the prophet would be arrested and thrown in jail for being intolerant or for uttering hate-speech. Can you imagine any of our presidents (including Barack Obama) setting aside their tailor-made suits and then broadcasting a message of national prayer, fasting, and repentance? That may seem completely absurd, but if a city as utterly depraved and wicked as Nineveh can repent, it's not impossible that our cities and nation cannot do likewise.

It may very well be that someday historians look back at America and say that the Third Great Awakening began in the months after the election of Barack Obama, the Great Recession, and the rise of the TEA Parties. And though America's future looks bleak, it has several times before. When the nation was on the very brink of destruction during the Revolutionary War and then the Civil War, men and women across the nation humbled themselves and beseeched God for His intervention and mercy.

If My People...

In the Bible, there's the story of another nation during that same time period as the Ninevites, who were once very familiar with God and His Laws: the nation of Israel. However, though they were given sign after sign and sent prophet after prophet that called them to repentance, they refused time and time again. Eventually, God was forced to judge them and completely destroyed the nation and sent them into Captivity for many, many years.

The message that God issued to ancient Israel is the same one that He holds out for any nation during any time, but especially those nations who were once well-versed in the Scriptures:

If My people who are called by My name will humble themselves, and pray and seek My face, and turn from their

514

wicked ways, then I will hear from heaven, and will forgive their sin and heal their land. – 2 Chronicles 7:14

If we really love America and not only want her to avoid certain judgment for her national sins and wickedness but yearn to see her restored and preserved, then let us all repent of our sins, fast and pray and earnestly seek God. Let us get down on our knees and implore Him once again on behalf of this great republic. Who knows? Like the king of Nineveh reasoned, who can tell if God will turn and relent, and turn away from His fierce anger, so that we may not perish?

After we repent, we must not stop there and return to our old ways – we must grow in the grace and knowledge of the God of the Bible, and then encourage others around us to do likewise. In the Old Testament, God admonished the people to consider and talk about His Commandments all the time, to keep the spiritual in the forefront rather than just being an afterthought (Deuteronomy 6, 11). We must do likewise – we should try to always keep these before us: the love of God, the love of our families, the love of our neighbors, and the love of our country.

We must talk regularly about America's incredible founding, our history, and the Colonists' dedication to God. Consider our great heritage and our forefathers, and all they sacrificed and fought and died for in order to create the free nation that we have enjoyed. Every year, make it a practice to read the Declaration of Independence with your family and friends on Independence Day and know what our Founders fought for. Read the Constitution and the writings of the great men and women of that founding generation. And then consider what you can do to keep America a nation of liberty and justice for all.

But more important than even the future of America, is where do you personally stand with God? After you die, will He be your Condemner or your Commender, your Judge or your Justifier?

If you haven't yet been saved, I beg you to become a Christian and join with us. Becoming a Christian could not be simpler: "Believe on the Lord Jesus Christ and you will be saved" (Acts 16:31). More specifically, believing that Jesus came as God in the Flesh, He died for our sins on the Cross, and was resurrected after three days (1 Corinthians 15).

Why Christianity and Jesus Christ? Because only He has the power to change people's hearts, to cause people to turn from death to life. Most of this book has been about Progressivism, politics, and Judeo-Christian values. However, values are only the outward expression of what's inside us – religions often don't change the heart, but relationships do. At their very core, Marxism and other forms of Progressivism are secular religions and belief systems. Progressivism changed the very heart of America from Judeo-Christianity to secularism. But there's no reason why it can't be changed back – that's the very nature of spiritual revivals and Great Awakenings.

Arthur Katz is one who exemplified the transformation which is possible throughout America, but it wasn't merely a change of values that so dramatically altered him, but a transformation of his heart. Art Katz was a deeply committed atheist, Marxist, and even communist – one of the many products of the Progressive system from UCLA and Berkeley in the early 1960s. After his divorce in 1963, he left his teaching position in Oakland and began traveling the world in an attempt to "find himself."

While on the trip, by chance Katz crossed paths with several Christians who not only believed the Scriptures and the Greatest Commandment, but lived them out in their daily lives. Being Jewish as well as an atheist, he was initially repulsed and suspiciously questioned their motives. However, as he saw the genuine love of Jesus Christ lived out through these average people, the icy walls of bitterness in his heart began to melt and he began to change.

Over the course of the next year, Katz underwent a radical heart transformation, though not of his own accord, but by the love of Jesus changing him from the inside out. Like millions who have undergone "conversions" or transformations of the heart, he wasn't reached by logic, rationalism, arguing and debates, but by real, genuine caring and sacrificial love. After he returned to his teaching position, he was an entirely different person, no longer even having the desire to partake in the endless debates and arguments he often used to initiate. He later began preaching around the world and eventually wrote several books and started several other ministries.

What has the power to change hearts? The Love of God – not the oozy, gooey, sappy love so often portrayed in the movies, but real, genuine love. The love that changes people is the sacrificial sort that causes one to lay down their lives for their friends – and even their enemies. The sort of love that requires us to turn the other cheek, go the extra mile, do good to those who hate us, pray for those who persecute us, and love even our enemies. That is the love that transforms individuals, families, communities, and nations. The Love of God has the power to transform the world. The Love of God has the power to revive a dying nation.

If you have already been saved, please join us in deep, regular prayer for our God-given republic. Immerse yourself in the Word and become "Doers, and not Hearers only." Whenever you leave your home or leave your church, try to have the perspective that "You're now entering the mission field!" If you don't have a church-home or there are no Bible believing churches near you, start your own in your home. That's how church is done in most of the world anyway.

Spiritual revival in America doesn't begin in a movement or a march, but with each of us as individuals. Samuel Adams was a lone voice for years crying out for his neighbors to repent and then throw off the chains of Great Britain. He was long-suffering and tireless in his efforts, and we must find that same strength. But that strength doesn't come from us, it comes from God.

Do your best to do what is right and good and encourage others to do likewise. Take the difficult roads rather than the easy shortcuts through life. Evil days provide enormous opportunities for the Kingdom. We must hold fast and strengthen what remains before it's swept away by those who would see America be turned into just another chaotic nation which can be ruled by Men rather than by Law.

We as brothers and sisters in faith may have differences of opinion from time to time, but we are still one in Christ. If the Puritans, the Quakers, the Anabaptists, the Methodists, the Presbyterians, the Catholics, and the Jews could put aside their theological differences to forge a new nation – One Nation Under God – then surely we can set aside our differences to revive it.

In the days, months, and years ahead – let us pray and fast and seek God once again with all our hearts. Let us remember our great heritage and live according to the ideals and virtues of our Founders. Let us continue to pray, fast, and humble ourselves and petition God to bring healing to this land that we love and hold so dear.

May the Third Great Awakening begin in our day and heal the heart, mind, and body of this great nation. May God bless America, so America can bless the world.

References and Recommended Reading

The Bible (New King James Version). Thomas Nelson, 1982.

Barton, David. *America's Godly Heritage.* WallBuilder Press, 1993.

Beck, Glenn. *Being George Washington: The Indispensable Man, As You've Never Seen Him.* Threshold Editions, 2011.

Bennett, Dr. William J. *America: The Last Best Hope (Volume I): From the Age of Discovery to a World at War.* Thomas Nelson, 2007.

Bennett, Dr. William J. *America: The Last Best Hope (Volume II): From a World at War to the Triumph of Freedom.* Thomas Nelson, 2008.

Bloom, Allan. *The Closing of the American Mind.* Simon & Schuster, 1988.

Bork, Robert H. *Slouching Towards Gomorrah: Modern Liberalism and American Decline.* Harper Perennial, 2003.

Churchill, Winston S. *The Great Republic: A History of America.* Modern Library, 2000.

Crosby, Jay; Bruun, Erik. *Our Nation's Archive: The History of the United States in Documents.* Black Dog & Leventhal Publishers, 1999.

DeMar, Gary. *America's Christian Heritage.* B&H Books, 2003.

Ferling, John. *A Leap in the Dark: The Struggle to Create the American Republic.* Oxford University Press, 2004.

Gibbs, Dr. David. *One Nation Under God: Ten Things Every Christian Should Know About the Founding of America.* Christian Law Association, 2005.

Hart, Benjamin. *Faith and Freedom – The Christian Roots of American Liberty.* Christian Defense Fund.

Hamilton, Alexander; Madison, James; Jay, John; Scigliano, Robert. *The Federalist: A Commentary on the Constitution of the United States.* Modern Library, 2000.

Langguth, A.J. *Patriots: The Men Who Started the American Revolution.* Simon & Schuster, 1989.

Levin, Mark R. *Liberty and Tyranny: A Conservative Manifesto.* Threshold Editions, 2009.

Levy, Leonard W. *Original Intent and the Framer's Constitution.* Ivan R. Dee, Publisher, 2000.

McCullough, David. *1776.* Simon & Schuster, 2005.

McCullough, David. *John Adams.* Simon & Schuster, 2008.

Murray, Iain. *The Really Inconvenient Truths: Seven Environmental Catastrophes Liberals Don't Want You to Know About–Because They Helped Cause Them.* Regnery Press, 2008.

Napolitano, Andrew. *Theodore and Woodrow: How Two American Presidents Destroyed Constitutional Freedom.* Thomas Nelson, 2012.

Prager, Dennis. *Still the Best Hope.* Broadside Books, 2012.

Spengler, Oswald. *The Decline of the West, 2 vols.* trans. by Charles Francis Atkinson, Alfred A. Knopf, 1926, 1928.

Steyn, Mark. *America Alone: The End of the World as We Know It.* Regnery Publishing, 2006.

Steyn, Mark. *After America: Get Ready for Armageddon.* Regnery Publishing, 2011.

Tocqueville, Alexis de. *Democracy in America.* Arlington House, written 1838.

About the Author

Chris Hambleton resides in Denver, Colorado, where he is employed as a software developer and consultant. He has authored more than a dozen books, as well as developed several websites, software applications, and written software-related articles. His other interests include hiking, studying the Bible, reading American history and politics, along with devouring good fiction books.

For more information about "Our American Awakening" and other conservative/patriotic resources, please visit the book's website at http://www.ouramericanawakening.com.

To learn more about Chris Hambleton and his other books, please visit his author website at http://www.cwhambleton.com.

Other Titles by Chris Hambleton

Speculative Fiction Titles
"The Seed of Haman" (2013)
"The Exchange" (2012)
"The Castors of Giza" (2012)
"The Cell" (2010)
"Endeavor in Time" (2008)

The Time of Jacob's Trouble Trilogy (2011)
"The Last Aliyah" (Book 1)
"The Son of Shinar" (Book 2)
"The Siege of Zion" (Book 3)

The Days of Noah Series (2013)

"Rise of the Anshar" (Book 1)

Non-Fiction Titles
"Our American Awakening" (2013)
"The American Tyrant" (2012)
"Ezekiel Watch" (2012)
"On the Precipice" (2011)

Connect with me Online at:
Website: http://www.cwhambleton.com
Blog: http://fictionsoftware.wordpress.com
Facebook: http://facebook.com/cwhambleton
Twitter: http://twitter.com/chris_hambleton

Author Biography

Chris Hambleton's first book, "The Time of Jacob's Trouble" was published in 2008 and later revised and expanded in 2011 as "The Time of Jacob's Trouble Trilogy" which chronicles the lives of an Israeli family as they experience the Magog Invasion and then the events of the Great Tribulation.

In "The Last Aliyah" (Book 1 of "The Time of Jacob's Trouble"), the tides of war are once again rising against the nation of Israel. Rocket attacks on Haifa and Sderot are increasing, and Israel cautiously prepares a response to a conflict that many fear will never end. And then a decision is made that will change the face of the Middle East forever.

The story of the Rosenberg family continues in "The Son of Shinar" (Book 2 of "The Time of Jacob's Trouble"), in which after the devastation of Israel's enemies in the Magog Invasion, Israel now has enough weapons and energy supplies for seven years. But now, rumors of a great leader and healer have begun sweeping through Baghdad. Has the Twelfth Imam returned? Could he be the long-awaited Jewish Messiah?

The End Times trilogy of the Rosenberg family concludes in "The Siege of Zion" (Book 3 of "The Time of Jacob's Trouble"). In one day, Supreme Leader David Medine has desecrated the Jewish Temple and Israel has fallen under the authority of the World Union. The Great Tribulation has begun and the future of Israel – along with all humanity – hangs in the balance.

After writing the "The Time of Jacob's Trouble" the next book published was, "Endeavor in Time." In this time-travel science-fiction story, Daniel Marks, the Chief Programmer on a cutting-edge research project, suddenly finds himself back nearly twenty years in the past. With his knowledge of the future before it happens, will he be able to prevent another disaster at NASA before Endeavor, the new shuttle is launched? The sequel to "Endeavor in Time" was published in mid-2012 called "The Exchange" in which Daniel Marks experiences a horrible personal loss and embarks on a hybrid-age journey which will cause him to not only question the entire purpose of his existence, but that very existence itself.

In 2010, "The Cell - Twilight's Last Gleaming" was published, a speculative fiction novel that examines America's future a decade after the financial crash of 2008. As America continues to slog through the Great Recession which has yet to end, the conservatives and the churches have been silenced, and law enforcement seems helpless against the growing gangs and vigilante groups. And though the light of many churches have been extinguished, tiny flames of faith flicker to life and begin to grow.

Late in 2011, Chris's first two non-fiction books were published, "On the Precipice" and "Ezekiel Watch." The book "On the Precipice - Hosea Speaks to America" explores America's current problems in comparison to the Book of Hosea in the Bible, in which the nation of Israel had turned away from her Scriptural foundations and was faced with judgment. "Ezekiel Watch - Then They Shall Know" provides a comprehensive examination of Ezekiel 36-39: Israel's restoration to her homeland and the massive attack on Israel by Russia, Iran, and the other Islamic nations of the Middle East.

"The Castors of Giza" is the first of several books that fictionalizes ancient history, with the subject of this story being the building of the Great Pyramid of Egypt. In the Fourth Dynasty of Kemet is growing stronger under its ambitious new leader, Pharaoh Khufu. His father, King Snefuru has established a legacy of extravagant monuments and massive building projects, and his son will not allow himself to become a lesser king. With the science of pyramid construction now perfected, Khufu has determined to build the grandest monument of all time: the Great Pyramid.

In Chris's first politically-oriented book, "The American Tyrant" Barack Obama's background, mentors, and presidency are explored. Who is Barack Obama? Where did he come from, what are his values, and where does he want to take the United States of America? Does his vision of America square with those of America's Founders and past presidents? Where are his czars, policies, and executive orders taking us? Could he really be America's Tyrant?

The latest book "Our American Awakening" is another politically-themed non-fiction book that explores America's founding, transition into Progressivism, and ways to restore America. What lies ahead for America in the years ahead? What changes can we make today that will improve America for our children and grandchildren?

Our American Awakening